Adobe Illustrator

2024 Release

Adobe Illustrator Classroom in a Book® 2024 release

© 2024 Adobe. All rights reserved.

Adobe Press is an imprint of Pearson Education, Inc. For the latest on Adobe Press books, go to *peachpit.com/adobepress*. To report errors, please send a note to errata@peachpit.com. For information regarding permissions, request forms and the appropriate contacts within the Pearson Education Global Rights & Permissions department, please visit *www.pearson.com/permissions*.

Cover Illustration: Marte (Martina Galarza), behance.net/martevisual

ISBN-13: 978-0-13-826382-9
ISBN-10: 0-13-826382-5

5 2024

WHERE ARE THE LESSON FILES?

Purchase of this Classroom in a Book in any format gives you access to the lesson files you'll need to complete the exercises in the book.

1 Go to peachpit.com/IllustratorCIB2024.

2 Sign in or create a new account.

3 Click Submit.

> **Note:** If you encounter problems registering your product or accessing the lesson files or web edition, go to peachpit.com/support for assistance.

4 Answer the questions as proof of purchase.

5 The lesson files can be accessed through the Registered Products tab on your Account page.

6 Click the Access Bonus Content link below the title of your product to proceed to the download page. Click the lesson file links to download them to your computer.

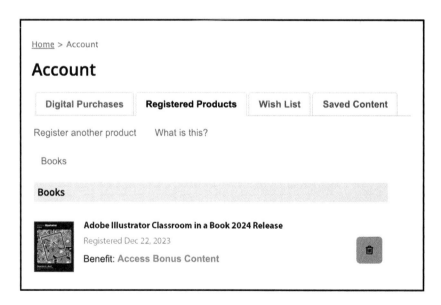

> **Note:** If you purchased a digital product directly from peachpit.com, your product will already be registered. Look for the Access Bonus Content link on the Registered Products tab in your account.

CONTENTS

8   USING COLOR TO ENHANCE ARTWORK   210

9 ADDING TYPE TO A PROJECT 240

12 USING BRUSHES TO CREATE AN AD 328

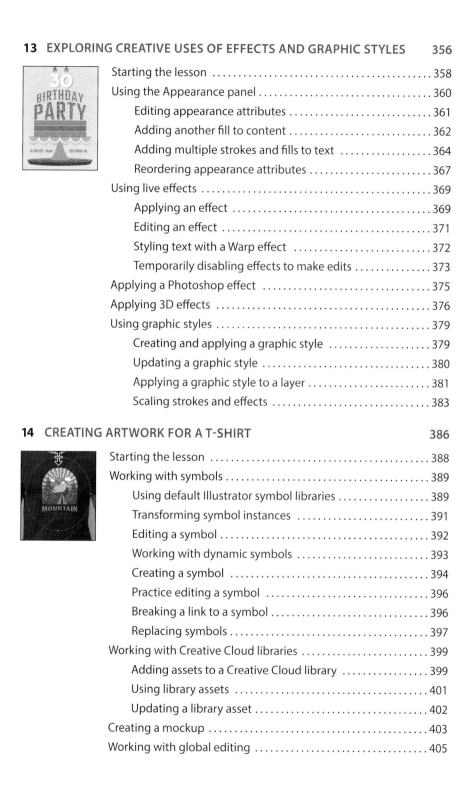

GETTING STARTED

Adobe® Illustrator® is an industry-standard print, multimedia, and online graphics illustration application. Whether you are a designer or a technical illustrator producing artwork for print publishing, an artist creating multimedia graphics, or a creator of web pages or online content, Adobe Illustrator offers you the tools you need to get professional-quality results.

About Classroom in a Book®

Adobe Illustrator Classroom in a Book® 2024 Release is part of the official training series for Adobe graphics and publishing software developed with the support of Adobe product experts. The features and exercises in this book are based on the 2024 release of Illustrator.

The lessons are designed so that you can learn at your own pace. If you're new to Adobe Illustrator, you'll learn the fundamentals you need to master to put the application to work. If you are an experienced user, you'll find that Classroom in a Book® also teaches some more advanced features, including tips and techniques for using the latest version of Adobe Illustrator.

Although each lesson provides step-by-step instructions for creating a specific project, there's room for exploration and experimentation. You can follow the book from start to finish or do only the lessons corresponding to your interests and needs. Each lesson concludes with a review section to quiz you on the main concepts.

Prerequisites

Before beginning to use *Adobe Illustrator Classroom in a Book® 2024 Release*, you should have working knowledge of your computer and its operating system. Ensure you know how to use the mouse and standard menus and commands and how to open, save, and close files. If you need to review these techniques, see the printed or online documentation for macOS or Windows.

Installing the program

Before you begin using *Adobe Illustrator Classroom in a Book® 2024 Release*, make sure that your system is set up correctly and that you've installed the required software and hardware.

You must purchase the Adobe Illustrator software separately. For complete instructions on installing the software, visit *helpx.adobe.com/support/ illustrator.html*. You must install Illustrator from Adobe Creative Cloud onto your hard disk. Follow the onscreen instructions.

Fonts used in this book

The Classroom in a Book lesson files use fonts that are included with your Creative Cloud subscription, and trial Creative Cloud members have access to a selection of fonts from Adobe for web and desktop use.

For more information about Adobe Fonts and installation, see the Adobe HelpX article at *helpx.adobe.com/creative-cloud/help/add-fonts.html*.

Online Content

Your purchase of this Classroom in a Book includes online materials, covered next, provided by way of your Account page on *peachpit.com/adobepress*.

Lesson files

To work through the projects in this book, you will need to download the lesson files using the following instructions.

Web Edition

The Web Edition is an online interactive version of the book providing an enhanced learning experience. Your Web Edition can be accessed from any device with a connection to the internet, and it contains:

* The complete text of the book.
* Hours of instructional video keyed to the text. Throughout the lessons, content that is available only as video content is marked with a video icon (■◀).
* Interactive quizzes.

Accessing the lesson files and Web Edition

You must register your purchase on *peachpit.com/adobepress* to access the online content:

1 Go to *peachpit.com/IllustratorCIB2024*.

2 Sign in or create a new account.

3 Click Register.

4 Answer the question as proof of purchase.

5 The lesson files can be accessed from the Registered Products tab on your Account page. Click the Access Bonus Content link below the title of your product to proceed to the download page. Click the lesson file link(s) to download them to your computer.

The Web Edition can be accessed from the Digital Purchases tab on your Account page. Click the Launch link to access the product.

● **Note:** If you purchased a digital product directly from *peachpit.com/adobepress*, your product will already be registered. Look for the Access Bonus Content link on the Registered Products tab in your account.

Restoring default preferences

The preferences file controls how command settings appear on your screen when you open the Adobe Illustrator program. Each time you quit Adobe Illustrator, the position of the panels and certain command settings are recorded in different preference files. If you want to restore the tools and settings to their original default settings, you can reset the Adobe Illustrator preferences.

You must restore the default preferences for Illustrator before you begin each lesson. This ensures that the tools function and the defaults are set exactly as described in this book.

To reset the current Illustrator preferences

1 Launch Adobe Illustrator.

2 Choose Illustrator > Settings > General (macOS) or Edit > Preferences > General (Windows).

3 In the Preferences dialog box, click the Reset Preferences button.

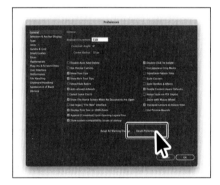

4 Click OK.

5 In the warning dialog that appears, click Restart Now.

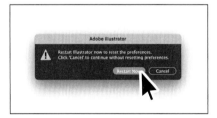

Illustrator will quit and then relaunch. When Illustrator reopens, the preferences will be reset.

Additional resources

Adobe Illustrator Classroom in a Book® 2024 Release is not meant to replace documentation that comes with the program or to be a comprehensive reference for every feature. Only the commands and options used in the lessons are explained in this book. For comprehensive information about program features and tutorials, please refer to these resources:

Adobe Illustrator Tutorials: *creativecloud.adobe.com/cc/learn/app/illustrator* is where you can find and browse tutorials on Adobe.com. In Illustrator, if you choose Help > Tutorials, the Discover panel will open where you can find and browse tutorials within the app.

Adobe Illustrator Learn & Support: *helpx.adobe.com/support/illustrator.html* is where you can find and browse tutorials, help, and support on Adobe.com. In Illustrator, if you choose Help > Illustrator Help, the Discover panel will open where you can find and browse hands-on tutorials, tutorials, and help articles within the app.

Adobe Community: *community.adobe.com* lets you tap into peer-to-peer discussions, questions, and answers on Adobe products.

Resources for educators: *adobe.com/education* and *edex.adobe.com* offer valuable information for instructors who teach classes on Adobe software. Find solutions for education at all levels, including free curricula that can be used to prepare for the Adobe Certified Associate exams.

Adobe Illustrator product home page: See *adobe.com/products/illustrator.html*.

Adobe add-ons: *exchange.adobe.com/creativecloud.html* is a central resource for finding tools, services, extensions, code samples, and more to supplement and extend Adobe Creative Cloud.

Adobe Authorized Training Partners

Browse a wealth of courses offered worldwide by our Adobe Authorized Training Partners at *learning.adobe.com/partner-finder.html*.

WHAT'S NEW IN ADOBE ILLUSTRATOR 2024 RELEASE

Adobe Illustrator 2024 release has new and innovative features to help you produce artwork more efficiently for print, web, and digital video publication. The features and exercises you'll learn about in this book are based on the Illustrator 2024 release. In this section, you'll preview many of these new features.

Mockup (Beta)

(found in Lesson 14)

With Mockup, currently in beta, you can create high-quality mockups of vector artwork (only) on raster images of mugs, totes, T-shirts—whatever you can think of.

Text to Vector Graphic (Beta)

(found in Lesson 3)

Using Text to Vector Graphic, you can generate all kinds of vector content based on a simple everyday language text prompt.

Generative Recolor

(found in Lesson 8)

In the Recolor Artwork dialog box, there is a feature called Generative Recolor. Generative Recolor is part of a suite of AI-powered capabilities powered by Adobe Firefly (*firefly.adobe.com*). With it you can recolor artwork using text prompts to achieve quick color variations.

Retype (Beta)

(found in Lesson 9)

With Retype, Illustrator can identify the fonts of text found in raster images, as well as those of outlined text. Once it's identified, you can apply the font to text and convert the text to live text that is editable.

Search and filter layers

(found in Lesson 10)

You can search for a layer or object name, or use the layer and object filters in the Layers panel, to locate specific layers and objects quickly.

Contextual Task bar

(found in Lesson 1)

In order to work faster, when you select things, you can access the most common actions and tools using the contextual Task bar. This can be faster than going to the Properties panel for common actions.

WebP export

You can now export in the WebP format.

Adobe is committed to providing the best tools possible for your publishing needs. We hope you enjoy working with Illustrator 2024 release as much as we do.

—The *Adobe Illustrator Classroom in a Book® 2024 Release* team

A QUICK TOUR OF ADOBE ILLUSTRATOR 2024 RELEASE

Lesson overview

In this interactive demonstration of Adobe Illustrator 2024 release you'll get an overview of the main features of the application.

 This lesson will take about 30 minutes to complete. To get the lesson files used in this lesson, download them from the web page for this book at *peachpit.com/IllustratorCIB2024*. For more information, see "Accessing the lesson files and Web Edition" in the Getting Started section at the beginning of this book.

Explore some of the essential features of
Adobe Illustrator as you create an advertisement for
an art supply store.

Starting the lesson

For the first lesson of this book, you'll get a quick tour of the most widely used tools and features in Adobe Illustrator, offering a sense of the many possibilities. Along the way, you'll create artwork for an art supply advertisement. First, you'll open the final artwork to see what you will create in this lesson.

Note: If you have not already downloaded the project files for this lesson to your computer from your Account page, make sure to do so now. See the "Getting Started" section at the beginning of the book.

1   To ensure that the tools and panels function exactly as described in this lesson, delete or deactivate (by renaming) the Adobe Illustrator preferences file. See "Restoring default preferences" in the "Getting Started" section at the beginning of the book.

2   Start Adobe Illustrator.

3   Choose File > Open, or click Open in the Home screen that is showing. Open the L00_end.ai file in the Lessons > Lesson00 folder.

4   Choose View > Fit Artboard In Window to see an example of the art supply ad you'll create in this lesson. Leave the file open for reference, if you'd like.

Creating a new document

In Illustrator, you can start a new document using preset options, depending on what you're making. In this case, you'll make an ad for social media, so you'll choose a preset from the Web presets to start.

1   Choose File > New.

2   In the New Document dialog box, select the Web preset category at the top of the dialog box.

Selecting the Web preset category gives you document sizes you might use when designing a project for the web. In the Preset Details area *on the right*, change the following:

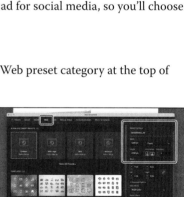

  • Enter a name for the document in the blank space: **SocialMedia_ad**.
  • Width: Select the Width value, and type **1080** (pixels).
  • Height: Select the Height value, and type **1080** (pixels).

3   Click Create, and a new, blank document opens.

Saving the document

Now let's save the project as an Illustrator document.

1 Choose File > Save.

2 If the Cloud Document dialog box opens, click Save On Your Computer to save the file on your computer (locally).

▷ **Tip:** Want to learn more about what a cloud document is? Explore the section "What are cloud documents?" in Lesson 3, "Make a Logo with Shapes."

3 In the Save As dialog box, set the following options:

- Leave the name as SocialMedia_ad.ai.

- Navigate to the Lessons > Lesson00 folder.

- Leave Adobe Illustrator (ai) chosen from the Format menu (macOS) or Adobe Illustrator (*.AI) chosen from the Save As Type menu (Windows).

- Click Save.

4 In the Illustrator Options dialog box that appears, simply click OK.

With the document saved to your computer, now let's make sure Illustrator is showing all of the tools and features you need.

5 Choose Window > Workspace > Essentials, and then choose Window > Workspace > Reset Essentials to reset the workspace.

6 Choose View > Fit Artboard In Window.

The white area you see is called the *artboard*, and it's where your artwork will go. Artboards are like pages in Adobe InDesign or a piece of paper on your desk. Your document can have multiple artboards, and each can be a different size.

Creating shapes

▶ **Tip:** Explore how to make and edit all kinds of different shapes in Lesson 3.

Shapes are the cornerstone of Illustrator, and you'll create a lot of them in the coming lessons. To start this project, you'll make several shapes that you'll combine to create a coloring marker, as you see at right.

1   Select the Rectangle tool (▨) in the toolbar on the left.

You'll start by making the narrower top of the marker body.

2   In the top part of the artboard, drag to make a rectangle.

After drawing it, the shape will be selected. Now let's make the rectangle a specific size.

3   In the Properties panel on the right, select the W value (Width) and change it to **80**.

4   Select the H value (Height) and change it to **110**. Press Return or Enter to accept the change.

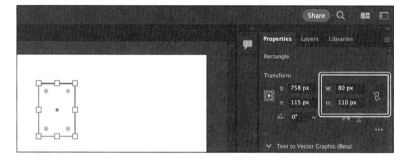

5   To hide the rectangle temporarily, choose Object > Hide > Selection.

That way, you can't accidentally move or edit it in any way. Now you'll make a larger rectangle that will become the wider marker body.

6   On the artboard, drag to make a much larger rectangle.

7   In the Properties panel, select the W (Width) value and change it to **280**. Select the H value (Height) and change it to **600**. Press Return or Enter to accept the change.

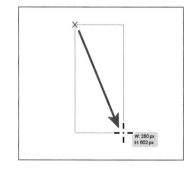

Editing shapes

Next you'll resize the larger rectangle by dragging an edge. This can make it so you don't have to be as exact as you just were in the Properties panel when creating shapes. You'll refer to a small measurement label that appears next to the cursor when you're resizing, to see how big it is.

▶ **Tip:** Explore shape editing in Lesson 3 and Lesson 4, "Editing and Combining Shapes and Paths."

1   Select the Selection tool (▶) in the toolbar on the left to be able to select shapes.

2   With the largest rectangle still selected, drag the bottom middle point on the box down to make the rectangle taller. When you see a height of about 800 pixels in the small gray measurement label next to the pointer, release the mouse button.

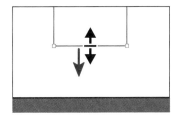 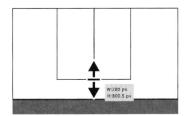

When you make a shape, that gray measurement label showing its size is a part of Smart Guides, which are turned on by default.

● **Note:** If you don't see the measurement label, make sure Smart Guides are on. Choose View > Smart Guides. A checkmark next to "Smart Guides" in the menu means they are on.

Rounding corners

To make the top of the marker look more natural, you'll round the top of the large rectangle, like you see at right.

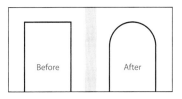

1   With the rectangle still selected, select the Direct Selection tool (▷) in the toolbar.

See the little blue squares on the corners of the rectangle? Those are called *anchor points*. They are used to control the shape of the path.

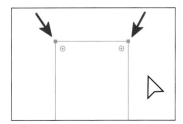

▶ **Tip:** Learn more about paths and anchor points in Lesson 7, "Drawing with the Pen Tool."

You will also see a bunch of small double circles called *corner radius widgets*. They control the roundness of the corners. To round two corners at once, you will select the anchor points on just those corners.

2 Drag across the top two corners of the rectangle. See the following figure.

3 Drag the double-circle (⊚) in either corner toward the center of the rectangle to round the corners as far as you can.

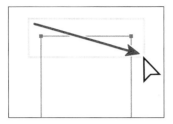 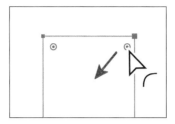 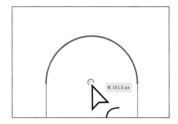

If you drag far enough, the top part that is curved will turn red, telling you that's as much as you can round the corners.

Copying shapes

Now you'll make a copy of the small rectangle you hid earlier. This new rectangle will be the tip of the marker.

1 Choose Object > Show All to see the small, hidden rectangle again. It should be selected now.

2 Select the Selection tool (▶) in the toolbar.

3 Drag the two rectangles like you see in the figure. *Make sure the small rectangle is under the larger rectangle a little!*

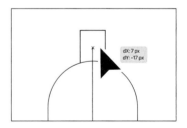

You'll see a vertical magenta guide as you drag, telling you that the shapes are aligned vertically.

4 With the small rectangle selected, choose Edit > Copy, and then choose Edit > Paste.

5 Drag the new copy above the original smaller rectangle like you see in the figure.

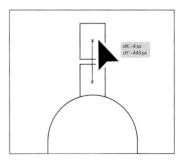

Don't worry right now if the shapes are off of the white artboard (page) area. You will move them soon.

6 Choose Select > Deselect so the shape is no longer selected.

7 Choose File > Save to save the document.

Combining shapes using the Shape Builder tool

You can make more complex artwork without having to "draw" it most of the time, by merging shapes with the Shape Builder tool (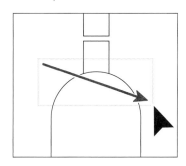). Next you'll merge the larger rectangle and one of the smaller rectangles to make the body of the marker.

1 Starting in an empty area of the artboard, drag across the two shapes you see in the figure to select them.

2 Select the Shape Builder tool (⊕) in the toolbar on the left.

3 Move the pointer to roughly where you see the pointer in the first part of the following figure.

4 Drag through all of the selected shapes to combine them, following the second part of the figure for where to drag. Release the mouse button, and the shapes are combined.

> **Tip:** Didn't drag through all of the shapes? Try again!

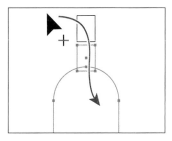 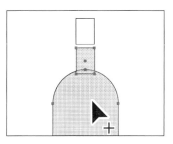 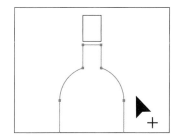

Now you'll practice rounding a few of the corners on the combined marker shapes like you did to the top of the rectangle previously.

5 Select the Direct Selection tool (▷) in the toolbar.

6 Drag across the two anchor points you see in the following figure.

7 Drag either double-circle (◉) away from the shape to round the corners as much as you want.

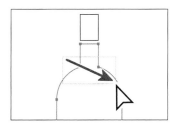 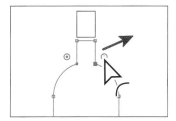 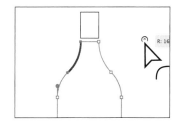

8 Save the file by choosing File > Save.

Applying and editing color

▶ **Tip:** Learn more about fill and stroke in Lesson 8, "Using Color to Enhance Artwork."

Applying color to artwork is a great way to express yourself creatively. Shapes you create can have a stroke (border) that goes around the edge and can be filled with a color. You can apply and edit swatches, which are saved colors that you make or that come with each document by default.

1   Select the Selection tool (▶) in the toolbar.

2   Click the small rectangle above the marker body shape to select it.

3   In the Properties panel on the right, click the white color box (☐) to the left of the word "Fill." In the Swatches panel that opens, make sure that the Swatches option (▦) is selected at the top. Move the pointer over the color swatches, and a tool tip appears, telling you the name of the swatch. Click an orange color with the tool tip "R=247, G=147, B=30" to change the fill color.

 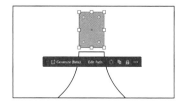

While you can use the default swatches, you can also create your own colors and save them to reuse later!

4   To remove the stroke (border) on the shape, in the Properties panel, click the down arrow for the stroke weight until it is gone.

5   Select the larger marker body shape to change its fill color as well.

6   Click the Fill color box (☐) to the left of the word "Fill" in the Properties panel. In the Swatches panel, click to apply a lighter orange color to the marker body. Leave the Swatches panel showing. Now you'll edit that color.

 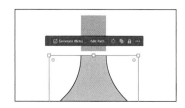

7   Double-click the swatch you applied in the Swatches panel (it has a white border around it).

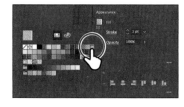

8 In the Swatch Options dialog box, select Preview to see the change to the marker body. Drag the G (green) slider to the right to make the color more yellow and make it a bit lighter. The swatch is made of red, green, and blue colors.

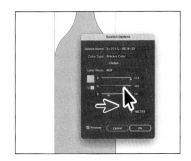

9 Click OK to save the change you made to the swatch.

10 To remove the stroke (border) on the shape, in the Properties panel, click the down arrow for the stroke weight until it is gone.

Transforming artwork

From rotating and scaling to moving, shearing, and reflecting, transforming artwork in Illustrator will allow you to make unique and creative content.

Now you'll reshape the marker tip and then make some copies of the whole marker, change the color, and rotate them.

1 Click the small rectangle above the marker body to select it.

2 Select the Direct Selection tool (⟜) in the toolbar,

3 Click the upper-left corner point on the rectangle to select it. Release the mouse button, and then drag that selected corner point down to give the marker tip a chiseled look.

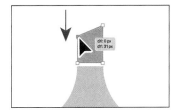

4 Select the Selection tool (▶) in the toolbar.

5 To deselect everything, choose Select > Deselect.

6 To select both shapes on the artboard, choose Select > All On Active Artboard.

7 Click the Group button toward the bottom of the Properties panel on the right.

Grouping treats the selected objects as one. The next time you want to select both the marker tip and the body, you can simply click one to select them as a group.

8 Choose Edit > Copy and then Edit > Paste to make a copy of the marker.

9 Drag the copy to the left, as in the figure.

10 To rotate the copy of the marker, move the pointer just off a corner of the box around it. When you see curved arrows, drag counterclockwise to rotate it a little.

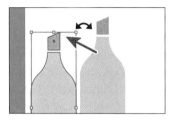 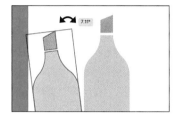

With one marker copy in place, you'll make another copy and flip it so it's on the other side of the original marker.

11 With the marker still selected, make a copy by choosing Edit > Copy. This time, choose Edit > Paste In Place to make a copy right on top of the original.

12 To flip the copy, in the Properties panel, click the Flip Horizontally button ().

13 Begin dragging the marker to the right, pressing the Shift key as you drag. When the marker is to the right of the other markers, release the mouse button and then the key. Leave the marker selected.

 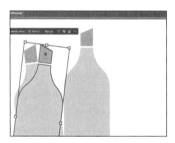 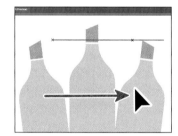

Recoloring artwork

In Illustrator, you can easily recolor artwork using the Recolor Artwork feature. Next, you'll recolor the two marker copies.

1 With the marker on the far right selected, Shift-click the marker on the far left to select the markers on either side of the marker in the center.

2 Click the Recolor button toward the bottom of the Properties panel to open the Recolor Artwork dialog box.

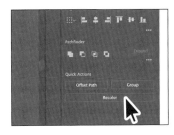 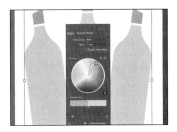

You can see the two colors from the bottle—the orange and lighter orange—as circles on the color wheel in the middle of the dialog box. Recolor Artwork lets you change color in selected artwork. Now, you'll display the swatches that are in the document and then change the two orange colors.

3   Choose Document Swatches from the Color Library menu at the top of the panel.

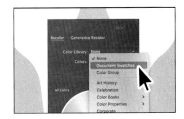

The color wheel now shows the swatches you saw when editing the fill color of the artwork in the Properties panel. You can drag the little color circles in the color wheel to change the corresponding color in the selected art. But by default, dragging one color circle drags all of them together.

4   To edit the two colors independently, click the link icon (🔗) beneath the color wheel to turn it off. It will look like this after you click it: 🔗. It's circled in the first part of the following figure.

5   Now, drag each of the orange circles, one at a time, into a different red/pink color to change the artwork.

Note: To get the first, darker color, make sure you drag to the edge of the color circle, as you see in the first part of the figure.

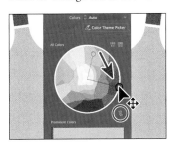 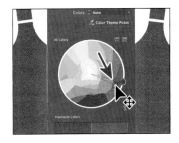

6   To select all of the markers, choose Select > All On Active Artboard.

This should also hide the Recolor Artwork dialog box.

7   Find the floating Task bar above or below the selected markers. Click the Group button in the Task bar to group them together.

8   Choose Select > Deselect.

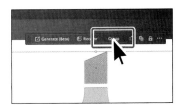

Tip: If you need to edit one of the markers, you can always click the Ungroup button in the Task bar or Properties panel to break the markers apart again.

Applying a gradient

▶ **Tip:** Learn more about working with gradients in Lesson 11, "Gradients, Blends, and Patterns."

A *gradient* consists of two or more colors that gradually blend one into another over a distance. Gradients can add a lot of creative flair and realism to your artwork. Next, you'll create a banner and apply a custom gradient to it.

1 Choose View > Zoom Out so it's easier to see the edges of the artboard.

2 Select the Rectangle tool (▢) in the toolbar.

● **Note:** Don't worry if the color of your rectangle doesn't match the figure. You'll change it next anyway.

3 Starting on the left edge of the white artboard, drag across to the right edge, making a rectangle the width of the artboard and with a height of approximately 375 pixels.

4 In the Properties panel, click the Fill color box, and select the White, Black swatch. Leave the Swatches panel showing.

5 At the bottom of the Swatches panel, click the Gradient Options button to open the Gradient panel.

    You can drag the Gradient panel by the title bar at the top to move it around.

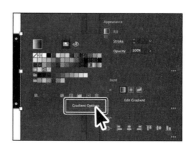

6 In the Gradient panel, do the following:

    • Click the Fill box to make sure you are editing the fill (circled in the figure).

    • Double-click the little black color stop (◉) on the right side of the gradient slider in the Gradient panel (an arrow is pointing to it in the figure).

    • Click the Swatches button (▦) in the panel that appears. Select a dark blue swatch.

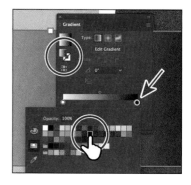

- Double-click the little white color stop (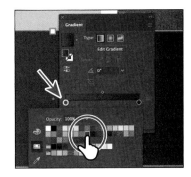) on the left side of the gradient slider in the Gradient panel (an arrow is pointing to it in the figure).
- Select a lighter blue swatch.

There are a lot of creative possibilities with gradients, from applying gradients to the stroke (border) of objects to making color transparent (see-through).

7 Click the X at the top of the Gradient panel to close it.

Editing strokes

A *stroke* is the outline (border) of artwork such as shapes and paths. There are lots of appearance properties you can change for a stroke, including width, color, dashes, and more. In this section, you'll adjust the stroke of the banner rectangle.

▶ **Tip:** Learn more about working with strokes in Lesson 3.

1 With the rectangle still selected, click the word "Stroke" in the Properties panel.

In the Properties panel, when you click an underlined word, a panel appears with more options for you.

2 In the Stroke panel, change the following options:

- Stroke Weight: **11 pt**
- Click Align Stroke To Inside (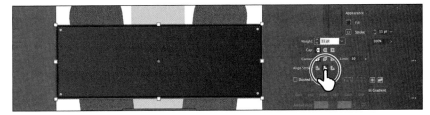) to align the stroke to the inside of the rectangle edge.

3 In the Properties panel, click the Stroke color box (◼), and select the white swatch.

4 Choose Select > Deselect.

Creating with the Curvature tool

▶ **Tip:** Learn more about working with the Curvature tool in Lesson 6, "Using the Basic Drawing Tools."

With the Curvature tool (✒), you can draw and edit smooth, refined paths and also straight lines. In this section, you'll explore the Curvature tool while creating a marker scribble.

1 Select the Curvature tool (✒) in the toolbar.

   Before you start drawing, you'll remove the fill and change the stroke color.

2 Click the Fill color box (■) in the Properties panel. In the Swatches panel that appears, click to apply the None (⊘) swatch to remove the fill.

3 Click the Stroke color box (▢) to the left of the word "Stroke" in the Properties panel. In the Swatches panel, click to apply an orange swatch. You can press the Esc key to hide the panel.

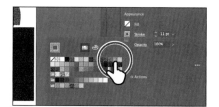

4 Move the pointer into the middle of the orange/yellow marker tip (see the first part of the following figure). Click and release to start drawing a shape.

5 To make a serpentine shape (like an "s"), move the pointer to the left, and click and release (see the second part of the figure). Move the pointer away after clicking to see a curving path.

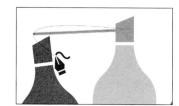

Every time you click, you are creating what is called an *anchor point*. As described earlier, anchor points you add (the circles you see on the path) control the shape of the path.

▶ **Tip:** After creating the path, you can move the pointer over any of the anchor points on the path—the circles—and drag to edit the path.

6 Make a scribble by clicking to the right, to the left, and then to the right. See the figure for where I clicked.

7 Press the Esc key to stop drawing.

   With the path selected, next you'll change the order of the artwork and put the path behind everything else on the artboard.

8   Click the Arrange button in the Quick Actions section of the Properties panel. Choose Send To Back to stack it behind everything. Leave it selected.

Applying a brush

With brushes, you can decorate paths with patterns, figures, brush strokes, textures, or angled strokes. You can also modify the brushes provided with Illustrator and create your brushes. Next, you'll apply a brush to the path you just drew to make it look more like a marker scribble.

▶ **Tip:** Learn more about getting creative with brushes in Lesson 12, "Using Brushes to Create an Ad."

1   Select the Selection tool (▶) in the toolbar.

2   With the path you drew still selected, choose Window > Brush Libraries > Artistic > Artistic_Ink. It's toward the bottom of the long menu.

    In the panel that opens, you see some brushes that come with Illustrator.

3   Scroll in the Artistic_Ink panel, and click the brush named Marker to apply it.

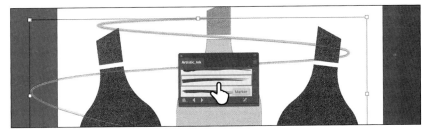

4   Close the Artistic_Ink panel by clicking the X in the top corner of the panel.

5   Change the Stroke Weight in the Properties panel to 6 pt by clicking the up arrow to the right of the word "Stroke."

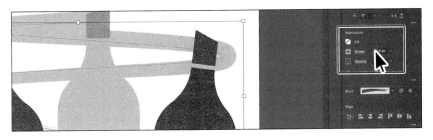

Working with type

▶ **Tip:** Learn more about working with type in Lesson 9, "Adding Type to a Project."

Next you'll add text to the project and make some formatting changes to it.

1   Select the Type tool (**T**) in the toolbar on the left, and click in the large rectangle with the gradient fill.

Placeholder text will appear with the selected placeholder text, "Lorem ipsum."

2   Type **ART SUPPLIES** in capital letters.

The text will be small and hard to read against the gradient. You'll remedy that next.

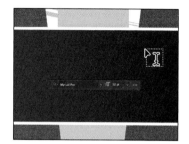

3   Select the Selection tool (▶) so the text object is selected.

4   Click the Fill color box (■) in the Properties panel. In the Swatches panel, click to apply an orange color.

5   In the Character section of the Properties panel, select the font size, and type **73**. Press Return or Enter to accept the size change.

6   In the same section of the Properties panel, change the Tracking (🔡) value by selecting the value in the field and typing **30** (highlighted in the following figure). Press Return or Enter to accept the change.

Tracking is how you can adjust spacing between characters. Leave the text selected.

Warping text

You can create some great design effects by warping text into different shapes using envelopes. You can make an envelope out of a custom shape, or you can use a preset warp shape or a mesh grid as an envelope.

▶ **Tip:** Learn more about warping text in Lesson 9.

1 With the Selection tool selected and the text still selected, copy and paste the text by choosing Edit > Copy and then Edit > Paste.

2 Drag the two text boxes so they are still within the bounds of the rectangle and stacked one on top of the other.

3 Select the Type tool (**T**), move the pointer over the top text, and triple-click to select it. Type **CRAFTY**.

4 Select the Selection tool (▶) so the CRAFTY text object is selected.

5 Change the font size to **190** in the Task bar below (or above) the selected text.

6 Choose Object > Envelope Distort > Make With Warp to open the Warp Options dialog box. In that dialog box, change the following:

- Style: Arch (*not Arc*)
- Bend: **20%**

7 Click OK. The text is now in a shape but is still editable.

▶ **Tip:** Want to edit the warp options again? Click the Warp Options button in the Quick Actions section of the Properties panel.

8 With the Selection tool selected, drag the curved text and the "ART SUPPLIES" text into position like you see in the figure.

Don't worry about having the text centered in the poster or blue shape—you'll do that shortly!

9 Choose File > Save.

Working with effects

▶ **Tip:** Learn more about effects in Lesson 13, "Exploring Creative Uses of Effects and Graphic Styles."

Effects, like drop shadows, let you really get creative with your artwork. Next you'll apply an effect to a sale sticker you make.

1   Press and hold on the Rectangle tool (▢) in the toolbar, and select the Ellipse tool (⬭).

2   Over the top of the banner rectangle, Shift-drag to make a circle like the one in the figure. Release the mouse button and then the key.

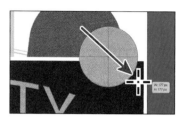

3   Click the Fill color in the Properties panel. In the panel that opens, select a light blue color.

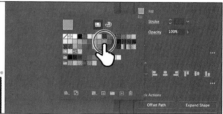

4   In the Properties panel, click the Choose An Effect button (*fx.*), and choose Distort & Transform > Zig Zag.

5   In the Zig Zag dialog box, select Preview to see your changes, if it isn't already selected, and then set the following options:

   • Size: **9 px**
   • Absolute: **Selected**
   • Ridges Per Segment: **9**
   • Points: **Corner**

6   Click OK.

Adding more text for practice

Now for a little practice! Try adding some text on top of the circle. You'll apply formatting you've already learned and a few more options. Here are the steps:

1   Select the Type tool (**T**), and click to add some text. To replace the text, type **30%**, press Return or Enter, and then type **OFF**.

2   Select the Selection tool (▶) so the text object is selected.

3 Set the following options in the Properties panel:

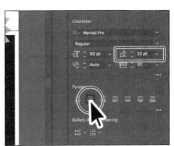

- Change the fill color to white.
- Change the font size to **60 pt**.
- Change the Leading (circled in the figure) to **50**. This changes the distance between the lines of text.
- In the Paragraph section of the Properties panel (below the formatting options you just set), click Align Center (▤) so the text is center aligned.

4 Drag the text so it is approximately centered on the circle.

⬤ **Note:** If your circle is too small, press the Shift key and drag a corner to make it larger. Release the mouse button and then the key.

Aligning artwork

Illustrator makes it easy to align or distribute multiple objects relative to each other, the artboard, or a key object. In this section, you'll move artwork into position and align some of it to the center of the artboard.

1 With the Selection tool (▶) selected, click to select the group of markers.

2 To select more content, press the Shift key and click the banner rectangle, the "CRAFTY" text, and the "ART SUPPLIES" text.

3 Click the Align To Selection menu (▦▾) in the Properties panel to the right of the document, and choose Align To Artboard from the menu.

4 Click the Horizontal Align Center button (▤) to align the selected artwork to the horizontal center of the artboard.

5 If necessary, drag the marker scribble and the 30% OFF graphic into position.

6 Choose File > Save, and then choose File > Close.

1 GETTING TO KNOW THE WORK AREA

Lesson overview

In this lesson, you'll explore the Illustrator workspace and learn how to do the following:

- Open an Adobe Illustrator file.

- Work with the toolbar, Properties panel, and Task bar.

- Move the toolbar. �

- Customize the toolbar. ■◀

- Work with panels.

- Scale the Illustrator interface. ■◀

- Reset and save your workspace.

- Use view options to change the display magnification.

- Pan with the Navigator panel. ■◀

- Rotate the canvas view.

- Navigate multiple artboards.

- Arrange multiple documents. ■◀

 This lesson will take about 45 minutes to complete. To get the lesson files used in this lesson, download them from the web page for this book at *peachpit.com/IllustratorCIB2024*. For more information, see "Accessing the lesson files and Web Edition" in the Getting Started section at the beginning of this book.

By learning how to navigate the workspace easily and efficiently, you'll be able to make the most of the extensive drawing, painting, and editing capabilities of Adobe Illustrator.

Welcome to Adobe Illustrator!

When I think of Illustrator, I think of an app for creating logos, posters, flyers, icons, and much more. Illustrator is about making and editing what are called *vector graphics* (sometimes called *vector shapes, art,* or *objects*).

Projects created using Adobe Illustrator.

Vector graphics are made of lines and curves defined by mathematical objects called *vectors*. You can resize vector graphics to cover the side of a building or use them as small as a social media icon without losing detail or clarity. As a result, vector graphics are the best choice for artwork, like logos, that will be used in various sizes and output media.

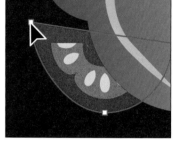

Vector graphics maintain crisp edges when printed to a PostScript printer, saved in a PDF file, or imported into a vector-based graphics application.

▶ **Tip:** To learn more about bitmap graphics, search for "Import bitmap images" in the Discover panel by choosing Help > Illustrator Help.

With Illustrator, you can also incorporate *bitmap images*—technically called *raster images*—made up of a rectangular grid of square pixels. Each pixel in the grid has a specific color. Take a look at the image below.

Example of a raster image and a zoomed-in portion to show the pixels. I added a grid to the zoomed-in part on the right to give you the idea.

Pictures you take with your phone camera are considered raster images. Raster images can be created and edited in a program like Adobe Photoshop.

Opening an Illustrator file

In this lesson, you'll open a document and explore Illustrator by navigating, zooming, and investigating in that document and the workspace. First, you'll restore the default preferences for Adobe Illustrator. You'll reset preferences at the start of each lesson in this book to ensure that the tools function as described in the lesson.

1 To delete or deactivate (by renaming) the Adobe Illustrator preferences file, see "Restoring default preferences" in the "Getting Started" section at the beginning of the book.

2 Double-click the Adobe Illustrator icon to launch Adobe Illustrator.

   With Illustrator open, you will see the Home screen showing starting file sizes, resources for Illustrator, and more.

3 Choose File > Open or click the Open button in the Home screen.

4 In the Lessons > Lesson01 folder on your hard disk, select the L1_start1.ai file, and click Open to open the design for a shoe ad.

   To start, with the file open, you'll reset the Illustrator interface so we all see the same thing.

Note: If you have not already downloaded the project files for this lesson to your computer from your Account page, make sure to do so now. See the "Getting Started" section at the beginning of the book.

5 Choose Window > Workspace and make sure Essentials is selected. A checkmark appears next to the name if selected.

6 Choose Window > Workspace > Reset Essentials to reset the workspace.

   The Reset Essentials command ensures that the workspace, which includes all of the tools and panels, is set to the default settings. You'll learn more about resetting the workspace later, in the section "Switching and resetting workspaces."

7 Choose View > Fit Artboard In Window.

   An *artboard* is the area that contains artwork that can be output and is like a page in Adobe InDesign or Microsoft Word.

   This command fits the whole artboard into the Document window so you can see the whole design. I added a red line around the artboard in the figure. You won't see the red line in your project.

Exploring the workspace

When Illustrator is launched and a file is open, the menus, Application bar, toolbar, and panels appear on the screen. The arrangement of these elements is called a *workspace*.

When you first start Illustrator, you see the default workspace, which you can customize. You can create and save multiple workspaces—one for editing and another for viewing, for example—and switch between them as you work.

A. Application bar

B. Panels

C. Toolbar

D. Document window

E. Status Bar

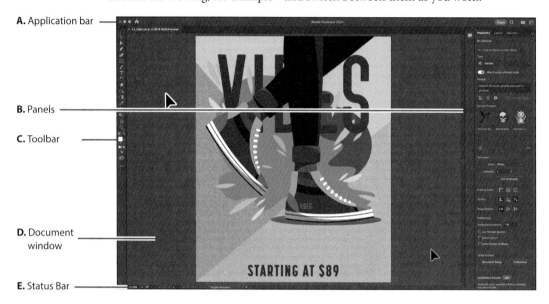

● **Note:** The screen captures in this lesson were taken using macOS and may look slightly different from what you see, especially if you are using Windows.

A. The **Application bar**, across the top by default, contains application controls, the workspace switcher, and search. On Windows, the main menu bar items appear *inline* with the Application bar—see the following figure.

B. **Panels** help you monitor and modify your work. Certain panels are displayed by default in the panel dock on the right side of the workspace, and you can display any panel by choosing it from the Window menu.

C. The **toolbar** contains tools for creating and editing images, artwork, artboard elements, and more. Related tools are grouped together.

D. The **Document window** displays the file(s) you're working on.

E. The **Status Bar** appears at the lower-left edge of the Document window. It displays file information, zooming, and navigation controls.

Getting to know the tools

The toolbar on the left side of the workspace contains tools for selecting, drawing, painting, editing, and viewing, as well as the Fill and Stroke boxes, drawing modes, and screen modes. As you work through the lessons, you'll learn about the specific function of many of these tools.

To start, you'll make a few changes to the design with the tools you select.

1 Move the pointer over the Selection tool (▶) in the toolbar on the left.

 Notice that the name (Selection tool) and keyboard shortcut (V) display in a tool tip. You might also see more information about the tool.

2 Select the Selection tool, if necessary, then select the purple text "STARTING AT $89."

Tip: You can turn the tool tips on or off by choosing Illustrator > Settings > General (macOS) or Edit > Preferences > General (Windows) and selecting or deselecting Show Rich Tool Tips.

3 Drag it up higher so it's more nearly centered in the area below the shoe.

Note: You need to drag the text from *within* the purple letters. You may find you accidentally dragged the shape in the background!

The Selection tool is one tool you will use a lot and is used for moving, resizing, scaling, and rotating content in your projects.

4 In the toolbar on the left, press and hold the Rectangle tool (▭) to reveal a menu of tools. Select the Star tool (☆).

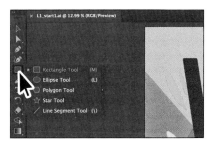
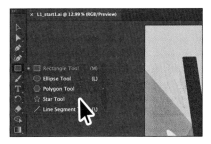

Any tool in the toolbar that displays a small triangle contains additional tools that can be selected this way.

Tip: Don't like where the star is? Don't forget about the Selection tool (▶)! You could select the Selection tool and move it.

5 To the left of the "STARTING AT $89" text in the ad, drag to draw a little star.

Notice that the star you made is probably purple. That's because you selected the text, which was purple, before making the star. Whatever you make next keeps the same color!

Working with the Properties panel

With a document open in Illustrator, you'll see the Properties panel on the right side of the workspace by default. The Properties panel displays options you can set for the active document when nothing is selected. It also shows appearance properties for any content you select. It's a panel you'll use quite a bit; it puts all the most commonly used options in one place. Using the Properties panel, you'll change the color of the star in the poster.

1 Select the Selection tool (▶) in the toolbar, and look in the Properties panel on the right.

2 Choose Select > Deselect so the star is no longer selected.

At the top of the Properties panel, you will see "No Selection." This is the *Selection Indicator*. It's a great place to see what type of content is selected (if any).

With nothing selected in the document, the Properties panel shows the current document properties and program preferences.

3 Click to select the large text "VIBES" in the background.

In the Properties panel, you should now see appearance options for the selected artwork, which is a group, as indicated

by "Group" at the top of the panel. You can change the size, position, color, and much more for the selected artwork.

4 Click the color box (■) to the left of the word "Fill" in the Properties panel to show a panel of colors.

5 In the panel that shows, make sure the Swatches option (▦) is selected at the top (circled in the following figure), and then click any color to apply it. I chose a pink.

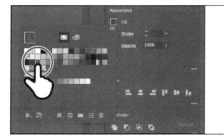 

6 Press Escape to hide the panel.

Exploring the Contextual Task Bar

To work faster, when you select things, you can access the most common actions and tools using the contextual Task bar. Using the Task bar options can be faster than going to the Properties panel for common actions. For the rest of the lessons, we will refer to this simply as the Task bar. Now, you'll try it out by copying the star.

1 Select the purple star you drew earlier.

You should see the Task bar showing above or below the selected artwork now. In that bar you can do things like duplicate, lock, repeat, or even recolor the text.

2 Click the Duplicate This Object (⊡) button in the Task bar to make a copy right on top of the original.

● **Note:** If you don't want the Task bar to show, you can turn if off by choosing Window > Contextual Task Bar.

▶ **Tip:** You can drag the Task bar by the little gripper area on the left edge. If you want to reset the position, choose Reset Bar Position from the More Options menu (▪▪▪) on the right end of the Task bar.

3 Start dragging the selected star to the right. As you drag, press the Shift key. Release the mouse and then the key when the star is on the right side of the "STARTING AT $89" text.

Finding more tools

In Illustrator, not all available tools are shown in the toolbar by default. As you go through this book, you'll explore some of those hidden tools. In this section, you'll see how to access all of the tools and then make an edit to the artwork.

1 Choose Window > Toolbars > Advanced.

The toolbar now contains every tool available to you in Illustrator.

Now you will use the Knife tool, which is a part of the Advanced toolbar, to cut a shape in the background so you can change the color.

2 Select the Selection tool (▶) in the toolbar. Click the lighter orange shape behind the "STARTING AT $89" text.

You'll learn more about how to use the Knife tool in Lesson 4, "Editing and Combining Shapes and Paths," but for now, know that you can cut only what is selected.

3 Press and hold on the Eraser tool (◆) in the toolbar and select the Knife tool (✏) from the menu.

4 To zoom out a little and give yourself some room to work, choose View > Zoom Out once or twice.

5 Drag across the selected shape to cut it into two pieces. Use the following figure as a guide for where to drag.

The cut line won't be perfectly straight—that's how the Knife tool is supposed to work!

● **Note:** If the design moves in the Document window, you can choose View > Fit Artboard In Window to recenter it.

6   Choose Select > Deselect so the two parts of the shape are no longer selected.

7   Select the Selection tool (▶) in the toolbar. Click the smaller orange shape behind the "STARTING AT $89" text.

8   Click the color box to the left of the word "Fill" in the Properties panel to show a panel of colors.

9   In the panel that shows, make sure the Swatches option (▦) is selected at the top, and then click any color to apply it. I chose a lighter yellow/orange color.

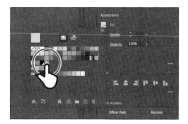 

10 Choose Window > Toolbars > Basic.

The toolbar is now reset to the basic toolbar again.

Moving the toolbar 📹

To learn about how to customize the appearance and location of the toolbar, check out the video *Moving the toolbar*, which is part of the Web Edition. For more information, see the "Web Edition" section of "Getting Started" at the beginning of the book.

Customizing the toolbar 📹

To learn about how to customize which tools appear in the toolbar, check out the video *Customizing the toolbar*, which is part of the Web Edition. For more information, see the "Web Edition" section of "Getting Started" at the beginning of the book.

Working with panels

On the right side of the workspace, the Properties panel is grouped with a few other panels by default. Sometimes those panels can get in the way. Next, you'll explore how to minimize panels and how to get them back the way they were.

1 In the upper-right corner of the application, click the Layers panel tab to the right of the Properties panel tab.

The Layers panel is grouped with two other panels—the Properties panel and the Libraries panel.

▶ **Tip:** Press Tab to toggle between hiding and showing panels. You can hide or show all open panels at once, except for the toolbar, by pressing Shift+Tab to toggle between hiding and showing them.

2 Click the double arrow at the top of the dock to collapse the panels.

▶ **Tip:** To expand or collapse the panel dock, you can also double-click the panel dock title bar at the top.

You can use this method of collapsing the panels to create a larger area for working on your document. You'll learn more about docking in the next section.

3 Drag the left edge of the docked panels (Properties, Layers, and Libraries) to the right until the panel text disappears.

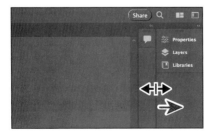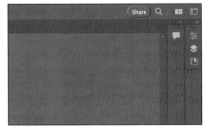

This hides the panel names and collapses the panel dock to icons only.

4 Click to select the large pink "VIBES" text in the background of the ad.

5 Click the Properties panel icon (⚏) to show the panel.

Now you'll change the color of the text again.

6 Click the color box to the left of the word "Fill" in the Properties panel to show a panel of colors, and select another color. I went back to the original purple.

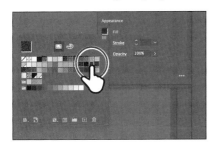

7 Click the Properties panel icon (⚏) to hide it.

● **Note:** You'll most likely need to click the icon twice. Once to hide the Swatches panel and a second time to hide the Properties panel.

8 Click the double arrow again to expand the panels.

9 Choose Window > Workspace > Reset Essentials to reset the workspace.

You'll learn more about resetting and switching workspaces in the section "Switching and resetting workspaces."

Moving and docking panels

Panels in Illustrator can be moved around in the workspace and organized to match your working needs. Next, you'll open a new panel and dock it with the default panels on the right side of the workspace.

1 Choose View > Fit Artboard In Window to fit the ad in the window.

Tip: A checkmark next to a panel name in the Window menu means it's already open and in front of other panels in its panel group. If you were to choose a panel name already selected in the Window menu, the panel and its group would either close or collapse.

2 Click the Window menu at the top of the screen to see all of the panels available in Illustrator. Choose Swatches from the Window menu to open the Swatches panel and the panels grouped with it by default.

Panels you open that do not appear in the default workspace are free-floating. That means they are not docked and can be moved around. You can dock free-floating panels on the right or left side of the workspace.

3 Drag the Swatches panel group *by the title bar above the panel names* to move the group closer to the docked panels on the right.

Next, you'll dock the Swatches panel with the Properties panel group.

Note: When dragging a panel to the dock on the right, if you see a blue line *above* the docked panel tabs before releasing, you'll create a new panel group above rather than docking the panel with the existing panel group.

4 Drag the Swatches panel *by its panel tab* onto the Properties, Layers, and Libraries panel tabs on the right. When a blue highlight appears *around* the entire panel dock, release the mouse button to dock the panel in the group.

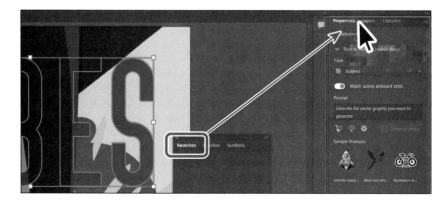

5 Click the X at the top of the Brushes and Symbols panel group, which is free-floating, to close it.

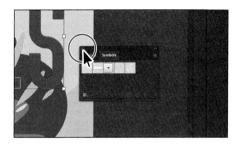

> **Tip:** To remove a panel from the dock, you can drag a panel by its tab away from the dock.

You might be thinking to yourself, "The Swatches panel has the same colors I see when clicking the Fill color in the Properties panel!" Why put the panel out here when you can see the same colors by clicking the Fill color in the Properties panel? I put the Swatches panel out here because with the Properties panel, artwork needs to be selected to see the swatches. If I want to make a color without having anything selected, I can use the Swatches panel!

Scaling the Illustrator interface ◼▶

To learn how to scale the user interface of Illustrator based on your screen resolution, check out the video *Scaling the Illustrator interface*, which is part of the Web Edition. For more information, see the "Web Edition" section of "Getting Started" at the beginning of the book.

Switching and resetting workspaces

As you've seen, you can customize the parts of your workspace, like rearranging panels. As you make changes, like opening, closing, and positioning panels, you can save that arrangement as a workspace—and switch between workspaces while you work. Illustrator also comes with a host of workspaces that are tailored to various tasks.

Next, you'll switch workspaces and learn about some new panels.

1 Above the docked panels, click the workspace switcher (▦) at the right end of the Application bar.

You'll see a number of workspaces listed; each has a specific purpose and will open panels and arrange your workspace accordingly.

> **Tip:** You can also choose Window > Workspace > Layout (or another workspace).

2 Choose Layout from the workspace switcher menu to change workspaces.

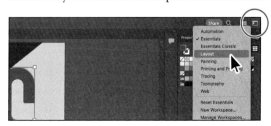

You'll notice a few major changes in the workspace. One of the biggest is the Control panel, which is now docked at the top of the workspace, just above the Document window (an arrow is pointing to it in the following figure). Similar to the Properties panel, it offers quick access to options, commands, and other panels relevant to the currently selected content.

Also, notice all of the collapsed panel icons on the right side of the workspace. In workspaces, you can create groups of panels that are stacked on top of others. That way, a lot more panels are visible.

3 Choose Essentials from the workspace switcher (▣) above the docked panels to switch back to the Essentials workspace.

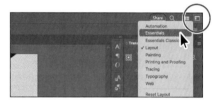

Notice that the Swatches panel is still docked in the panels.

4 Choose Reset Essentials from the workspace switcher in the Application bar.

When you switch back to a previous workspace, it remembers any changes you made, like grouping the Swatches panel. To completely reset a workspace to its default settings, the Essentials workspace in this case, you'll need to reset it.

Saving your own workspace

If you get all the panels you want out and set them right where you want them, you can save a custom workspace.

To save your own workspace, make sure your panels are where you want them and then choose Window > Workspace > New Workspace. Change its name to whatever makes sense to you in the New Workspace dialog box, and click OK.

You can now select that workspace from the workspace switcher!

Using panel and context menus

Most panels in Illustrator have more options available in a panel menu, found by clicking the panel menu icon (▤ or ▤) in the upper-right corner of a panel. These additional options can be used to change the panel display, add or change panel content, and more. Next, you'll change the display of the Swatches panel using its panel menu.

1   With the Selection tool (▶) selected in the toolbar, make sure the large "VIBES" text is selected.

2   Click the Fill color box, to the left of the word "Fill," in the Properties panel.

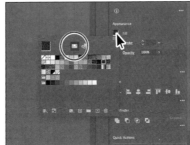

3   In the panel that appears, called the Swatches panel, make sure that the Swatches option (▦) (near the top of the panel) is selected. It's circled in the figure at right.

4   Click the panel menu icon (▤) in the upper-right corner of the panel, and choose Small List View from the panel menu.

This displays the swatch names, together with thumbnails. Because the options in the panel menu apply only to the active panel, only the Swatches panel view is affected.

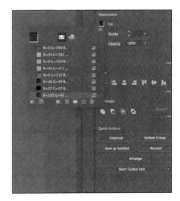

5   Click the same panel menu icon (▤) in the panel showing, and choose Small Thumbnail View to return the swatches to their original view.

6   Press Escape to hide the Swatches panel.

7   Choose Select > Deselect so the text is no longer selected.

Another type of menu you can show is a context menu, which appears wherever you right-click. In addition to the panel menus, context-sensitive menus display commands relevant to the active tool, selection, or panel. Usually the commands in a context menu are also available in another part of the workspace, but using a context menu can save you time.

▶ **Tip:** If you move the pointer over the tab or title bar for a panel and right-click, you can close a panel or a panel group from the context menu that appears.

8 Move the pointer over the dark gray area surrounding the ad. Then, right-click to show a context menu that displays commands specific to the open document.

9 Choose Zoom Out to make the ad appear a little smaller.

The content of context-sensitive menus will change depending on what the pointer is positioned over; in other words, it changes depending on its context.

Adjusting the brightness of the user interface

As with Adobe InDesign and Adobe Photoshop, Illustrator supports a brightness adjustment for the application user interface. This is a program-wide preference setting that allows you to choose a brightness setting from four preset levels.

To change the user-interface brightness, you can choose:

- Illustrator > Settings > User Interface (macOS)
- Edit > Preferences > User Interface (Windows)

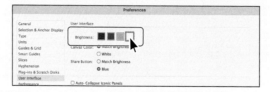

Changing the view of artwork

While working in files, you'll likely need to change the magnification level and navigate between artboards. The magnification level, which can range from 3.13% to 64000%, is displayed in the title bar (or document tab) next to the filename and in the lower-left corner of the Document window.

There are many ways to change the zoom level in Illustrator, and in this section, you'll explore several.

Using view commands

One way to zoom in or out of your project is to use view commands. They are found in the View menu and are an easy way to enlarge or reduce the view of artwork. I zoom in to and out of my artwork most often using these commands.

1   Choose View > Zoom In twice to enlarge the display of the artwork.

Using the viewing tools and commands affects only the display of the artwork, not the actual size of the artwork. Each time you choose a zoom option, the view of the artwork is resized to the closest preset zoom level. The preset zoom levels appear in a menu in the lower-left corner of the Document window, identified by a down arrow next to a percentage.

Tip: The keyboard shortcut for the View > Zoom In command is Command and + (macOS) or Ctrl and + (Windows). You can zoom out using the keyboard shortcut Command and − (macOS) or Ctrl and − (Windows).

2   Choose View > Fit Artboard In Window to see the entire ad again.

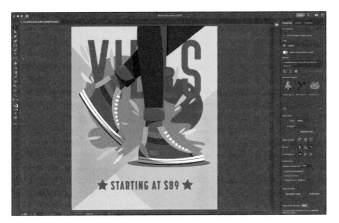

By choosing View > Fit Artboard In Window or using the keyboard shortcut Command+0 [zero] (macOS) or Ctrl+0 [zero] (Windows), the entire artboard (page) is centered in the Document window.

Tip: If you need to zoom in to a specific area of your design—like the "STARTING AT $89" text, you can select that content first and then use the View > Zoom In command to zoom in to what's selected.

3 Click the text "STARTING AT $89" to select it.

4 Choose View > Zoom In.

5 Press the Shift key and select each star to select them as well.

6 Choose Object > Group to group the text and star together. You'll learn more about grouping in Lesson 2, "Techniques for Selecting Artwork."

7 Choose View > Fit Artboard In Window to see the whole ad.

8 Choose Select > Deselect so the group is no longer selected.

Using the Zoom tool

In addition to the View menu commands, you can use the Zoom tool ($\mathbb{Q}$) to magnify and reduce the view of artwork to predefined magnification levels. I tend to use the Zoom tool when I need to zoom in to a particular area and zoom in or out a lot.

1 Select the Zoom tool ($\mathbb{Q}$) in the toolbar, and then move the pointer over the ad.

Notice that a plus sign (+) appears at the center of the pointer.

2 Move the Zoom tool pointer over the word "VIBES" on the shoe, and click once.

The artwork is displayed at a higher magnification, depending on your screen resolution. Notice that where you clicked is now in the center of the Document window.

3 Keep clicking the same "VIBES" text until you are close enough to see the cartoon eyes in the "B."

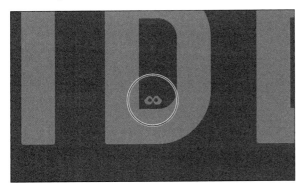

Being this close to the artwork can make it easier to see smaller details and possibly make it easier to select things. Let's remove the eyes.

4 Select the Selection tool and click the eyes artwork. Press Delete or Backspace to remove it.

5 Select the Zoom tool and press the Option (macOS) or Alt (Windows) key. A minus sign (–) appears at the center of the Zoom tool pointer. With the Option or Alt key pressed, click the artwork a few times to *reduce* the view of the artwork.

Using the Zoom tool, you can also drag in the document to zoom in and out. By default, if your computer meets the system requirements for GPU performance and it's enabled, zooming is animated. To find out if your computer meets the system requirements, see the sidebar "GPU performance" following this section.

6 Choose View > Fit Artboard In Window.

Note: If your
computer does not
meet the system
requirements for
GPU performance,
you will instead draw
a dotted rectangle,
called a *marquee*, when
dragging with the
Zoom tool.

7 With the Zoom tool still selected, drag from the left side of the document to the
right to zoom in. The zooming is animated. Drag from right to left to zoom out.

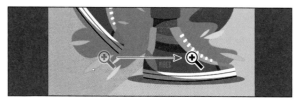

Zooming this way can be challenging at first. If you pause before dragging, it will
zoom without control. The secret is not to pause—rather, just drag.

8 Choose View > Fit Artboard In Window to fit the artboard in the
Document window.

The Zoom tool is used frequently during the editing process to enlarge and
reduce the view of artwork. Because of this, Illustrator allows you to select the
Zoom tool using the keyboard at any time without first deselecting any other
tool you may be using.

- To access the Zoom tool using your keyboard, press spacebar+Command
  (macOS) or Ctrl+spacebar (Windows).

- To access the Zoom Out tool using your keyboard, press
  spacebar+Command+Option (macOS) or Ctrl+Alt+spacebar (Windows).

Note: In certain
versions of macOS,
the keyboard
shortcuts for the Zoom
tool (Q) open Spotlight
or the Finder. If you
decide to use these
shortcuts in Illustrator,
you may want to turn
off or change those
keyboard shortcuts
in macOS System
Preferences.

GPU performance

The Graphics Processing Unit (GPU), found on video cards and as part of display
systems, is a specialized processor that can rapidly execute commands for
manipulating and displaying images. GPU-accelerated computing offers faster
performance across a broad range of design, animation, and video applications.

This feature is available on compatible macOS and Windows computers and means
you get a big performance boost.

It is turned on by default in the latest version of Illustrator, and options can be
accessed in Preferences by choosing Illustrator > Settings > Performance (macOS) or
Edit > Preferences > Performance (Windows).

To learn more about GPU performance, visit
helpx.adobe.com/illustrator/kb/gpu-performance-preview-improvements.html.

Panning in a document

In Illustrator, you can use the Hand tool (✋) to pan to different areas of a document. Using the Hand tool allows you to push the document around much like you would a piece of paper on your desk. This can be a useful way to move around in a document with a lot of artboards or when you are zoomed in. In this section, you'll access the Hand tool a few different ways.

1   Select the Selection tool (▶) and select the "STARTING AT $89" group again.

2   Choose View > Zoom In twice to zoom in to the text.

Now, suppose you need to look at the top of the ad. This is where, instead of zooming out and then zooming in to the other area, you could simply pan or *drag* to see it.

3   Press and hold on the Zoom tool in the toolbar, and select the Hand tool (✋).

4   Drag down in the Document window. As you drag, the artboard and the artwork on it move with the hand.

As with the Zoom tool (🔍), you can select the Hand tool with a keyboard shortcut without first deselecting the active tool.

5   Click any tool other than the Type tool (T) in the toolbar, and move the pointer into the Document window. Hold down the spacebar on the keyboard to temporarily select the Hand tool, and then drag to bring the artwork back into the center of your view. Release the mouse button and then the spacebar.

6   Choose View > Fit Artboard In Window.

Panning with the Navigator panel 🎥

To learn about a different way to pan around in a document, check out the video *Panning with the Navigator panel*, which is part of the Web Edition. For more information, see the "Web Edition" section of "Getting Started" at the beginning of the book.

Note: The spacebar shortcut for the Hand tool (✋) does not work when the Type tool (T) is active and the cursor is in the text. To access the Hand tool when the cursor is in text, press the Option (macOS) or Alt (Windows) key. Note that the text in the open document is not text you can edit—it is shapes. So this shortcut won't work in the document!

Rotating the view

Projects like packaging designs, logos, or any projects that contain rotated text or artwork can be easier to work on when you rotate the document temporarily. Think of a large drawing on paper. If you wanted to edit part of the drawing, you might turn the paper on your desk. In this section, you'll see how to rotate the whole canvas with the Rotate View tool to make editing text easier.

1 Choose File > Open. In the Open dialog box, navigate to the Lessons > Lesson01 folder, and select the L1_start2.ai file on your hard disk. Click Open to view two more versions of the ad.

2 Choose View > Fit All In Window to see two different ads.

3 Press and hold on the Hand tool in the toolbar, and select the Rotate View tool ().

▶ Tip: To automatically align the canvas view to a rotated object, you can choose View > Rotate View To Selection to rotate the canvas.

4 Drag clockwise in the Document window to rotate the entire canvas. As you drag, press the Shift key to rotate the view in 15-degree increments. When you see −90 degrees in the measurement label, release the mouse button and then the key.

The artboards, which are on the canvas, rotate as well.

5 Select the Type tool (**T**) in the toolbar. Now you'll edit the "STARTING AT $89" text to change the price. Drag to select the "89" text and type **98** to replace it. The text now reads "STARTING AT $98."

When finished, you can reset the canvas.

6 Select the Selection tool (▶), and click in an empty area to deselect.

7 Click the −90° you see in the Status Bar below the document to show a menu of canvas rotation values. Choose 0 from that menu to set the canvas back to the default rotation.

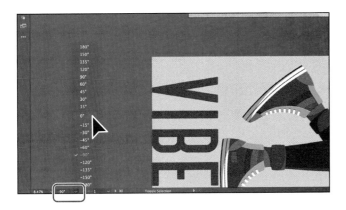

▶ **Tip:** To reset the rotated canvas view, you can also press the Esc key, choose View > Reset Rotate View, or press Shift+Cmd+1 (macOS) or Shift+Ctrl+1 (Windows).

8 Choose View > Fit All In Window.

Viewing artwork

When you open a file, the artwork is displayed in Preview mode. Illustrator offers other ways of viewing your artwork, such as outlined and rasterized. Next, you'll take a look at the different methods for viewing artwork and understand why you might view artwork each of these ways.

When working with large or complex illustrations, you may want to view only the outlines or paths of objects in your artwork. That way, the artwork doesn't have to be redrawn each time you make a change. This is called *Outline mode*. Outline mode can also be helpful for selecting objects, as you will see in Lesson 2.

1 Choose View > Outline.

Only the outlines of objects are displayed. You can also use this view to find and select things that might be hiding behind other objects. Do you see the very small "VIBES" text in the ad on the right? I circled it in the figure so you can see it. It was hidden behind the other art.

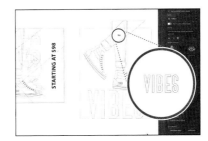

▶ **Tip:** You can press Command+Y (macOS) or Ctrl+Y (Windows) to toggle between Preview and Outline modes.

2 With the Selection tool (▶) selected, click that small text, and press Delete or Backspace to remove it.

3 With Outline mode still active, choose View > Preview (or GPU Preview) to see all the attributes of the artwork again.

4 Choose View > Pixel Preview.

5 Click the white shoelaces on the shoe on the far right. See the figure.

6 Choose 600% (or something around there) from the zoom level menu in the lower-left corner of the application window to more easily see the edges of the artwork.

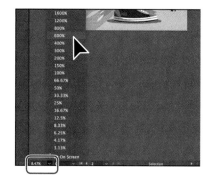

Pixel preview shows you how the artwork would look if it were rasterized and viewed onscreen in a web browser. Note the "jagged" edge on some of the artwork. Arrows are pointing to it in the figure.

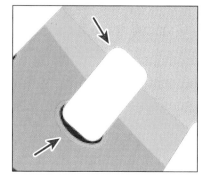

7 Choose View > Pixel Preview to turn off Pixel preview.

8 Choose Select > Deselect so the laces are no longer selected.

Navigating multiple artboards

As you may recall, artboards contain artwork that will be output, similar to pages in Adobe InDesign. You can use artboards to crop areas to be output or for placement purposes. Multiple artboards help you to create a variety of products, such as multipage PDFs, printed pages with different sizes or different elements, independent elements for websites, video storyboards, social media content, or individual items for animation in Adobe Animate or Adobe After Effects.

Illustrator allows for up to 1,000 artboards within a single file (depending on their dimensions). Multiple artboards can be added when you initially create an Illustrator document, or you can add, remove, and edit artboards after the document is made.

Tip: You'll learn about another method for navigating artboards, the Artboards panel, in Lesson 5, "Transforming Artwork."

Next, you'll learn how to navigate the artboards in the open document.

1   Choose View > Fit All In Window to make sure that you see both ads.

Notice that there are two artboards in the document; as I said earlier, these are two different versions of the ad from L1_start1.ai.

You can arrange the artboards in a document in any order, orientation, or size—they can even overlap. Suppose that you want to create a four-page brochure. You can create different artboards for every page of the brochure, all with the same size and orientation. They can be arranged horizontally or vertically or in whatever way you like.

2   Select the Selection tool (▶) in the toolbar, and click to select the vertical "STARTING AT $98" text on the artboard to the left.

3   Choose View > Fit Artboard In Window.

When you select artwork, it makes the artboard that the artwork is on the *active*, or selected, artboard. By choosing the Fit Artboard In Window command, the currently active artboard is fit into the Document window.

You can tell which is the active artboard by looking at the Artboard Navigation menu in the Status Bar below the document. Currently, it's artboard 1.

4 Choose Select > Deselect to deselect the text.

5 Choose 2 from the Artboard menu in the Properties panel.

Notice the arrows to the right of the Artboard menu in the Properties panel. You can use these to navigate to the previous (◀) and next (▶) artboards.

6 Click the Previous navigation button (◀) in the Status Bar *below the document* to view the previous artboard (artboard 1) in the Document window.

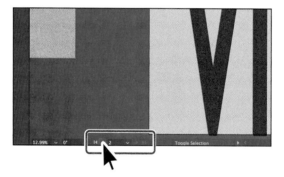

The Artboard menu and navigation arrows always appear in the Status Bar below the document, but they appear in the Properties panel only when you're not in Artboard Editing mode, the Selection tool is active, and nothing is selected.

Arranging multiple documents ◼◀

To learn about arranging multiple open documents, check out the video *Arranging multiple documents,* which is part of the Web Edition. For more information, see the "Web Edition" section of "Getting Started" at the beginning of the book.

Review questions

1 What is the Properties panel for?

2 Describe two ways to change the view of a document.

3 How do you save the locations and visibility of panels?

4 Describe a few ways to navigate between artboards in Illustrator.

5 How can you rotate the canvas view?

Review answers

1 The Properties panel in Illustrator is in the default workspace; it allows you to access settings and controls for items that are selected on the artboard, as well as settings and controls for the entire document when nothing is selected.

2 You can choose commands from the View menu to zoom in or out of a document or to fit it to your screen; you can also use the Zoom tool (Q) in the toolbar and click or drag over a document to enlarge or reduce the view. In addition, you can use keyboard shortcuts to magnify or reduce the display of artwork.

3 You can save panel locations and visibility preferences by choosing Window > Workspace > New Workspace to create custom work areas and to make it easier to find the controls you need.

4 To navigate between artboards in Illustrator, you can choose the artboard number from the Artboard Navigation menu at the lower left of the Document window. With nothing selected and while not in Artboard Editing mode, you can choose the artboard number from the Artboard menu or use the Active Artboard arrows in the Properties panel. You can use the Artboard Navigation arrows in the Status Bar in the lower left of the Document window to go to the first, previous, next, and last artboards. You can also use the Artboards panel to navigate to artboards, or you can use the Navigator panel to drag the proxy view area to navigate between artboards.

5 To rotate the canvas view, drag in the Document window with the Rotate View tool (🖐), choose a rotate value from the Rotate View menu in the Status Bar, or (bonus!) choose a rotate value from the View > Rotate View menu.

2 TECHNIQUES FOR SELECTING ARTWORK

Lesson overview

In this lesson, you'll learn how to do the following:

- Discover the various selection tools and use selection techniques.
- Recognize Smart Guides.
- Save selections for future use.
- Hide, lock, and unlock items.
- Use tools and commands to align shapes and points to each other and the artboard.
- Group items.
- Work in Isolation mode.
- Arrange objects.

This lesson will take about 45 minutes to complete. To get the lesson files used in this lesson, download them from the web page for this book at *peachpit.com/IllustratorCIB2024*. For more information, see "Accessing the lesson files and Web Edition" in the Getting Started section at the beginning of this book.

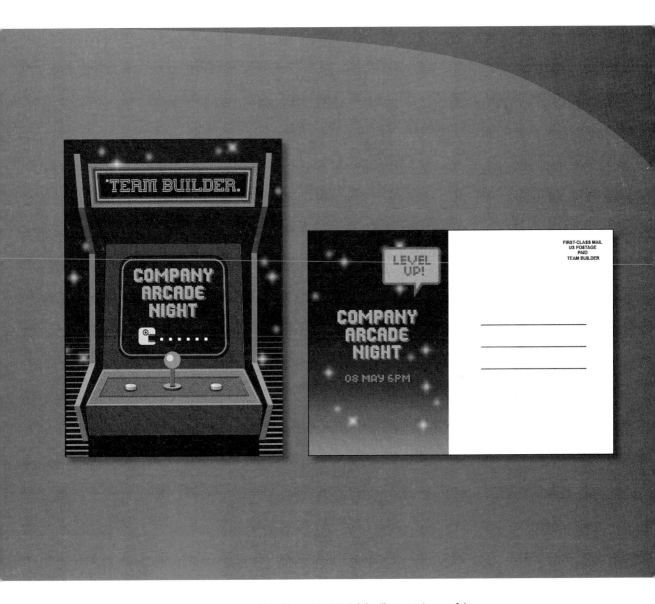

Selecting content in Adobe Illustrator is one of the
most important tasks you can master. In this lesson,
you'll learn how to select objects using selection
tools; protect objects by grouping, hiding, and locking
them; align objects to each other and to the artboard;
and much more.

Starting the lesson

Creating, selecting, and editing are the cornerstones of creating in Adobe Illustrator. In this lesson, you'll learn the fundamentals of selections—which includes selecting, hiding, locking, aligning, and grouping artwork—using different methods to finish a postcard for a team-building event at an old-school video arcade. You'll begin by resetting the preferences in Illustrator and opening the lesson files.

Note: If you have not already downloaded the project files for this lesson to your computer from your Account page, make sure to do so now. See the "Getting Started" section at the beginning of the book.

1 To ensure that the tools function and the defaults are set exactly as described in this lesson, delete or deactivate (by renaming) the Adobe Illustrator preferences file. See "Restoring default preferences" in the "Getting Started" section at the beginning of the book.

2 Start Adobe Illustrator.

3 Choose File > Open. Locate the file named L2_end.ai, which is in the Lessons > Lesson02 folder that you copied onto your hard disk, and click Open.

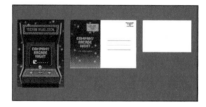

This file contains the postcard that you'll finish in this lesson.

4 Choose File > Open. Open the L2_start.ai file in the Lessons > Lesson02 folder on your hard disk.

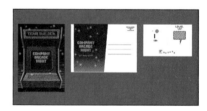

You'll save this starter file so you can work on it.

5 Choose File > Save As.

When saving as in Illustrator, you may see the following dialog box. If you do, you can choose to save either to Creative Cloud as a cloud document or to your computer. For this lesson, you'll save the lesson file to your computer.

Note: To learn more about saving as a cloud document, visit the sidebar "What are cloud documents?" in Lesson 3, "Make a Logo with Shapes."

6 If the Cloud Document dialog box opens, click Save On Your Computer to show the Save As dialog box.

7 In the Save As dialog box, name the file **GameNight.ai**, and save it in the Lessons > Lesson02 folder. Leave Adobe Illustrator (ai) chosen from the Format menu (macOS) or Adobe Illustrator (*.AI) chosen from the Save As Type menu (Windows), and click Save.

8 In the Illustrator Options dialog box, simply click OK.

9 Choose Window > Workspace > Essentials and make sure "Essentials" is selected.

10 Then choose Window > Workspace > Reset Essentials to reset the workspace.

Selecting objects

Whether creating artwork from scratch or editing existing artwork in Illustrator, you'll need to become familiar with how best to select objects. It will help you to understand what artwork you make in Illustrator, called *vector artwork*, is all about. There are many methods and tools for selecting and editing, and in this section, you'll explore the most widely used, which are the Selection (▶) and Direct Selection (▷) tools.

Using the Selection tool

The Selection tool (▶) is one tool you will use a lot. You can select, move, rotate, and resize objects with it. In this section, you'll put together the pieces for an arcade joystick using the Selection tool.

1 Choose 3 Pieces from the Artboard Navigation menu below the Document window.

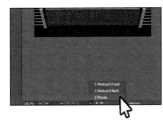 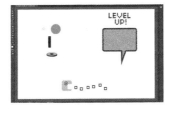

This should fit the Pieces artboard into the Document window. If the artboard *doesn't* fit in the window, you can choose View > Fit Artboard In Window.

2 Select the Selection tool (▶) in the toolbar on the left. Move the pointer over the different artwork on the artboards, *but don't click.*

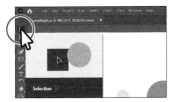 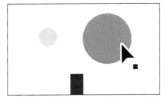

The little box that appears next to the pointer (▶) as it passes over objects indicates that there is artwork under the pointer. When you hover over something, that object has a color outline, like blue in this instance.

3 Move the pointer over the *edge* of the larger green circle.

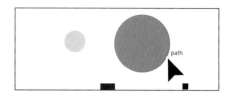

A word such as "path" or "anchor" might show next to the pointer because Smart Guides are on by default (View > Smart Guides). Smart Guides are temporary guides that help you align, edit, and transform things.

▶ **Tip:** The color of the bounding box tells you which layer the object is on. Layers are discussed more in Lesson 10, "Organizing Your Artwork with Layers."

4 Click anywhere inside the larger green circle to select it.

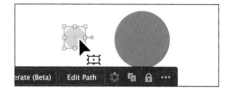

A *bounding box* with eight handles appears around the circle. All content shows a bounding box when selected, and it can be used to make changes to the selected content like resizing or rotating.

5 Click in the smaller light green circle to the left.

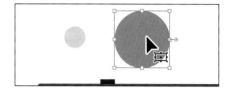

Notice that the larger circle is now deselected and only the smaller circle is selected.

6 Drag the smaller circle onto the larger circle, like you see in the first part of the following figure.

7 Pressing the Shift key, click in the larger circle to select it as well, and then release the key, like you see in the second part of the following figure.

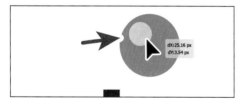
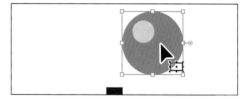

Both circles are now selected, and a larger bounding box surrounds them.

8 Drag either circle down onto the dark gray rectangle handle to move both.

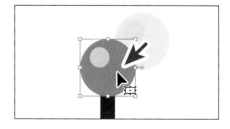

As you drag, magenta lines, called *alignment guides*, and gray boxes next to the pointer, called *measurement labels*, may appear. They are visible because Smart Guides are turned on (View > Smart Guides); they help you align with other artwork in the document (the guides), and they note the distances dragged (the gray labels).

Selecting and editing with the Direct Selection tool

Shapes and paths are composed of *anchor points* (sometimes just called *points*) and path segments. Anchor points control the shape of a path segment and work like pins holding a wire in place.

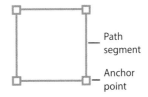

Path segment

Anchor point

A shape, like a square, is made of at least four anchor points on the corners with path segments connecting the anchor points.

One way to change the shape of a path or shape is by dragging its anchor points or path segments with the Direct Selection tool (▷). Next, you'll become familiar with selecting anchor points using the Direct Selection tool to reshape a thought bubble.

1   Select the Direct Selection tool (▷) in the toolbar on the left. Click inside the pink thought bubble to see its anchor points.

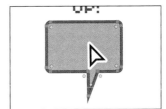

Notice the square anchor points on the edge of the shape that are all filled with a blue color, which means they are all selected. Also notice the little double-circles in the shape. Those are for rounding the path around the anchor points.

2   Choose View > Zoom In once so it's easier to see the shape up close.

3   Move the pointer directly over the anchor point on the end of the tail of the thought bubble (indicated in the figure).

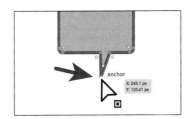

With the Direct Selection tool selected, when the pointer is right over an anchor point, the word "anchor" appears.

Also, notice the little white box next to the pointer (▷). A tiny dot in the white box indicates that the pointer is over an anchor point.

4   Click to select that anchor point, and then move the pointer away from it.

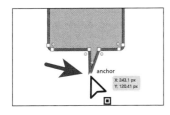
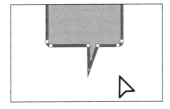

Notice that only the anchor point you clicked is now filled with blue, indicating that it's selected. The other anchor points in the shape are now hollow (filled with white), indicating that they are not selected.

5 With the Direct Selection tool still selected, move the pointer over the selected anchor point, and then drag it up to make that part shorter.

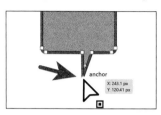 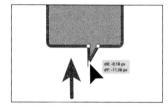

6 Try clicking another point on the shape. Notice that when you select the new point, the previous point is deselected.

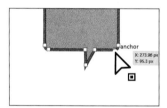

7 Choose Select > Deselect so the anchor point is no longer selected.

Anchor points too small?

The anchor points, handles, and bounding box points may be difficult to see at times. In the Illustrator preferences, you can adjust the size of those features.

- On macOS, choose Illustrator > Settings > Selection & Anchor Display.
- On Windows, choose Edit > Preferences > Selection & Anchor Display.

In the Anchor Points, Handle, and Bounding Box Display section of the Preferences dialog box, drag the Size slider to change the size!

Selecting with a marquee

Another way to select content is by dragging across what you want to select, called a *marquee selection*, which you can do with either the Selection tool or the Direct Selection tool selected.

1 Choose View > Fit Artboard In Window.

2 Select the Selection tool (▶) in the toolbar.

3 To select the circles and rectangle that make up part of the joystick, move the pointer above and to the left of all objects. Drag to overlap at least part of them. Release the mouse button.

Selecting by dragging is the same as Shift-clicking to select multiple objects. Know that when dragging with the Selection tool (▶), you only need to encompass a small part of something to select it.

4 Drag the selected content down onto the pink joystick base.

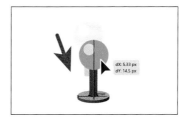

Now, the speech bubble needs to be a little shorter in height. With the Direct Selection tool, you can select multiple anchor points by dragging around anchor points, which allows you to edit them as one.

▶ **Tip:** You might have seen the magenta alignment guides when the content came close to the joystick base. Those are the Smart Guides I mentioned, trying to help you align the content you are dragging to other content.

5 Select the Direct Selection tool (▷) in the toolbar.

6 Drag across the bottom half of the pink speech bubble shape, like you see in the first part of the following figure, and release the mouse button.

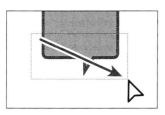 

7 Press the Up Arrow key a few times to see how the selected anchor points move together. I added a dashed line in the figure to show where it was.

▶ **Tip:** Why didn't we just drag the anchor points like we did earlier? Because dragging would snap the anchors to a lot of other content and it would be challenging to put them where we want to with Smart Guides on.

8 Select the Selection tool (▶) and drag the "LEVEL UP!" text down onto the speech bubble. Center it as best you can.

9 Choose Select > Deselect and then choose File > Save.

Locking objects

Selecting artwork can be challenging in Illustrator when objects are stacked one on another or when there are lots of objects in a small area. In this section, you'll learn a common way to make selecting objects easier by locking content.

You'll select a bunch of lines on the postcard design so you can move them all.

1 Choose 1 Postcard Front from the artboard navigation menu in the lower left.

2 With the Selection tool (▶) selected, click the black shape in the background to select it.

▶ **Tip:** You can also press Command+2 (macOS) or Ctrl+2 (Windows) to lock selected content.

3 Choose Object > Lock > Selection.

You can no longer select it. Locking objects prevents you from selecting and editing them.

4 Click the very small star to the left of the arcade game to select it—see the figure. Press the Shift key and click the other star in the same area to select it as well.

Yes, they might be challenging to select. When selecting in Illustrator, not everything is super easy!

5 Choose Object > Lock > Selection.

6 Starting off the left edge of the postcard, drag across just the lines toward the bottom of the postcard to select just them.

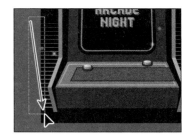

Be careful not to select the arcade machine! If you select more than the lines, choose Select > Deselect and try again.

7 Drag the lines down so the bottom line is at the bottom of the postcard.

Be careful! To drag the lines, you need to drag by one of the lines—not *between* the lines.

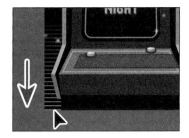

Unlocking objects

If you find you want to edit something that is locked, you can easily unlock it later. In this case, the black shape in the background needs to have a different color fill to look better. To do so, you first need to unlock it.

1 Choose Object > Unlock All to unlock everything in the document.

2 Choose Select > Deselect.

▶ **Tip:** You can also press Shift+Command+A (macOS) or Shift+Ctrl+A (Windows) to deselect.

3 Select the black shape in the background again.

4 To change the color of the shape, click the Fill color box to the left of the word "Fill" in the Properties panel and select a new color.

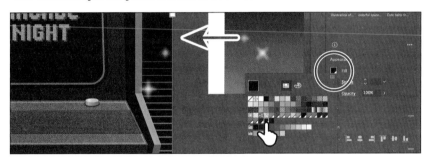

5 Choose Object > Lock > Selection to lock the background shape again.

Selecting similar objects

Using the Select > Same command, you can select artwork based on similar fill color, stroke color, stroke weight, and more. This can make selecting objects with a similar appearance easy. Next, you'll select several objects with the same fill and stroke applied.

1 Choose 3 Pieces from the Artboard Navigation menu below the Document window.

2 With the Selection tool (▶), click to select one of the white squares to the right of the orange character at the bottom of the artboard.

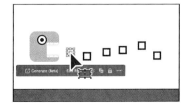

Tip: In Lesson 14, you'll learn about another method for selecting similar artwork using Global Edit.

3 Choose Select > Same > Fill & Stroke.

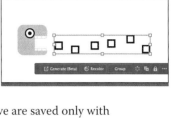

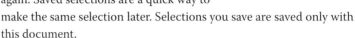

All the shapes with the same fill color and stroke weight and color are now selected.

You can also save a selection if you know that you need to reselect a series of objects again. Saved selections are a quick way to make the same selection later. Selections you save are saved only with this document.

You'll save the current selection next.

4 With the shapes still selected, choose Select > Save Selection. Name the selection **Dots** in the Save Selection dialog box, and click OK.

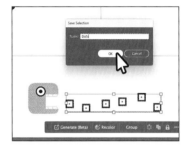

Now that you've saved it, you'll be able to choose this selection quickly and easily from the bottom of the Select menu when you need it.

5 Choose Select > Deselect, and then choose File > Save.

Hiding objects

Another way to focus on specific content and make selections easier is to temporarily hide content. To select the arcade game more easily, you'll hide the stars.

1 Choose 1 Postcard Front from the Artboard Navigation menu below the Document window.

2 Click any one of the stars in the background.

3 Choose Select > Same > Appearance to select all of the stars in the document.

In Illustrator, selecting artwork with the same "appearance" means selecting everything that matches the star's specific combination of fill and stroke color, stroke width, opacity, effects, and so on.

4 Choose Object > Hide > Selection.

▶ **Tip:** You can also press Command+3 (macOS) or Ctrl+3 (Windows) to hide content.

The stars are now hidden so that you can more easily focus on other objects.

Selecting in Outline mode

By default, Adobe Illustrator displays all artwork with its attributes showing, like fill and stroke (border). However, you can view artwork in Outline mode to display artwork so that attributes like fill and stroke are temporarily removed and only outlines (or paths) are visible.

Outline mode can be useful if you want to more easily select objects within a series of stacked objects. Now you'll use Outline mode to select a series of letters.

1 Choose View > Outline to view artwork as outlines.

2 With the Selection tool (▶), drag across the "COMPANY ARCADE NIGHT" text.

3 Press the Up Arrow key several times to move the text up a little bit.

4 Click the Group button in the Task bar beneath the artwork to group the text shapes together.

You'll learn more about groups in a few sections.

5 Choose View > Preview (or GPU Preview) to see the painted artwork.

Aligning objects

Say you have a bunch of fence posts you made and you need them all to line up with each other. Or you need to align your artwork to the center of a poster. Illustrator makes it easy to align or distribute multiple objects relative to each other, the artboard, or a key object. In this section, you'll explore the different options for aligning objects.

Aligning objects to each other

One way to align objects is to each other. This can be useful if, for instance, you want to align the top edges of a series of selected shapes to each other. Next you'll align the white dot shapes to each other.

1 Choose 3 Pieces from the Artboard Navigation menu.

2 Choose Select > Dots to reselect the white shapes on the 3 Pieces artboard.

3 Click the Vertical Align Center button () in the Properties panel on the right.

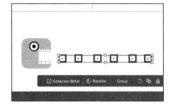

Notice that all of the selected objects moved to align to the vertical center of the shapes. The horizontal spacing between them is still not the same, but you will fix that in a few sections using *distributing*.

Aligning to a key object

A *key object* is an object that you want other objects to align to. This can be useful when you want to align a series of objects and one of them is already in the perfect position. You specify a key object by selecting all the objects you want to align, including the key object, and then clicking the key object again. Next, you'll align some buttons to a part of the game console using a key object.

1 Choose 1 Postcard Front from the Artboard Navigation menu below the Document window.

● **Note:** The key object outline color is determined by the layer color that the object is on. You'll learn about layers in Lesson 10.

2 Click one of the green game buttons in the bottom half of the artboard.

3 Shift-click the other green button and the darker pink shape behind them to select all three. Make sure to release the Shift key.

The buttons need to align to the pink shape because that shape is already where it needs to be; it can't move. You will make the pink shape the key object so the buttons align to it.

4   Click the darker pink shape again.

That object is now the key object. When selected, the key object has a thick outline, indicating that other objects will align to it.

5   Click the Vertical Align Center button () in the Properties panel.

Notice that the button shapes moved to align to the vertical center of the pink key object.

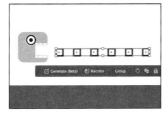

Distributing objects

Aside from aligning, you can also distribute objects. *Distributing* objects means you distribute the spacing equally between the centers or edges of those objects. For instance, maybe you have a series of icons in a web page design and they need to be spaced evenly.

Next, you will make the spacing between shapes the same.

1   Choose 3 Pieces from the Artboard Navigation menu below the Document window.

2   Choose Select > Dots to select those white shapes again.

3   Click More Options (•••) in the Align section of the Properties panel (circled in the figure). Click the Horizontal Distribute Center button (⬚) in the panel that appears.

● **Note:** You'll need to hide the panel to continue. To do that, press the Escape key. I won't always tell you to hide these panels, so it's a good habit to get into.

Distributing this way moves all of the selected shapes, except for the first and last, so that their centers are spaced an equal distance apart. This looks okay, but you need the shapes to be closer, so you can set that distance using distribution.

4   With the shapes still selected, click the leftmost shape to make it the key object.

5   Click More Options (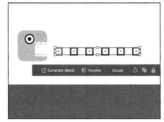) in the Align section of the Properties panel (circled in the following figure). Ensure that the Distribute Spacing value is 7 pixels, and then click the Horizontal Distribute Space button ( ).

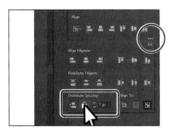

Distribute Spacing distributes the spacing between selected objects, whereas the Distribute Objects options distribute the spacing between the center points of selected objects. The value you can set is a great way to set a specific distance between objects.

6   Click the Group button in the Task bar beneath (or above) the shapes to group them together. As I said before, you'll learn more about groups in a few sections.

7   Choose Select > Deselect, and then choose File > Save.

Aligning anchor points

Next, you'll align two anchor points to each other using the Align options. As with setting a key object in the previous section, you can also align anchor points to a key anchor point you select.

1   Choose 2 Postcard Back from the Artboard Navigation menu below the Document window.

2   Choose View > Zoom Out so you can see more area around the postcard.

3   Select the Direct Selection tool ( ) in the toolbar, and select the rectangle in the background with the color gradient (blend of color from lighter blue to indigo) to see its anchor points.

4   Click the upper-right corner point of the shape (see the first part of the following figure).

5   Press the Shift key, and click to select the lower-right point of the same shape to select both anchor points (second part of the following figure).

The last selected anchor point is the *key anchor point.* All other selected anchor points will align to that point.

6 Click the Horizontal Align Right button (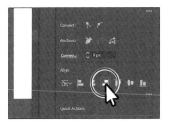) in the Properties panel to the right of the document.

The first anchor point selected aligns to the last-selected anchor point selected, making the right edge of the shape straight.

7 Choose Select > Deselect.

Aligning to the artboard

You can also align content to the active artboard (page) rather than to a selection or a key object. Aligning to the artboard aligns each selected object *separately* to the edges of the artboard.

Next, you'll align the selected shape to the left edge of the artboard.

1 Select the Selection tool (▶) in the toolbar, and select the same rectangle you just edited.

See how it has a white gap on the left side between the edge of the artboard and itself? You could try to drag it to snap to the edge of the artboard, but to ensure that it's properly aligned, using alignment methods is sometimes best.

2 Click the Align To button (⬚▾) in the Align section of the Properties panel, and make sure that Align To Artboard is chosen from the menu that appears.

Any content you align will now align to the artboard.

3 Click the Horizontal Align Left button (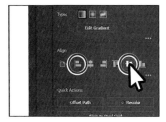), and then click the Vertical Align Center button (🔲) in the Align section of the Properties panel to align the shape to the left edge and vertical center of the artboard.

4 Choose Select > Deselect, and then choose File > Save.

Working with groups

Earlier you grouped something and I said you would learn more about that later. Well, it's now later! You can combine objects into a group so that the objects act as a single unit. That way, you can move or transform several objects without affecting their individual attributes or positions relative to each other. It can also make selecting artwork easier.

Grouping items

Next you'll select the pieces of the joystick and create a group from them.

1 Choose 3 Pieces from the Artboard Navigation menu below the Document window.

2 Drag across the joystick objects to select them. See the figure.

Tip: After this step is performed, the Group button in the Properties panel now shows as Ungroup. Clicking the Ungroup button will remove the objects from a group.

3 Click the Group button in the Task bar beneath the artwork to group the selected artwork together.

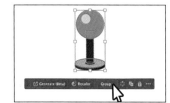

4 Choose Select > Deselect.

5 With the Selection tool (▶) selected, click one of joystick shapes in the new group. Because they are grouped together, all are now selected.

6 Practice by grouping the "LEVEL UP!" text and the pink speech bubble. Drag across them and click the Group button in the Task bar beneath the artwork.

Editing a group in Isolation mode

Isolation mode lets you isolate groups to easily select and edit specific objects or parts of objects without having to ungroup the objects. In Isolation mode, all objects outside the isolated group are locked and dimmed so that they aren't affected by your edits. Next, you will edit a group using Isolation mode.

1   Double-click any part of the joystick group to enter Isolation mode.

● **Note:** You'll learn more about layers in Lesson 10.

Notice that the rest of the content in the document appears dimmed (you can't select it). At the top of the Document window, a gray bar appears with the words "Layer 1" and "<Group>." That bar indicates that you have isolated a group of objects on Layer 1, and they are now temporarily ungrouped.

2   Click to select the dark gray rectangle (the part that connects the green ball to the base). Click the Fill color box in the Properties panel on the right, and making sure the Swatches option (▦) is selected in the panel that appears, click to select a different color. I chose a lighter gray.

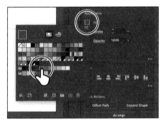

3   Double-click outside the shapes within the group to exit Isolation mode.

You can also click the gray arrow in the upper-left corner of the Document window or press the Escape key when in Isolation mode. The joystick is once again grouped, and you can also now select other objects.

4   Choose View > Fit All In Window.

5   Click to select the joystick group again. Drag it onto the video game console where the buttons are.

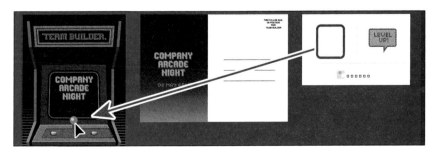

Creating a nested group

Groups can also be *nested*—grouped within other objects or grouped to form larger groups. Nesting is a common technique and a great way to keep associated content together. In this section, you'll explore how to create a nested group.

1 Choose 3 Pieces from the Artboard Navigation menu below the Document window.

2 Choose View > Fit Artboard In Window.

3 Click any of the white shapes next to the orange character at the bottom of the artboard to select the entire group.

Now you'll group the orange character together with the white group of shapes.

4 Click any of the shapes that make up the orange character.

If you look at the top of the Properties panel, you can see that it is already a group because it shows "Group" in the Selection Indicator.

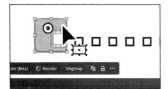 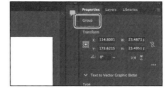

5 Shift-click the group of white shapes to the right.

6 Click the Group button in the Task bar beneath (or above) the artwork.

You have created a *nested group*—a group that is combined with other objects or groups to form a larger group.

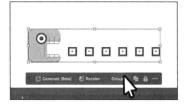

7 Choose Select > Deselect.

Editing a nested group

You can edit the content in a nested group the same way you edit content in a group: by double-clicking the nested group to enter Isolation mode.

1 With the Selection tool, click the orange character or white shapes to select the nested group.

2 Double-click the orange character to enter Isolation mode.

3 Click to select the orange character, and notice that it is still grouped.

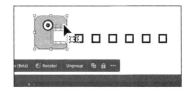

▶ Tip: Instead of either ungrouping a group or entering Isolation mode to select the content within, you can select with the Group Selection tool (▷⁺). Nested within the Direct Selection tool (▷) in the toolbar, the Group Selection tool lets you select an object within a group, a single group within multiple groups, or a set of groups within the artwork.

4 Double-click the orange character to edit the content in that group.

5 Click the orange shape to select it, if necessary.

6 Click the Fill color in the Properties panel and select another color.

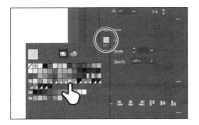 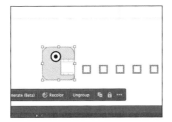

7 Double-click away from any artwork to exit Isolation mode.

Now to drag that nested group into place.

8 Choose View > Fit All In Window.

9 Drag the nested group just below the "COMPANY ARCADE NIGHT" text on the leftmost artboard.

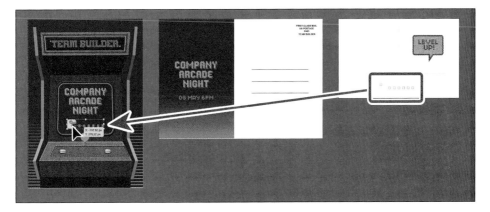

10 Drag the LEVEL UP! group above the "COMPANY ARCADE NIGHT" text in the middle artboard.

Exploring object arrangement

Illustrator puts objects one on top of another in order as you create them, beginning with the first object created. This ordering of objects, called *stacking order*, determines how they display when they overlap. You can change the stacking order of objects in your artwork at any time, using either the Layers panel or the Arrange commands.

Arranging objects

Next you'll work with the Arrange commands to finish the postcard artwork.

1   Choose 1 Postcard Front from the Artboard Navigation menu.

2   With the Selection tool (▶) selected, click the joystick group to select it (see the following figure).

Right now, it is behind the pink rectangle and needs to be on top of it.

3   Click the Arrange button in the Properties panel. Choose Bring To Front to bring the group on top of all the other shapes.

4   Select the pink rectangle behind the joystick and buttons.

5   Click Horizontal Align Center in the Properties panel to center align it.

6   Choose Object > Show All to see the stars on the left artboard that you previously hid.

7   Choose View > Fit All In Window to see both sides of the postcard in the Document window.

8   Choose Select > Deselect.

9   Choose File > Save and then File > Close.

Review questions

1 How can you select an object that has no fill?

2 Explain how you can select an item in a group without ungrouping.

3 Of the two selection tools (Selection [▶] and Direct Selection [▷]), which allows you to edit the individual anchor points of an object?

4 What should you do after creating a selection that you are going to use repeatedly?

5 To align objects to the artboard, what do you first need to change in the Properties panel or Align panel before you choose an alignment option?

6 Sometimes you are unable to select an object because it is underneath another object. Explain a way to get around this issue.

Review answers

1 You can select an object that has no fill by clicking the stroke or by dragging a marquee across any part of the object.

2 You can double-click the group with the Selection tool selected to enter Isolation mode, edit the shapes as needed, and then exit Isolation mode by pressing the Escape key or by double-clicking outside the group. Read Lesson 10 to see how you can use layers to make complex selections. Also, using the Group Selection tool (▷⁺), you can click once to select an individual item within a group (not discussed in the lesson). Click again to add the next grouped items to the selection.

3 Using the Direct Selection tool (▷), you can select one or more individual anchor points to change the shape of an object.

4 For any selection that you anticipate using again, choose Select > Save Selection. Name the selection so that you can reselect it at any time from the Select menu.

5 To align objects to an artboard, first choose the Align To Artboard option.

6 If your access to an object is blocked, you can select the blocking object, then choose Object > Hide > Selection to hide the blocking object. The object is not deleted. It is just hidden in the same position until you choose Object > Show All. *BONUS!* You can also use the Selection tool (▶) to select an object that's behind other objects by pressing the Command (macOS) or Ctrl (Windows) key and then clicking the overlapping objects until the object you want to select is selected.

3 MAKE A LOGO WITH SHAPES

Lesson overview

In this lesson, you'll learn how to do the following:

- Create a new document.
- What is a bleed? ◼
- Use tools and commands to create a variety of shapes.
- Understand Live Shapes.
- Create rounded corners.
- Discover other ways to round corners. ◼
- Work with drawing modes.
- Use the Place command.
- Use Image Trace to create shapes.
- Work with Draw Behind mode. ◼
- Simplify paths.
- Explore Text to Vector Graphic (Beta).
- See the latest Text to Vector Graphic feature. ◼

This lesson will take about 60 minutes to complete. To get the lesson files used in this lesson, download them from the web page for this book at *peachpit.com/IllustratorCIB2024*. For more information, see "Accessing the lesson files and Web Edition" in the Getting Started section at the beginning of this book.

Creating and editing shapes are essential to creating
Illustrator artwork. In this lesson, you'll create a new
document and then use the shape tools to create and
edit a series of shapes for a logo.

Starting the lesson

In this lesson, you'll explore the different methods for creating artwork by using the shape tools and other methods to create a logo for an adventure company.

● **Note:** If you have not already downloaded the project files for this lesson to your computer from your Account page, make sure to do so now. See the "Getting Started" section at the beginning of the book.

1 To ensure that the tools function and the defaults are set exactly as described in this lesson, delete or deactivate (by renaming) the Adobe Illustrator preferences file. See "Restoring default preferences" in the "Getting Started" section at the beginning of the book.

2 Start Adobe Illustrator.

3 Choose File > Open. Locate the file L3_end.ai, which is in the Lessons > Lesson03 folder that you copied onto your hard disk, and click Open.

This file contains the finished illustrations that you'll create in this lesson.

4 Choose View > Fit Artboard In Window; leave the file open for reference, or choose File > Close.

Creating a new document

To start, you'll create a new document for the logo.

1 Choose File > New.

2 In the New Document dialog box, change the following options:

- Click the Print category at the top of the dialog box.

- Click the Letter blank document preset, if it isn't already selected.

You can set up a document for different kinds of output, such as print, web, video, and more, by choosing a category. For example, if you are designing a flyer or poster, you can select the Print category and select a document preset (size). The document will be set with the units in points (most likely), the color mode as CMYK, and the raster effects to High (300 ppi)—all optimal settings for a print document.

3 On the right side of the dialog box, in the Preset Details area, change the following:

- Enter a name for the document in the blank space under Preset Details: **AdventureLogo**.

The name will become the name of the Illustrator file when you save it later.

- Units: Choose Inches from the units menu to the right of the Width field.

- Width: Select the Width value, and type **8**.

- Height: Select the Height value, and type **8**.

- Orientation: Portrait ().

- Artboards: 1 (the default setting).

At the bottom of the Preset Details section on the right side of the dialog box, you will also see Advanced Options and a More Settings button (you may need to scroll to see it). They contain more settings for document creation that you can explore on your own.

4 Click Create to create a new document.

Note: You can set the units to whatever makes sense to you. Know that throughout the lesson I use inches. There is a note in the "Creating rectangles" section that will help when it comes to entering the value I give you in inches.

Saving your document

With the document open, now you'll save it locally.

1 Choose File > Save.

2 If the Cloud Document dialog box opens, click Save On Your Computer to save the document locally.

To learn more about cloud documents, see the sidebar "What are cloud documents?" after this section.

3 In the Save dialog box, set the following options:

- Filename: **AdventureLogo.ai**

- Saved in the Lessons > Lesson03 folder.

- Leave Adobe Illustrator (ai) chosen from the Format menu (macOS) or Adobe Illustrator (*.AI) chosen from the Save As Type menu (Windows).

4 Click Save.

Adobe Illustrator (.ai) is called a *native format* and is your working file. That means it preserves all Illustrator data so you can edit everything later.

5 In the Illustrator Options dialog box that appears, leave the options at their default settings, and click OK.

The Illustrator Options dialog box is full of options for saving the Illustrator document, from specifying a version for saving to embedding any files that are linked to the document. You usually won't have to change anything in there.

6 Choose Window > Workspace > Essentials (if it's not already selected).

7 Choose Window > Workspace > Reset Essentials to reset the panels and settings for the Essentials workspace.

8 Look in the Properties panel on the right.

With nothing selected in the document, you'll see settings for the document like the units, navigating and editing artboards, showing and hiding useful features like rulers and guides, and much more. The Document Setup button is where you can set options like the document bleed and more. To learn more about bleeds, check out the video at the end of this section.

9 Choose View > Fit Artboard In Window to ensure that you can see the entire artboard (page).

What is a bleed? ▬◀

To learn about document bleed, check out the video *Edit document settings*, which you'll find in the Web Edition. For more information, see the "Web Edition" section of "Getting Started" at the beginning of the book.

What are cloud documents?

Aside from saving your Illustrator documents locally, you can also save them as cloud documents. A cloud document is an Illustrator document that is stored in Adobe Creative Cloud and can be accessed *anywhere* you sign in to Illustrator.

Here's how to save as a cloud document and access cloud documents.

- After you create a new document or open a document from your hard drive, you save the file as a cloud document by choosing File > Save As.

  The first time you do this, you will see a Cloud Document dialog box with options to save as a cloud document or save on your computer.

- To save as a cloud document, you would click the Save To Creative Cloud button. You can see it in the previous figure.

  If instead of the Cloud Document dialog box you see the Save As dialog box and want to save as a cloud document, you can click the Save Cloud Document button.

- In the dialog box that appears, you can change the name and click the Save button to save the document to Creative Cloud.

  When working on cloud documents, changes are automatically saved, so the document is always up to date.

  Tip: If you change your mind and want to save the file locally, you can click On Your Computer in that dialog box (an arrow is pointing to it in the figure).

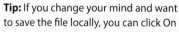

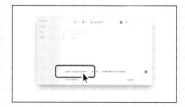

Want to open a cloud document? Choose File > Open. In the Open dialog box, click the Open Cloud Document button.

You can then open a cloud document from the dialog box that appears.

Working with basic shapes

In the first part of this lesson, you'll create all kinds of shapes, including rectangles, ellipses, and polygons.

Shapes you create are made of *anchor points,* with paths connecting the anchor points.

For instance, a basic square is made of four anchor points on the corners, with paths connecting those anchor points (see the upper figure at right). A shape is referred to as a *closed path* because the ends of the path are connected.

A path like a line is an open path. An *open path* has distinct anchor points on each end, called *endpoints* (see the figure at right). You can fill both open and closed paths with color, gradients, or patterns.

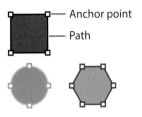

Anchor point

Path

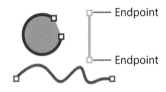

Examples of closed paths

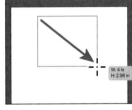

Endpoint

Endpoint

Examples of open paths

Creating rectangles

The main logo art for the adventure company will be a bear. You'll start by creating a few rectangles, and you'll explore creating them using two different methods.

1   Select the Rectangle tool (▧) in the toolbar.

First we'll create the larger rectangle that will be the body of the bear.

2   Near the top of the artboard, drag to create a rectangle, and then release the mouse button.

Don't worry about the size yet; you'll resize it shortly.

As you drew the shape, did you happen to notice the width and height in the little gray tool tip next to the pointer? That is called the *measurement label.* That label is a part of Smart Guides (View > Smart Guides).

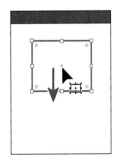

3   Move the pointer over the small blue dot in the center of the rectangle (called the *center point widget*). When the pointer changes (▶▦), drag the shape so it's roughly in the middle of the artboard.

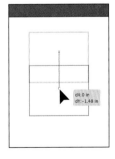

With the Rectangle tool selected (or any other shape tool), this is how you need to move a shape. Otherwise, you will draw a new one!

Next, you'll create a smaller rectangle using a more precise method to serve as the head of the bear.

4   With the Rectangle tool (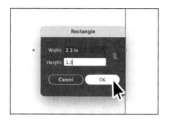) still selected, click in an empty area of the artboard to open the Rectangle dialog box.

5   In the dialog box, change the Width to **2.3** inches and the Height to **1.3** inches. Click OK to create a new rectangle.

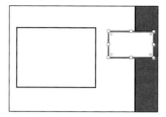

Creating a rectangle by clicking rather than dragging is useful when you need to make a shape of a specific size. For most drawing tools, you can either draw with the tool or click to create a shape this way.

Editing rectangles

All of the shape tools, except for the Star tool and Flare tool (currently), create Live Shapes. Live Shapes have attributes, such as width, height, rotation, and corner radius, that are editable without switching from the drawing tool you are using.

With two rectangles created, you'll make some changes to them so they look more like the body and head of a bear and are scaled relative to each other.

1   Select the Selection tool (▶) in the toolbar.

2   Click the View menu and make sure that Smart Guides are on. A checkmark will appear next to Smart Guides in the menu if they are.

You can turn the Smart Guides on when they are useful. In this case, when you resize one of the rectangles, you will see a gray measurement label telling you its size.

3   Click anywhere in the larger rectangle to select it.

4   Drag the bottom, middle point of the rectangle until you see a height of approximately 4.6 inches in the measurement label (the gray tool tip next to the pointer), release the mouse button.

Since your rectangle might be bigger or smaller, I didn't tell you which way to drag (up or down).

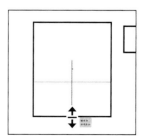

You can also resize shapes with more precision in the Properties panel, which is what you'll do next.

5 In the Transform section of the Properties panel on the right, make sure Maintain Width And Height Proportions to the right of Width (W:) and Height (H:) is *deselected* (it looks like this: ⧉).

Setting Maintain Width And Height Proportions (turning it on) is useful when you change the height or the width and want the other value to change proportionally.

Tip: Why are we being so precise? In Illustrator you can work as loosely or precisely as you need. I want all of our bear logos to be about the same size and shape, so some precision is necessary!

6 Select the Width (W:) value, and type **2.9 in**. Press Return or Enter to accept the change.

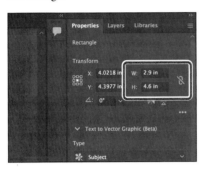

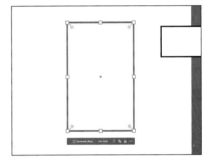

Now you'll rotate the larger rectangle so the bear body is horizontal.

7 Move the pointer just off a corner of the selected (larger) rectangle. When you see rotate arrows (↱), drag clockwise to rotate the shape. As you drag, press the Shift key to constrain the rotation to increments of 45 degrees. When an angle of 270° shows in the measurement label, release the mouse button and then the key. Leave the shape selected.

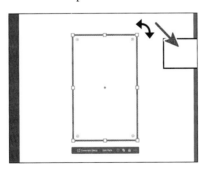

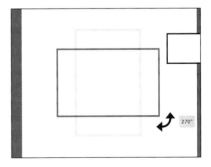

Tip: If you look in the Properties panel, you will also see a Rotate value. There are multiple ways to do almost everything in Illustrator. For instance, if you wanted to rotate more freely—at some random angle—you might do it by dragging, rather than choosing a rotation angle in the Properties panel.

Now you'll drag the smaller rectangle onto the larger rectangle. With the Selection tool selected, you can drag from *anywhere* within the shape bounds, as long as it is filled with a color, pattern, or gradient. You don't have to use the center point like you did previously with the Rectangle tool selected.

8   Drag the smaller rectangle onto the larger rectangle where the head of the bear should go. See the figure.

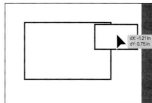

Changing the color of the shapes

By default, shapes are filled with white and have a black stroke (border). Next, you'll change the color of both rectangles to brown so they start to look more like a bear.

1   With the smaller rectangle still selected, click the Fill color box (☐) in the Properties panel on the right. It may be lower in the panel.

2   In the panel that opens, make sure that the Swatches option (▦) is selected at the top. Select a brown color to fill the shape.

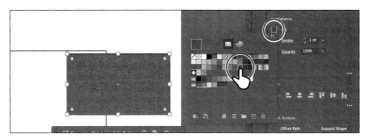

3   Press the Escape key to hide the Swatches panel before moving on.

4   Change the Stroke Weight in the Properties panel to 0 (zero).

5   Click the larger rectangle to select the body of the bear.

6   For practice, change the fill color to the same brown and set the Stroke Weight to 0 (zero) following the previous steps.

7   Choose Select > Deselect.

Rounding rectangle corners by dragging

The rectangles you created don't look very much like a bear yet. Luckily, we can round the corners of the rectangles to make them more interesting.

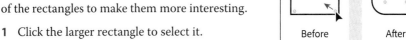

Before   After

1 Click the larger rectangle to select it.

2 Choose View > Zoom In once or twice.

You need to see the Live Corners widgets (⊙) in each corner of the rectangle. If you are zoomed out far enough, the Live Corners widgets are hidden on the shape. Zoom in until you see them.

3 Drag any of the Live Corners widgets (⊙) in the rectangle toward the center to round all of the corners. Drag until the corners are as round as they can be.

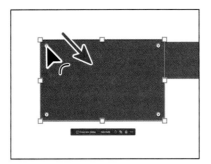
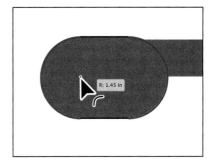

The more you drag toward the center, the more rounded the corners become. If you drag a Live Corners widget far enough, a red arc appears on the shape, indicating you've reached the maximum corner radius.

4 Click to select the smaller brown rectangle (the head of the bear), and drag any of the Live Corners widgets (⊙) to round the corners a little.

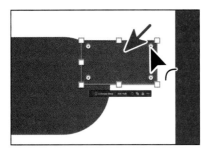
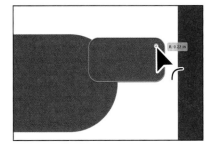

5 Leave the smaller rectangle selected.

6 Choose File > Save to save the file.

Rounding individual corners

You can also round individual corners using the Selection tool. Next, you'll explore rounding the individual corners of the head of the bear.

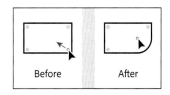

Before   After

1   With the smaller rectangle selected, click the Live Corners widget (◉) in the upper-right corner to select it, and then release.

    If you move the pointer away, you will see that the widget has changed in appearance, from this (◉) to this (◯). If you drag that corner widget now, it will be the only one that changes.

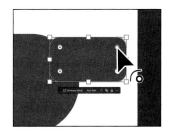

2   Now, drag the selected corner widget away from the center of the shape to remove the rounding.

    Be careful! If you don't click, release, and then drag, you won't select just the one corner widget. Instead, you'll round them all!

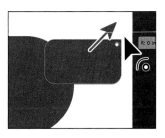

3   Follow the previous steps to remove the rounding from the lower-left corner of the rectangle as well.

4   Click the corner widget in the lower-right corner and release to select it.

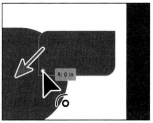

5   Then drag it toward the opposite corner, rounding the corner as much as possible.

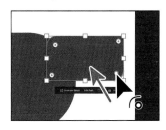
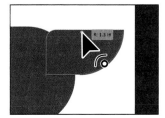

6   Choose Select > Deselect, and then choose File > Save.

Discover other ways to round corners ■◄

There are so many ways to round corners. To learn more ways, check out the video *Discover other ways to round corners*, which you'll find in the Web Edition. For more information, see the "Web Edition" section of "Getting Started" at the beginning of the book.

Changing a corner type

Aside from dragging to round corners, you can also use the Properties panel to change the type of corner radius and make more precise adjustments. The three types are shown in the figure at right.

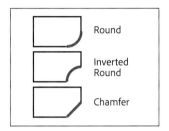

Round

Inverted Round

Chamfer

Now you'll make a copy of the larger rectangle and change the corner types for a few corners. This rectangle will become the belly of the bear.

1   Choose View > Fit Artboard In Window to see the entire artboard.

2   Select the larger rectangle, and to copy it, choose Edit > Copy, and then paste it by choosing Edit > Paste.

3   Drag the copy just below the other rectangles.

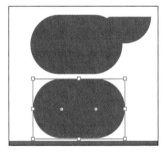

You might need to select the two original rectangles and move them up a bit. If you do, make sure to select the copy again before continuing.

4   In the Properties panel, click More Options (■■■) in the Transform section to show more options. It's circled in the following figure.

5   Ensure that Link Corner Radius Values is off—it should look like this: 🗝. You can click the button to toggle it on and off. It's circled in the figure.

Each corner value in the panel corresponds to a corner in the shape.

For the next step, *pay attention to which corner is adjusted in the figure.* Since the rectangle was rotated earlier, the corner values in the panel no longer seem to correspond to the correct corner in the shape.

6 Change the lower-left and lower-right corners of the rectangle to 0 (zero).

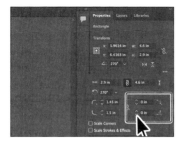 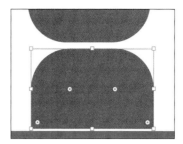

Aside from changing the corner radius, you can also change the corner type. You can choose between Round (default), Inverted Round, and Chamfer.

7 Change the Corner Type setting for the upper-left corner and upper-right corner of the rectangle to Chamfer (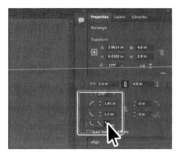).

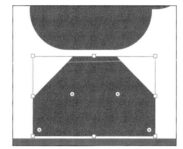

8 Make the corner radius for the same corners smaller. Make them both around 1 inch.

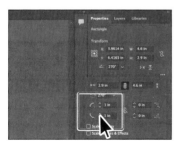 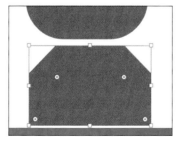

9 Press the Escape key to close the options panel, and leave the rectangle selected.

10 Drag a side handle to make the shape narrower. See the figure.

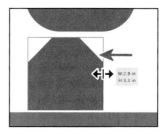

Creating an ellipse

The Ellipse tool is used to create ellipses and perfect circles. Next, you'll create an ellipse with the Ellipse tool (⬭) to make an eye for the bear.

1   Press and hold the mouse button on the Rectangle tool (▢) in the toolbar, and select the Ellipse tool (⬭).

When you draw the circle that will become the eye of the bear, make it bigger than an eye should be so you can work with it more easily.

▶ **Tip:** When an ellipse is a perfect circle, you will see magenta crosshairs in it as you are drawing it (with Smart Guides turned on [View > Smart Guides]).

2   In an empty area of the artboard, Shift-drag to make a perfect circle that will become the eye of the bear. As a reference, I made mine about 1 inch in width and height. Release the mouse button and then the key.

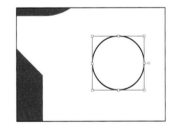

3   Zoom in to the circle by choosing View > Zoom In a few times or by pressing Command and + (macOS) or Ctrl and + (Windows) a few times.

Editing an ellipse

With the eye shape (circle) created, now you'll change the appearance and put it in place.

1   Press the letter D on your keyboard to apply the default of a white fill and black stroke.

This is a keyboard shortcut that I use a lot to remove formatting from shapes and get them back to a default (that's what the "D" stands for) appearance of a white fill and black stroke!

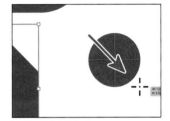

2   Change the Stroke Weight setting in the Properties panel to **19 pt**.

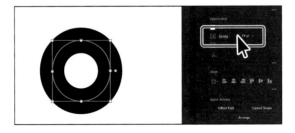

We need the fill to be black and the stroke to be white. So the opposite of what is applied to the current shape.

3 To swap the fill and stroke colors, click the Swap Fill And Stroke arrow (↰) toward the bottom of the toolbar on the left.

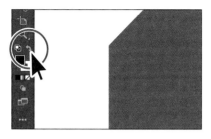 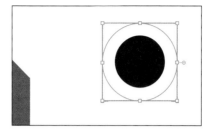

4 To see everything, choose View > Fit Artboard In Window.

5 Drag the circle by the blue center dot (the center point widget) onto the head of the bear, as you see in the figure.

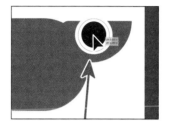

Next you'll make the eye smaller. By default, stroke weights do not scale (they stay the same). So if you were to make the circle a lot smaller, for instance, the stroke weight would stay 19 pt and look rather large. See the figure for an example. To scale the stroke as the circle scales, you can turn on an option.

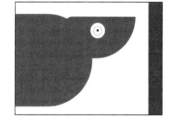

6 Click the More Options button (•••) in the Transform section of the Properties panel. Select Scale Strokes & Effects in the panel that opens.

7 Shift-drag the circle to make it smaller. When it's small enough to look good, release the mouse button and then the key.

8 Drag the eye where you want it on the bear head.

9 Choose File > Save.

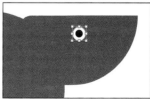

Changing stroke alignment

As you've seen, strokes are borders of an object or path. By default, strokes *center* on a path, which means that along the path, half the stroke weight is on one side and half is on the other.

You can adjust this alignment so the stroke appears in the center (default), inside, or outside. Next, you'll change the stroke so you can still see the fill of the eye.

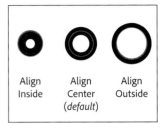

Align Inside   Align Center (*default*)   Align Outside

1   With the eye circle still selected, zoom in by pressing Command and + (macOS) or Ctrl and + (Windows) a few times.

2   Click the word "Stroke" in the Properties panel to open the Stroke panel.

3   In the Stroke panel, click the Align Stroke To Outside button ( ) to align the stroke to the outside edge of the circle.

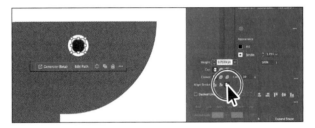

I hope you can see the difference when the stroke is aligned to the outside. Zoom in if you need. I made the eye a little smaller after aligning the stroke.

4   Choose Select > Deselect.

Creating a pie shape from an ellipse

Ellipses have a pie widget that you can drag to create a pie shape. Next, you'll make a new circle and turn it into an ear.

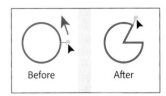

Before   After

1   With the Ellipse tool ( ) still selected, change the Stroke Weight in the Properties panel to **0**.

2   Shift-drag to make another circle in an empty area of the artboard.

This circle will become the ear of the bear—but you can make it bigger and scale it down later, if you want.

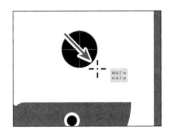

With it selected, *do you see the pie widget (─⊙) on the right side of the shape?* You can drag that to make a pie shape.

3 Drag the pie widget clockwise around the bottom of the ellipse, and then release.

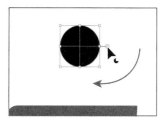 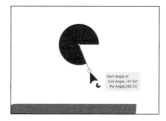

Notice that there is another pie widget in the same place from which you started dragging this one. The pie widget you just dragged is called the *pie start angle*, and the other pie widget is called the *pie end angle*.

4 Drag the other pie widget (the *pie end angle*) from the same place counterclockwise around the top of the ellipse. Don't worry about how far.

▶ **Tip:** Need to remove the pie angle change and go back to a whole circle? Double-click either pie widget!

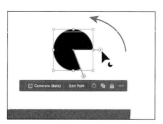 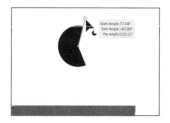

The ear shape you are making will look best if we see exactly half of it. That requires the two pie widgets you dragged to be at precise angles to each other—showing 180 degrees of the circle. You can adjust them with precision in the Properties panel.

5 In the Properties panel to the right, click More Options (●●●) in the Transform section to show more options. Choose 90° from the Pie Start Angle (◢) menu.

6 Choose 270° from the Pie End Angle (◢) menu.

◯ **Note:** The figure shows after choosing 270° from the Pie End Angle menu.

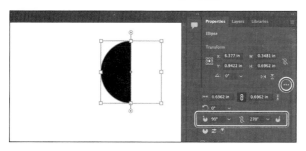

7 Press the Escape key to hide the panel.

8 Drag the half-circle ear on top of the bear head.

9 With the ear still selected, change the Fill color in the Properties panel to a lighter brown than the bear head.

10 Try adjusting the size of the ear if you need to make it look better, and rotate it slightly.

Want a little practice? You could make a new ear (or copy) to give the bear two ears! The new ear might look better if it were behind the bear head—so you can choose Arrange > Send To Back.

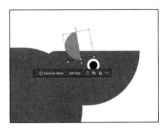

Drawing lines

Lines created with the Line Segment tool are Live, and similarly to Live Shapes, they have many editable attributes after they are drawn. Next, you'll create a line with the Line Segment tool. This line will become a leg of the bear.

1 Press and hold on the Ellipse tool (⬤) in the toolbar, and select the Line Segment tool (╱).

2 In an empty area of the artboard, press and drag in any direction to draw a line. *Don't release the mouse button yet.*

3 As you drag, press the Shift key to constrain the line to a multiple of 45 degrees. Notice the length and angle in the measurement label next to the pointer as you drag. Drag directly to the right until the line is around 0.5 inches in length. Release the mouse button and then the key.

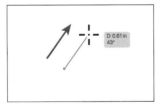

Editing a line

Now you'll rotate and change the stroke weight and color of the line.

● **Note:** The stroke color is white, so the path will be challenging to see.

1 With the line selected, change the stroke weight to **90 pt** in the Properties panel to the right of the document.

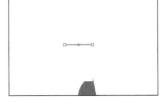

2 Click the Stroke color box in the Properties panel, and make sure that the Swatches option () is selected in the panel that appears. Select the same brown color as the body of the bear.

Since this is a leg, and a bear leg is not horizontal, it needs to be rotated. Yes, you could have drawn it that way, but then we wouldn't explore rotating lines!

3 With the new line selected, move the pointer just off the right end. When the pointer changes to a rotate arrow (↷), press and drag up until you see an angle of 90° in the measurement label next to the pointer. That will make the line vertical.

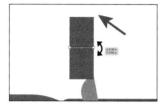 

4 Choose View > Fit Artboard In Window.

5 Select the Selection tool (▶) in the toolbar, and drag the line by the center point to make it a leg for the bear.

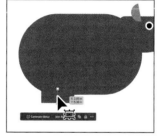

It's a little short—so let's make it longer. For the following figures, I moved the belly shape that was below the bear out of the way.

6 Drag the end of the line to make the leg longer.

7 Make a copy by Option-dragging (macOS) or Alt-dragging (Windows) the line to where the other leg should be. Release the mouse button and then the key.

Note: If you resize a line in the same trajectory as the original path, it will snap to that same trajectory. You will also see the words "Line Extension" and "on" appear at opposite ends of the line. These appear because the Smart Guides are turned on.

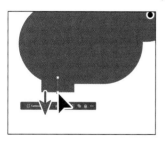 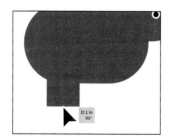 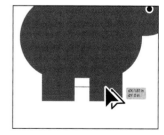

Creating polygons

Using the Polygon tool (⬡), you can create shapes with multiple straight sides. By default, the Polygon tool draws hexagons (six-sided shapes). What's different about polygons is that they are drawn from the center. Polygons are also Live Shapes, which means attributes such as size, rotation, number of sides, and more remain editable after you create them.

Now you'll create several polygons to make the claws of the bear.

1   Press and hold the Line Segment tool (╱) in the toolbar, and select the Polygon tool (⬡).

2   Choose View > Smart Guides to turn them off.

3   Choose Select > Deselect.

4   Press the letter D on your keyboard to apply the default of a white fill and black stroke. Otherwise, the stroke will be a rather large 90 point!

5   Move the pointer into an empty area of the artboard. Drag to the right to draw a polygon. As you drag, press the Shift key to straighten the shape. Release the mouse button and then the key.

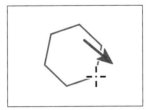 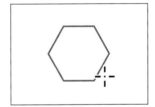

Notice that you didn't see the gray measurement label (the tool tip), since it's part of the Smart Guides that you turned off. Smart Guides can be helpful in certain situations, such as when more precision is necessary—maybe you want to know how large the shape is—and can be toggled on and off when needed.

6   Click the Fill color box (▨) in the Properties panel, make sure that the Swatches option (▦) is selected, and change the color to a lighter brown.

7   Change the Stroke Weight in the Properties panel to 0 (zero).

8   Choose View > Smart Guides to turn them back on.

Now you'll make it look more like a claw, by turning the shape into a triangle.

9   With the Polygon tool still selected, drag the little side widget (◇) on the right side of the bounding box up to change the number of sides to 3—making a triangle.

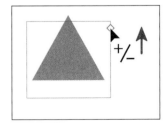

10 Choose File > Save.

Editing a polygon

Now you'll change the size of the polygon and create a nail from it.

1 Select the Selection tool (▶) in the toolbar.

2 Drag the polygon to the bottom of one of the legs. See the figure for where.

3 Zoom in to the claw shape by pressing Command and + (macOS) or Ctrl and + (Windows) a few times.

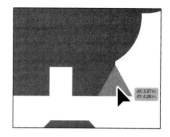

4 To make it smaller, press the Shift key and drag a corner to change the width and height proportionally (together). When it looks like the size of a proper claw, release the mouse button and then the key.

Note: Depending on how big your polygon was to start, you made it either larger or smaller in this step to match the height we suggest.

With the polygon shape now created, you'll round one of the corners so the claw is a little less sharp. We need to round only one of the corners, so you will select the corner you want to round.

With the Selection tool selected, a polygon shows only a single Live Corner widget, so you can't round just one corner with the Selection tool. To round only one corner, you will use the Direct Selection tool.

5 Select the Direct Selection tool in the toolbar. Click the Live Corners widget (◉) in the corner showing in the figure.

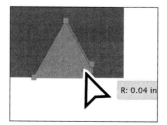

6 Drag the selected Live Corners widgets toward the center of the triangle to round the one corner a little.

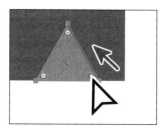

7   Select the Selection tool (▶) and drag the triangle into position like you see in the figure.

8   To make a copy, choose Edit > Copy and then Edit > Paste In Front.

A copy is placed directly on top of the original.

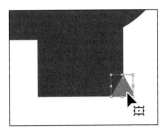

9   Drag it into place on the other leg, like you see in the figure.

Creating a star

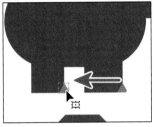

Next, you'll use the Star tool (★) to create a star that will become the tail of the bear. Currently, the Star tool doesn't create Live Shapes, so editing the star after the fact can be challenging.

When drawing with the Star tool, you use keyboard modifiers to get the number of points you want and to change the radius of the star's arms (the length of the arms). Here are the keyboard modifiers you'll use in this section when drawing the star:

- **Arrow keys:** Pressing the Up Arrow key adds arms to the star as you draw it, and the Down Arrow key removes them.
- **Shift:** This straightens the star (constrains it).
- **Command (macOS) or Ctrl (Windows):** Pressing this key and dragging while creating a star allows you to change the radius of the arms of the star (make the arms longer or shorter).

Creating a star will take a few keyboard commands, so *don't release the mouse button* until you are told. This section may take a few tries!

1   Press and hold the Polygon tool (⬡) in the toolbar, and select the Star tool (★).

▶ **Tip:** You can also click in the Document window with the Star tool (★) and edit the options in the Star dialog box instead of drawing it.

2   In an empty area of the artboard, press and drag to create a star shape. Drag until the measurement label shows a width of about 1 inch and then stop dragging. *Don't release the mouse button!*

3   Press the Up Arrow key a few times to increase the number of points on the star to eight. *Don't release the mouse button!*

4 Press Command (macOS) or Ctrl (Windows), and start dragging again, toward the center of the star a short distance, as you see in the figure, and then stop dragging *without releasing the mouse button*. Release Command or Ctrl but *not the mouse button*.

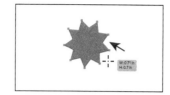

Pressing Command/Ctrl when drawing a star keeps the inner radius constant, making the arms longer or shorter, depending on how you drag.

5 Press the Shift key. When the star straightens out, release the mouse button and then the key.

6 Select the Selection tool (▶), and drag the star onto the back end of the bear like you see in the following figure.

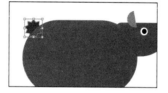

7 Click the Fill color box (■) in the Properties panel, make sure that the Swatches option (■) is selected, and change the color to a darker brown.

8 Click the Arrange button in the Properties panel and choose Send To Back to send the star behind the rest of the bear.

9 Drag it into position as you see in the figure.

Working with drawing modes

Illustrator has three different drawing modes that allow you to draw shapes in different ways. They are found near the bottom of the toolbar: Draw Normal, Draw Behind, and Draw Inside.

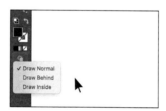

- **Draw Normal mode:** Every document starts by drawing in Normal mode, which stacks shapes on top of each other.

- **Draw Behind mode:** This allows you to draw behind all artwork on a layer if no artwork is selected. If artwork is selected, the new object is placed beneath the selected object.

- **Draw Inside mode:** This mode lets you draw objects or place images inside other objects, automatically creating a clipping mask of the selected object.

● **Note:** A clipping mask is a shape that hides parts of other artwork. You will learn more about clipping masks in Lesson 15, "Placing and Working with Images."

Using Draw Inside mode

Now you'll add a nose to the bear (and a few other things) by drawing and pasting inside of shapes using the Draw Inside drawing mode. This can be useful if you want

Note: If the toolbar you see is displayed as a double column, you will see all three of the drawing modes as buttons toward the bottom of the toolbar.

to hide (mask) part of the artwork. You can draw, place, or paste content into a shape with Draw Inside mode active. Let's add a nose to the bear, and a few other things.

1   Click to select the bear's head.

2   Choose Draw Inside from the Drawing Modes menu ( ), near the bottom of the toolbar.

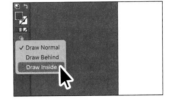

3   Press and hold on the Star tool ( ) in the toolbar and select the Ellipse tool ( ). Draw a circle on the bear head that will become a nose. See the following figure.

4   Change the fill color to black.

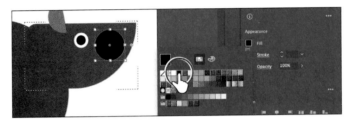

5   With the Selection tool selected, drag the circle into position where the nose might go.

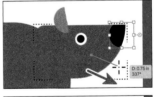

If you drag the circle so it extends beyond the edges of the bear's head, you will see that part is hidden because it is inside of the bear head.

Now you'll draw a line to give the bear a smile.

6   Press and hold on the Ellipse tool in the toolbar and select the Line Segment tool. Draw a straight line that will be the mouth of the bear.

7   Change the Stroke Weight to 2 pt and the Stroke Color to black.

8   Click the Drawing Modes button ( ) toward the bottom of the toolbar. Choose Draw Normal.

When you're finished adding content inside a shape, you can choose Draw Normal so that any new content you create will be drawn normally (stacked rather than drawn inside).

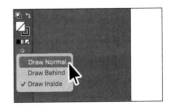

Practicing with Draw Inside mode

Now you'll take the brown chamfered corner rectangle and paste it into the body of the bear to make the belly.

1   With the Selection tool (▶), click the rectangle with chamfered edges to select it.

2   Change the fill color to a lighter brown.

3   Choose Edit > Cut to cut it from the artboard.

4   Select the body of the bear.

5   Choose Draw Inside from the Drawing Modes menu (⬛), near the bottom of the toolbar.

6   Choose Edit > Paste.

The artwork is pasted within the bear body shape. You'll get it into place in the next section.

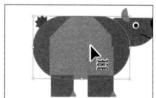

● **Note:** If the toolbar you see is displayed as a double column, you will see all three of the drawing modes as buttons toward the bottom of the toolbar.

7   Click the Drawing Modes button (⬛) toward the bottom of the toolbar. Choose Draw Normal.

8   Choose Select > Deselect, and then choose File > Save.

Editing content drawn inside

Next you'll make adjustments to the bear's belly to see how you can edit an object inside another object after you create it.

1   With the Selection tool (▶) selected, try clicking the lighter bear belly shape. You'll wind up selecting the darker brown bear body that it's inside of.

The bear body is now a mask (called a *clipping path)*. The bear body and the belly artwork you pasted inside make a *clip group*. Looking at the top of the Properties panel, you will see "Clip Group."

2   With the clip group selected, click the Isolate Mask button in the Properties panel to enter Isolation mode. Now you can select either the clipping path (the brown bear body shape) or the lighter brown artwork pasted within.

▷ **Tip:** As with a group, you can also double-click the clip group to enter Isolation mode.

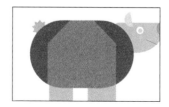

3 Drag the lighter brown belly shape to look more like you see in the figure. You can use the arrow keys to move it, make it smaller, and perform any other type of transformation as well.

4 Press the Escape key to exit Isolation mode.

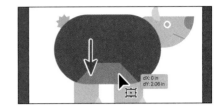

You'll probably see that the legs are in front of the bear body. Let's put them behind.

5 Drag across both the legs and the claws (triangles). Choose Object > Arrange > Send To Back.

I moved my legs up and farther apart.

6 Choose Select > Deselect.

Working with Draw Behind mode

To learn about drawing behind existing content, check out the video *Working with Draw Behind mode*, which you'll find in the Web Edition. For more information, see the "Web Edition" section of "Getting Started" at the beginning of the book.

Pasting artwork between documents

Next you'll paste the bear logo you've created so far into another Illustrator document that contains a flyer design.

1 To select all of the bear artwork, choose Select > All On Active Artboard.

2 Copy it by choosing Edit > Copy.

3 Choose File > Open. In the Open dialog box, select the L3_flyer.ai file in the Lessons > Lesson03 folder on your hard disk, and click Open.

4 Click in the blank artboard on the right to make it active and fit the artboard in the window by pressing Command+0 (macOS) or Ctrl+0 (Windows).

5 Choose Edit > Paste to paste the bear logo.

6 Click the Group button in the Task bar below (or above) the artwork to group it.

7 Choose Select > Deselect.

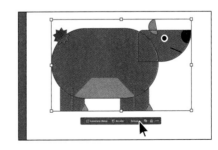

Using Image Trace to convert images into editable vector art

In this part of the lesson, you'll learn how to work with the Image Trace command, which converts a raster image, like a JPEG, into editable vector artwork. Tracing can help turn something you drew on paper—for instance, a logo, a pattern or texture, or hand-drawn type—into editable vector art. In this section, you'll trace hand-drawn text that is part of the logo type.

1   Choose File > Place. In the Place dialog box, select the hand-drawn-text.jpg file in the Lessons > Lesson03 folder on your hard disk, leave all options at their defaults, and click Place.

2   Click in the artboard to place the image.

3   If you need to, drag the image you just placed and the bear so they don't overlap.

4   Select the TREK image, and to center the image in the Document window, choose View > Zoom In a few times.

5   With the image selected, click the Image Trace button in the Properties panel to the right of the document, and choose 3 Colors from the menu.

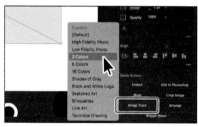

This image is converted into vector and is now called an *image tracing object*. You can't edit the vector content yet, but you can still try other tracing settings.

● **Note:** You can also choose Object > Image Trace > Make, with raster content selected, or begin tracing from the Image Trace panel (Window > Image Trace).

An image tracing object comprises the source image and the tracing result, which is the vector artwork. By default, only the tracing result is visible. However, you can change the display of both the original image and the tracing result.

6   Click the Open The Image Trace Panel button (▣) in the Properties panel.

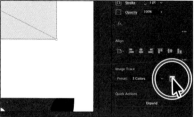

The buttons at the top of the Image Trace panel are for converting the image to grayscale, black and white, and more.

▷ **Tip:** The Image Trace panel can also be opened by choosing Window > Image Trace.

Below the buttons at the top, you'll see the Preset menu. This menu has the same options that you saw in the Properties panel.

The Mode menu allows you to change the color mode of the resulting artwork (color, grayscale, or black and white). The Palette menu is also helpful in limiting the color palette or assigning colors from a color group.

► **Tip:** You can deselect Preview at the bottom of the Image Trace panel when modifying values so Illustrator won't apply the trace settings to what you are tracing every time you make a change.

7   In the Image Trace panel, click the triangle to the left of the Advanced options to reveal them. Change the following options in the Image Trace panel, using these values as a starting point:

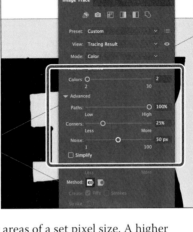

-   Colors: **2**

-   Paths: **100%** (For path fitting. A higher value means a tighter fit. We get to keep some of the rough edge on the letters.)

-   Corners: **25%** (A higher value means more corners.)

-   Noise: **50 px** (Reduce noise by ignoring areas of a set pixel size. A higher value means less noise.)

8   In the panel still, select Ignore Color. This lets you sample a color that will be excluded from the tracing.

9   Click the Eyedropper icon (✎) next to the Ignore Color option and click to sample the yellow color in the text background.

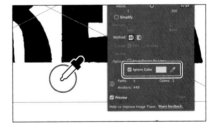

There are a lot of options in the Image Trace panel for you to explore. You will see an option for Simplify. I'm pointing that out because you will learn about a Simplify command with more options in the next section.

10 Close the Image Trace panel.

11 With the text still selected, click the Expand button in the Properties panel.

The text is no longer an image tracing object but is composed of shapes and paths that are grouped together.

Cleaning up traced artwork

Since the text image has been converted to shapes using the Image Trace command, you can refine the shapes to make the text look better. You'll apply the Simplify command to make the edges a bit smoother. The Simplify command reduces the number of anchor points the path is made of without affecting the overall shape much. It can be used to remove imperfections in the traced path when using Image Trace.

1 With the text selected, choose Object > Path > Simplify.

   In the Simplify options that appear, the Reduce Anchor Point slider is set to an auto-simplified value by default.

2 Drag the slider all the way to the left to remove a lot of points and see what the text looks like.

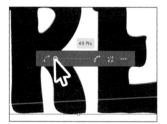 

Dragging the slider to the left reduces the anchor points and simplifies the path. The closer the slider is to the minimum value on the left, the fewer the anchor points there are, but the path will most likely look different. The closer the slider is to the maximum value, the more it will look like it did before you applied the Simplify command.

3 Click the Auto-Simplify button (⊡) in the Simplify options bar to set the default amount again.

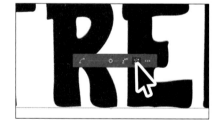

4 Click More Options (⋯) in the Simplify options bar to open a dialog box with more options. In the dialog box that opens, make sure Preview is selected to see the changes happen.

   You can see the original number of anchor points (Original) of the text and the number of anchor points after applying the Simplify command (New).

5 In the Simplify dialog box, drag the Simplify Curve slider all the way to the right (Maximum).

   This is a great starting point, and the artwork will look like it did before you applied the Simplify command.

6 Drag the same Simplify Curve slider to the left until you think it looks smoother on the edges. I set the Simplify Curve option to around 65%. See the following figure.

7 Do the same for the Corner Point Angle Threshold. Drag the slider until there are fewer ripples in the edge of the text. I set it to 94°.

For the Corner Point Angle Threshold, if the angle of a corner point is less than the angle threshold, the corner point is not changed. This option helps keep corners sharp, even if the value for Curve Precision is low.

8 Click OK.

9 Choose View > Fit All In Window.

10 Select the Eyedropper tool (✐) from the toolbar and click in the "OUTDOORS" text in the flyer to sample the color and apply it to the "TREK" text.

Adding the text and bear logo to the flyer

Now you'll move the bear logo artwork and the text into place.

1 With the Selection tool (▶) selected, drag the bear logo and the text into the flyer and arrange them however you like. Refer to the figure for how I did it.

If you want to resize either, do so with the Selection tool, pressing the Shift key to maintain proportions.

2 Choose File > Save.

Using Text to Vector Graphic (Beta)

This feature is going to be super useful for some of us! Using Text to Vector Graphic, you can generate all kinds of vector content based on a simple everyday language text prompt. Be aware that as of the writing of this book, this feature is still in beta and is the first iteration, *so it will change over time*. Keep that in mind as you go through this section. We will use Text to Vector Graphic to create a compass icon for our flyer.

1   Choose View > Fit Artboard In Window to fit the flyer in the Document window.

 To generate artwork with Text to Vector Graphic, you can either select a placeholder shape—like a rectangle—and replace it or generate artwork that is added to your design. You'll add a rectangle to the flyer so it is used as a placeholder and sized roughly as we need it to be.

2   Select the Rectangle tool (▢) from the shape tools in the toolbar.

3   Draw a rectangle at the top of the design. Use the figure for guidance.

4   Choose Window > Text To Vector Graphic (Beta) to open the panel.

> **Tip:** You can also click the Generate button in the taskbar beneath the artwork or generate content in the Properties panel.

5   Choose Icon from the Type menu.

 Right now, there are four types of artwork that you can generate:

- **Subject:** This option creates artwork without a background. Choose it if you want to add something to an existing scene or design.

> **Note:** You currently need an internet connection to generate artwork with Text to Vector Graphic (Beta).

- **Scene:** An entire artwork scene is generated with this chosen.

- **Icon:** Creates simpler artwork (usually) that is more icon-like in appearance.

- **Pattern:** This option creates repeatable artwork patterns.

6   Now type in a prompt to make the sun. I typed **warm yellow sun**.

 Most of the time you want to be more descriptive with your prompts to get the desired artwork. But this prompt worked well for me.

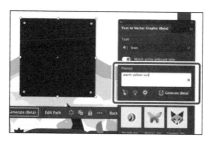

7 Click Generate in the panel.

The first time you generate, a dialog box may appear asking you to agree with the user guidelines. Then, after a short time, the rectangle will be replaced with generated artwork. The generated artwork is vector—which means it is completely editable!

● **Note:** The sun artwork that you see will definitely be something different when you generate your own artwork. Every time you generate, brand new artwork is created!

8 In the Text To Vector Graphic (Beta) panel, click one of the other variation thumbnails to replace the selected compass artwork in the flyer.

9 Click the Generate button again to generate more artwork based on the same text prompt.

10 If you want, try changing your prompt text and click Generate again!

There are other options to explore related to the Text to Vector Graphic feature, but I just wanted to give you a taste of what is to come. As time goes on, this feature will only get better!

11 Close the Text To Vector Graphic (Beta) panel.

12 Choose File > Save, and then choose File > Close for all open files.

See the latest Text to Vector Graphic feature ◼️▶

To see the latest version of the Text to Vector Graphic feature, check out the video *Exploring Text to Vector Graphic*, which you'll find in the Web Edition. For more information, see the "Web Edition" section of "Getting Started" at the beginning of the book.

Review questions

1 When creating a new document, what is a document category?

2 What are the basic tools for creating shapes?

3 What is a Live Shape?

4 Describe what Draw Inside mode does.

5 How can you convert a raster image into editable vector shapes?

Review answers

1 You can set up a document for different kinds of output, such as print, web, video, and more, by choosing a category. For example, if you are designing a web page mockup, you can select the Web category and select a document preset (size). The document will be set with the units in pixels, the color mode as RGB, and the raster effects to Screen (72 ppi)—all optimal settings for a web design document.

2 There are five shape tools in the Essentials workspace: Rectangle, Ellipse, Polygon, Star, and Line Segment (the Rounded Rectangle and Flare tools are not in the toolbar in the Essentials workspace).

3 After you draw a rectangle, ellipse, or polygon (or a rounded rectangle, which wasn't covered) using a shape tool, you can continue to modify its properties, such as width, height, rounded corners, corner types, and radii (individually or collectively). This is what is known as a Live Shape. The shape properties, such as corner radius, are editable later in the Transform panel, in the Properties panel, or directly on the art.

4 Draw Inside mode lets you draw objects or place images inside other objects, including live text, automatically creating a clipping mask of the selected object.

5 You can convert a raster image into editable vector shapes by selecting it and then clicking the Image Trace button in the Properties panel. To convert the tracing to paths, click Expand in the Properties panel, or choose Object > Image Trace > Expand. Use this method if you want to work with the components of the traced artwork as individual objects. The resulting paths are grouped.

4 EDITING AND COMBINING SHAPES AND PATHS

Lesson overview

In this lesson, you'll learn how to do the following:

- Cut with the Scissors tool.
- Join paths.
- Work with the Knife tool.
- Work with the Eraser tool.
- Create a compound path.
- Outline strokes.
- Work with the Shape Builder tool.
- Use Pathfinder effects to create shapes.
- Work with the Reshape tool.
- Edit strokes with the Width tool.
- Use Intertwine.

This lesson will take about 45 minutes to complete. To get the lesson files used in this lesson, download them from the web page for this book at *peachpit.com/IllustratorCIB2024*. For more information, see "Accessing the lesson files and Web Edition" in the Getting Started section at the beginning of this book.

After you begin creating simple paths and shapes, you will likely want to use them to create more complex artwork. In this lesson, you'll explore how to edit and combine shapes and paths.

Starting the lesson

In Lesson 3, you learned about creating and making edits to basic shapes. In this lesson, you'll take basic shapes and paths and learn how to edit and combine them to create artwork for a diner (restaurant) poster.

● **Note:** If you have not already downloaded the project files for this lesson to your computer from your Account page, make sure to do so now. See the "Getting Started" section at the beginning of the book.

1 To ensure that the tools function and the defaults are set exactly as described in this lesson, delete or deactivate (by renaming) the Adobe Illustrator preferences file. See "Restoring default preferences" in the "Getting Started" section at the beginning of the book.

2 Start Adobe Illustrator.

3 Choose File > Open. Locate the file named L4_end.ai, which is in the Lessons > Lesson04 folder that you copied onto your hard disk, and click Open. This file contains the finished artwork.

4 Choose View > Fit All In Window; leave the file open for reference, or choose File > Close (I closed it).

5 Choose File > Open. In the Open dialog box, navigate to the Lessons > Lesson04 folder, and select the L4_start.ai file on your hard disk. Click Open.

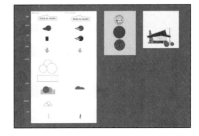

● **Note:** You need an internet connection to activate fonts. The process may take a few minutes.

6 The Missing Fonts dialog box will most likely appear. Click Activate Fonts to activate all the missing fonts. After they are activated and you see the message stating that there are no more missing fonts, click Close.

If you see another dialog box asking about font auto-activation, click Skip.

7 Choose File > Save As. If the Cloud Document dialog box opens, click Save On Your Computer to save it locally.

8 In the Save As dialog box, change the name to **DinerPoster.ai** (macOS) or **DinerPoster** (Windows), and choose the Lesson04 folder. Leave Adobe Illustrator (ai) chosen from the Format menu (macOS) or Adobe Illustrator (*.AI) chosen from the Save As Type menu (Windows), and then click Save.

9 In the Illustrator Options dialog box, leave the Illustrator options at their default settings, and click OK.

10 Choose Window > Workspace > Reset Essentials.

Note: If you don't see Reset Essentials in the Workspace menu, choose Window > Workspace > Essentials before choosing Window > Workspace > Reset Essentials.

Editing paths and shapes

In Illustrator, you can edit and combine paths and shapes in many ways to create your artwork. Sometimes, that may mean starting with more straightforward paths and shapes and using different methods to produce more complex artwork. The methods and tools you will use in this lesson include working with the Scissors tool (✂), the Knife tool (✒), and the Eraser tool (◆), outlining strokes, joining paths, and more.

Cutting with the Scissors tool

Several tools allow you to cut and divide shapes. You'll start with the Scissors tool (✂), which splits a path at an anchor point or on a line segment to create an open path.

Next, you'll cut a shape for the restaurant sign with the Scissors tool and reshape it to look more like a building shape.

1 Click the View menu, and make sure that the Smart Guides option is selected. A checkmark appears when it's selected.

2 Choose 1 Poster Parts from the Artboard Navigation menu in the lower-left corner of the Document window.

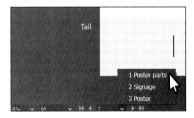

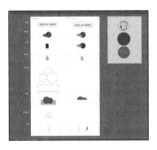

You can see examples of what you will make in the column labeled "Final Examples." You will work on the artwork in the Work Area column.

3 Select the Selection tool (▶) in the toolbar, and click the gray shape with the green stroke behind the "OPEN 24 HOURS" text on the top-left side of the artboard.

4 Press Command and + (macOS) or Ctrl and + (Windows) several times to zoom in to the selected artwork.

5 With the shape selected, in the toolbar press and hold on the Eraser tool (◆), and select the Scissors tool (✂).

6 Move the pointer over the top edge of the shape (see the first part of the following figure). When you see the word "intersect" and a vertical magenta line, click to cut the path at that point, and then move the pointer away.

 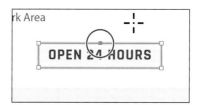

● **Note:** To learn more about open paths and closed paths, see the section "Working with basic shapes" in Lesson 3.

Cuts made with the Scissors tool must be somewhere on a line or a curve rather than on the end of an open path, as with a line. With the Scissors tool, when you click the stroke of a closed shape, like the shape in this example, the path is cut where you click so that it becomes an open path.

7 Select the Direct Selection tool (▷) in the toolbar.

8 Move the pointer over the selected (blue) anchor point, and drag it up and a little to the left.

9 From where you originally cut the shape, drag the other anchor point up and a little to the right.

Notice that the stroke (the green border) doesn't go around the shape. Cutting a shape with the Scissors tool makes it an open path. It doesn't have to be a closed path if you only want to fill the shape with a color. However, a path must be closed if you want a stroke to appear around the entire fill area.

Joining paths

Suppose you have a "U" shape and want to close the shape, joining the ends of the "U" with a straight path. You can use the Join command to create a line segment between the end points, closing the path.

before joining   after joining

When more than one open path is selected, you can join their ends to create a closed path. You can also join specific end points of two separate paths. Next, you'll join the ends of the sign shape you just edited to create a closed shape again.

1 Select the Selection tool (▶) in the toolbar.

2 Click away from the path to deselect it, and then click in the gray fill to reselect it.

This step is important! Only one anchor point was left selected from the previous section. If you were to choose the Join command with only one anchor point selected, an error message would appear.

Tip: If you want to join specific anchor points from separate paths, select the anchor points and choose Object > Path > Join or press Command+J (macOS) or Ctrl+J (Windows).

By selecting the whole path, when you apply the Join command, Illustrator simply finds the two ends of the path and connects them with a straight line.

3 Click the Join Path button in the Task bar below the artwork (or the Join button in the Quick Actions section of the Properties panel).

When you apply the Join command to two or more open paths, by default Illustrator first looks for and joins the paths that have end points located closest to each other. This process is repeated every time you apply the Join command until all paths are joined.

Tip: In Lesson 6, "Using the Basic Drawing Tools," you'll learn about the Join tool (✂), which allows you to join two paths at a corner, keeping the original curve intact.

4 Shift-click the "OPEN 24 HOURS" text to select it as well.

5 Click the Group button in the Task bar beneath (or above) the artwork to group them together so they move as one.

6 Choose Select > Deselect, and then choose File > Save.

Cutting with the Knife tool

You can also use the Knife tool (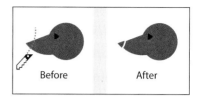) to cut vector artwork. You drag across a shape using the Knife tool, and instead of creating open paths like the Scissor tool, you end up with closed paths. The Knife tool is a great way to make multiple shapes from a single shape—maybe so you can apply different colors.

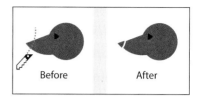

Before   After

In this section and the next, you'll cut a shape into multiple shapes to make the head of the dog.

1   Press the spacebar to access the Hand tool (✋), and drag up in the document window to see the brown shapes just below the "OPEN 24 HOURS" sign.

2   With the Selection tool (▶) selected, click the brown shape you see to the right.

Now you need to access the Knife tool, but it's not in the default toolbar. You'll switch over to a more advanced toolbar for the moment so you can access the tools you need.

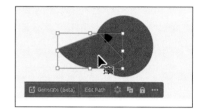

3   Choose Window > Toolbars > Advanced.

You should now see a lot more tools in the toolbar on the left.

4   Press and hold on the Scissors tool (✂) in the toolbar, and select the Knife tool (✐) from the menu of tools.

First, you'll use the Knife tool to make a freeform cut from the brown shape, making the nose of the dog.

5   With the Knife tool selected in the toolbar, move the Knife pointer (✐) above the selected shape. Drag to cut a nose out of the shape. See the figure for where!

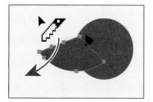   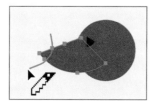   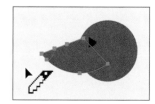

Only selected objects will be cut by the Knife tool. If nothing is selected, it will cut any vector objects it touches.

▶ **Tip:** Don't like your cut? Try again! Choose Edit > Undo Knife Tool and try cutting again.

6   Choose Select > Deselect.

7   Select the Selection tool (▶), and click the new nose shape (see the following figure).

8   Click the Fill color box in the Properties panel, make sure the Swatches option (▦) is selected in the panel that appears, and select black.

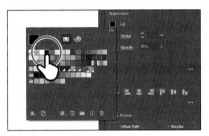 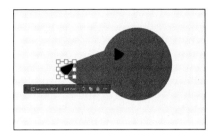

9   Press the Escape key to hide the Swatches panel, if it's showing.

10 Choose Select > Deselect.

Cutting in a straight line with the Knife tool

By default, as you just saw, dragging across a shape with the Knife tool makes a freeform cut that is not straight.

Next, you'll see how to cut artwork in a straight line with the Knife tool to give the dog a different color muzzle.

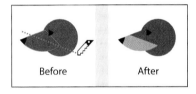

Before   After

1   With the Selection tool (▶) selected, click what is left of the same brown shape. See the following figure.

2   Select the Knife tool (✐) in the toolbar.

3   Move the pointer just above the top of the shape.

4   Press the Caps Lock key to turn the Knife tool pointer into crosshairs (-¦-).

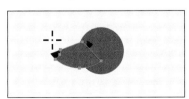

The crosshairs pointer is more precise and can make it easier to see exactly where you begin cutting.

Note: Pressing the Option/Alt key keeps the cut straight. Adding the Shift key (Option/Alt-Shift) would constrain the cutting to a multiple of 45°.

5 Press and hold Option (macOS) or Alt (Windows), and begin dragging across the shape to cut it into two. *Don't release the key or mouse button yet!* Keep dragging over the anchor point on the right. See the figure.

6 Release the mouse button and then the key to make the cut.

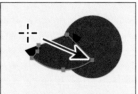
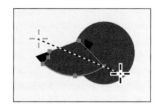
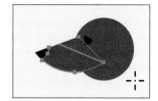

7 Choose Select > Deselect.

8 Select the Selection tool (▶), and click the left half of the original shape (see the following figure).

9 Click the Fill color box in the Properties panel, make sure the Swatches option (▦) is selected in the panel that appears, and click to select a lighter brown.

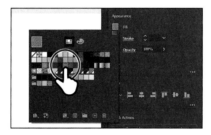
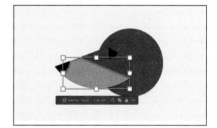

10 Drag across all of the dog head shapes to select them.

11 Click the Group button in the Task bar.

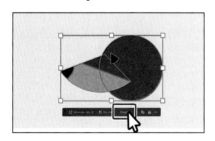
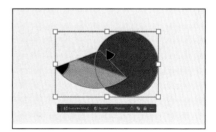

12 Press the Caps Lock key to turn off the pointer crosshairs.

Using the Eraser tool

The Eraser tool (◆) lets you erase areas of your vector artwork. With nothing selected, you can erase any object that the tool touches. If any artwork is selected, only that artwork can be erased.

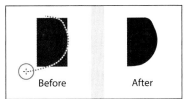

Before   After

Note: You cannot erase raster images, text, symbols, graphs, or gradient mesh objects.

Next, you'll use the Eraser tool to erase part of a rounded rectangle so it looks more like the ear of a dog.

1 Choose Select > Deselect.

2 Press the spacebar to select the Hand tool (✋). Drag up in the Document window so you can see the brown rectangle below the dog's head.

3 Press and hold down the mouse button on the Knife tool (✐), and select the Eraser tool (◆) in the toolbar.

4 Double-click the Eraser tool (◆) in the toolbar to edit the tool properties. In the Eraser Tool Options dialog box, change Size to **60 pt** to make the eraser larger. Click OK.

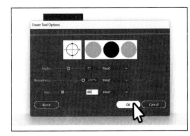

Tip: With the Eraser tool selected and nothing selected in the document, you could also click the Tool Options button at the top of the Properties panel to see the Eraser Tool Options dialog box.

5 Move the pointer above the brown rectangle. Drag down in an arc to remove part of the right side. See the figure.

When you release the mouse button, part of the shape is erased, and the shape is still a closed path. If you missed a part, drag across the shape again to smooth it out.

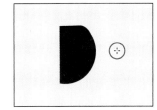

If you find that you haven't quite erased enough, drag across the right side again until it looks the way you want. At any point, if you've erased too much, you can choose Edit > Undo Eraser and try again.

Now you'll round the corners on the left side of the same shape.

6 Select the Direct Selection tool (▷), and click in the brown shape to select it.

7 Click the Corner Radius widget in the upper-left corner and Shift-click the lower-left corner widget to select both.

8 Drag one of the selected widgets to round the corners a bit.

 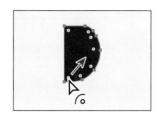 

Now you will add the ear to the dog's head and group them together.

9 Select the Selection tool and drag the ear of the dog you just erased part of onto the head of the dog directly above it. You may need to zoom out to see both.

10 Move the pointer just off a corner until you see the rotate arrows (↰). Drag to rotate it a bit.

11 Drag across the combined artwork and click the Group button in the Task bar below (or above) the artwork.

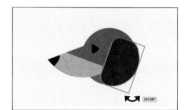

Toward the end of the lesson, you will drag the head over to the sign and add it there.

Erasing in a straight line

Next, you'll erase a circle in a straight line to make a bush.

1 Choose 3 Poster from the Artboard Navigation menu in the lower-left corner of the Document window.

2 With the Selection tool (▶) selected, click the larger green circle.

3 Choose View > Zoom In a few times to see more detail.

4 Double-click the Eraser tool (◆) to edit the tool properties. In the Eraser Tool Options dialog box, change Size to **300 pt** to make the eraser much bigger. Click OK.

5 With the Eraser tool (◆) selected, move the pointer to where you see the red "X" in the first part of the following figure. Press the Shift key, and drag straight across to the right. Release the mouse button and then the Shift key.

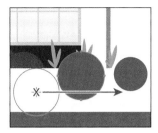  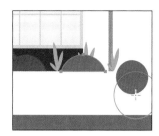

If nothing is erased, try again. Also, it may look like you erased other parts of the shape, but if nothing else was selected, you didn't.

6 Select the smaller green circle to the right and practice by erasing the bottom half to make another bush.

7 Choose File > Save.

Tip: While using almost any tool, pressing Command/Ctrl turns the tool into a temporary Selection tool.

Creating a compound path

Compound paths let you use a vector object to cut a hole in another vector object. If you were to select two vector objects, the "cutting" object would be the top object.

Before   After

Whenever I think of a compound path, I think of a doughnut shape created from two circles. Holes appear where paths overlap. A compound path is like a group, and the individual objects in the compound path can still be edited or released (if you don't want them to be a compound path anymore).

Next, you'll create a compound path to make the rest of the diner sign.

1 Choose 2 Signage from the Artboard Navigation menu in the lower-left corner of the Document window.

2 With the Selection tool (▶), select the red circle at the bottom of the artboard.

3 Shift-click the dark green circle above it to select both. Release the Shift key.

4 Click the larger dark green circle to make it the key object so the red circle will align with it.

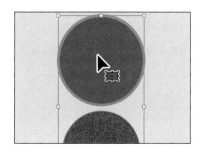

5 In the Properties panel, click the Horizontal Align Center button () and the Vertical Align Center ( ) button to center the red circle on the green circle.

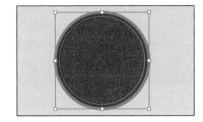

▶ **Tip:** You can still edit the original shapes in a compound path like this one. To edit them, select each shape individually with the Direct Selection tool (▷), or double-click the compound path with the Selection tool to enter Isolation mode and select individual shapes.

6 With both circles selected, choose Object > Compound Path > Make, and leave the artwork selected.

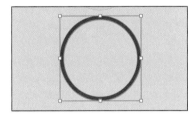

You can now see that the red circle has seemingly disappeared, and you can see through the green circle to the gray background. The red circle "punched" a hole in the green shape.

With the shape still selected, you should see "Compound Path" at the top of the Properties panel to the right. A compound path is a special group and is treated as a single object.

7 Shift-click the light green circle that is the background of the "DACHSHUND DINER" text above it to select it as well. Release the Shift key.

Now you'll align the compound path you just made to the light green circle above it.

8 Click the same light green circle to make it the key object.

9 In the Properties panel, click the Horizontal Align Center button ( ) and the Vertical Align Center ( ) button to center the compound path on the light green circle.

10 Choose Select > Deselect, and then choose File > Save.

Outlining strokes

A path, like a line, can have only so many things done to it. For example, you can only erase a line to shorten it. To erase a line to look like what you see in the figure, you need to turn it into a shape by outlining the stroke.

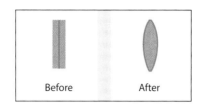

Before   After

Next, you'll outline the stroke of a line so you can make it look like a plant leaf.

1   Choose 1 Poster Parts from the Artboard Navigation menu in the lower-left corner of the Document window.

2   With the Selection tool (▶), click a green plant path in the Work Area column.

    To erase part of the path and make it look like a plant leaf, the path will need to be a filled shape, not a path.

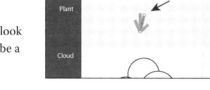

3   Choose View > Zoom In a few times to see the path more easily.

    Look in the Properties panel and you can see that the path has a stroke but no fill.

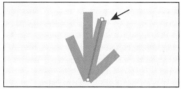

4   Choose Object > Path > Outline Stroke.

    The path with a stroke is now a shape with a fill. Next, you'll erase parts of the shape so it looks more like a plant.

5   Select the Eraser tool (◆) in the toolbar.

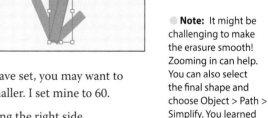

    Before erasing with the rather large brush size you have set, you may want to double-click the Eraser tool and set the size to be smaller. I set mine to 60.

6   With the shape selected, drag from the top down along the right side.

7   Do the same for the left side to make a leaf shape.

Note: It might be challenging to make the erasure smooth! Zooming in can help. You can also select the final shape and choose Object > Path > Simplify. You learned about the Simplify command in Lesson 3.

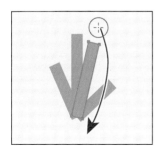

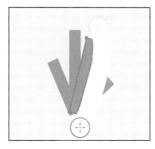

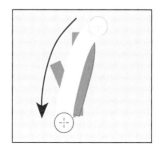

Now for some practice!

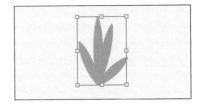

Tip: I always strive to work smarter, not harder. If this were a real-world project, I would outline and then erase one, and then copy it a few times, scaling each copy!

8 Select another green path in the plant, outline the stroke (Object > Path > Outline Stroke), and erase it!

If you want some more practice, try outlining and erasing the next two paths in the plant.

9 When you are finished, with the Selection tool selected, drag across the parts of the plant and group them by clicking the Group button in the Task bar.

Combining shapes

Creating more complex shapes from simpler shapes can be easier than making them with drawing tools like the Pen tool. In Illustrator, you can combine vector objects in different ways. The resulting paths or shapes differ depending on the method you use to combine the paths. This section explores a few more widely used methods for combining shapes.

Working with the Shape Builder tool

The first method you'll learn for combining shapes involves working with the Shape Builder tool (⊕). This tool allows you to visually and intuitively merge, delete, fill, and edit overlapping shapes and paths directly in the artwork. You will likely use it a lot once you see how easy it is! In this section, you'll create a cloud from a series of circles using the Shape Builder tool.

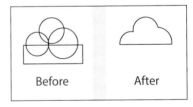

Before   After

1 Choose View > Zoom Out a few times.

2 Press the spacebar to select the Hand tool (✋). Drag up in the Document window so you can see the cloud artwork below the plant artwork.

3 Select the Selection tool (▶), and drag across the three white circles.

To edit shapes with the Shape Builder tool (⊕), they need to be selected. Using the Shape Builder tool, you will now combine, delete, and paint these simple shapes to create a cloud.

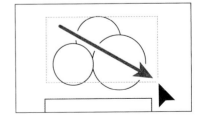

4 Select the Shape Builder tool (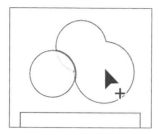) in the toolbar. Move the pointer off the left side of the shapes and drag to the right through some of the shapes. Release the mouse button to combine those shapes.

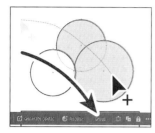

When you select the Shape Builder tool, the overlapping shapes are temporarily divided into separate objects. As you drag from one part to another, a red outline appears, showing you the shape that will result when the existing shapes are merged.

You may notice that not everything combined! To add parts of the shapes to the final combined shape, you needed to drag through *all* of them. You'll fix that next.

5 Press the Shift key and drag a marquee across *all* of the cloud shapes to combine everything.

Dragging a marquee with the Shift key can be an easier way to combine a bunch of shapes, since you don't have to drag through each shape; they just need to be within the marquee.

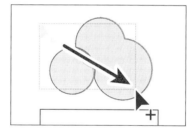

▶ **Tip:** Pressing Shift+Option (macOS) or Shift+Alt (Windows) and dragging a marquee across selected shapes with the Shape Builder tool (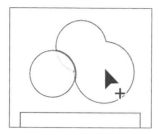) allows you to delete a series of shapes within the marquee.

Now you will add a rectangle and use it to subtract the bottom part of the cloud, making a flat bottom.

6 Select the Selection tool and drag the white rectangle that's beneath the cloud up onto the cloud, covering roughly the bottom half of the cloud.

7 Shift-click the cloud shape to select it as well.

8 Select the Shape Builder tool (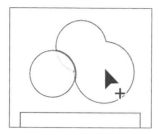) again.

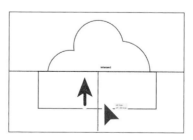

9 Press the Option (macOS) or Alt (Windows) key. Notice that, with the modifier key held down, the pointer shows a minus sign (▶_). Drag from off the left side of the rectangle through the bottom of the cloud. Release the mouse button, and then the key.

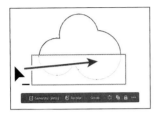  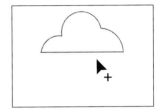

10 Choose View > Fit Artboard In Window.

11 Select the Eyedropper tool (⚲) in the toolbar. With the cloud still selected, click the cloud to the right in the Final Example column to sample the color and apply it to your cloud.

12 Choose Select > Deselect.

Combining objects using Pathfinder effects

Pathfinder effects, found in the Properties panel or the Pathfinder panel (Window > Pathfinder), are another way to combine shapes in a variety of ways.

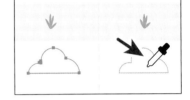

Before   After

By default, when a Pathfinder effect such as Unite is applied, the original objects selected are *permanently* transformed. Now you'll make a bush from a few shapes.

1 Zoom in to the Bush shapes (the green circles and orange rectangle).

2 With the Selection tool (▶) selected, drag across the two green circles to select them.

> ● **Note:** The Unite button in the Properties panel produces a similar result as the Shape Builder tool by combining multiple shapes into one.

3 With the shapes selected, in the Pathfinder section of the Properties panel on the right, click the Unite button (▣) to *permanently* combine the two shapes into one.

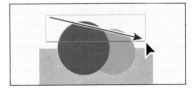

Notice that the color of the final, combined shape is the darker green. That's because the color of the final shape is taken from the topmost shape that is combined.

4   Shift-click the orange rectangle that is behind the new green shape.

5   In the Properties panel, click More Options () in the Pathfinder section to show more options.

6   Click the Minus Back (⬛) button to knock the orange rectangle, which is in the back, from the green shape, which is in front.

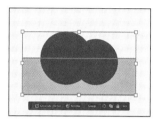

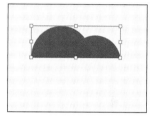

Know that using any of the options you saw in the Pathfinder section of the Properties panel makes a permanent change to the shapes.

Understanding shape modes

If you Option-click (macOS) or Alt-click (Windows) any of the default set of pathfinders showing in the Properties panel, called *Shape modes*, the result is not permanent. A compound shape rather than a standard shape (path) is created. The original underlying objects are preserved. As a result, you can still select each original object within a compound shape. Using a shape mode to create a compound shape can be useful if you think that you may want to retrieve the original shapes at a later time.

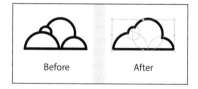

Now you'll create another cloud from a series of shapes, and you'll be able to edit the underlying shapes later.

1   Press the spacebar to select the Hand tool (✋). Drag up in the Document window so you can see the Cloud 2 artwork below the bush artwork.

2   Drag across all of the cloud shapes.

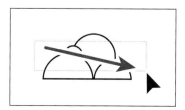

3 Press the Option (macOS) or Alt (Windows) key, and click the Unite button (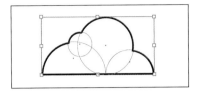) in the Properties panel.

This creates a compound shape that traces the outline of what's left after the shapes are combined. You'll still be able to edit the original shapes separately.

4 Choose Select > Deselect to see the final shape.

5 With the Selection tool, double-click within the cloud to enter Isolation mode.

As when a regular group is in Isolation mode, the parts of the compound shape are temporarily ungrouped!

6 Click in the larger ellipse to select it.

7 Make the shape smaller by Shift-dragging the bounding point on the top.

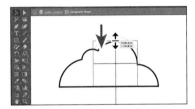

Notice that the outline around the cloud changes.

8 Press the Escape key to exit Isolation mode.

You will now expand the artwork appearance. Expanding the appearance of a compound shape maintains the shape, but you can no longer select or edit the original shapes. You will typically expand an object when you want to modify the appearance attributes and other properties of the entire shape.

9 Click away from the cloud to deselect it, and then click to select it again.

That way, the entire object is selected, and not just the one shape.

10 Choose Object > Expand Appearance.

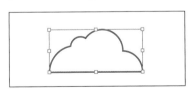

The Pathfinder effect is now *permanent,* and the shapes are a single shape.

11 Choose View > Fit Artboard In Window.

12 Select the Eyedropper tool (✎) in the toolbar. With the cloud selected, click the cloud to the right in the Final Example column to sample the color and apply it to your cloud.

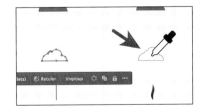

Reshaping a path

Using the Reshape tool, you can stretch parts of a path without distorting its overall shape. In this section, you'll change the shape of a line, giving it a bit of curve, so you can add a tail to the dog.

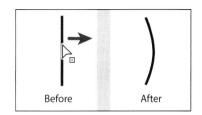

Before   After

1 Make sure the Smart Guides are on (View > Smart Guides).

2 With the Selection tool (▶) selected, select the vertical line at the bottom of the artboard in the "Tail" Work Area section.

3 To make it easier to see, press Command and + (macOS) or Ctrl and + (Windows) several times to zoom in.

4 In the toolbar, press and hold on the Scale tool (⊡) and select the Reshape tool (↘).

5 Move the pointer over the middle of the path. When the pointer changes (△), drag to the right to add an anchor point and reshape the path.

● **Note:** You can use the Reshape tool on a closed path, like a square or circle, but if the entire path is selected, the Reshape tool will add anchor points and move the path.

 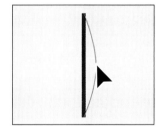 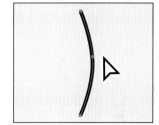

The Reshape tool can be used to drag an existing anchor point or path segment. If you drag from an existing path segment, an anchor point is created.

● **Note:** Only selected anchor points are adjusted when dragging with the Reshape tool.

6 Move the pointer over the bottom third of the path, and drag it to the left a little. Leave the path selected.

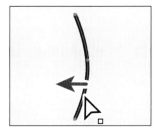 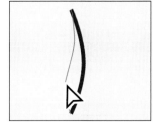 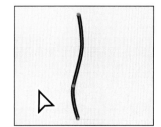

Using the Width tool

Not only can you adjust the weight of a stroke, as you did in Lesson 3, but you can alter regular stroke widths either by using the Width tool (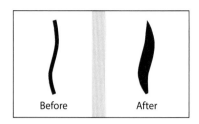) or by applying width profiles to the stroke. This allows you to create a variable width along the stroke of a path. Next, you will use the Width tool to adjust the path you just reshaped to finalize the tail.

Before   After

▶ **Tip:** You can drag one width point on top of another width point to create a discontinuous width point. If you double-click a discontinuous width point, the Width Point Edit dialog box allows you to edit both width points.

1 Select the Width tool (🖉) in the toolbar.

2 Move the pointer over the middle of the path you just reshaped, and notice that the pointer has a plus symbol next to it (▸₊) when it's positioned over the path. If you were to drag, you would edit the width of the stroke. Drag away from the line, to the right. Notice that, as you drag, you are stretching the stroke to the left and right equally. Release the mouse button when the measurement label shows a Width of approximately 44 pixels.

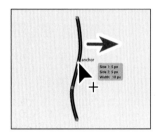
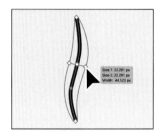

You just created a variable stroke on a path, not a shape with a fill. The new point on the original path is called the *width point*. The lines extending from the width point are the *handles*.

▶ **Tip:** If you select a width point by clicking it, you can press Delete to remove it. When there is only one width point on a stroke, removing that point removes the width adjustment completely.

3 Click in an empty area of the artboard to deselect the point.

4 Move the pointer anywhere over the path. You should see the width point you just created (an arrow is pointing to it).

5 Move the pointer over the original width point, and when you see lines extending from it and the pointer changes (▸～), drag it up and down to see the effect on the path. See the last part of the following figure for where it should approximately land.

In addition to dragging to reposition a width point, you can double-click and enter values in a dialog box. That's what you'll do next.

6 Move the pointer over the top anchor point of the path.

Notice that the pointer has a wavy line next to it (▶~) and the word "anchor" appears (see the first part of the following figure).

7 Double-click the point to create a new width point and to open the Width Point Edit dialog box.

8 In the Width Point Edit dialog box, change Total Width to **0 in**, and click OK.

▶ **Tip:** You can select a width point and Option-drag (macOS) or Alt-drag (Windows) one of the width point handles to change one side of the stroke width.

▶ **Tip:** After defining the stroke width, you can save the variable width as a *profile* that you can reuse later from the Stroke panel or the Control panel.

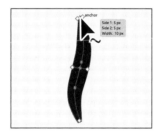
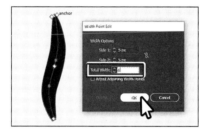

The Width Point Edit dialog box allows you to adjust the length of the width point handles, together or separately, with more precision. Also, if you select the Adjust Adjoining Width Points option, any changes you make to the selected width point affect neighboring width points as well.

9 Move the pointer over the handle on either side of the bottom anchor point of the path. Drag so that the width is roughly 12 pixels.

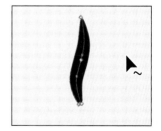

You could also have double-clicked the anchor point at the bottom to set the total width to 12 pixels in the Width Point Edit dialog box, like you did in the previous step.

Using Intertwine

A time-saving feature in Illustrator is Intertwine. With Intertwine, you can take a path like you see in the figure and make part of it appear on top of another object or behind that same object. This can give the appearance of the path "intertwining" around the other object.

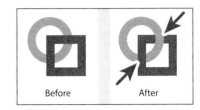

Before   After

In this section, you will intertwine a scarf on the dog so it looks like it goes behind and in front of the body of the dog.

1   Choose 2 Signage from the Artboard Navigation menu in the lower-left corner of the Document window.

2   With the Selection tool selected, click the white serpentine shape (the scarf) on the dog's body.

3   Choose View > Zoom In several times to see it better.

The white scarf would look good if it appeared to wrap around the dog—going behind and in front of the body of the dog. You can do that manually using the Scissors tool to cut the white scarf path and send paths behind, but using Intertwine is much easier.

4   Shift-click the body of the dog to add it to the selection.

Currently, you need to have more than one object selected for this to work.

5   Choose Object > Intertwine > Make.

The scarf and dog are now a grouped Intertwine object. If you look at the top of the Properties panel, you'll see "Intertwine."

Now that the objects are an Intertwine object, you can tell Illustrator what parts of the white scarf, in this case, should go behind the dog body. To tell Illustrator which parts, you drag a selection around it.

▶ **Tip:** You can also click on the white scarf where it overlaps the dog body to send it behind or bring it to front!

6   Drag a selection around where the white scarf and dog body intersect. See the first part of the following figure. When you release, the scarf in that small area will be behind the dog!

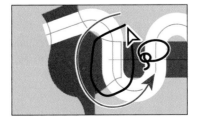
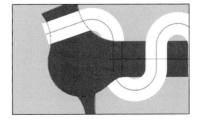

If it doesn't look right—maybe you didn't select enough of the overlapping area—you can choose Edit > Undo Rearrange and try again!

7 Try dragging around another part of the white scarf where it overlaps the dog.

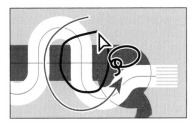 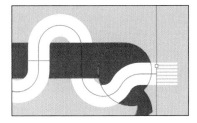

8 When finished, choose Select > Deselect.

9 With the Selection tool, click the white scarf to select the Intertwine object again.

If you wanted to continue telling Illustrator what parts of the scarf to bring in front, or reverse parts you already did, you could click the Edit button in the Quick Actions section of the Properties panel and make more selections.

Assembling the sign

To complete the sign, you'll drag and position the dog's head and the tail onto the sign, resize them, and reposition them. You'll need to zoom in and out a fair amount to move and resize things.

1 Choose View > Fit All In Window.

2 With the Selection tool (▶) selected, drag the dog's head you worked on onto the body of the dog in the middle artboard.

3 Drag the tail of the dog from the bottom of the leftmost artboard onto the sign as well.

4 Choose View > Zoom In a few times to zoom in to the dog.

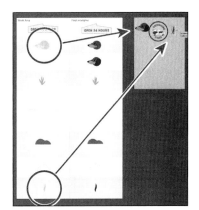

5 Resize the head by Shift-dragging a corner to make it smaller, and then drag it into place on the body of the dog.

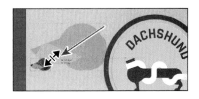

6 Select the tail.

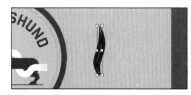

Since the tail is a path with a stroke, to resize it and scale the stroke weight as well, you need to turn on Scale Strokes & Effects.

7 Click More Options () in the Transform section of the Properties panel. Select Scale Strokes & Effects. Press the Esc key to hide the panel.

8 Shift-drag the tail to make it smaller.

Note: If either the head or the tail is behind the body, click the Arrange button in the Properties panel and choose Bring To Front.

9 To rotate the tail, move the pointer just off a corner and rotate to make it look like you see in the following figure.

10 Drag each into the position like you see in the figure.

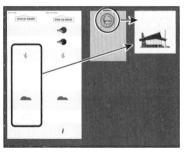

11 Drag across all of the pieces in the "DACHSHUND DINER" sign and choose Object > Group.

Assembling the poster

To finish up, you will now drag what you have made in the other artboards onto the poster in the far-right artboard.

1 Choose View > Fit All In Window.

2 Drag all of the pieces—the sign from the middle artboard, the clouds, the bush, and the plant—into the poster on the far right.

I put dashed line shapes in the poster where they might go!

3 Resize the "OPEN 24 HOURS" sign to make it smaller and fit nicely. Make sure you drag with the Shift key to maintain the proportions!

4 Switch the toolbar back to the basic toolbar by choosing Window > Toolbars > Basic.

5 Choose File > Save and then File > Close.

Review questions

1 Name two ways you can combine several shapes into one.

2 What is the difference between the Scissors tool (✂) and the Knife tool (✐)?

3 How can you erase with the Eraser tool (◆) in a straight line?

4 What is the main difference between shape modes and Pathfinder effects in the Properties panel or Pathfinder panel?

5 Why would you outline strokes?

Review answers

1 Using the Shape Builder tool (⊕), you can visually and intuitively merge, delete, fill, and edit overlapping shapes and paths directly in the artwork. You can also use the Pathfinder effects, which can be found in the Properties panel, the Effects menu (not mentioned in this lesson), or the Pathfinder panel, to create new shapes out of overlapping objects.

2 The Scissors tool (✂) is meant to split a path, graphics frame, or empty text frame at an anchor point or along a segment. The Knife tool (✐) cuts objects along a path you draw with the tool, dividing objects. When you cut a shape with the Scissors tool, it becomes an open path. When you cut a shape with the Knife tool, the resulting shapes become closed paths.

3 To erase in a straight line with the Eraser tool (◆), press and hold the Shift key before you begin dragging with the Eraser tool.

4 In the Properties panel, when a shape mode (such as Unite) is applied, the original objects selected are permanently transformed, but you can hold down the Option (macOS) or Alt (Windows) key to preserve the original underlying objects. When a Pathfinder effect (such as Merge) is applied, the original objects selected are permanently transformed.

5 A straight path (line) can show a stroke color but not a fill color by default. If you create a line in Illustrator and want to apply both a stroke and a fill, you can outline the stroke, which converts the line into a closed shape (or compound path).

5 TRANSFORMING ARTWORK

Lesson overview

In this lesson, you'll learn how to do the following:

- Add, edit, rename, and reorder artboards in an existing document.

- Navigate artboards.

- Change the order of artboards. ■◄

- Work with rulers and guides.

- Edit the ruler origin. ■◄

- Position objects with precision.

- Move, scale, rotate, and shear objects using a variety of methods.

- Transform with the Free Transform tool. ■◄

- Explore the mirror repeat.

- Use grid and radial repeats. ■◄

- Work with the Puppet Warp tool.

 This lesson will take about 60 minutes to complete. To get the lesson files used in this lesson, download them from the web page for this book at *peachpit.com/IllustratorCIB2024*. For more information, see "Accessing the lesson files and Web Edition" in the Getting Started section at the beginning of this book.

As you create artwork, you can modify it by quickly and precisely controlling objects' size, shape, and orientation. In this lesson, you'll explore creating and editing artboards, the various Transform commands, and specialized tools while creating several pieces of artwork.

Starting the lesson

In this lesson, you'll transform artwork and use it to complete a few ads. Before you begin, you'll restore the default preferences for Adobe Illustrator and then open a file containing the finished artwork to see what you'll create.

Note: If you have not already downloaded the project files for this lesson to your computer from your Account page, make sure to do so now. See the "Getting Started" section at the beginning of the book.

1   To ensure that the tools function and the defaults are set exactly as described in this lesson, delete or deactivate (by renaming) the Adobe Illustrator preferences file. See "Restoring default preferences" in the "Getting Started" section at the beginning of the book.

2   Start Adobe Illustrator.

3   Choose File > Open, and open the L5_end.ai file in the Lessons > Lesson05 folder on your hard disk.

    This file contains the artboards that make up a few different versions of an ad.

Note: For more information on installing fonts, visit *helpx.adobe.com/ creative-cloud/help/add-fonts.html*.

4   In the Missing Fonts dialog box, ensure that each missing font is selected, and click Activate Fonts. After some time, the font(s) should be activated, and you should see a success message in the Missing Fonts dialog box. Click Close.

    If a dialog box appears discussing font auto-activation, you can click Skip.

5   Choose View > Fit All In Window, and leave the artwork onscreen as you work.

6   Choose File > Open. In the Open dialog box, navigate to the Lessons > Lesson05 folder, and select the L5_start.ai file on your hard disk. Click Open.

7   Choose File > Save As. If the Cloud Document dialog box opens, click Save On Your Computer.

8   In the Save As dialog box, name the file **Vacation_ads.ai**, and navigate to the Lesson05 folder. Leave Adobe Illustrator (ai) chosen from the Format menu (macOS) or Adobe Illustrator (*.AI) chosen from the Save As Type menu (Windows), and click Save.

Note: If you don't see Reset Essentials in the Workspace menu, choose Window > Workspace > Essentials before choosing Window > Workspace > Reset Essentials.

9   In the Illustrator Options dialog box, leave the Illustrator options at their default settings, and then click OK.

10 Choose Window > Workspace > Reset Essentials.

How can you use artboards?

By now, you probably have an idea of what
artboards generally are. They represent the
regions containing printable or exportable
artwork, similar to pages in Adobe InDesign or
Microsoft Word.

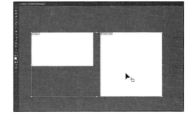

But how can you use artboards?
You can use them however you like, but here
are a few of the more widely used ways:

- Multi-page documents—each "page" is on an artboard.
- Multiple *projects* in the same document, each artboard being the same or
  different sizes—doesn't matter.
- A scratch pad for creative ideas. *You can also just use the gray canvas area for that!*
- Independent elements for websites or apps on a single artboard, exported
  separately via Asset Export or other method.

Creating and editing artboards

In this section, you'll explore creating and editing artboards so that you can put three
different ads on separate artboards that you can then export however you need.

Making a custom-sized artboard

Each document starts with one artboard. You can add and remove artboards at any
time while working on a document, and they can be different sizes, as needed. You
can resize, position, reorder, and rename them in Artboard Editing mode.

To start, you'll add a few artboards to your document.

1 Choose View > Fit Artboard In Window.

   There is only one artboard in document right now, so it is fit into the
   Document window.

2 To zoom out, press Command and – (macOS) or Ctrl and – (Windows) twice.

3 Press the spacebar to temporarily access
   the Hand tool (✋). Drag to the left
   in the Document window so the tree off
   the right side of the artboard is more in
   the center of the window.

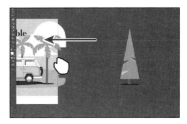

4 Select the Selection tool (▶).

   Now you'll create a new artboard.

5 Click the Edit Artboards button in the Properties panel.

Clicking the Edit Artboards button enters Artboard Editing mode and selects the Artboard tool in the toolbar.

You'll now see a dashed line around the only artboard in the document and, if it's in view, a label showing "01 - Artboard 1" in the upper-left corner of the artboard. Note that artwork, like the tree sitting in the gray canvas area by itself, doesn't have to be on an artboard.

6 Like drawing a rectangle, drag across the tree to make an artboard. Don't worry about the size; you're going to change it soon.

The tree is now on that new artboard.

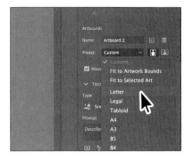

In the Properties panel on the right, in Artboard Editing mode, you'll see lots of options for editing the selected artboard.

For instance, when an artboard is selected, the Preset menu lets you change the artboard to a set size, like Letter. The sizes in the Preset menu include typical print, video, tablet, and web sizes.

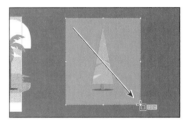

7 In the Properties panel on the right, select the Width and type **336**. Select the Height value, and type **280**. Press Return or Enter to accept the height.

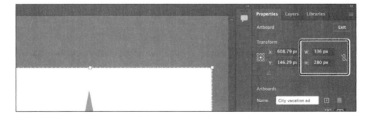

Note: The unit of measurement in this document is the pixel, but you don't have to type the "px" in.

8 Change the name to **City vacation ad** in the Artboards section of the Properties panel. Press Return or Enter to make the change.

9 Out in the document, drag the selected artboard to the right a bit to make more room between the artboards.

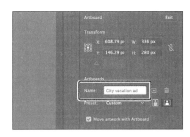

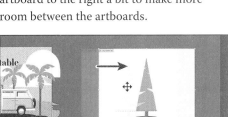

Did you notice that the tree moved with it? By default, content on an artboard that isn't locked moves with the artboard.

▶ **Tip:** Looking in the Properties panel, you'll see the Move Artwork With Artboard option is selected. If you deselect that option before moving an artboard, the artwork won't move with it.

Creating a new same-sized artboard

Next, you'll create another artboard that's the same size as the City Vacation Ad artboard for another ad.

1 Click the New Artboard button (▣) in the Properties panel to create a new artboard that's the same size as the City Vacation Ad artboard and to its right.

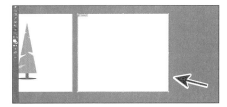

2 Change the name of the new artboard to **Mountain vacation ad** in the Properties panel. Press Return or Enter to make the change.

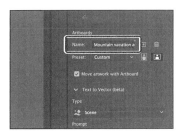
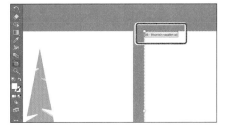

Remember that when editing artboards in Artboard Editing mode, you can see the name of each artboard in the upper-left corner of the artboard.

3 Choose View > Fit All In Window to see all of your artboards.

Tip: To exit Artboard Editing mode, you can also select another tool in the toolbar besides the Artboard tool (⛶) or press the Escape key.

4 Click the Exit button at the top of the Properties panel to exit Artboard Editing mode.

Exiting Artboard Editing mode deselects all artboards and selects the tool that was active before you entered the mode. In this case, the Selection tool is selected.

Moving and resizing artboards

After creating artboards, you can edit or delete them by using the Artboard tool (⛶), menu commands, Properties panel, or Artboards panel. Next, you'll move and change the size of two artboards using the Artboard tool.

1 Press Command and – (macOS) or Ctrl and – (Windows) *twice* to zoom out.

2 Select the Artboard tool (⛶) in the toolbar.

This is another way to enter Artboard Editing mode and can be useful when artwork is selected, since you can't see the Edit Artboards button in the Properties panel with artwork selected.

Tip: I'm asking you to drag the artboard a little higher so when you align the artboards later, they will move.

3 Drag the rightmost artboard, named Mountain Vacation Ad, to the left of the original artboard *and a little higher*. Don't worry about its exact position yet, but make sure it doesn't cover any artwork.

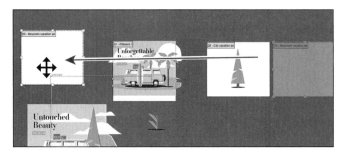

4 Click in the artboard with the "Unforgettable Beaches" text to select that artboard.

5 Choose View > Fit Artboard In Window to fit that artboard in the Document window.

Commands such as View > Fit Artboard In Window typically apply to the selected, or *active*, artboard.

6 Drag the bottom-middle point of the artboard up to resize it. When the point snaps to the bottom of the yellow-orange shape, release the mouse button.

You can resize artboards to fit content or the other way around—whatever you need. Next, you'll delete the artboard named City Vacation Ad on the right since you'll copy an artboard from another document to replace it.

7 Choose View > Fit All In Window to see all of your artboards.

8 Click the City Vacation Ad artboard, and press Delete or Backspace to remove it.

▶ **Tip:** With an artboard selected with the Artboard tool (⊕), you can also click the Delete Artboard button (🗑) in the Properties panel to delete an artboard.

When you delete an artboard, the artwork that was on that artboard remains. In any document, you can delete all but one artboard.

9 Select the Selection tool (▶), which exits Artboard Editing mode, and drag the tree artwork below the artboard with the "Unforgettable Beaches" text on it to move it out of the way.

Copying artboards between documents

You can copy or cut artboards from one document and paste them into another, and the artwork on those artboards comes with them. Copying artboards makes it easy to reuse content across documents. For this project, you'll copy the start of another ad design into the project you're working on to keep it all in one file.

1 Choose File > Open. Open the Bus.ai file in the Lessons > Lesson05 folder on your hard disk.

2 Choose View > Fit Artboard In Window to see the entire artboard.

Notice that the van is a light blue. A color swatch named Van is applied to it. That will be important soon!

3 Select the Artboard tool (⊡) in the toolbar, and the only artboard in the document is selected. If it isn't, click within the artboard to select it.

Be careful about clicking the artboard if it's already selected! You may make a copy on top.

4 Choose Edit > Copy to copy the artboard and the artwork on it.

Artwork not on the artboard—like the palm tree off the right side of the artboard—isn't copied. Depending on how the artboard fits, you may not see it.

5 Choose File > Close to close the file without saving.

6 Back in the Vacation_ads.ai document, choose Edit > Paste to paste the artboard and the artwork.

7 In the Swatch Conflict dialog box that appears, make sure that Merge Swatches is selected, and select Apply To All so any other swatches do the same. Click OK.

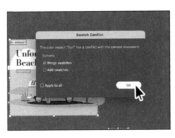

Swatches applied to any content on the artboard that you paste are imported. If those imported swatches have the same name as but different color values than swatches already in the document, a swatch conflict occurs.

In the Swatch Conflict dialog box, by selecting the Add Swatches option, any swatches from the Van.ai document with the same name found in the Vacation_ads.ai file are added by appending a number to the conflicting swatch names. If you select Merge Swatches, swatches with the same name from the pasted content are merged using the color values of the existing swatches. The blue van from the Bus.ai file is now green because the swatch named Van in the Vacation_ads.ai file is green.

Aligning and arranging artboards

To keep artboards tidy in your document, you can move and align them to suit your working style. One example is aligning artboards so that the top edges of all artboards line up. Next, you'll select all of the artboards and align them.

1   With the Artboard tool (⌐) still selected, Shift-click the other two artboards to select them as well.

> **Tip:** With the Artboard tool (⌐) selected, you can also press the Shift key and drag across a series of artboards to select them.

When the Artboard tool is selected, the Shift key allows you to select more artboards by clicking or dragging across them. Without the Shift key held down, dragging would draw a new artboard.

2   Click the Vertical Align Top button (▣) in the Properties panel on the right to align the artboards to each other.

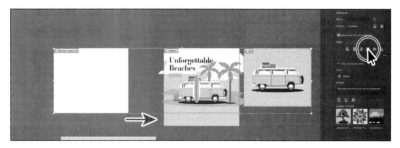

You *might* have seen that the light orange background shape on the artboard with the "Unforgettable Beaches" text didn't move with the artboard. An arrow is pointing to it in the previous figure. That rectangle is locked, and locked objects don't move when artboards move.

3   Choose Edit > Undo Align to get the artboards back where they were.

4   To unlock the background object (and any other locked objects), choose Object > Unlock All.

5   Now click the Vertical Align Top button (⬛) in the Properties panel again to align the artboards to each other and also move the background shape.

In Artboard Editing mode, you can also arrange your artboards however you like using the Rearrange All Artboards command, which is what you'll do next.

6   Click the Rearrange All button in the Properties panel to open the Rearrange All Artboards dialog box.

In the Rearrange All Artboards dialog box, you can arrange your artboards in columns or rows and set the spacing between each artboard to a set amount.

7   Click Arrange By Row (➡) so the three artboards can remain next to each other horizontally. Set Spacing to **40 px** to set an exact spacing between them. Click OK.

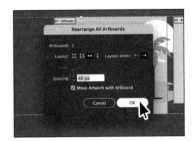

The artboard that was in the middle is now first in the row of artboards, and the other artboards are to the right of it. That's because the Arrange By Row option ordered the artboards based on the order that the artboards were created.

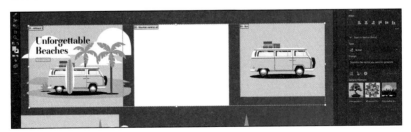

Setting options for artboards

By default, artboards are assigned a number and a name, as you've seen. When you navigate the artboards in a document, it can be helpful to name them, as you have been doing. Next, you'll learn how to *rename* artboards so that the names help identify artboards more quickly, and you'll see other options you can set for each artboard.

1 While still in Artboard Editing mode, click to select the artboard named Artboard 1. It's the artboard with the "Unforgettable Beaches" text on it.

2 Click the Artboard Options button in the Properties panel.

3 In the Artboard Options dialog box, change the name to **Beach vacation ad** and click OK.

The Artboard Options dialog box has lots of extra options for artboards, as well as a few you've already seen, like width and height.

4 Select the Selection tool (▶) so you can exit Artboard Editing mode.

5 Choose Select > Deselect, if necessary.

6 Choose File > Save.

Changing the order of artboards 🎥

To learn how to reorder artboards and navigate between them, check out the video *Changing the order of artboards*, which is part of the Web Edition. For more information, see the "Web Edition" section of "Getting Started" at the beginning of the book.

Working with rulers and guides

With the artboards set up, now you'll learn about aligning and measuring content using rulers and guides. Rulers help you accurately place and measure objects and distances. They appear along the top and left sides of the Document window and can be shown and hidden. *Guides* are nonprinting lines that help you align objects. To create guides, you can drag them from the rulers into the document.

Creating guides

Next, you'll create a guide so you can accurately align content to an artboard.

► **Tip:** You can also choose View > Rulers > Show Rulers.

1   Click the Show Rulers button () in the Properties panel to show the rulers.

2   With the Selection tool, click the text "Unforgettable Beaches" in the leftmost artboard.

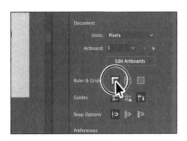

See the *very* subtle black outline around that artboard? You should also see "1" showing in the Artboard Navigation menu (below the Document window), which indicates that the Beach Vacation Ad artboard is the active artboard.

3   Choose View > Fit Artboard In Window.

Look at the rulers along the top of the Document window and the left. The point on each ruler (horizontal and vertical) where the 0 (zero) shows is the *ruler origin*. The ruler origin (0,0) starts in the upper-left corner of the artboard. Next you'll create a guide on the active artboard.

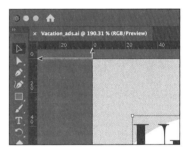

4   Choose Select > Deselect so you can see the document properties in the Properties panel on the right.

5   Click the Units menu in the Properties panel, and choose Inches to change the units for the entire document.

You can now see that the rulers show inches instead of pixels. For this example, we need the text to be at least 0.25 inches (1/4 inch) from the edge of the ad.

► **Tip:** Dragging from a ruler while pressing the Shift key "snaps" a guide to the measurements on the ruler.

► **Tip:** You can double-click the horizontal or vertical ruler to add a new guide.

6   From the ruler on the left, drag into the artboard to make a vertical guide. Keep dragging until you reach about 1/2 inch on the ruler above the document, and then release the mouse button.

Don't worry about the guide being at precisely 1/2 inch.

After creating a guide, it's selected. When selected, the color of a guide matches the color of the layer it's on (blue in this case) when you move the pointer away from it.

7 With the guide still selected, change the X value in the Properties panel to **0.25** (inch), and press Return or Enter to reposition the guide.

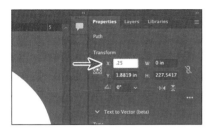 

8 Choose Select > Deselect to deselect the guide.

In the section "Working with the bounding box," you'll drag content to align with the guide.

Positioning artwork using the Properties panel

At times, you may want to position things more precisely—relative either to other objects or to the artboard. You could use the alignment options, as you saw in Lesson 2. You can also use Smart Guides (View > Smart Guides) and Transform options in the Properties panel to move objects to exact coordinates on the x and y axes and control the positioning of objects relative to the edge of the artboard.

Next, you'll add content to an artboard and position it precisely.

1 Choose View > Fit All In Window to see all three artboards.

2 Click in the blank artboard in the middle to make it the active artboard.

3 Click the group of artwork with the "Untouched Beauty" text, beneath the artboards, to select it.

You may need to zoom out or pan to see it!

4 In the Transform section of the Properties panel, click the upper-left point of the reference point locator (⊞).

The points in the reference point locator represent the points of the bounding box around the selected content. In this case, the upper-left reference point refers to the upper-left point of the bounding box.

> **Tip:** You could have also aligned the content to the artboard using the alignment options. You'll find there are at least a few ways to accomplish most tasks in Illustrator.

5 Change the X value to **0** and the Y value to **0**, and press Return or Enter.

The selected artwork is moved into the upper-left corner of the *active* artboard.

6 Shift-drag the lower-right corner to make the selected artwork smaller. Make sure the pink rectangle in the background just fits on the artboard. Other artwork will hang off and that's okay.

7 Choose Select > Deselect, and then choose File > Save.

Editing the ruler origin ■◀

You can move the ruler origin to start the horizontal and vertical measurements at another location. To learn how to work with the ruler origin, check out the video *Editing the ruler origin,* which is part of the Web Edition. For more information, see the "Web Edition" section of "Getting Started" at the beginning of the book.

Transforming content

In Lesson 4, you learned how to take simple paths and shapes and create more complex artwork by editing and combining that content. In this lesson, you'll learn how to scale, rotate, and transform content in other ways, using various tools and methods.

Working with the bounding box

As you've seen so far, a bounding box appears around selected content. You can resize and rotate content using the bounding box, but you can also turn it off.

Turning off the bounding box makes it so you *can't* resize or rotate content with the Selection tool by dragging anywhere on the bounding box, but it makes it easier to drag and snap content.

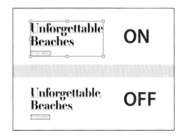

Bounding box

1 With the Selection tool (▶) selected, click to select the "Unforgettable Beaches" text to select the text and the button that are grouped together.

2 Choose View > Fit Artboard In Window.

3 Move the pointer over the lower-left corner of the selected group. If you were to drag right now, you would resize the content.

4 Choose View > Hide Bounding Box.

This command hides the bounding box that surrounded all of the selected artwork. Now, you can't resize the group by dragging with the Selection tool.

5 Move the pointer over the lower-left point on the LEARN MORE button, and drag the group to the left, onto the vertical guide you created. When the pointer arrow changes (▶), the artwork is snapped to the guide, and you can release the mouse button.

● **Note:** If the group is not aligning to the guide, or in other words it's not snapping, and the pointer isn't changing, you need to zoom in closer.

6 Choose View > Show Bounding Box to turn it back on for all artwork.

Scaling objects precisely

So far in this book, you've scaled most content with the selection tools. In this part of the lesson, you'll scale artwork using the Properties panel and use an option called Scale Strokes & Effects.

1 Choose View > Fit All In Window.

2 With the Selection tool (▶) selected, drag across the plant shapes to select them.

3 Press Command and + (macOS) or Ctrl and + (Windows) a few times to zoom in to them.

4 Choose View > Hide Edges so you hide the inside edges.

Hiding the edges will make it easier to see the stroke weight change when you scale the artwork.

▶ **Tip:** When typing values to transform content, you can type different units, such as percent (%) or pixels (px), and they will be converted to the default unit, which is inches (in) in this case.

5 In the Properties panel, click the center reference point of the reference point locator (), if it's not selected, to resize from the center.

6 Ensure that Maintain Width And Height Proportions is set (🔗), type **40%** in the Width (W) field, and then press Return or Enter to make it less than half the size.

Notice that the artwork is smaller, but the vertical stem is still the same width. That's because the stem is a path with a stroke applied.

By default, strokes are *not* scaled along with objects. For instance, if you make a circle with a 1-pt stroke bigger, the stroke remains 1 pt. By selecting Scale Strokes & Effects before you scale—and then scaling the object—that 1-pt stroke would scale (change) relative to the amount of scaling applied to the object.

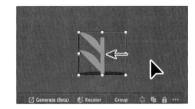

7 Choose Edit > Undo Scale.

8 In the Properties panel, click More Options (•••) in the Transform section. Select Scale Strokes & Effects.

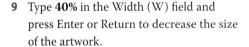

9 Type **40%** in the Width (W) field and press Enter or Return to decrease the size of the artwork.

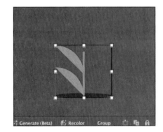

Now any strokes applied to any paths are scaled proportionally.

10 Choose View > Show Edges to show the inside edges again.

Rotating objects with the Rotate tool

There are many ways to rotate artwork, including methods that range from precise to more free-form rotation. In previous lessons, you learned that you could rotate selected content with the Selection tool. In this part of the lesson, you'll rotate artwork using the Rotate tool.

1 Choose View > Fit All In Window.

2 With the Selection tool (▶) selected, on the "Unforgettable Beaches" artboard, click to select the palm tree to the right of the van.

3 Choose View > Fit Artboard In Window.

The palm tree would look better if it were rotated, giving it a more wind-blown look. You could rotate it with the Selection tool and then drag it into place, but to save a step, you can rotate it with the Rotate tool around its bottom.

4 Select the Rotate tool (↻) in the toolbar. Move the pointer over the bottom of the tree trunk—click and release to set the point that the palm tree will rotate around. It looks like an aqua crosshairs and is called the *reference point*.

5 Move the pointer anywhere over the palm tree, and drag clockwise to give the tree a bit of a lean.

> ▷ **Tip:** If you want to make the bottom of the palm tree look flatter, you can erase it with the Eraser tool (◆) in the toolbar.

Scaling using Transform Each

You've been scaling artwork to make it bigger or smaller throughout this book. Sometimes, however, you want to make *multiple* objects bigger or smaller at once. Using the Transform Each command, objects you scale or rotate are done in place—they don't move, and they are all transformed at once using the same settings.

Now you'll scale three clouds at one time.

1   With the Selection tool (▶) selected, click to select one of the white clouds in the sky. Shift-click the other two clouds in the sky to select all three.

2   Choose Object > Transform > Transform Each.

The Transform Each dialog box opens with multiple options, like scale, moving, rotation, and more.

3   In the Transform Each dialog box, change the Horizontal Scale and Vertical Scale values to **70%**. Click OK.

Each of the clouds is smaller and still in the same place. In other words, each cloud scaled individually from its center.

4   Choose File > Save.

Shearing objects

Shearing an object slants, or skews, the sides of the object along the axis you specify, keeping opposite sides parallel and making the object asymmetrical. Next, you'll apply shear to a rectangle to make a reflection in the window of the van.

1   Click to select the van, and press Command and + (macOS) or Ctrl and + (Windows) a few times to zoom in.

2   Select the Rectangle tool (▢) in the toolbar. Drag to create a small rectangle in the middle of the front window of the van.

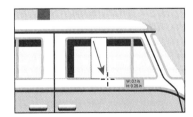

3   Make sure that the fill color in the Properties panel is white, and the Stroke Weight is **0**.

Now you'll skew the shape to give it perspective.

4   With the shape selected, select the Shear tool (➡), nested within the Rotate tool (↻) in the toolbar.

5 Move the pointer above the shape, press the Shift key to constrain the artwork to its original height, and drag to the left. Release the mouse button and then the Shift key when you see a shear angle (S) of approximately −45.

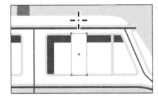 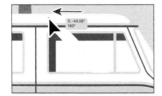

6 Change the opacity of the rectangle in the Properties panel by clicking the arrow to the right of 100% in the Opacity field and dragging the slider to change it. I changed it to 60%.

Transforming using menu commands

The transform tools you find in the toolbar—Selection, Rotate, Scale, Shear, and Reflect—are also represented as menu items when you choose Object > Transform. In a lot of cases, you can use any of those menu commands in place of a tool.

Now you'll make a copy of the window reflection using the Move command.

1 To make a copy of the rectangle, choose Object > Transform > Move.

2 In the Move dialog box, change Horizontal Position to **0.12 in** to move the rectangle that distance to the right, and make sure the Vertical Position is **0** to keep it in the same vertical position. Click Copy.

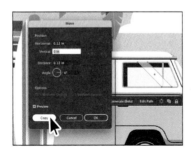

Now, you'll make the rectangle narrower. It's a bit more challenging than just dragging the bounding box, since the shape is skewed. You'll drag anchor points instead to maintain the skew angle while transforming the shape.

3 Select the Selection tool (▶) and double-click the duplicate rectangle.

This enters Isolation mode and makes it much easier to select part of the rectangle, since everything else is dimmed and can't be selected.

4 Select the Direct Selection tool (▷). Click the top-right anchor and Shift-click the bottom-right anchor to select both.

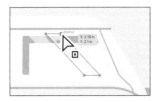 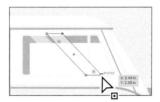

5 Press the Left Arrow key on your keyboard several times to move the selected anchor points to the left, making the shape narrower.

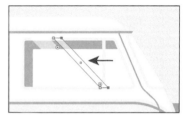

6 Press the Esc key to exit Isolation mode.

7 Choose View > Fit All In Window, and then choose File > Save.

Transforming with the Free Transform tool ▰◀

To learn how to transform artwork freely with the Free Transform tool, check out the video *Transforming with the Free Transform tool,* which is part of the Web Edition. For more information, see the "Web Edition" section of "Getting Started" at the beginning of the book.

Using repeats

You can easily repeat objects by applying one of the available repeat types: Radial, Grid, or Mirror. When you apply one of the repeats to selected artwork, Illustrator auto-generates artwork using your chosen method. If you update one of the repeat instances, all instances are modified to reflect the change.

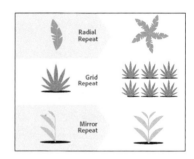

Applying a mirror repeat

For this section, you'll focus on applying a mirror repeat to artwork. Mirror repeats help create symmetrical artwork. You create half of the artwork, and Illustrator automatically makes the other half for you. In this case, you'll finish a plant that will become part of one of the ads.

1 Select the Zoom tool (🔍) and zoom in to the green plant below the artboards.

2 Select the Selection tool (▶), and drag across the green plant shapes *except for the dark oval shadow* to select them.

3 Choose Object > Repeat > Mirror.

As soon as you choose Mirror, Illustrator enters Isolation mode. The rest of the artwork is dimmed and cannot be selected, as is typical for Isolation mode.

The vertical dashed line you see is called the *symmetry axis*. It shows the center of the symmetrical artwork, and you use it to change the distance between the halves and rotate the auto-generated half.

4 Find the circle control handle on the symmetry axis, just below the plant. Drag it left and right to change the distance between the halves.

Make sure there is no gap between the plant halves.

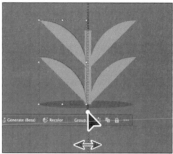

5 Drag either circle control handle at the very top or bottom of the symmetry axis to rotate the mirrored content.

6 To reset the angle of the mirror repeat, choose 90 degrees from the Angle Of Mirror Axis menu in the Properties panel.

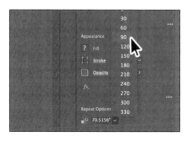

Not only can you use Mirror to copy and flip artwork you've already created, but you can also add or remove artwork while editing the mirror repeat.

7 Choose Select > Deselect so no plant artwork is selected.

Note: The Shift key constrains the movement, and the Option/Alt key copies the artwork.

8   To copy one of the leaves, Shift+Option-drag (macOS) or Shift+Alt-drag (Windows) the top leaf up. Make sure to drag it to the very top of the green plant stem (the vertical green path). Release the mouse button and then the keys.

Notice that the generated artwork on the right mirrors what you are doing in real time. Any changes you make to the artwork are visible in the mirrored half.

9   Shift-drag the upper-left corner to make the leaf smaller.

10 To stop editing the mirror repeat, exit Isolation mode by pressing the Esc key. The plant should now be deselected.

Editing a mirror repeat

When you create a mirror repeat, or any type of repeat, the artwork becomes a repeat object. In this case, the plant is now a mirror repeat object—sort of like a special group. Now, you'll learn how to edit the mirror repeat.

1   Click the plant to select it.

At the top of the Properties panel, you'll see "Mirror Repeat," which tells you that it's a mirror repeat object group.

2   Double-click the plant to enter Isolation mode.

You can now see the symmetry axis and can edit the original artwork you created on the left.

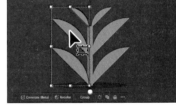

Tip: To edit the auto-generated half of the mirrored artwork, you need to expand the mirror repeat object. Choose Object > Expand. Know that if you expand a mirror repeat object, you cannot edit the mirror repeat using the symmetry axis, and the artwork is simply a group of individual objects.

3   Click away from the plant to deselect it, and then click one of the leaves and change the fill color in the Properties panel to another color. I chose a lighter green.

4   Press the Escape key or double-click in an empty area to exit Isolation mode.

5   Choose View > Fit All In Window.

6   Drag across the plant art and oval shadow to select them. Choose Object >
    Group. Drag the group onto the artboard on the right with the van by itself.

    If the plant is behind the artwork on the artboard, choose Bring To Front from
    the Arrange menu in the Properties panel.

Using grid and radial repeats ▰◢

To learn how to work with the other repeat options, check out the video *Using grid
and radial repeats,* which is part of the Web Edition. For more information, see the
"Web Edition" section of "Getting Started" at the beginning of the book.

Working with the Puppet Warp tool

In Illustrator, you can easily twist and distort artwork into different positions using
the Puppet Warp tool. In this section, you'll warp one of the palm trees.

Adding pins

With the tool now showing in the toolbar, you'll use it to warp the palm tree so it
looks a little more natural and less like it's falling over.

1   Click the palm tree you rotated on the "Unforgettable Beaches" artboard. Zoom in
    by pressing Command and + (macOS) or Ctrl and + (Windows) several times.

2   Choose Window > Toolbars > Advanced.

3   Press and hold on the Free Transform tool (▧) and select the
    Puppet Warp tool (✦).

    By default, Illustrator identifies the best
    areas to transform your artwork and
    automatically adds pins to the artwork. The
    pin is circled in the figure.

    Pins are used to hold part of the selected
    artwork to the artboard, and you can add
    or delete pins to transform your object.
    You can rotate the artwork around a pin,
    reposition pins to move artwork, and more.

4   In the Properties panel on the right, you
    should see Puppet Warp options. Deselect
    Show Mesh.

    That will make it easier to see the
    pins and provide a clearer view of any
    transformations you make.

Note: The pins
Illustrator adds to the
artwork by default
may not look like what
you see in the figure.
If that is the case, pay
attention to the notes
along the way.

5 Click the one pin on the tree to select it. You can tell that a pin is selected because it has a white dot in the center. Drag the selected pin to the left to see how the artwork reacts.

Notice that the whole tree moves. That's because there is only one pin. By default, pins on the artwork help to keep (pin) parts in place. Having at least three pins on your artwork usually achieves a better result.

6 Choose Edit > Undo Puppet Warp as many times as necessary to return the tree to its original position.

7 Click the bottom of the brown tree trunk to add a pin. Click in the middle of the brown tree trunk to add another pin.

The pin at the bottom is meant to pin, or hold, the bottom of the tree trunk in place so that part won't move as much. The pin in the middle of the tree trunk is the one you will drag to reshape the tree.

8 Drag the pin in the middle of the trunk to reshape the tree.

You'll find that if you drag too far, odd things like path twisting may happen.

You can't move pins on the artwork without moving the artwork, so if they're not in the right place for the warping you want, you need to remove pins and add them where they are needed.

9 Click the pin in the leaves to select it, and press Delete or Backspace to remove it. It would better if it were in the middle of the leaves for rotation.

Notice that the leaves move once the pin is deleted.

10 Click in the middle of the leaves to add a new pin.

11 Drag the new pin approximately back to where the original was. Leave the pin selected.

Rotating pins

Another helpful thing you can do to pins is rotate them. In this section, you'll rotate all of the leaves and then warp one of the leaves without affecting the rest as much.

1 With the pin in the middle of the leaves still selected, you will see a dashed circle around the pin. You drag that to rotate it. Move the pointer over the dashed circle, and drag to rotate the leaves around the pin until you think it looks good.

Now you'll warp a single leaf. This will require adding some more pins.

2 Click in the end of one of the leaves on the right to add a pin.

You might see the other parts of the artwork change in reaction. If that happens, select the pin in the center of the leaves again and rotate it back.

Tip: Pressing the Option/Alt key limits the affected area directly around the pin you are dragging.

3 Drag the new pin on the end of the leaf to stretch the leaf a bit and to see how the artwork reacts.

You might see the other leaves moving as well. In this case, you want to pin the parts that are moving to keep them still.

4 Choose Edit > Undo Puppet Warp as many times as necessary to return the leaf to its original position.

5 Click to set pins on the leaves to hold them in place.

6 Drag the pin at the end of the leaf to stretch the leaf a little and see how everything reacts.

The last thing you'll do is rotate and drag the pin at the bottom of the tree trunk.

7 Click the pin at the bottom of the tree trunk. Move it to see how the rest of the tree artwork reacts.

8 Move the pointer over the dashed circle around the pin, and drag to rotate the bottom until you think it looks good.

9 Choose Window > Toolbars > Basic to reset the toolbar.

10 Choose Select > Deselect, and then choose View > Fit All In Window.

11 Choose File > Save and then File > Close.

Review questions

1 Name three ways to change the size of an existing active artboard.

2 What is the ruler origin?

3 What is a bounding box used for?

4 Briefly describe what the Scale Strokes & Effects option in the Properties panel or Transform panel does.

5 Briefly describe what the Puppet Warp tool does.

Review answers

1 To change the size of an existing artboard, you can do any of the following:

- Double-click the Artboard tool (⊡), and edit the dimensions of the active artboard in the Artboard Options dialog box.

- With nothing selected and the Selection tool selected, click the Edit Artboards button in the Properties panel to enter Artboard Editing mode. With the Artboard tool selected, position the pointer over an edge or corner of the artboard, and drag to resize.

- With the Artboard tool selected, click an artboard in the Document window, and change the dimensions in the Properties panel.

2 The ruler origin is the point where 0 (zero) appears on each ruler. By default, the ruler origin is set to be 0 (zero) in the upper-left corner of the active artboard.

3 A bounding box is a rectangular border around an image, shape, or text that you can drag to move, transform, rotate, or scale.

4 The Scale Strokes & Effects option, which can be accessed from the Properties panel or the Transform panel, scales any strokes and effects as the object is scaled. This option can be turned on and off as needed.

5 In Illustrator, you can use the Puppet Warp tool to easily twist and distort artwork into different positions while adding pins to hold parts of it stationary.

6 USING THE BASIC DRAWING TOOLS

Lesson overview

In this lesson, you'll learn how to do the following:

- Draw curves and straight lines with the Curvature tool.

- Edit paths with the Curvature tool.

- Create dashed lines.

- Draw and edit with the Pencil tool.

- Join paths with the Join tool.

- Add arrowheads to paths.

 This lesson will take about 30 minutes to complete. To get the lesson files used in this lesson, download them from the web page for this book at *peachpit.com/IllustratorCIB2024*. For more information, see "Accessing the lesson files and Web Edition" in the Getting Started section at the beginning of this book.

In previous lessons, you created and edited shapes. Next you'll learn how to create straight lines, curves, or more complex shapes using the Pencil and Curvature tools. You'll also explore creating dashed lines, arrowheads, and more.

Starting the lesson

In the first part of this lesson, you'll start by creating and editing freeform paths with the Curvature tool and exploring other drawing methods to create a series of logos.

● **Note:** If you have not already downloaded the project files for this lesson to your computer from your Account page, make sure to do so now. See the "Getting Started" section at the beginning of the book.

1 To ensure that the tools function and the defaults are set exactly as described in this lesson, delete or deactivate (by renaming) the Adobe Illustrator preferences file. See "Restoring default preferences" in the "Getting Started" section at the beginning of the book.

2 Start Adobe Illustrator.

3 Choose File > Open. Locate the file named L6_end.ai, which is in the Lessons > Lesson06 folder that you copied onto your hard disk, and click Open.

This file contains the finished logos that you'll create in this lesson.

4 Choose View > Fit All In Window; leave the file open for reference, or you can close it by choosing File > Close.

5 Choose File > Open, and open the L6_start.ai file in the Lessons > Lesson06 folder on your hard disk.

6 Choose File > Save As.

7 If the Cloud Document dialog box opens, click Save On Your Computer.

8 In the Save As dialog box, navigate to the Lesson06 folder, and open it. Rename the file **Outdoor_logos.ai**.

Choose Adobe Illustrator (ai) from the Format menu (macOS), or choose Adobe Illustrator (*.AI) from the Save As Type menu (Windows). Click Save.

9 In the Illustrator Options dialog box, leave the default settings, and then click OK.

● **Note:** If you don't see Reset Essentials in the menu, choose Window > Workspace > Essentials before choosing Window > Workspace > Reset Essentials.

10 Choose Window > Workspace > Reset Essentials.

Creating with the Curvature tool

With the Curvature tool (✒), you can create freeform paths with straight lines and smooth, refined curves. It's one of the easier drawing tools to start with and master. The Curvature tool creates paths made of *anchor points* (also just called *anchors* or *points*) that are editable with any drawing or selection tools.

Drawing paths with the Curvature tool

In this first part, you'll draw a curved path with the Curvature tool that will become a horizon in a logo (the red path in the figure).

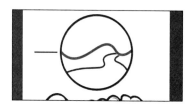

1   Choose 1 Logo 1 from the Artboard Navigation menu below the Document window to fit the first artboard in the window.

2   Select the Selection tool (▶), and click the edge of the circle.

3   To lock it, choose Object > Lock > Selection. That way, you can draw without accidentally editing the circle.

4   Select the Curvature tool (✒) in the toolbar and move the pointer into the document—an asterisk (*) next to the pointer means you're going to draw a new path.

5   To set the stroke and fill before you draw, make sure that the Fill is set to None (▱), that the stroke color is a dark gray swatch with the tool tip "C=0 M=0 Y=0 K=90," and that the stroke weight is 4 pt.

    With the Curvature tool, you click and release to start drawing and make the first point. Where the path's direction and/or the amount of curve needs to change, you set more points.

> **Note:** The stroke and fill should be already set, since you just selected the circle and Illustrator remembers the fill and stroke of the last selected object.

> **Note:** You might see the word "anchor" if you move the pointer over the anchor point of the circle. That's okay.

6   On the left edge of the circle, click and release to start the path that will become the horizon.

7   Move the pointer to the right, click and release to create a new point, and then move the pointer away.

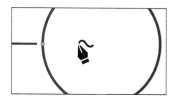
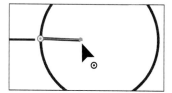
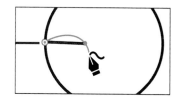

Notice the blue rubber band preview of the curve before and after the new point. The Curvature tool works by creating anchor points where you click. The path will "flex" around the points dynamically.

8 Move the pointer to the right. Click and release to create a point. Then, move the pointer around to see how the path reacts.

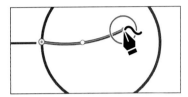 

If you add an anchor in the wrong spot at any point, you can always move the pointer over the anchor, drag it, and then continue drawing. You'll learn all about editing paths with the Curvature tool in a few sections.

9 Click and release to the right to create another anchor point.

10 Finally, to complete the horizon, move the pointer over the right edge of the circle; click and release to create the last anchor point.

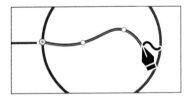 

11 To stop drawing and lock the path so you can't accidentally edit it in the next section, choose Object > Lock > Selection.

Drawing a river path

To continue with the Curvature tool, next you'll draw a river that begins at the horizon path you just created. You'll draw one side of the river and then the other. The figure at the right shows an example of how the river might look when you're finished. Yours may look different, and that's okay.

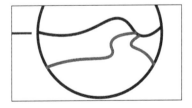

You may want to zoom in to the artwork for this section.

1 Move the pointer over the horizon path as you see in the figure. Click and release to start a new path.

For the next steps, use the figures as a guide, but experiment a little!

2 Move the pointer down and to the left, and click. Continue moving the pointer down, clicking three more times to create one side of the river. Make sure the last point you create is on the edge of the circle.

  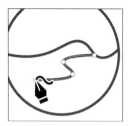 

When learning the Curvature tool, it helps to click, release, and then move the pointer around to get a feel for how it affects the path.

3 Press the Escape key to stop drawing the path.

Next you'll draw the other side of the river using a similar technique.

4 Choose Select > Deselect.

5 Move the pointer over the horizon path just to the right of the start of the path you just drew.

Make sure you see the asterisk (*) next to the pointer! The asterisk means you will start a new path.

6 Click and release to start a new path.

It's important not to click too close to the first river path you drew, because you may edit that path instead of starting a new one. If you click and begin editing the other path, press the Escape key to stop editing the first river path.

7 Move the pointer down, and click to set another point.

8 Do this two more times to add points to create the other side of the river. Make sure the last point you create is on the edge of the circle.

9 To stop drawing the river path, press the Escape key.

Editing a path with the Curvature tool

You can also edit paths with the Curvature tool by moving or deleting anchor points or adding new ones. You can use the Curvature tool to edit a path regardless of the drawing tool used to create it. Next, you'll edit the paths you've created so far.

1   With the Curvature tool selected, click the first river path you drew on the left to select it and show the anchor points.

To edit a path with the Curvature tool, it needs to be selected.

▶ **Tip:** To close a path with the Curvature tool, hover the pointer over the first point you created in the path. When a circle appears next to the pointer (✎₀), click to close the path.

2   Move the pointer over the anchor point circled in the first part of the following figure. When the point changes appearance (▶₀), click to select the point. Drag that point to reshape the curve a little.

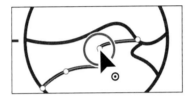 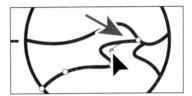

3   Try dragging other points in the path.

You'll find that you don't need to click and release to select a point first and then drag. You can simply drag the anchor point.

Next, you'll unlock the horizon path and edit it.

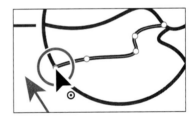

4   Choose Object > Unlock All to be able to edit the horizon path you drew.

5   With the Curvature tool selected, click the horizon path to select just that path and see the anchor points on it.

6   Move the pointer over the path just to the right of the first anchor (on the left). When a plus sign (+) appears next to the pointer (✎₊), click to add a new point.

7   Drag the new point down a bit to reshape the path.

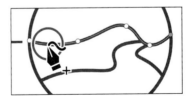 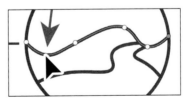

You'll remove the point just to the right of the new point you just added so the path can have more curve.

8   Click the point to the right to select it, and to remove it press Delete or Backspace.

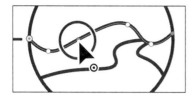 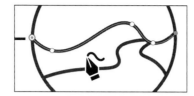

If you're wondering, instead of adding and deleting anchors, you could have just moved the anchor you deleted to reshape the path.

9 To lock the path so you don't accidentally edit it in the next section, choose Object > Lock > Selection.

Creating corners with the Curvature tool

By default, the Curvature tool creates smooth anchor points—points that cause the path to curve. Paths can have two kinds of anchor points: corner points and smooth points. At a *corner point*, a path abruptly changes direction. At a *smooth point*, path segments are connected as a continuous curve. With the Curvature tool, you can also create corner points to create straight paths.

Next, you'll draw a mountain for the logo using corner points.

1 With the Curvature tool (✎) selected, move the pointer over the left side of the horizon path. When the word "path" appears, telling you the point you add will start on the path, click to set the first point.

● **Note:** If the word "path" doesn't appear, make sure Smart Guides are turned on (View > Smart Guides).

2 Move the pointer up and to the right, and click to start a mountain peak.

3 Move the pointer down and to the right, and click to create a new point.

 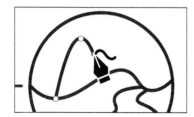

To make the mountain peak have a point to it and not be curved, you'll convert the anchor point you just created to a corner point.

4 Move the pointer over the top anchor point on the mountain path, and when the pointer changes (▸₀), double-click to convert it to a corner point.

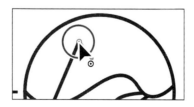

You can tell which points are smooth and which are corners by their appearance. Each point you create with the Curvature tool can have three appearances, indicating their current state: a selected point (●), a corner point that is not selected (◉), and a smooth point that is not selected (○).

5 To continue drawing, move the pointer over and up, and click to create another point and start another mountain peak.

The point you just created and the point before it also need to be converted to corner points. All of the anchor points you create for the mountain path need to be corners. You'll convert the two anchor points to corner points next.

6 Double-click the last *two* anchor points you made to make them corners.

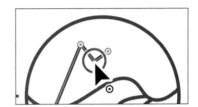

To finish the mountain path, you'll create a few more anchor points, but you will make corner points instead of smooth points by pressing a key as you create them.

7 Press Option (macOS) or Alt (Windows), and the pointer will change (⬐). Click to make a corner anchor.

8 While still pressing Option (macOS) or Alt (Windows), click a few more times to finish the mountain path. Make sure the last point you create is on the horizon path.

Feel free to adjust any anchor points. Drag a point to reshape the path, double-click a point to convert it between a corner and smooth point, or select an anchor and press Delete or Backspace to remove it from the path.

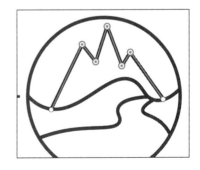

9 Press the Escape key to stop drawing.

10 Choose Select > Deselect, and then choose File > Save.

Creating dashed lines

To add some design flair to your artwork, you can add dashes to the stroke of a closed path (like a square) or an open path (like a line). You add dashes to paths in the Stroke panel, where you can specify a sequence of dash lengths and the gaps between them. Next, you'll add a dash to lines to add sun rays around the circle.

1 Select the Selection tool (▶), and click the line to the left of the circle.

2 In the Properties panel, click the word "Stroke" to show the Stroke panel. Change the following options in the Stroke panel:

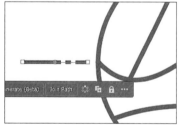

- Weight: **3 pt** (should already be set)
- Dashed Line: Selected
- Preserves Exact Dash and Gap Lengths (▨): Selected (The dashes won't be adjusted at all.)
- First Dash value: **35 pt** (This creates a 35-pt dash, 35-pt gap pattern.)
- First Gap value: **4 pt** (This creates a 35-pt dash, 4-pt gap pattern.)
- Second Dash value: **5 pt** (This creates a 35-pt dash, 4-pt gap, 5-pt dash, 5-pt gap pattern.)
- Second Gap value: **4 pt** (This creates a 35-pt dash, 4-pt gap, 5-pt dash, 4-pt gap pattern.)

After entering the last value, press Return or Enter to accept the value and close the Stroke panel.

> ▶ **Tip:** The Preserves Exact Dash And Gap Lengths button (▨) allows you to retain the appearance of the dashes without aligning to the corners or the dash ends.

> ● **Note:** If pressing Return or Enter doesn't close the panel, press the Esc key. Pressing Return or Enter works only if your cursor is in a field.

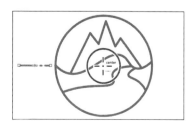

Now you'll make copies of the dashed line around the circle.

3 With the dashed line selected, select the Rotate tool (↻) in the toolbar.

4 Move the pointer into the center of the circle, and when you see the word "center," Option-click (macOS) or Alt-click (Windows).

Pressing the key and clicking sets a reference point—the point the artwork rotates around—*and also* opens the Rotate dialog box in one step.

> ● **Note:** If the word "center" doesn't appear, make sure Smart Guides are turned on (View > Smart Guides).

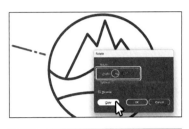

Note: To preview the rotation, you may need to turn off Preview and then turn it back on.

5 Select Preview to see the results of the changes you make in the dialog box. Change the Angle to **–15**, and click Copy.

6 To copy the dashed line again using the same rotation, choose Object > Transform > Transform Again.

7 To make 10 more copies, press Command+D (macOS) or Ctrl+D (Windows) 10 times.

Command/Ctrl+D is the keyboard command for the Transform Again command.

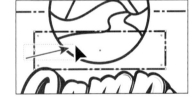

To finish the artwork, you'll cut off part of the circle and drag the text at the bottom of the artboard onto the logo.

8 Select the Rectangle tool (▢) in the toolbar, and draw a rectangle that covers the lower part of the circle (see the following figure). Notice that the dashed stroke is applied to the rectangle.

9 Select the Selection tool (▶) and drag, touching *only* the rectangle and circle!

10 Select the Shape Builder tool (⬚) in the toolbar. Press the Option key (macOS) or Alt key (Windows) and drag across the rectangle and bottom part of the circle to remove them. Release the mouse button and then the key.

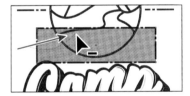

You removed the bottom part of the circle so it won't show when you drag the text into place.

11 Select the Selection tool and drag the text at the bottom of the artboard up onto the logo.

12 Click the Arrange button in the Properties panel and choose Bring To Front so the text is in front.

13 Choose Select > Deselect, and choose File > Save.

Creating with the Pencil tool

Another drawing tool in Illustrator is the Pencil tool. The Pencil tool (✐) lets you draw freeform open and closed paths that contain curves and straight lines and is similar to drawing with a pencil on paper. As you draw with the Pencil tool, anchor points are created on the path, where necessary, according to the Pencil tool options you set. The path can easily be adjusted when the path is complete.

Drawing paths with the Pencil tool

Next you'll draw and edit a simple path to make fire for one of the logos, using the Pencil tool.

1   Choose 2 Pencil from the Artboard navigation menu in the lower-left corner of the Document window.

2   Select the Pencil tool (✐) from the Paintbrush tool (✐) group in the toolbar.

3   Double-click the Pencil tool. In the Pencil Tool Options dialog box, set the following options:

- Drag the Fidelity slider all the way to the right to Smooth. This will smooth the path and reduce the number of points on a path drawn with the Pencil tool.

- Keep Selected: Selected (the default setting)

4   Click OK.

If you move the pointer into the Document window, the asterisk (*) that appears next to the Pencil tool pointer indicates that you're about to create a new path.

▶ **Tip:** When it comes to the Fidelity value, dragging the slider closer to Accurate usually creates more anchor points and more accurately reflects the path you've drawn. Dragging the slider toward Smooth makes fewer anchor points and a smoother, less complex path.

5   In the Properties panel, make sure that the fill color is None (⬜), the stroke color is the dark gray swatch with the tool tip "C=0 M=0 Y=0 K=90," and the stroke weight is 3 pt.

6   Starting at the red dot on the template labeled "A," drag clockwise around the dashed template path. When the pointer gets close to where you started the path (the red dot), a small circle displays next to it (✐₀). This means that if you release the mouse button, the path will be closed. When you see the circle, release the mouse button to close the path.

● **Note:** If the pointer looks like ✕ instead of the Pencil icon (✐), the Caps Lock key is active. Caps Lock turns the Pencil tool icon into an X for increased precision.

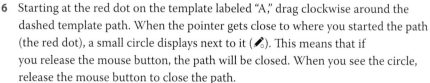

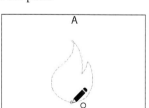

Notice that as you draw, the path may not look perfectly smooth. After releasing the mouse button, the path is smoothed based on the Fidelity value that you set in the Pencil Tool Options dialog box. Next, you'll redraw a part of the path with the Pencil tool.

7   Move the pointer on or near the path to redraw a part of it. When the asterisk next to the pointer disappears, press and drag to reshape the path, making sure the pointer begins on the original path and returns to it before you release the mouse button. If both ends of the redrawn path don't intersect with the original path, you'll end up creating a separate path alongside the original one.

8   With the fire shape selected, change the fill color to a red in the Properties panel.

Drawing straight lines with the Pencil tool

In addition to drawing curved paths, you can use the Pencil tool to create straight lines that can be constrained to 45-degree angles. Next, you'll create a log for the fire using the Pencil tool. The shape you draw could be created by drawing a rectangle and rounding the corners, but we want it to look more hand-drawn, which is why you're drawing it with the Pencil tool.

1   Move the pointer over the red dot labeled "B" on the left side of the path. Press and drag up and around the top of the shape, and release the mouse button when you get to the blue dot and move the pointer away.

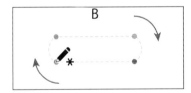 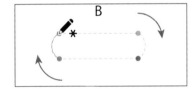

The next part of the path you draw will be straight. As you draw with the Pencil tool, you can easily continue drawing paths.

2   Move the pointer over the end of the path you just drew. When a line appears next to the Pencil tool pointer (✏), indicating that you can continue drawing the path, press Option (macOS) or Alt (Windows) and drag to the right to the orange dot. When you reach the orange dot, release the key but *not the mouse button*.

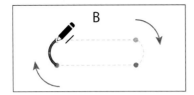 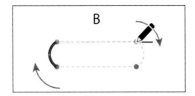

Pressing the Option (macOS) or Alt (Windows) key when you're drawing with the Pencil tool lets you create a straight path in any direction.

3   With the mouse button still held down, continue drawing around the bottom of the template path. When you reach the purple dot, keep the mouse button held down and press the Option (macOS) or Alt (Windows) key. Continue drawing to the left until you reach the start of the path at the red dot. When a small circle displays next to the Pencil tool pointer (✎), release the mouse button and then the modifier key to close the path.

▶ **Tip:** You can also press the Shift key before or while drawing with the Pencil tool and drag to create a straight line that is constrained to 45°.

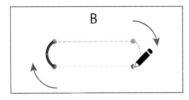 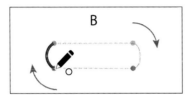

4   With the path selected, change the fill color to a brown swatch in the Properties panel.

5   Select the Selection tool (▶), and drag the fire shape down onto the log shape.

6   To bring the fire shape on top of the log shape, click the Arrange button in the Properties panel and choose Bring To Front.

7   Drag across both shapes to select them.

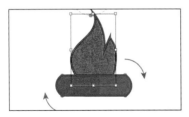  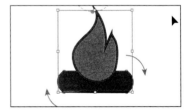

8   Copy the two shapes by choosing Edit > Copy.

9   To move to the next artboard, click the Next Artboard button (▶) below the Document window in the Status Bar.

10 To paste the shapes, choose Edit > Paste.

11 Drag the shapes onto the artwork as you see in the figure.

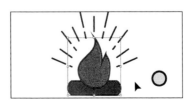

Joining with the Join tool

In earlier lessons, you used the Join command (Object > Path > Join) to join and close paths. You can also join paths using the Join tool. With the Join tool (⟩⟨), you can use scrubbing gestures to join paths that cross, overlap, or have open ends.

1. Select the Direct Selection tool (▷), and click the yellow circle on the artboard. The yellow circle will be used as the center of the flame.

2. Choose View > Zoom In a few times to zoom in.

3. Select the Scissors tool (✂), which is grouped with the Eraser tool (◆), in the toolbar.

4. Move the pointer over the top blue anchor point. When you see the word "anchor," click to cut the path there.

   A quick message telling you that the shape has been expanded appears at the top of the Document window. This circle, by default, was a Live Shape. After cutting the path, it's no longer a Live Shape.

5. Select the Direct Selection tool and drag the top anchor point up and slightly to the right.

 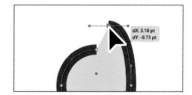

6. Drag the anchor point on the other end of the path up just to the left. A horizontal purple alignment guide will appear when the anchor point is aligned with the first anchor point.

 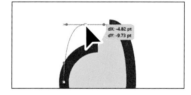

Right now the two endpoints are curved, but they need to be straight.

7. With the Direct Selection tool selected, drag across the two end points.

8. In the Properties panel on the right, click the Convert Selected Anchor Points To Corner button (⬧) to straighten the ends of the path.

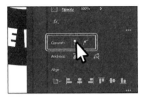

You'll learn more about converting anchor points in the next lesson.

9 Choose Window > Toolbars > Advanced.

10 Press and hold the Pencil tool (✏) and select the Join tool (⤲) from the menu.

11 With the Join tool now selected, drag across the top two ends of the path (see the following figure).

When dragging (also called *scrubbing*) across paths, they will be either "extended and joined" or "trimmed and joined." In this example, the ends of the path were extended and joined. Also, the resulting joined artwork is deselected to allow you to continue working on other paths.

Note: If you were to instead join the ends of the open path by pressing Command+J (macOS) or Ctrl+J (Windows), a straight line would connect the ends.

12 Choose Window > Toolbars > Basic.

Finishing the Camp logo

Now you'll put everything together to finish the logo.

1 Choose View > Fit Artboard In Window.

2 Select the Selection tool (▶), and select the yellow shape.

3 To bring the yellow shape on top of the other artwork, click the Arrange button in the Properties panel and choose Bring To Front.

4 Drag the yellow shape onto the fire shape, aligning it with the bottom of the shape.

5 Drag the "Camp" text at the bottom of the artboard onto the rest of the logo.

6 To bring the text on top of the other artwork, click the Arrange button in the Properties panel and choose Bring To Front.

7 Choose Select > Deselect, and choose File > Save.

Adding arrowheads to paths

You can add arrowheads to both ends of a path using the Stroke panel. There are many different arrowhead styles to choose from in Illustrator, as well as arrowhead editing options. Next, you'll apply arrowheads to a few paths to finish a logo.

1 Choose 4 Logo 3 from the Artboard Navigation menu below the Document window to switch artboards.

2 Click the curved pink path on the left to select it. Press the Shift key, and click the curved pink path to the right to select it as well.

● **Note:** When you draw a path, the beginning is where you start drawing, and the "end" is where you finish. If you need to swap the arrowheads, you can click the Swap Start And End Arrowheads button (⊟) in the Stroke panel.

3 With the paths selected, click the word "Stroke" in the Properties panel to open the Stroke panel. In the Stroke panel, change only the following options:

- Stroke Weight: **3 pt**
- Choose Arrow 5 from the Arrowheads menu on the right. This adds an arrowhead to the end of lines.
- Scale (*directly beneath where you chose Arrow 5*): **70%**
- Choose Arrow 17 from the Arrowheads menu on the left. This adds an arrowhead to the beginning of lines.
- Scale (*directly beneath where you chose Arrow 17*): **70%**

Experiment with some of the arrowhead settings. Maybe try changing the Scale values or choosing different arrowheads.

4 With the paths selected, change the stroke color to white in the Properties panel.

5 Choose Select > Deselect.

6 Choose File > Save, and then choose File > Close.

Review questions

1 By default, what type of path is created by the Curvature tool, curved or straight?

2 How do you create a corner point when working with the Curvature tool?

3 How can you change the way the Pencil tool (✏) works?

4 Explain how you can redraw parts of a path with the Pencil tool.

5 How do you draw a straight path with the Pencil tool?

6 How is the Join tool different from the Join command (Object > Path > Join)?

Review answers

1 When drawing paths with the Curvature tool, curved paths are created by default.

2 When drawing with the Curvature tool, either double-click an existing point on a path to convert it to a corner or, while drawing, press Option (macOS) or Alt (Windows) and click to create a new corner point.

3 To change the way the Pencil tool (✏) works, double-click the Pencil tool in the toolbar or click the Tool Options button in the Properties panel to open the Pencil Tool Options dialog box. There you can change the fidelity and other options.

4 With a path selected, you can redraw parts of it by moving the Pencil tool pointer over the path and redrawing part of it, ending up back on the path.

5 Paths you create with the Pencil tool are freeform by default. To draw a straight path with the Pencil tool, press the Option (macOS) or Alt (Windows) key and drag to create a straight line.

6 Unlike the Join command, the Join tool can trim or extend overlapping paths or the ends of an open path as it joins, and it doesn't simply create a straight line between the anchor points you are joining. The angle created by the two paths to be joined is taken into account.

7 DRAWING WITH THE PEN TOOL

Lesson overview

In this lesson, you'll learn how to do the following:

- Draw straight and curved lines with the Pen tool.

- Edit curved and straight lines.

- Add and delete anchor points.

- Convert between smooth points and corner points.

 This lesson will take about 60 minutes to complete. To get the lesson files used in this lesson, download them from the web page for this book at *peachpit.com/IllustratorCIB2024*. For more information, see "Accessing the lesson files and Web Edition" in the Getting Started section at the beginning of this book.

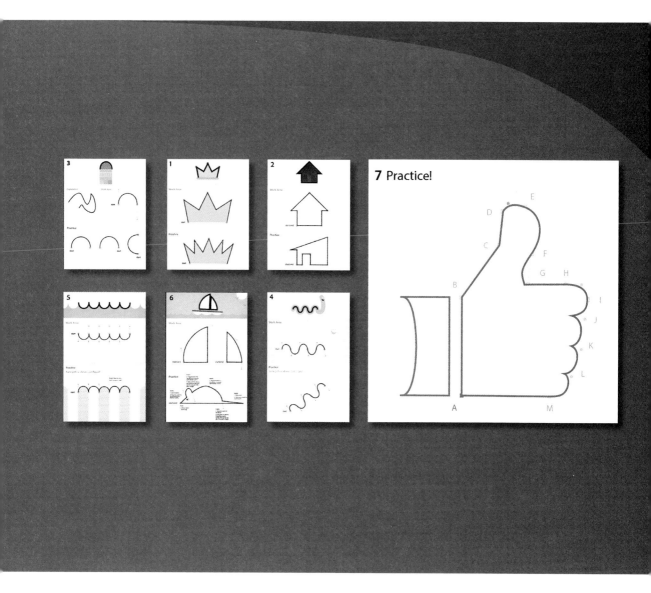

7 Practice!

In the previous lesson you started working with the basic drawing tools in Illustrator. In this lesson, you'll learn how to create and refine artwork using the Pen tool.

Starting the lesson

In this lesson, you'll focus on creating and editing with the Pen tool. You'll start by working through some exercises to learn the fundamentals of the tool, and then you'll put the Pen tool into practice!

Note: If you have not already downloaded the project files for this lesson to your computer from your Account page, make sure to do so now. See the "Getting Started" section at the beginning of the book.

1 To ensure that the tools function and the defaults are set exactly as described in this lesson, delete or deactivate (by renaming) the Adobe Illustrator preferences file. See "Restoring default preferences" in the "Getting Started" section at the beginning of the book.

2 Start Adobe Illustrator.

3 Choose File > Open, and open the L7_start.ai file in the Lessons > Lesson07 folder on your hard disk.

4 Choose File > Save As.

5 If the Cloud Document dialog box opens, click Save On Your Computer; otherwise, continue.

6 In the Save As dialog box, navigate to the Lesson07 folder, and open it. Rename the file **Pen_drawing.ai**. Choose Adobe Illustrator (ai) from the Format menu (macOS), or choose Adobe Illustrator (*.AI) from the Save As Type menu (Windows). Click Save.

7 In the Illustrator Options dialog box, leave the default settings, and then click OK.

8 Choose Window > Workspace > Reset Essentials.

9 Choose View > Fit All In Window.

Note: If you don't see Reset Essentials in the menu, choose Window > Workspace > Essentials before choosing Window > Workspace > Reset Essentials.

Why use the Pen tool?

In the previous chapter, you created curved and straight paths with the Curvature and Pencil tools. With the Pen tool (✐) you can also create and edit curved and straight paths, but you have even more control over the shape of the paths you draw.

Since the Pen tool is in other Adobe apps, such as Photoshop and InDesign, understanding how to work with it will give you more creative freedom in Illustrator as well as in those other apps.

Learning and mastering the Pen tool takes lots of practice. So go through the steps in this lesson and *practice, practice, practice.*

Starting with the Pen tool

In this section, you'll set up your document so you can get started exploring the Pen tool.

1 Choose 1 from the Artboard Navigation menu in the lower-left corner of the Document window, if it's not already chosen.

● **Note:** If the artboard does not fit in the document window, choose View > Fit Artboard In Window.

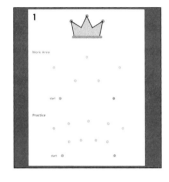

2 Select the Zoom tool (🔍) in the toolbar, and click in the area labeled Work Area to zoom in.

3 Choose View > Smart Guides to turn *off* Smart Guides.

   Smart Guides can be helpful when you draw, helping you align anchor points, among other things, but they make *learning* the Pen tool chaotic.

Creating straight lines to make a crown

You'll start drawing straight lines with the Pen tool to create the main path for a royal crown, like the one you see at the top of the artboard.

1 Select the Pen tool (✒) in the toolbar.

2 In the Properties panel, click the Fill color box. In the panel that opens, make sure the Swatches option (▦) is selected, and select None (◻).

3 Click the Stroke color box, and make sure that the color black is selected.

4 Make sure the stroke weight is **4 pt** in the Properties panel.

   When you start drawing with the Pen tool, it's usually best to have no fill on the path you draw, because the fill can cover parts of the path you are trying to create. You can add a fill later if you want.

5 Move the pointer anywhere into the area labeled Work Area on the artboard.

   Notice the asterisk (✳) next to the Pen icon. That asterisk means you'll create a new path if you start drawing.

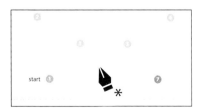

● **Note:** If you see ✕ instead of the Pen icon (✳), the Caps Lock key is active. Caps Lock turns the Pen tool icon into ✕ for increased precision. After you begin drawing with the Caps Lock key active, the Pen tool icon looks like this: -¦-.

6 Move the pointer over the orange start point, 1. Click and release to set the first anchor point.

This is the start of your crown. You learned about anchor points in Lessons 2 and 3 (and others). They control where your paths go and how they look.

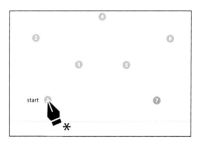

7 Move the pointer away from the point you just created.

See the blue line connecting the first point and the pointer, no matter where you move the pointer? That line is called the *Pen tool preview* (also known as the *rubber band*).

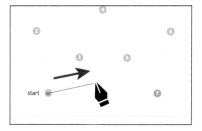

Later, as you create curved paths, it will make drawing them easier because it is a preview of what the path will look like. Also notice that the asterisk has disappeared from next to the pointer, indicating that you are now drawing a path.

8 Move the pointer over the gray dot labeled 2. Click and release to create another anchor point.

You just created a straight path. A path is made of two anchor points and a line segment connecting those anchor points. The type of anchor point you just created is called a *corner point.* Corner points make straight lines.

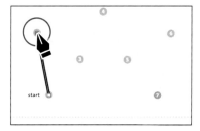

● **Note:** Unlike the Curvature tool, the Pen tool creates corner points and straight lines by default.

9 Continue clicking points 3 through 7, releasing the mouse button after every click to create new anchor points and paths.

▶ **Tip:** If you make a mistake as you draw, you can undo creating points by choosing Edit > Undo Pen and then drawing the last point(s) again.

10 Select the Selection tool (▶) to stop drawing and leave the crown path selected.

Continuing to draw a path

At times, you might draw a path and later want to continue drawing from the end of that path. Next, you'll see how to select and edit paths with the Direct Selection tool, and how to continue drawing from the end of a path.

1 With the crown path selected, click the Fill color box (▨) in the Properties panel on the right to reveal a panel.

2 Click the Swatches button (▦) toward the top of the panel, if it isn't already selected, to show the default swatches (colors). Click to apply a yellow color to change the color of the fill for the crown.

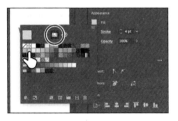 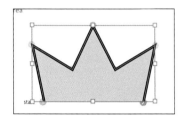

3 Click in an empty area of the artboard to deselect.

4 Select the Direct Selection tool (▷) and move the pointer over the path between points 5 and 6. When the pointer changes (▷.), click to select the line segment.

5 Choose Edit > Cut.

Note: If the entire path disappears, choose Edit > Undo Cut, and try selecting the line segment again.

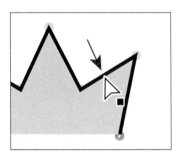 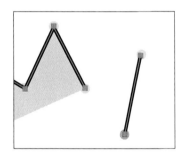

This removes the selected segment between anchor points 5 and 6. The crown is now two separate paths, and it no longer shows the yellow fill in the whole object. Next you'll learn how to connect the paths again.

6 Select the Pen tool (✒), and move the pointer onto the anchor point labeled 5. Notice that the Pen tool shows a forward slash (✒/), indicating that if you click, you will continue drawing from that anchor point.

7 Click the point.

This tells Illustrator that you want to continue drawing from that anchor point.

8 Move the pointer over the anchor point labeled 6. The pointer now shows a merge symbol next to it (◻), indicating that, if you click, you are connecting to another path. Click the point to reconnect the paths.

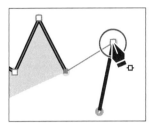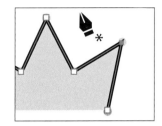

9 Choose Select > Deselect.

Practicing by making another crown!

Below the crown you just made on the artboard is another crown for practice!

1 Select the Hand tool (✋) and drag up to see the practice area on the same artboard.

2 Select the Pen tool and get creating!

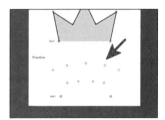

Drawing a house with the Pen tool

In previous lessons, you learned that using the Shift key and Smart Guides with the shape tools constrains the shape of objects. The Shift key and Smart Guides can also constrain paths drawn with the Pen tool, allowing you to create straight paths with 45-degree angles.

Next, you'll learn how to draw straight lines *and* constrain angles as you draw a house with the Pen tool.

1 Choose 2 from the Artboard Navigation menu.

2 Select the Zoom tool (🔍) in the toolbar, and click in the area labeled Work Area to zoom in.

3 Click the View menu, and choose Smart Guides to turn them *on*.

4 Select the Pen tool (✒), and in the Properties panel, change the fill color to None (⬜), ensure the stroke color is Black, and ensure the stroke weight is still 4 pt.

5 In the area labeled Work Area, click the orange point labeled 1, where you see "start/end," to set the first anchor point.

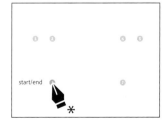

6 Move the pointer over the point labeled 2.

Notice the gray measurement label that appears next to the pointer. As you've learned in previous lessons, the measurement label is a part of the Smart Guides. In this case, the measurement label shows the distance from the last point and can be helpful when precision matters when drawing with the Pen tool.

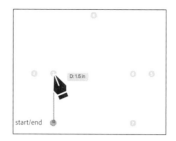

7 Click to set another anchor point.

8 Move the pointer over point 3 to the left.

When the pointer is aligned with point 2 to the right, it will "snap" in alignment. You may want to move the pointer around to feel this.

9 Click to make the third anchor.

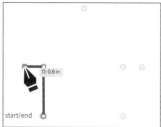

Note: You may see a vertical magenta alignment guide telling you that the point will be lined up with content like the orange house in the top half of the artboard. This is a part of the Smart Guides.

10 Click point 4, and then click to set point 5.

When making those points, you may have seen other magenta alignment guides telling you that the point will be lined up with other content. These guides and the snapping can sometimes make it challenging to draw freeform paths with the Pen tool.

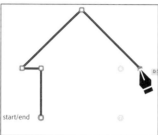

11 Choose View > Smart Guides to turn *off* the Smart Guides.

With Smart Guides turned off, you'll need to press the Shift key to align points.

12 Press the Shift key, click to set point 6, and then click to set point 7. Release the Shift key.

With Smart Guides off, there is no measurement label, and the point is only aligning with the previous point because you are pressing the Shift key.

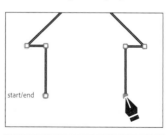

13 Move the pointer over point 1 (the first point). When the pointer shows a small circle next to it (○), click to close the path.

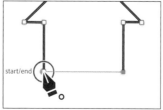

Practicing by making another house!

Below the house you just made on the artboard is another house for practice!

1 Select the Hand tool (✋) and drag up to see the practice area on the same artboard.

2 Select the Pen tool and get creating!

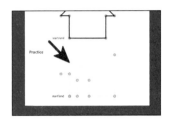

Exploring curved paths

Now that you can create corners with the Pen tool, you'll learn how to create curves. To create a curve with the Pen tool, instead of clicking to make an anchor point, you drag. This creates *direction lines* (some people call them *handles*) that define the shape of the curve. This type of anchor point, with direction lines, is called a *smooth point*.

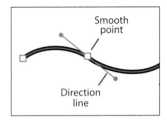

Drawing curves gives you some of the greatest control and flexibility in creating paths. However, mastering this technique does take some time. The goal for this particular exercise is not to create anything specific but to play a little and get accustomed to the feeling of creating curves.

1 Choose 3 from the Artboard Navigation menu.

2 Select the Zoom tool (🔍) in the toolbar, and click once or twice in the area labeled "Exploration" to zoom in.

3 Select the Pen tool (✒) in the toolbar. In the Properties panel, make sure that the fill color is None (◻), the stroke color is Black, and the stroke weight is still 4 pt.

4 With the Pen tool selected, click and release in an empty area of the artboard to create a starting anchor point. Move the pointer away.

Like before, you'll see the Pen tool preview showing what the path will look like if you click and release.

5 In an empty area, *press and drag* to create a curved path. Release the mouse button.

As you drag away from the point, two direction lines appear. A *direction line* has a round *direction point* at its end. The angle and length of direction lines determine the shape and size of the curve.

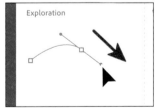

6 Move the pointer away from the anchor point and move it around a bit to see the path preview.

7 Continue pressing, dragging, and releasing to create some more points.

8 Choose Select > Deselect.

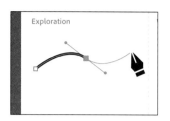

Drawing a curve with the Pen tool

In this part of the lesson, you'll use what you just learned about drawing curves to trace a curved shape with the Pen tool. This will require a little more precision.

1 Press the spacebar to temporarily select the Hand tool (✋), and drag to the left to get to the area labeled Work Area to the right.

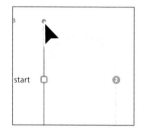

2 With the Pen tool (✏️) selected, move the pointer over the point labeled 1. Press and drag up to the red dot, and then release the mouse button.

Note: The artboard may scroll as you drag. If you lose visibility of the curve, choose View > Zoom Out until you see the curve and anchor point. Pressing the spacebar allows you to use the Hand tool to reposition the artboards in the canvas area.

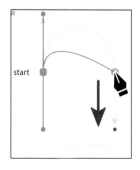
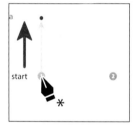

Up to this point (pun intended), you've clicked and released to start paths. You can also start a path by creating a smooth (curved) point so your path can be extra curvy. By dragging first, you made an anchor point that has direction lines.

3 Press and drag from point 2 down to the red dot, but don't let go yet. Drag the pointer around to see how the path reacts. Pulling the direction line longer makes a steeper curve; when the direction line is shorter, the curve is flatter. With the pointer over the red dot, release the mouse button.

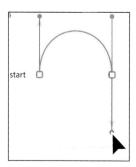
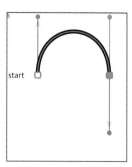

> ▶ **Tip:** If the path you created is not aligned precisely with the template, select the Direct Selection tool (▷), and select an anchor point to show the direction lines. You can then drag the ends of the direction lines (called direction points) until your path better follows the template!

4   Select the Selection tool (▶), and click the artboard in an area with no objects, or choose Select > Deselect.

Deselecting the path allows you to create a new path. If you click somewhere on the artboard with the Pen tool while the path is still selected, the new path connects to the last point you drew.

Practicing by creating more curves!

Below the pencil eraser you made are more eraser for practice!

1   Select the Hand tool (✋) and drag up to see the practice area on the same artboard.

2   Select the Pen tool and get creating!

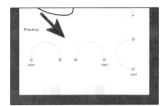

Drawing a series of curves with the Pen tool

Now that you've experimented with drawing a curve, you'll draw a worm character that contains several continuous curves.

1   Choose 4 from the Artboard Navigation menu.

2   Select the Zoom tool (🔍), and click several times in the Work Area to zoom in.

3   Select the Pen tool (✒). In the Properties panel to the right of the document, make sure that the fill color is None (▢), the stroke color is black, and the stroke weight is still 4 pt.

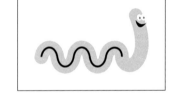

> ▶ **Tip:** As you are dragging out the direction lines for an anchor point, you can press and hold the spacebar to reposition the anchor point. When the anchor point is where you want it, release the spacebar and continue drawing.

4   Press and drag up from point 1, labeled "start," in the direction of the arc, stopping at the red dot.

This is exactly how you started the last path.

5   Move the pointer over the point labeled 2 and drag down to the red dot, adjusting the path between points 1 and 2 by dragging before you release the mouse button.

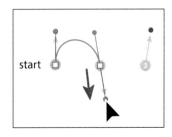

When you drag to create a curve with the Pen tool, you create a *leading* direction line and a *trailing* direction line on the anchor point. By default, they are equal and paired together.

Leading direction line

Trailing direction line

When it comes to curves, you'll find that you spend a lot of time focusing on the path segment *behind* the anchor point you're making. The trailing direction line controls the shape of the segment behind the anchor point.

6 Continue along the path, alternating between dragging up and down. Drag up at point 3.

7 Drag down at point 4

8 Drag up at point 5. Put anchor points only where there are numbers

9 Finish dragging down at the point labeled 6.

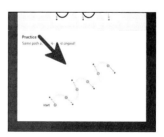

If you make a mistake as you draw, you can undo the last anchor(s) by choosing Edit > Undo Pen and then draw the last point again.

10 When the path is complete, select the Direct Selection tool (▷), and click to select any anchor point in the path to see the direction lines. You can then readjust the curve of the path, if necessary.

With a curve selected, you can also change the stroke and fill. When you do this, the next line you draw will have the same attributes.

11 Choose Select > Deselect, and then choose File > Save.

Practicing by creating continuous curves!

Below the worm body you made is a snake for practice!

1 Select the Hand tool (✋) and drag up to see the practice area on the same artboard.

2 Select the Pen tool and get creating!

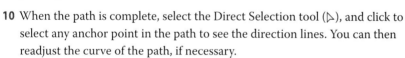

Changing path direction

When you make curves, the path is smooth—like you see in the figure. But what if you want to change the path direction in the middle of a curve, like you see in a series of waves?

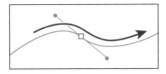

In this next part of the lesson, you'll change the direction of paths when making curves. You'll do this by moving the direction lines for anchor points in different directions, called *splitting* direction lines, to make some waves.

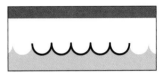

1   Choose 5 from the Artboard Navigation menu.

2   Select the Zoom tool (🔍), and click several times in the Work Area to zoom in.

3   Select the Pen tool (✒). In the Properties panel, make sure that the fill color is None (▢), the stroke color is Black, and the stroke weight is still 4 pt.

4   Press and drag down from point 1 to the red dot.

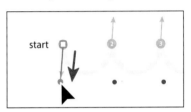

5   From point 2, drag up. When the curved path between points 1 and 2 looks right, release the mouse button.

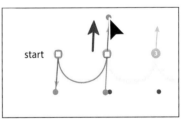

This is the first time I'm not asking you to drag to a colored dot in the template! In the real world those obviously won't be there, so for the next point you will create a point without much guidance, except an arrow pointing in the right direction. Don't worry, you can always choose Edit > Undo Pen and try again! I want you to focus on making sure the path looks right instead.

Now you need the path to switch directions and go down. You will *split* the direction lines or move them in different directions from each other.

▶ **Tip:** You can watch these steps in a video! Check out the videos that are a part of the Web Edition. For more information, see the "Web Edition" section of "Getting Started" at the beginning of the book.

6   Move the pointer over the anchor point you just created at point 2.

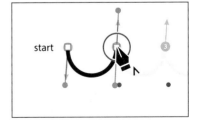

You should see the convert-point icon (^) next to the Pen tool pointer (✎₄) when it's right over the anchor point. That icon means you can drag a new leading direction line out.

7 Press the Option (macOS) or Alt (Windows) key, and drag from the anchor point down to the red dot to redirect the leading direction line. Release the mouse button and then the key.

 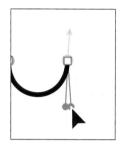

The Option (macOS) or Alt (Windows) key is what allows you to *split* the direction lines so that they are independent of each other for that anchor point.

8 Drag up from point 3. When the curved path between points 2 and 3 looks right, release the mouse button.

9 Press the Option (macOS) or Alt (Windows) key, and move the pointer over point 3. When a convert-point icon (^) appears next to the Pen tool pointer (🖊ₙ), press and drag a direction line down to the red dot below. Release the mouse button, and then release the modifier key.

● **Note:** For the next point, you will work faster by not releasing the mouse button to split the direction lines, so pay close attention and read the step before doing it!

10 Press and drag from anchor 4 up until the path looks correct. *Without releasing*, press the Option (macOS) or Alt (Windows) key, and drag down to the red dot for the next curve. Release the mouse button, and then release the modifier key.

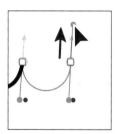 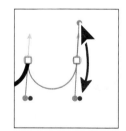 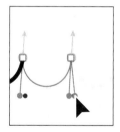

11 Continue this process using the Option (macOS) or Alt (Windows) key to create point 5, and then create point 6.

Practicing by creating more curves!

Below the waves you made is some practice!

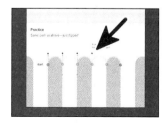

1 Select the Hand tool (🖐) and drag up to see the practice area on the same artboard.

2 Select the Pen tool and get creating!

Combining curves and straight lines

When you're drawing your own artwork with the Pen tool, you'll need to transition easily between curves and straight lines. In this next section, you'll learn how to go from curves to straight lines and from straight lines to curves, making a sail.

1 Choose 6 from the Artboard Navigation menu.

2 Select the Zoom tool ($\mathbb{Q}$), and click several times in the Work Area part of the artboard to zoom in.

3 Select the Pen tool (✒). In the Properties panel, make sure that the fill color is None (◻), the stroke color is Black, and the stroke weight is still 4 pt.

4 Move the pointer over point 1, labeled "start/end," and press and drag up to the red dot. Release the mouse button.

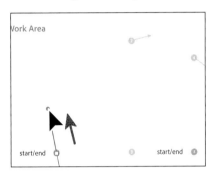

5 Press and drag from point 2, and release the mouse button when the path between 1 and 2 roughly matches the gray template path.

This method of creating a curve should be familiar to you by now.

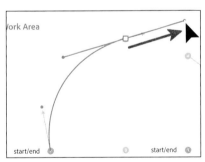

If you were to continue drawing by clicking point 3, even pressing the Shift key (to produce a straight line), the path would be curved (don't do either). The last point you created has a curve and a leading direction line (the one you pulled out). You will now continue the path as a straight line by removing the leading direction line.

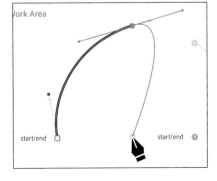

6 Move the pointer over point 2 at the top. When the convert-point icon appears (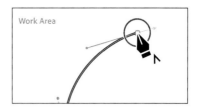), click.

This deletes the *leading* direction line from the anchor point (not the trailing direction line), as shown in the figure.

Work Area

Note: The figure shows what the path looks like after clicking.

7 Move the pointer over point 3. Pressing the Shift key, click and release to create the next point.

Releasing the Shift key after clicking creates a straight line.

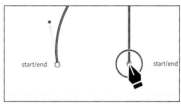

start/end   start/end

8 Finally, move the pointer over point 1. When the pointer shows a small circle next to it (○), click to close the path.

9 Choose File > Save.

start/end   start/end

Practicing by making the other sail!

Now you'll make another sail. For this sail, you'll remove a direction line from a point and add one to another.

1 Select the Hand tool (✋). If necessary, drag to the left to see the sail to the right.

2 Click point 1 to add the first anchor.

3 To make a straight line, Shift-click point 2 above point 1.

Now you need the next part of the path to curve. To do that, you will need a direction line coming out of the anchor you just made, so you will drag one out.

4 Move the pointer back over the anchor 2. When the convert-point icon appears (✒), press and drag from that point to the red dot.

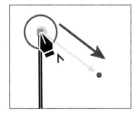 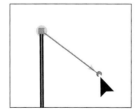

This creates a new, independent direction line that will control the curve of the path. The following part of the path needs to be straight, so you'll remove the leading direction line.

5 Drag from point 3 to the red dot.

6 Click the last anchor point you created (point 3) to remove the direction line.

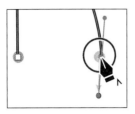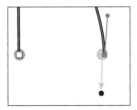

7 Click the first point to close the path.

Practicing by creating more curves!

Below the sails you just made is another path for practice!

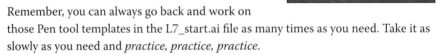

1 Select the Hand tool (✋) and drag up to see the practice area on the same artboard.

2 Select the Pen tool and get creating!

Remember, you can always go back and work on those Pen tool templates in the L7_start.ai file as many times as you need. Take it as slowly as you need and *practice, practice, practice.*

Putting your learning into practice

▶ **Tip:** Don't forget you can always undo a point you've drawn (Edit > Undo Pen) and then try again.

● **Note:** You do not have to start at the blue square (point A) to draw this shape. You can set anchor points for a path with the Pen tool in a clockwise or counterclockwise direction.

Next, you'll take what you've learned and create some artwork. To start you'll draw a hand giving the thumbs-up, which combines curves and corners. Then you'll edit the paths using a few new tools and techniques.

This section has more steps than a normal section—so take your time as you practice with this shape, and use the template guides provided.

1 Choose 7 Artboard 7 from the Artboard Navigation menu.

2 Select the Pen tool (✒). In the Properties panel, make sure that the fill color is None (▱), the stroke color is a *blue*, and the stroke weight is 6 pt.

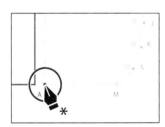

3 Click the blue square labeled "A" on the hand template to set the starting anchor point.

4 Shift-click point B to make a straight line.

5 Move the pointer over point B again, and when the pointer changes (✒ₓ), drag away from the point to the red dot to create a new direction line.

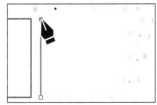

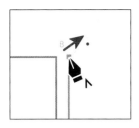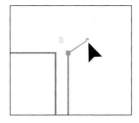

We created a direction line because the next part of the path has a slight curve.

6 Click point C to make a line with a slight curve to it.

7 Click point D to make a straight line.

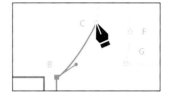

The next part of the path needs to be curved. *Can you guess what you need to do next?*

8 Move the pointer over point D again, and when the pointer changes (🖊), drag away from the point to the red dot to create a short new direction line. Release the mouse button and then the key.

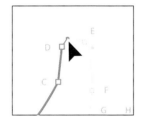

9 Drag from point E to make a curve.

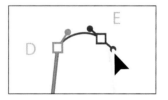

The part of the path to pay attention to is highlighted in red in the figure.

Notice that the red dot on the template is faint? As I said previously, remember to pay attention to how the path you are creating looks as you drag. It's easier when dragging to color dots on a template, but when you're creating your own content, you'll need to focus on what the path looks like.

10 Click points F and G to make the segments between those points straight lines.

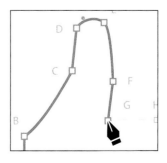

You will curve this part of the path next using a different method. Sometimes it's easier to quickly get the anchor points out and then go back and refine them to make your shape.

You can edit part of a path you previously drew while still drawing with the Pen tool. By pressing a modifier key with the Pen tool selected, you can drag a path segment you've drawn to modify it, which is what you'll do next.

Tip: You can also press Option+Shift (macOS) or Alt+Shift (Windows) to constrain the handles on each anchor point to a perpendicular direction.

11 Move the pointer over the path between points F and G. Press the Option (macOS) or Alt (Windows) key. When the pointer has this ($\curvearrowright$) next to it, drag the path to make it curved, as you see in the figure. Release the mouse button and then the key.

This adds direction lines to the anchor points at both ends of the line segment. After releasing the mouse button, notice that as you move the pointer around, you can see the Pen tool rubber-banding, which means you are still drawing the path.

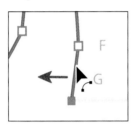 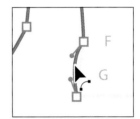

The path from point G to point H needs to be straight, followed by a curve, so you'll need to add a leading direction line to the point.

12 With the Pen tool pointer over point H, Shift-drag to the light red dot.

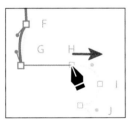 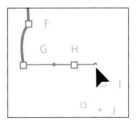

This creates a new leading direction line and sets up the next path to be a curve. Also, pressing the Shift key kept the line straight.

13 Move the Pen tool pointer over point I and begin dragging down. Press the Shift key to constrain the path, following the template path!

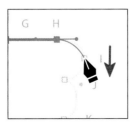 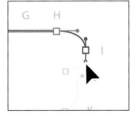

The part of the path to pay attention to is highlighted in red in the figure.

For the next three points, you will split the direction handles so you can make the knuckles. *Don't release the mouse button until you are told!*

For the next steps you may want to zoom in to the remaining points.

14 Move the Pen tool pointer over point J and drag to make the path behind curved, following the template path. *Without releasing the mouse button*, press Option (macOS) or Alt (Windows) and drag to the light red dot to split the direction lines.

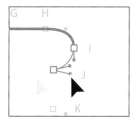

▶ **Tip:** I've said this a few times, but don't forget you can always undo a point you've drawn (Edit > Undo Pen) and then try again.

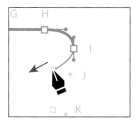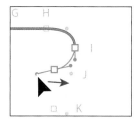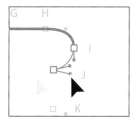

That is the faster method for splitting direction lines. If you don't feel comfortable doing it this way, you can also follow the method in the section "Changing path direction."

15 Repeat the previous step for points K and L for a little practice!

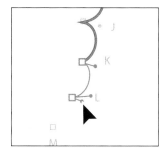

16 For point M, start dragging from the point to the left, and press the Shift key as you drag. Drag until the curve looks right. Release the mouse button and then the key.

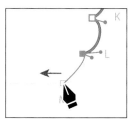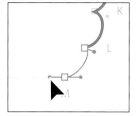

Next, you'll complete the drawing by closing the path.

17 Move the Pen tool pointer over point A and click to close the path.

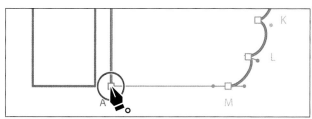

18 In the Properties panel, click the Fill color and select white (if it isn't already).

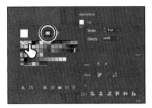 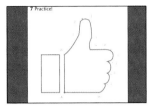

19 Command-click (macOS) or Ctrl-click (Windows) away from the path to deselect it, and then choose File > Save.

This is a shortcut method for deselecting a path while keeping the Pen tool selected. You could also choose Select > Deselect, among other methods.

Editing paths and points further

Next you'll edit a few of the paths and points for the art you just created. You'll start by reshaping the thumb a little.

1 Select the Direct Selection tool (▷), and click the anchor point labeled "G" to select it.

2 Begin dragging the anchor point to the left. As you drag, press the Shift key. When it looks like the figure, release the mouse button and then the key.

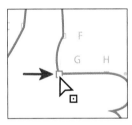 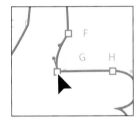

Pressing the Shift key when dragging will constrain the movement to multiples of 45°.

▶ **Tip:** You can drag the line segment (path) between the anchor points without selecting Option/Alt, as you did with the Pen tool earlier, because at least one of the anchor points has direction lines. This won't work on a straight path.

3 Move the pointer over the part of the path between points E and F. When the pointer has this (🖰) next to it, drag the path a little to the right to change the curve of the path.

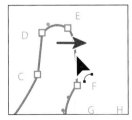 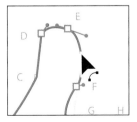

As you drag the path using this method, the anchor points and direction lines are adjusted. This is an easy way to make edits to a curved path without having to edit the direction lines for each anchor point. You might notice that point F now looks more like a corner—a more V-shaped path, rather than a smooth path going through it.

4   To make the thumb a bit rounder, click point F and drag one of the direction lines to make the path appear smoother.

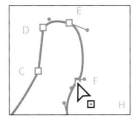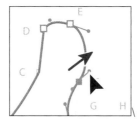

I dragged the direction line just a little, so it's a subtle change.

5   Choose Select > Deselect, and then choose File > Save.

Deleting and adding anchor points

Most of the time, the goal of drawing paths with a tool like the Pen tool or Curvature tool is to avoid adding more anchor points than necessary. You can reduce a path's complexity or change its overall shape by deleting unnecessary points (and therefore gain more control over the shape), or you can extend a path by adding points to it. Next you'll delete anchor points from, and add anchor points to, different parts of the path.

1   Open the Layers panel (Window > Layers).

2   In the Layers panel, click the eye icon () for the Template Content layer to hide the template.

▶ **Tip:** You'll learn all about layers in Lesson 10, "Organizing Your Artwork with Layers."

3   With the Direct Selection tool (▷) selected, click in the white fill of the blue hand to select it.

You should see the selected anchor points on the path now, but it's challenging because the path is blue and the anchor points are also blue! To see the anchor points more easily, you will change the layer color.

4 In the Layers panel, double-click the thumbnail to the left of the Practice layer.

5 In the Layer Options dialog box, choose Light Red from the Color menu and click OK.

  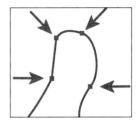

Now that you can more easily see the anchor points (they are now red), you'll delete a point in the hand to simplify the path.

Tip: With an anchor point selected, you can also click Remove Selected Anchor Points (⬛) in the Properties panel to delete the anchor point.

6 Select the Pen tool (✍) in the toolbar, and move the pointer over the anchor point on the top knuckle of the hand. When a minus sign (−) appears next to the Pen tool pointer (✎_), click to remove the anchor point.

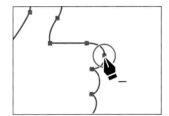

Next you'll reshape the remaining path a little so the curve looks better.

7 With the Pen tool selected, press Command (macOS) or Ctrl (Windows) to temporarily select the Direct Selection tool so you can edit an anchor.

Note: It can be tricky to drag the end of a direction line. If you wind up missing and deselecting the path, with the modifier key still held down, click the path and then click the anchor point to see the direction lines and try again.

8 With the key still held down, begin dragging the direction line you see in the first part of the figure. Drag it to the right. As you drag, press the Shift key as well. Release the mouse button and then the keys.

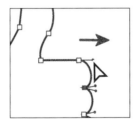 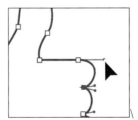

With that part of the path reshaped, now you'll add a new anchor point to the path so you can reshape it further.

9 Move the pointer over the bottom knuckle of the hand. See the figure for where. When a plus sign (+) appears to the right of the Pen tool pointer (✎₊), click to add an anchor point.

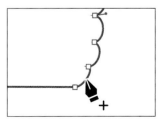

10 Press Command (macOS) or Ctrl (Windows) to temporarily select the Direct Selection tool, and drag the new anchor to the right to reshape the path. Release the key.

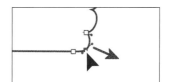

Converting between smooth points and corner points

To more precisely control the path you create, you can convert points from smooth points to corner points and the other way around, using several methods. Next, you'll round the corners of the rectangle to the left of the hand you drew.

1 Select the Direct Selection tool (▷). Click in the rectangle to the left of the hand.

2 Select the upper-left anchor point.

3 In the Properties panel, click the Convert Selected Anchor Points To Smooth button (▰) to add direction lines to the anchor point.

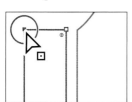
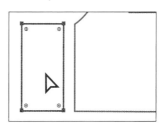
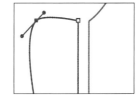

▶ **Tip:** You could also convert between corner and smooth points by double-clicking (or Option-clicking [macOS] or Alt-clicking [Windows]) an anchor point with the Curvature tool.

4 Select the lower-left anchor point and do the same—click the Convert Selected Anchor Points To Smooth button (▰) to round the anchor point. An arrow is pointing to it in the figure.

Now you'll fix up the two corners to look better.

5 With the Direct Selection tool selected, move the pointer over the path between the two anchor points you just rounded. When the pointer has this (✐) next to it, begin dragging to the right to change the curve of the path. As you drag, press the Shift key to constrain the movement. Release the mouse button and then the key.

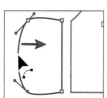
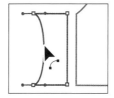

6 Choose Select > Deselect and then File > Save.

Converting anchor points with the Anchor Point tool

The Anchor Point tool is another way to convert anchor points between smooth and corner points (‸). With this tool, you can convert anchor points as you did in the previous section, but you can adjust the paths with it at the same time. You'll use the tool to finish the art.

1   With the Direct Selection tool (▷) selected, select the point in the hand you see in the figure.

    You can see a single direction line on the point.

2   Press and hold on the Pen tool (✎) in the toolbar to reveal another tool. Select the Anchor Point tool (‸).

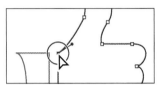

● **Note:** Don't drag if the pointer has this (⌒) next to it. This means that the pointer is not over the anchor point, and if you drag, you will reshape the curve.

3   Move the pointer over the point you see in the following figure. The pointer should still look like this: ‸. Click that point to remove the direction line.

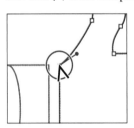 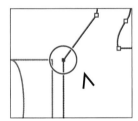

▶ **Tip:** If you move the Anchor Point tool pointer over the end of a direction line that is split, you can press the Option (macOS) or Alt (Windows) key and, when the pointer changes (▸), click to make the direction lines a single straight line again (not split).

Clicking a point that has one or both direction lines removes them, making the point a corner.

4   Click the point you see in the following figure to remove the direction lines.

5   Drag from the same point to add direction lines again. Drag until you think the curve of the thumb looks good!

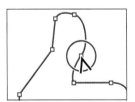 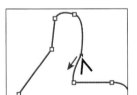 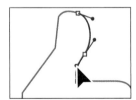

Good job! You've explored the Pen tool and a lot of the methods for making and editing your very own art. The only thing left to do is to keep practicing!

6   Choose View > Fit All In Window.

7   Choose File > Save and then File > Close.

Review questions

1 Describe how to draw straight vertical, horizontal, or diagonal lines using the Pen tool (✐).

2 How do you draw a curved line using the Pen tool?

3 What are the two types of anchor points you can create with the Pen tool?

4 Name two ways to convert a smooth point on a curve to a corner point.

5 Which tool would you use to edit a segment on a curved line?

Review answers

1 To draw a straight line, click with the Pen tool (✐) and then move the pointer and click again. The first click sets the starting anchor point, and the second click sets the ending anchor point of the line. To constrain the straight line vertically, horizontally, or along a 45° diagonal, press the Shift key as you click to create the second anchor point with the Pen tool.

2 To draw a curved line with the Pen tool, click to create the starting anchor point, drag to set the direction of the curve, and then click to end the curve.

3 With the Pen tool, you can create corner points or smooth points. Corner points allow the path to change direction and have either no direction lines or split direction lines. Smooth points have direction lines that form a straight line.

4 To convert a smooth point on a curve to a corner point, use the Direct Selection tool (▷) to select the anchor point and then use the Anchor Point tool (⋏) to drag a direction line to change the direction. Another method is to select a point or points with the Direct Selection tool and then click the Convert Selected Anchor Points To Corner button (⬕) in the Properties panel.

5 To edit a segment on a curved line, select the Direct Selection tool and drag the segment to move it; or drag a direction line on an anchor point to adjust the length and shape of the segment. Here's a tip: pressing the Option (macOS) or Alt (Windows) key and dragging a path segment with the Pen tool is another way to reshape a path.

8 USING COLOR TO ENHANCE ARTWORK

Lesson overview

In this lesson, you'll learn how to do the following:

- Understand color modes and the main color controls.

- Create, edit, and apply colors using a variety of methods.

- Name and save colors.

- Copy and paste appearance attributes from one object to another.

- Explore color groups.

- Be inspired creatively with the Color Guide panel.

- Explore the Recolor Artwork command.

- Get started with Generative Recolor.

- Work with Live Paint groups.

This lesson will take about 75 minutes to complete. To get the lesson files used in this lesson, download them from the web page for this book at *peachpit.com/IllustratorCIB2024*. For more information, see "Accessing the lesson files and Web Edition" in the Getting Started section at the beginning of this book.

Spice up your illustrations with color by taking advantage of color controls in Adobe Illustrator. In this information-packed lesson, you'll discover how to create and apply fills and strokes, use the Color Guide panel for inspiration, work with color groups, recolor artwork, and more.

Starting the lesson

In this lesson, you'll learn about the fundamentals of color by using the Swatches panel and more to create and edit the colors in artwork for tea labels.

● **Note:** If you have not already downloaded the project files for this lesson to your computer from your Account page, make sure to do so now. See the "Getting Started" section at the beginning of the book.

● **Note:** For more information on activating fonts, visit *helpx.adobe.com/ creative-cloud/help/add-fonts.html*.

1 To ensure that the tools function and the defaults are set exactly as described in this lesson, delete or deactivate (by renaming) the Adobe Illustrator preferences file. See "Restoring default preferences" in the "Getting Started" section at the beginning of the book.

2 Start Adobe Illustrator.

3 Choose File > Open, and open the L8_end.ai file in the Lessons > Lesson08 folder to view a final version of the artwork.

4 In the Missing Fonts dialog box, ensure that the checkboxes to the right of the names of the missing fonts are selected, and click Activate Fonts. After some time, the font(s) should be activated, and you should see a success message in the Missing Fonts dialog box. Click Close.

5 If you see a dialog box about font auto-activation, click Skip.

6 Choose View > Fit All In Window. You can leave the file open for reference or choose File > Close to close it.

7 Choose File > Open. In the Open dialog box, navigate to the Lessons > Lesson08 folder, and select the L8_start.ai file on your hard disk. Click Open to open the file. This file has all the pieces already in it; they just need to be painted.

8 Choose View > Fit All In Window.

9 Choose File > Save As. If the Cloud Document dialog box opens, click Save On Your Computer.

10 In the Save As dialog box, navigate to the Lesson08 folder, and name the file **TeaPackaging.ai**. Leave Adobe Illustrator (ai) chosen from the Format menu (macOS) or Adobe Illustrator (*.AI) chosen from the Save As Type menu (Windows), and click Save.

● **Note:** If you don't see Reset Essentials in the menu, choose Window > Workspace > Essentials before choosing Window > Workspace > Reset Essentials.

11 In the Illustrator Options dialog box, leave the options at their default settings and then click OK.

12 Choose Window > Workspace > Reset Essentials.

Exploring color modes

There are many ways to experiment with and apply color to your artwork in Adobe Illustrator. As you work with color, it's important to consider the medium in which the artwork will be published, such as print or web. The colors you create need to be suitable for that medium. This usually requires that you use the correct color mode and color definitions for your colors.

Before starting a new document, you should decide which color mode the artwork should use, *CMYK* or *RGB*.

- **CMYK**—Cyan, magenta, yellow, and black are the colors of ink used in four-color process printing. These four colors are combined and overlapped in a pattern of dots to create a multitude of other colors.

- **RGB**—Red, green, and blue light are added together in various ways to create an array of colors. Select this mode if you are using images for onscreen presentations, the internet, or mobile apps, or maybe for printing to desktop inkjet printers.

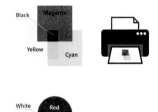

When you create a new document by choosing File > New, each new document preset, like Print or Web, has a specific color mode. For instance, the presets in the Print category use the CMYK color mode by default. You can easily change the color mode by choosing a different option from the Color Mode menu in the Advanced Options area of the New Document dialog box.

Note: You may see a series of templates in the New Document dialog box that are different than those you see in the figure.

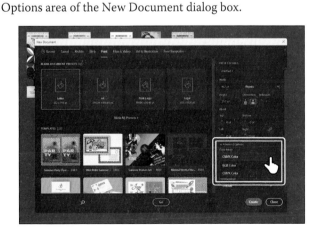

Once a color mode is chosen, colors in the document are displayed in and created from that color mode. Once a document is created, you can change the color mode of a document by choosing File > Document Color Mode and then switching to either CMYK Color or RGB Color in the menu.

Working with color

In this lesson, you'll learn about the many ways of coloring objects in Illustrator using a combination of panels and tools, such as the Properties panel, Swatches panel, Color Guide panel, Color Picker, and paint options in the toolbar.

● **Note:** The toolbar you see may be a double column, depending on the resolution of your screen.

In previous lessons, you learned that objects can have a fill, a stroke, or both. At the bottom of the toolbar, notice the Fill and Stroke boxes. The Fill box is white (in this case), and the Stroke box is black. If you click those boxes one at a time, you'll see that whichever is clicked is brought in front of the other (it's selected).

When a color is chosen, it is applied to the fill or stroke, whichever is *selected*. As you explore more of Illustrator, you'll see these fill and stroke boxes in lots of other places, like the Properties panel, Swatches panel, and more.

Applying an existing color

● **Note:** Throughout this lesson, you'll be working on a document with a color mode that was set to CMYK when the document was created. That means that colors you create will, by default, be composed of cyan, magenta, yellow, and black.

Every new document in Illustrator has some default saved colors you can use in your artwork in the form of swatches in the Swatches panel. The first color method you'll explore is applying one of those existing colors to a shape.

1 With the TeaPackaging.ai document showing, choose 1 Tea - Start from the Artboard Navigation menu in the lower-left corner of the Document window (if it's not chosen already)

2 Then, choose View > Fit Artboard In Window.

3 With the Selection tool (▶), click one of the gray leaf shapes to select it. Shift-click the other two gray leaves and the gray saucer under the coffee cup to select them as well.

4 Click the Fill box (■) in the Properties panel on the right to reveal a panel.

5 In the panel, click the Swatches button (▦) toward the top of the panel, if it isn't already selected, to show the default swatches (colors), as well as the custom colors defined specifically for this document. Then, click to apply a darker green swatch to change the color of the fill for the selected shape.

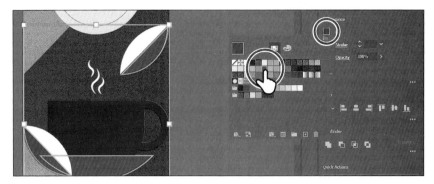

6 Press the Escape key to hide the Swatches panel.

Making a custom color

Using the Color panel (Window > Color) or Color Mixer, you can make custom colors and apply them to an object's fill and stroke. You can also edit and mix colors using different color models (CMYK, for example).

In the Color panel and Color Mixer, you can either visually select a color from the color spectrum bar at the bottom of the panel or mix colors in various ways.

Next, you'll create a custom color using the Color Mixer.

1 Select the black coffee cup, and then click the Fill box (■) in the Properties panel.

2 Click the Color Mixer button (🎨) at the top of that panel (circled in the following figure).

3 At the bottom of the panel, click in the yellow-green part of the color spectrum to sample a yellow-green color, and apply it to the fill.

> **Tip:** To see a larger color spectrum, you can open the Color panel (Window > Color) and drag the bottom of the panel down.

Since the spectrum bar is so small, you most likely won't achieve the same color as you see in the book. That's okay, because you'll edit it to match next.

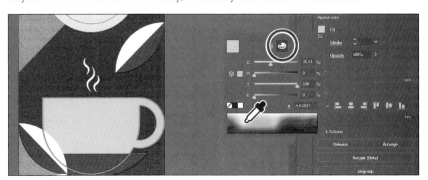

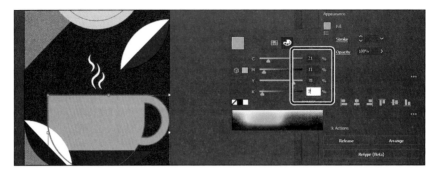

Tip: Don't see CMYK in the panel? Choose CMYK from the Swatches panel menu ().

4 In the Color Mixer panel, which should still be showing, type the following values in the CMYK fields: C=**21**, M=**11**, Y=**78**, K=**7**. Press Return or Enter after the last value entered to make a yellow-green color and close the panel. Leave the shape selected.

Colors created in the Color Mixer panel are not saved anywhere except in the fill or stroke of the selected artwork. If you want to easily reuse the color you just created elsewhere in this document, you can save it as a swatch in the Swatches panel, which is what you'll do next.

Saving a color as a swatch

You can save different types of colors, gradients, and patterns in the document as swatches so that you can apply and edit them later. Swatches are listed in the Swatches panel in the order in which they were created, but you can reorder or organize the swatches into groups to suit your needs.

All documents start with a default number of swatches, as mentioned earlier. Any colors you save or edit in the Swatches panel are available only to the current document, by default, since each document has its own defined swatches.

Next, you'll save the color you just created as a swatch so you can reuse it later.

1 With the coffee cup still selected, click the Fill box (■) in the Properties panel to show the panel again.

2 Click the Swatches button (▦) at the top of the panel to see the swatches.

3 Click the New Swatch button (⊞) at the bottom of the panel to create a swatch from the fill color of the selected artwork.

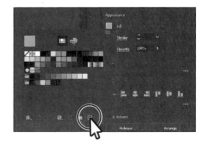

4 In the New Swatch dialog box that appears, change the swatch name to **Light Green**.

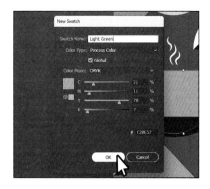

Notice the Global option that is selected by default? New swatches you create are global by default.

A *global swatch* is a swatch that is updated everywhere it's applied anytime the color is changed, regardless of whether the artwork is selected. Also, the Color Mode menu lets you change the color mode of a specific color to RGB, CMYK, Grayscale, or another mode.

Tip: Naming colors can be an art form. You can name them according to their values (C=45, ...), appearance (light orange), or description (like "text header"), among other attributes.

5 Click OK to save the swatch.

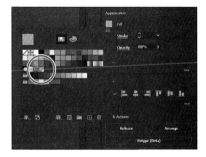

Notice that the new Light Green swatch is highlighted in the Swatches panel (it has a white border around it). That's because it's applied to the selected coffee cup automatically.

Also, notice the little white triangle (△) in the lower-right corner of the swatch, which indicates that it's a global swatch.

Leave the coffee cup selected and the panel showing for the next section.

Creating a copy of a swatch

One of the easiest ways to create and save a color as a swatch is to make a copy of an existing swatch and edit the color of the copy. Follow these steps to create a swatch copy:

1 With a shape selected, click the Fill or Stroke color box in the Properties panel.

2 Make sure the swatches are showing. Click the New Swatch button (🔲) at the bottom of the panel.

This creates a copy of the selected swatch and opens the New Swatch dialog box.

Tip: You can also choose Duplicate Swatch from the Swatches panel menu (▦) to create a copy of a selected swatch.

Editing the global swatch

Next you'll edit the global color you just made. When you edit a global color, all artwork with that swatch applied is updated, regardless of which artwork is and isn't selected.

1   With the Selection tool (▶), click the bottom-most green leaf.

You'll apply the Light Green swatch to the shape and then change the color.

2   Click the Fill box (■) in the Properties panel, and click to apply the swatch named Light Green. Leave the panel of swatches showing.

3   Double-click the Light Green swatch in the Swatches panel to edit it. In the Swatch Options dialog box:

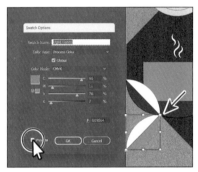

   • Select Preview to see the change.

   • Change the C (Cyan) value to **90**, and click in another field in the dialog box to see the change happen.

You may need to drag the dialog box by the top title bar to see the coffee cup and leaf shape. Notice that both shapes with the global swatch applied are updated—even though the coffee cup isn't selected.

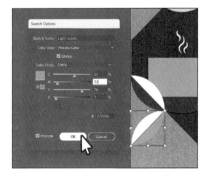

4   Change the C (Cyan) value to **57** and click OK.

Editing a non-global swatch

The default color swatches that come with each Illustrator document are *non-global* swatches by default. As a result, when you edit one of those color swatches, the artwork that uses the color will update only if that artwork is selected.

Next, you'll edit the non-global green swatch you applied to the fill of the dark green leaves.

1   With the Selection tool (▶) selected, click to select one of the dark green leaves you first changed the color for.

2   Click the Fill box (■) in the Properties panel, and you'll see that the dark green swatch is applied to the fill.

This was the first color you applied at the beginning of this lesson.

You can tell that the dark green swatch is *not* a global swatch because it doesn't have the small white triangle in the lower-right corner of the swatch in the Swatches panel.

3   Press the Escape key to hide the Swatches panel.

4   Choose Select > Deselect.

Most of the formatting options you find in the Properties panel can also be found in separate panels. Opening the Swatches panel, for instance, can be a useful way to work with color without having to select artwork.

5   Choose Window > Swatches to open the Swatches panel as a separate panel.

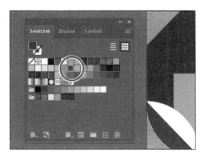

6   Double-click the same dark green swatch to edit it.

7 In the Swatch Options dialog box, change the name to **Dark Green** and the K (Black) value to **30**, select Global to ensure that it's a global swatch, and select Preview.

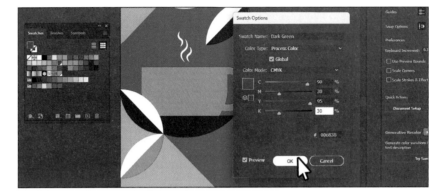

Notice that none of the dark green leaves changed. That's because Global wasn't selected in the Swatch Options dialog box when the color was applied to them. After changing a non-global swatch, you need to reapply it to artwork that wasn't selected when you made the edit.

8 Click OK.

9 Click the X at the top of the Swatches panel group to close it.

10 Select one of the dark green leaves, and then Shift-click to select the other *dark* green leaf and dark green cup saucer (under the coffee cup).

11 Click the Fill box (■) in the Properties panel, and notice that what was the dark green color swatch is no longer applied.

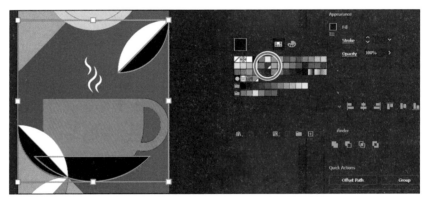

12 Click the Dark Green swatch you just edited to apply it.

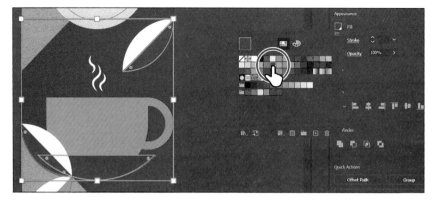

13 Choose Select > Deselect, and then choose File > Save.

Using the Color Picker to create color

Another method for creating color is to use the Color Picker. The Color Picker lets you select a color in a color field or spectrum by defining colors numerically or clicking a swatch. You'll also find the Color Picker in Adobe applications like InDesign and Photoshop. Next, you'll create a color using the Color Picker and then save that color as a swatch in the Swatches panel.

1 Select the deep royal blue shape behind the coffee cup.

2 Double-click the deep royal blue Fill box (■) at the bottom of the toolbar, to the left of the document, to open the Color Picker.

Note: You can't double-click the Fill box in the Properties panel to open the Color Picker.

In the Color Picker dialog box, the larger color field shows saturation (horizontally) and brightness (vertically). The color spectrum bar to the right of the color field shows the hue.

3 In the Color Picker dialog box, drag up and down in the color spectrum bar to change the color range. Make sure that you wind up with the triangles in a red color—it doesn't have to match the figure exactly.

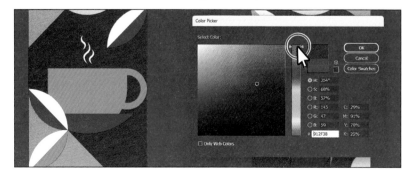

4 Drag in the color field (where you see the circle in the following figure). As you drag right and left, you adjust the saturation, and as you drag up and down, you adjust the brightness. The color you create when you click OK (don't click yet) appears in the New Color rectangle (an arrow is pointing to it in the figure).

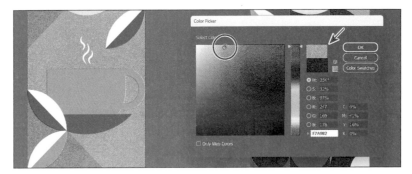

Next, you'll enter color values so we all have the same color.

5 In the CMYK fields, change the values to C=**2**, M=**31**, Y=**23**, and K=**0**.

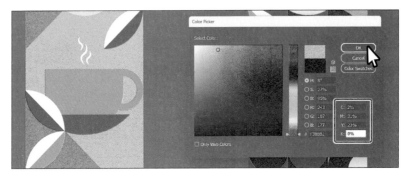

● **Note:** The Color Swatches button in the Color Picker shows you the swatches in the Swatches panel and the default color books (the sets of swatches that come with Illustrator). It also lets you select a color from one. You can return to the color spectrum by clicking the Color Models button and then editing the swatch color values, if necessary.

6 Click OK, and you should see that the pink color is applied to the background shape.

7 To save the color as a swatch so you can reuse it, click the Fill box (▣) in the Properties panel to show the swatches.

8 Click the New Swatch button (▣) at the bottom of the panel, and change the following options in the New Swatch dialog box:

   • Swatch Name: **Pink**
   • Global: Selected (the default setting)

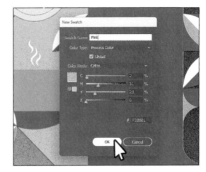

9 Click OK to see the color appear as a swatch in the Swatches panel.

10 Choose Select > Deselect.

11 Choose File > Save.

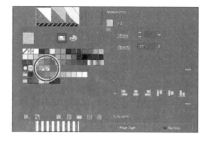

Using Illustrator swatch libraries

Swatch libraries are collections of preset colors, such as TOYO and others, as well as thematic libraries, such as Earthtone and Ice Cream. Illustrator has default swatch libraries that appear as separate panels and can't be edited when you open them. Swatch libraries are a great starting point for creating colors.

Let's apply a color from a library to the artwork.

1 Choose 2 Tea - Tint from the Artboard Navigation menu in the lower-left corner of the Document window.

2 Choose Window > Swatch Libraries > Art History > Impressionism.

The Swatch Libraries option is toward the bottom of the Window menu.

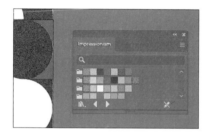

3 With the Selection tool (▶), click one of the red shapes. A group of red shapes is now selected.

▶ **Tip:** If you know the name of a color, you can type the name in the find field at the top of the panel to filter the list.

4 In the Impressionism panel, find a lighter green color. Click the color swatch to apply it to the shape.

I chose a color with a value of C=36, M=15, Y=33, K=0. See the figure for which.

● **Note:** If you exit Illustrator with a color library panel still open and then relaunch Illustrator, the panel does not reopen. To automatically open the panel whenever Illustrator opens, choose Persistent from the panel menu (▤).

5 Close the Impressionism panel.

6 Click the Fill box (⬜) in the Properties panel to show the swatches, click the New Swatch button (⊞) at the bottom of the panel, and change the following options in the New Swatch dialog box:

- Swatch Name: **Pale Green**
- Global: Selected (the default setting)

7 Click OK.

You should see the color now in the Swatches panel.

8 Choose Select > Deselect, and then choose File > Save.

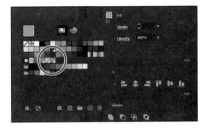

Pantone colors

Color system manufacturers like Pantone create standardized colors for relaying color information across apps like Adobe Photoshop, Illustrator, and InDesign.

To learn more about these color libraries, visit *helpx.adobe.com/illustrator/kb/pantone-color-books-illustrator.html*.

Creating and saving a tint of a color

A tint is a lighter version of a color. You can create a tint from a global process color, like CMYK, or from a spot color. Next, you'll create a tint of the pale green swatch you added to the document to make the background a new color.

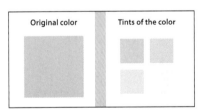

Original color	Tints of the color

1 With the Selection tool (▶), click the yellow shape at the bottom of the tea label.

2   Click the Fill box in the Properties panel () on the right. Select the
    Pale Green swatch to fill the shape. Leave the panel open.

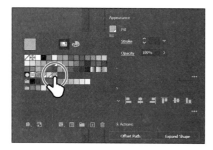

3   Click the Color Mixer button () at the top of the panel.

    In the section "Making a custom color," you created a custom color using the
    Color Mixer sliders. In that section, you were creating a custom color from
    scratch—that's why there were CMYK sliders. Now you'll see a single slider
    labeled "T" for tint. When using the color mixer for a global swatch, you create a
    tint instead of mixing CMYK values.

4   Drag the tint slider to the left to change the tint value to 40%.

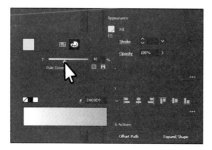

5   Click the Swatches button () at the top of the panel to show the swatches.
    Click the New Swatch button () at the bottom of the panel to save the tint.

6   Move the pointer over the swatch icon to see its name, which is
    Pale Green 40%.

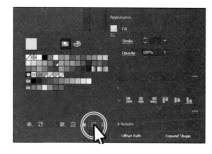
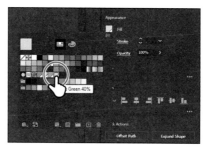

7   Choose Select > Deselect, and then choose File > Save.

Converting colors

Illustrator offers commands for selected artwork that allow you to convert colors between color modes—maybe to make color artwork grayscale, blend colors, invert colors, and much more. Perhaps you can no longer justify the added cost of adding a spot color. You can convert the spot color to CMYK and get something close to the original result at a lower price.

- Select all artwork you want to convert.
- Choose Edit > Edit Colors > Convert To CMYK (or whichever mode you want).

Copying appearance attributes

Using the Eyedropper tool (✐), you can copy appearance attributes, such as text formatting, fill, and stroke, from one object to another. This can speed up your creative process.

There is another shape in the background of the tea label that needs the pale green color applied. You could have applied it in the last section, or you could simply apply the Pale Green swatch now. But sometimes you just need to get a color applied quickly.

1 Using the Selection tool (▶), select the light gray shape behind the text at the top of the tea label.

▶ **Tip:** You can double-click the Eyedropper tool in the toolbar before sampling to change the attributes that the Eyedropper picks up and applies.

2 Select the Eyedropper tool (✐) in the toolbar on the left. Click in the shape to which you applied the tint at the bottom of the label. See the figure.

The once gray shape now has the attributes from the tint-filled shape.

3 Select the Selection tool (▶).

4 Choose Select > Deselect and then choose File > Save.

Exploring color groups ■◀

In Illustrator, you can save colors in color groups, consisting of related color swatches in the Swatches panel. To learn how to create and organize colors in groups, check out the video *Exploring color groups*, which is part of the Web Edition. For more information, see the "Web Edition" section of "Getting Started" at the beginning of the book.

Using the Color Guide panel for creative inspiration

The Color Guide panel can provide you with color inspiration as you create your artwork. You can use it to pick color tints, analogous colors, and much more and then apply them directly to artwork, edit them using several methods, or save them as a group in the Swatches panel.

Next, you'll select a color from another tea label and then use the Color Guide panel to create new colors based on that original color.

1 Choose 3 Tea - Recolor 1 from the Artboard Navigation menu in the lower-left corner of the Document window.

2 With the Selection tool (▶), click the light pink background behind the Tea Time text.

3 Make sure that the Fill box is selected (near the bottom of the toolbar).

4 Choose Window > Color Guide to open the panel.

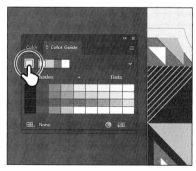

5 In the Color Guide panel, click the Set Base Color To The Current Color button (☐) (circled in the figure).

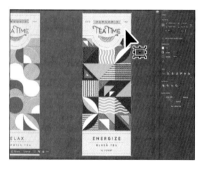

The Color Guide panel suggests colors based on the color showing in the Set Base Color To The Current Color button. The colors you see in the Color Guide panel may differ from what you see in the figure. That's okay.

Next, you'll experiment with colors using harmony rules.

6 Choose Right Complement from the Harmony Rules menu (circled in the first part of the following figure) in the Color Guide panel.

> **Tip:** You can also choose a different color variation (different from the default Tints/Shades), such as Show Warm/Cool or Vivid/Muted, by clicking the Color Guide panel menu icon (▤) and choosing one.

A base group of colors is created to the right of the base color (light pink), and a series of tints and shades of those colors appears in the body of the panel. There are lots of harmony rules to choose from, each instantly generating a color scheme based on any color you want. The base color you set (light pink) is the basis for generating the colors in the color scheme.

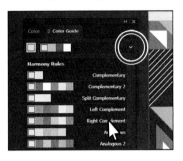 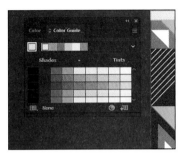

Applying colors from the Color Guide panel

▶ Tip: If you click the Save Color Group To Swatch Panel button () at the bottom of the Color Guide panel, the top colors in the Color Group panel are saved in the Swatches panel as a group.

After creating colors with the Color Guide panel, you can either click a color in the Color Guide panel to apply it to selected artwork or apply colors you saved in the Swatches panel as a color group. Next, you'll apply a color from the Color Guide panel to the tea label for the packaging.

1 Select one of the bright green shapes in the tea label artwork.

2 To select all of the shapes with the same fill, choose Select > Same > Fill Color.

3 Select a pink color in the Color Guide panel to apply it.

After selecting a color, it becomes the base color.

4 Click the base color (see the figure). The colors in the panel are now based on that new color, using the Right Complement rule you set previously.

Using this method, you could continually explore different colors based on the current color.

5 Close the Color Guide panel group.

6 Choose File > Save.

Using Recolor Artwork to edit colors in artwork

Updating a series of colors in artwork one at a time may take too long, but using Recolor Artwork you can manually edit colors, sample colors from other artwork or an image, change the number of colors, map an existing color to a new color, and do much more. Next, you'll open a new document and get it ready.

Recoloring artwork

With the document open you can now recolor artwork using the Recolor Artwork dialog box.

1   Choose 4 Tea - Recolor 2 from the Artboard Navigation menu in the lower-left corner of the Document window.

2   To select the entire tea package label, choose Select > All On Active Artboard.

3   Click the Recolor button in the Task bar below (or above) the artwork, to open the Recolor Artwork dialog box.

Note: If you don't see the Recolor button in the Task bar, you can click the Recolor button in the Properties panel.

The options in the Recolor Artwork dialog box allow you to edit, sample, or reduce the colors in your selected artwork and to save colors you create in groups.

Tip: If you need to move the Recolor dialog box, you can drag it by the top.

You'll see a big color wheel in the middle of the dialog box. The colors in the selected tea label artwork are each represented on the color wheel as circles, called *handles*. You can edit the colors individually or together visually by dragging, or precisely by double-clicking a handle and entering specific color values in the Color Picker dialog box.

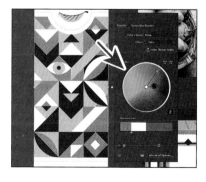

Note: The Recolor Artwork dialog box will close if you click away from the selected artwork.

You can choose colors from a color library to change the number of colors in the selected artwork—maybe to make the artwork a single color with tints of that color applied.

4 Make sure that the Link Harmony Colors icon is *disabled* so you can edit colors independently. The Link Harmony Colors icon should look like this: 🔓, not like this: 🔒.

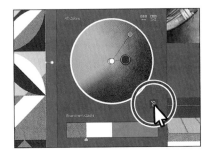

The lines between the color handles (circles) and the center of the color wheel are now dotted, telling you that you can edit them independently. If the Link Harmony Colors option were on and you edited one of the colors, the rest would change relative to your edited color.

Tip: Know that if you make a mistake when editing the colors and want to start over, you can click the Reset button in the upper-right corner of the dialog box to reset the colors to their original values.

5 Drag the largest *dark* brown handle (circle) to change the color.

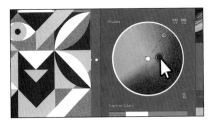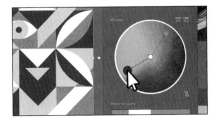

The largest handle (circle) indicates the base color. If you were to pick a color harmony, like in the Color Guide panel as you did previously, the base color is what the resulting colors would be based on. You can set a color harmony after clicking the Advanced Options button at the bottom of the Recolor Artwork dialog box.

6 Double-click that same handle (circle) to open the Color Picker. Change the color to something else, like a blue. Click OK.

After clicking OK, notice that the handle has moved in the color wheel, and it's the only one that moved. That's because you unlinked the harmony colors before you started editing the color.

Sampling color in Recolor Artwork

Next, you'll see how to use Recolor Artwork to sample color from an image and vector artwork to apply that color to the tea label.

1 Click the Color Theme Picker button in the Recolor Artwork dialog box. The pointer becomes an eyedropper (![eyedropper]) that you can then click to sample color from a single raster image or vector art, for instance. You may want to drag the dialog box by the top so you can see the image of fruit and the shop artwork. Click in the image of the fruit to sample the colors from the entire image and apply them to the artwork.

2 Click the shop artwork below the fruit image to sample the colors and apply them to the tea label.

If you click a single vector object, like a shape, the color is sampled from that single object. If you click a group of objects, like the shop artwork, the color is sampled from all the objects within the group. With vector artwork that you sample color from, you can also select part of the artwork to sample color from. You don't need to switch tools; simply drag a selection around the artwork to sample color within the selected area.

3 Drag around a smaller area of the shop artwork to sample just those colors within the selection.

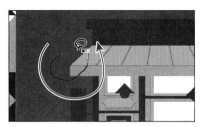

Depending on what color objects were within the selection area, your tea label may look different, and that's okay.

To ensure that we all see the same colors in the tea label art going forward, next you'll click to sample the color from the shop artwork again.

4 Click the shop artwork again to sample the colors and apply them to the tea label.

5 Click the Show Saturation And Hue On Color Wheel button toward the bottom to see brightness and hue on the color wheel (circled in the following figure).

6 Drag the slider to the right to adjust the overall saturation. When you release it, the colors will change.

The colors in the tea label are also shown in the Prominent Colors section below the color wheel. The size of the color areas in that bar is meant to give you an idea of how much area each color occupies in the artwork. In this case, the aqua color is a bit more prominent, so it shows as larger in the Prominent Colors section.

As a last step, you'll save the colors as a group in the Swatches panel.

7 Click the folder icon (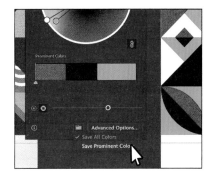) at the
bottom of the panel and choose
Save Prominent Colors to save the
prominent colors as a group in the
Swatches panel.

If the Swatches panel opens, you can
close it.

8 Choose Select > Deselect, and then
choose File > Save.

Making color variations with sample prompts using Generative Recolor

In the Recolor Artwork dialog box, there is a feature called Generative Recolor.
Generative Recolor is part of a suite of AI-powered capabilities powered by Adobe
Firefly (firefly.adobe.com). You can recolor artwork using text prompts to achieve
quick color variations with it.

Let's experiment with Generative Recolor; then, you can explore on your own!

1 To select the entire same tea package label again, choose Select > All On
Active Artboard.

2 Click the Recolor button in the Task bar below the artwork or in the Properties
panel to open the Recolor Artwork dialog box.

3 Select the Generative Recolor option at
the top of the dialog box.

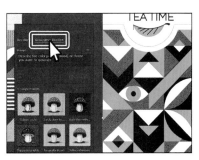

With Generative Recolor, you can
either try one of the sample prompts
to generate color variations of your
artwork or enter your custom prompt
to see color variations.

4 Select one of the sample prompts in
the dialog box. I chose the prompt
"Dark blue midnight."

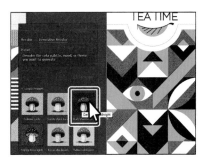

Color variations of your selected
artwork are showing in the panel.

⬤ **Note:** You may see a dialog box if you are using
the Generative Recolor option for the first time. Click
Agree, if that is the case.

5 Click one of the variation thumbnails to apply it to your tea packaging artwork.

Let's say you don't like what was generated. You can always ask Illustrator to generate more variations.

6 Click Generate to try again.

More variations are made and shown in the dialog box. You can either select one to apply the color to your artwork, generate more variations, or create a custom prompt, which is what you'll do next.

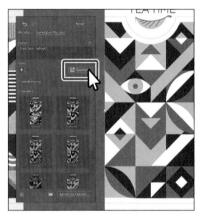

Making color variations with custom prompts using Generative Recolor

You'll add a custom prompt to make some color variations this time. Crafting your text prompts is a bit of an art form.

Let's try our hand at writing an effective text prompt. For this example, the tea brand wants to go with vibrant pinks and purples and a color palette closer to a carnival theme.

1 In the Generative Recolor dialog box, type **vibrant pink purple neon carnival** in the Prompt field.

2 Click Generate.

A selection of variations is made. If you don't like any of them, you can click Generate again and select one you like!

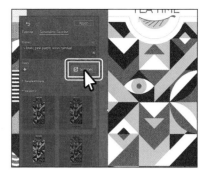

3 Click a variation thumbnail you would like to apply to the tea label.

Here's a tip for you. You aren't stuck with what it makes for you. Think about the previous sections, where you explored the Recolor options! You can click the Recolor option at the top of the dialog box and continue exploring color by editing the number of colors, the colors together, and each color independently.

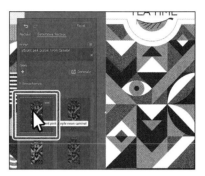

Working with Live Paint

Live Paint lets you paint vector graphics intuitively by automatically detecting and correcting gaps that might otherwise affect the application of fills and strokes. Painting objects with Live Paint is like coloring in a coloring book or using watercolors to paint a sketch. The underlying shapes are not edited.

Note: To learn more about Live Paint and all that it can do, search for "Live Paint groups" in Illustrator Help (Help > Illustrator Help).

Creating a Live Paint group

To start, you'll turn another tea label design into a Live Paint group so you can edit the colors using the Live Paint Bucket tool (⬧) .

1 Choose 5 Tea - Live Paint from the Artboard Navigation menu in the lower-left corner of the Document window.

2 Select the Selection tool (▶), and double-click the coffee cup in the center of the artboard to enter Isolation mode for the group that it's in.

3 Select the Line Segment tool (✏) in the toolbar so you can draw a few lines.

4 Drag to make a line across the pink background shape, like you see in the figure.

5 Ensure that the Stroke and Fill color are both None (⊘) in the Properties panel.

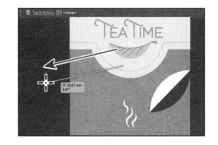

6 Now make another line below the coffee cup, starting where the leaves meet, down past the corner of the pink background. See the figure.

Right now, the lines aren't making a visual difference. But soon you'll be able to use them to define where a fill color ends.

7 Press the Escape key to exit Isolation mode.

8 Select the Selection tool and click the coffee cup to select the group again.

▶ **Tip:** You can convert selected artwork to a Live Paint group by clicking it with the Live Paint Bucket tool selected. You'll explore the Live Paint Bucket tool next.

9 With the group still selected, choose Object > Live Paint > Make.

The whole coffee cup group is now a Live Paint object. You can now see that the points on the bounding box have changed (⊞). One of them is circled in the figure.

Painting with the Live Paint Bucket tool

With objects converted to a Live Paint group, you can paint them with the Live Paint Bucket tool using several methods, which is what you'll do next.

1 Choose Window > Toolbars > Advanced.

2 Press and hold on the Shape Builder tool (🔍) in the toolbar, and select the Live Paint Bucket tool (🪣) from the menu.

3 Open the Swatches panel by choosing Window > Swatches.

You don't have to have the Swatches panel open when working with the Live Paint Bucket tool. You can just select a color from the Fill color box in the Properties panel. It helps to have the Swatches panel open so you can understand how color selection works with the tool.

4 Select the swatch you made earlier named "Pink" in the Swatches panel.

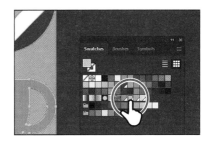

5 Move the pointer into an empty area of the artboard to see the three little swatches above the pointer.

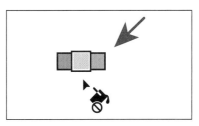

The three colors above the pointer represent the selected color (the middle, Pink color), the color before it in the color group (the Light Green), and the color after it in the group (the Pale Green).

6 Move the pointer into the area above the coffee cup, shown in the figure. *Can you see the red outline?* That shows you the edges where the color will fill up to.

7 Click to apply the color to the area.

You just filled a *face*, which is an enclosed area. The color fills the area you click up to the path edges it finds.

8 Click to apply the color to the areas shown in the figure.

You can select another color to paint with from the Swatches panel, or you can work faster and switch to another color using the arrow keys.

9 Close the Swatches panel.

Modifying a Live Paint group

When you make a Live Paint group, each path remains editable. When you move or adjust a path, the colors that were previously applied don't just stay where they were, as they do in natural media paintings or with image-editing software. Instead, the colors are automatically reapplied to the new regions that are formed by the intersecting paths. Next you'll edit a path in the same Live Paint group.

> **Tip:** A Live Paint group is similar to a regular group of objects. The individual objects in the artwork are still accessible when you double-click to enter Isolation mode. When you enter Isolation mode, you can move, transform, add, or remove shapes as well.

1 Select the Direct Selection tool (⯆).

2 Choose View > Outline to see the outlines of the artwork.

3 Move the pointer over the end of the top path you drew and click to select the anchor point. See the figure.

4 Choose View > Preview to see the color of the artwork again.

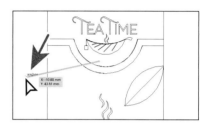

> **Note:** Can't see the line? Make sure Edges are showing (View > Show Edges).

5 Drag the selected anchor point to reshape the line.

This is the magic of Live Paint! The line position and shape determines where each fill is.

6 Choose Select > Deselect.

7 Choose Window > Toolbars > Basic to reset the toolbar.

8 Choose View > Fit All In Window to see everything you've done.

9 Choose File > Save and then choose File > Close as many times as necessary to close all open files.

Review questions

1 Describe what a global color is.

2 How can you save a color?

3 Describe what a tint is.

4 How can you choose color harmonies for color inspiration?

5 Name two things that the Recolor Artwork dialog box allows you to do.

6 Explain what Live Paint allows you to do.

Review answers

1 A global color is a color swatch that, when you edit it, automatically updates all artwork to which it is applied. All spot colors are global; however, process colors you save as swatches are global by default, but they can be either global or non-global.

2 You can save a color for painting other objects in your artwork by adding it to the Swatches panel by doing one of the following:

   • Drag the color from a Fill box, and drop it over the Swatches panel.

   • Click the New Swatch button (▣) at the bottom of the Swatches panel.

   • Choose New Swatch from the Swatches panel menu (▤).

   • Choose Create New Swatch from the Color panel menu (▤).

3 A *tint* is a lighter version of a color. You can create a tint from a global process color, like CMYK, or from a spot color.

4 You can choose color harmonies from the Color Guide panel. Color harmonies are used to generate a color scheme based on a single color.

5 You use the Recolor Artwork dialog box to change the colors used in selected artwork, create and edit color groups, reassign or reduce the colors in your artwork, and quickly explore color combinations using Generative Recolor, among other functions.

6 Live Paint lets you paint vector graphics intuitively by automatically detecting and correcting gaps that might otherwise affect the application of fills and strokes. Paths divide the drawing surface into areas, any of which can be colored, regardless of whether the area is bounded by a single path or by segments of multiple paths. If you edit those paths, the color reflows to fill the new shape.

9 ADDING TYPE TO A PROJECT

Lesson overview

In this lesson, you'll learn how to do the following:

- Create and edit area and point type.
- Import and thread text.
- Change text formatting.
- Fix missing fonts. ■◀
- Work with glyphs. ■◀
- Vertically align area type.
- Snap to glyphs. ■◀
- Create columns of text.
- Create and edit paragraph styles.
- Create and edit character styles. ■◀
- Add bullet and number lists.
- Wrap type around an object.
- Curve text on a path.
- Reshape text with a warp.
- Create text outlines.
- Explore Retype (Beta).

 This lesson will take about 75 minutes to complete. To get the lesson files used in this lesson, download them from the web page for this book at *peachpit.com/IllustratorCIB2024*. For more information, see "Accessing the lesson files and Web Edition" in the Getting Started section at the beginning of this book.

Text is an important design element in your illustrations. Like other objects, type can be painted, scaled, rotated, and more. In this lesson, you'll create basic text and add interesting text effects.

Starting the lesson

You'll be adding type to three projects during this lesson, but before you begin, you'll restore the default preferences for Adobe Illustrator. Then you'll open the finished art file for this lesson to see the illustration.

Note: If you have not already downloaded the project files for this lesson to your computer from your Account page, make sure to do so now. See the "Getting Started" section at the beginning of the book.

1   To ensure that the tools function and the defaults are set exactly as described in this lesson, delete or deactivate (by renaming) the Adobe Illustrator preferences file. See "Restoring default preferences" in the "Getting Started" section at the beginning of the book.

2   Start Adobe Illustrator.

3   Choose File > Open. Locate the file named L9_end.ai in the Lessons > Lesson09 folder. Click Open.

You will most likely see a Missing Fonts dialog box, since the file is using specific Adobe Fonts. *Do not activate the fonts.* Simply click Close in the Missing Fonts dialog box. You will learn all about Adobe Fonts later in this lesson.

Leave the file open for reference later in the lesson, if you like. I closed it.

4   Choose File > Open. In the Open dialog box, navigate to the Lessons > Lesson09 folder, and select the L9_start.ai file on your hard disk. Click Open to open the file.

You'll add text and formatting to complete a flyer and recipe card.

5   Choose File > Save As. If the Cloud Document dialog box opens, click Save On Your Computer.

6   In the Save As dialog box, navigate to the Lesson09 folder, and name the file **Recipes.ai**. Leave Adobe Illustrator (ai) chosen from the Format menu (macOS) or Adobe Illustrator (*.AI) chosen from the Save As Type menu (Windows), and click Save.

Note: If you don't see Reset Essentials in the Workspace menu, choose Window > Workspace > Essentials before choosing Window > Workspace > Reset Essentials.

7   In the Illustrator Options dialog box, leave the Illustrator options at their default settings, and then click OK.

8   Choose Window > Workspace > Reset Essentials.

Adding text

Type features are some of the most powerful in Illustrator. As in Adobe InDesign, you can create columns and rows of text, place text, flow text into a shape or along a path, work with letterforms as graphic objects, and more.

In Illustrator, you can create text in three main ways: point type, area type, and type on a path.

Adding text at a point

Point type is a horizontal or vertical line of text that begins where you click and expands as you enter characters. Entering text this way is perfect for small amounts of text, like a headline or button text. To start, you'll add a heading using point type.

1 Choose 1 Flyer from the Artboard Navigation menu below the document, if it's not already selected.

2 Zoom in to the top of the artboard.

   You will add some text above the cooking pot artwork.

3 Select the Type tool (**T**) in the toolbar on the left. Click (*don't drag*) toward the top of the artboard. Type **Learn to cook!** (*with* the exclamation point).

   The "Lorem ipsum" text you saw is just placeholder text that you can replace.

4 Press the Escape key to select the Selection tool (▶).

   When the cursor is in text, this is a fast way to get to the Selection tool so you can move or resize the text.

5 Zoom in to the text by pressing Command and + (macOS) or Ctrl and + (Windows). Don't zoom in too far, because you will make the text larger in the next step.

6 Shift-drag the lower-right bounding point to make the text much larger.

 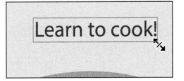

   If you scale point type without the Shift key held down, the text stretches when you resize it this way.

7 Practice by selecting the Type tool again and clicking to add more text below the text you just added. Type **with chef Hodgman**.

8 Select the Selection tool. Shift-drag a corner to make it about as wide as the other text you made.

 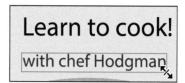

As you go through this chapter, you will refine the appearance of this text and get it into place.

Adding area type

Area type uses the edges of an object, like a rectangle, to control how text flows either horizontally or vertically. When text reaches an edge, it automatically wraps to fit inside the object. Entering text in this way is useful when you want to create one or more paragraphs, such as for a poster or a brochure.

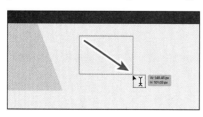

Text flowing within a frame.

To create area type with the Type tool (**T**), you drag where you want the text—which creates an area type object (also called a *type object, text box, text area*, or *text object*). Next, you'll create some area type and add a heading to the ad.

1 Choose 2 Recipe card from the Artboard Navigation menu below the document.

In the lesson, you will be moving between artboards a lot!

2 With the Type tool (**T**) selected, move the cursor to the right of the pink box at the top of the artboard. Press and drag to make a small area that is about 150 pixels in width and 100 pixels in height.

▶ **Tip:** Filling type objects with placeholder text is a preference you can change. Choose Illustrator > Settings (macOS) or Edit > Preferences (Windows), select the Type category, and deselect Fill New Type Objects With Placeholder Text to turn the option off.

By default, area type objects are filled with selected placeholder text that you can replace with your own.

3 Zoom in to the text by pressing Command and + (macOS) or Ctrl and + (Windows) a few times.

4 With the placeholder text selected, type **Avocado beet salad with citrus vinaigrette dressing**. *(Without the period!)*

Notice how the text wraps horizontally to fit within the type object.

5 Press the Escape key to select the Selection tool (▶). Drag the lower-right bounding point to the left and then back to the right to see how the text wraps within but doesn't resize.

You can drag any of the eight bounding points on the type object to resize it.

6 Drag the lower-right bounding point to make the type object shorter so that you still see all of the text and it wraps as you see in the figure.

7 Double-click the text to switch to the Type tool.

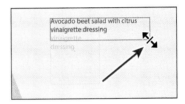

8 Put the cursor before the word "citrus" and press Shift+Return or Shift+Enter to break the line using a soft return.

Soft returns keep the lines of text a single paragraph rather than breaking it into two paragraphs. Later, when you apply paragraph formatting, this can make applying the formatting easier.

Converting between area type and point type

You can easily convert a text object from area type to point type and vice versa. This can be useful if you type a headline by clicking, which creates point type, but later want to resize and add more text without stretching the text inside.

Point type

Area type

Next, you will convert a type object from point type to area type.

1   Select the Hand tool (✋) and drag so you can see the upper-left corner of the artboard.

2   With the Type tool (T) selected, near the upper-left corner of the artboard, click to add some point type.

3   Type **Starters • Salads Recipe #1**

▶ **Tip:** To add the bullet, choose Type > Insert Special Character > Symbols > Bullet.

Notice that the text keeps going. We need to have the text wrap, so area type might be a better choice in this case.

4   Press the Escape key to select the Selection tool (▶).

▶ **Tip:** With a type object selected, you can also choose Type > Convert To Point Type or Convert To Area Type, depending on what the selected type object is.

5   Move the pointer over the annotator (—O) off the right edge of the type object. A hollow end on the annotator means it's point type. When the pointer changes (▶ₘ), double-click the annotator to convert the point type to area type.

The annotator end should now be filled (—●), indicating that it is area type.

6   Drag the lower-right bounding point to wrap the text within until it looks like the figure.

Area type auto sizing 🎬

To learn about setting text object auto-resize, check out the video *Area type auto sizing*, which you'll find in the Web Edition. For more information, see the "Web Edition" section of "Getting Started" at the beginning of the book.

Importing a plain-text file

You can import text into your Illustrator document from a text file created in another application. One of the advantages of importing text from a file, rather than copying and pasting it, is that imported text retains its character and paragraph formatting (by default). For example, text from an RTF file retains its font and style specifications in Illustrator, unless you remove formatting when you import the text.

In this section, you'll place text from a plain-text file into your design to get the bulk of the text for the flyer and recipe card in place.

1   Choose 1 Flyer from the Artboard Navigation menu below the Document window to switch to the flyer.

2   Zoom in to the aqua guide box at the bottom of the artboard. Make sure you can see the whole thing.

3   Choose Select > Deselect.

4   Choose File > Place. In the Place dialog box, navigate to the Lessons > Lesson09 folder, and select the L9_text.txt file.

5   Click Place.

In the Text Import Options dialog box that appears, you can set some options prior to importing text.

6   Leave the default settings, and click OK.

7   Move the loaded text icon into the lower-left part of the artboard, in the aqua box. Drag from the upper-left corner to make a text box. Use the figure as a guide.

▶ **Tip:** I made a rectangle and a few lines and converted them to guides by choosing View > Guides > Make Guides. This is useful for creating custom guides, for instance.

If you were to simply click with the loaded text pointer, a type object would be created that is smaller than the size of the artboard.

Threading text

When working with area type, each area type object has an *in port* and an *out port*. Those ports enable you to link type objects and flow text between them.

In port ———

 Out port

- An empty out port indicates that all the text is visible and that the type object isn't linked.

- An small arrow in a port indicates that the type object is linked to another type object.

- A red plus sign (⊞) in an out port indicates that the object contains additional text called *overflow text*. You can adjust the text, resize the type object, or thread the text to another type object to show all of the overflow text.

To *thread* or continue text from one object to the next, you have to link the objects. Linked type objects can be of any shape; however, the text must be entered in an object or along a path, not as point type (simply clicking to create text).

Next, you'll thread text between two type objects.

Note: If you double-click an out port, a new type object appears. If this happens, you can either drag the new object where you would like it to be positioned or choose Edit > Undo Link Threaded Text, and the loaded text icon will reappear.

1 With the Selection tool (▶) selected, click the out port (⊞) in the lower-right corner of the type object. The out port is most likely pretty small and zooming won't make it bigger.

2 Then, move the pointer away.

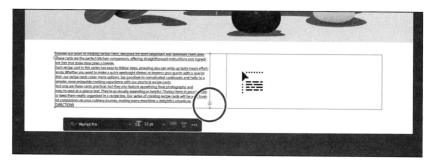

The pointer changes to a loaded text icon (⌷≣) when you move it away from the original type object.

3 Choose View > Fit All In Window.

4 Move the pointer to the upper-left corner of the aqua box on the recipe card on the right. Drag across the aqua box to make an area type object. Use the figure as a guide.

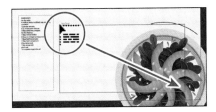 

With the second type object still selected, do you see a line connecting the two type objects? (An arrow is pointing to it in the figure.)

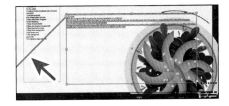

Tip: Another way to thread text between objects is to select an area type object, select the object (or objects) you want to link to, and then choose Type > Threaded Text > Create.

If you don't see this thread (line), choose View > Show Text Threads. This (non-printing) line is the *text thread* that tells you that the two objects are connected. The out port (▶) of the type object on the leftmost artboard and the in port (▶) of the type object on the top-right artboard contain small arrows indicating how the text is flowing from one to the other.

5 Click the placed text at the bottom of the flyer artboard on the left.

6 Zoom in to the text by pressing Command and + (macOS) or Ctrl and + (Windows) a few times.

7 Drag the right-middle point to the right to make it as wide as you see in the figure.

The text will flow between the type objects. If you were to delete the second type object, the text would be pulled back into the original object as overflow text. Although not visible, the overflow text isn't deleted.

After resizing your text area, you may see more or less text on the recipe card artboard on the right, and that's okay.

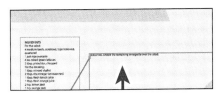

8 Choose File > Save.

Formatting type

You can format text in a lot of creative ways. You can apply formatting to one character, a range of characters, or all characters. As you'll soon see, selecting the type object, rather than selecting the text inside, lets you apply formatting options to all of the text in the object, including options from the Character and Paragraph panels, fill and stroke attributes, and transparency settings.

In this section, you'll discover how to change text attributes, such as size and font, and later learn how to save that formatting as text styles.

Changing font family and font style

In this section, you'll apply a font to text. In addition to local fonts, Creative Cloud members have access to a library of fonts for use in desktop applications such as InDesign or Microsoft Word and on websites. Trial Creative Cloud members can also access select fonts from Adobe. Fonts you choose are activated and appear alongside other locally installed fonts in the fonts list in Illustrator. By default, Adobe Fonts are turned on in the Creative Cloud desktop application to activate fonts and make them available in your desktop applications.

● **Note:** The Creative Cloud desktop application must be installed on your computer, and you must have an internet connection to initially activate fonts. The Creative Cloud desktop application is installed when you install your first Creative Cloud application, like Illustrator.

Activating Adobe Fonts

Next, you'll select and activate Adobe Fonts so that you can use them in your project.

● **Note:** To learn about the Creative Cloud desktop application, visit *adobe.com/ creativecloud/ desktop-app.html.*

1 Ensure that the Creative Cloud desktop application has been launched and you are signed in with your Adobe ID (this requires an internet connection).

2 Select the Type tool (**T**), and click in the text at the bottom of the flyer artboard on the left.

3 Choose Select > All or press Command+A (macOS) or Ctrl+A (Windows) to select all of the text in both threaded type objects.

4 In the Properties panel, click the arrow to the right of the Font Family menu (where you see Myriad Pro), and notice the fonts that appear in the menu.

The fonts you see by default are those that are installed locally. In the font menu, an icon appears to the right of the font names in the list, indicating what type of font it is. For some examples: $\circlearrowleft$ is an activated Adobe Font, O is OpenType, $\boxed{\scriptstyle{VAR}}$ is a variable font, $\boxed{\scriptstyle{SVG}}$ is an SVG font, and Π is TrueType.

5 Click Find More to see a list of Adobe Fonts you can choose from.

The menu content may take a few seconds to initialize. My list will look different from yours, since Adobe is constantly updating the font selections.

6 Click the Filter Fonts icon (▼▾) to open a menu. You can filter the font list by selecting classification and property criteria. Click the Sans Serif option under Classification to filter the fonts.

7 Scroll down in the font list to find Oswald.

8 Click the arrow to the left of Oswald, if necessary, to see the font styles.

▶ **Tip:** The fonts are activated on all computers where you've installed the Creative Cloud application and logged in. To view fonts you've activated, open the Creative Cloud desktop application and click the Fonts icon (f) in the upper right.

9 Click the Activate icon (△) to the far right of the name Oswald SemiBold.

If you see $\circlearrowleft$ or, when the pointer is over the font name in the list, $\leftslice$, then the font is already activated, so you don't need to do anything.

10 Click OK in the dialog box that appears.

11 Click the Activate button (△) to the far right of the following names: Oswald Medium, Oswald Regular, and Oswald Light. Make sure to click OK in the dialog box that appears each time.

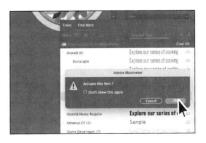

Once the fonts are activated (be patient; it may take some time), you may begin to use them.

12 After activating the fonts, click the words "Clear All" toward the top of the menu to remove the Sans Serif filtering and see all of the fonts again.

Applying fonts to text in Illustrator

Now that the Adobe Fonts are activated, you can use them in any application. Next, you'll apply the fonts to text.

1 With the threaded text still selected and the Font Family menu still showing, click the Show Activated Fonts button (![icon]) to filter the font list and show only activated Adobe Fonts.

The list in the figure may be different than yours, and that's okay as long as you see the Oswald fonts.

2 Move the pointer over the fonts in the menu. You should see a preview of the font the pointer is over, which is applied to the selected text.

3 Click the arrow to the left of Oswald in the menu, and choose Light (or simply choose Oswald Light).

4 Zoom out so you can see the flyer and the recipe card to the right of the flyer.

5 With the Selection tool (![icon]) selected, click the "Learn to cook" text and Shift-click the "with chef Hodgman" text to select both.

If you want to apply the same font to all of the text in a point type or area type object, you can simply select the object, not the text, and then apply the font.

6 With the type objects selected, click the font name in the Properties panel (I see Myriad Pro). Begin typing the letters **os** (you may need to type more of the word "Oswald").

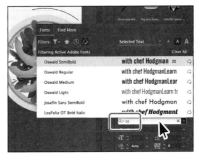

Tip: With the cursor in the Font Name field, you can also click the X on the right side of the Font Family field to clear the search field.

A menu appears above or below where you are typing. Illustrator filters through the list of fonts and displays the font names that contain "os," regardless of where "os" is in the font name and regardless of whether it's capitalized. The Show Activated Fonts (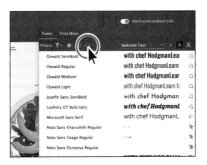) filter is still turned on from before, so you'll turn it off next.

7 Click Clear Filter (⊘) in the menu that is showing to see all of the available fonts.

8 In the menu that appears beneath where you are typing, move the pointer over the fonts in the list (my list will be different from yours because of the other fonts I already had activated). Illustrator shows a live font preview of the text.

9 Click to select Oswald Medium to apply the font.

10 Click the "Avocado Beet Salad with Citrus Vinaigrette Dressing" text on the recipe card. Shift-click the "Starters • Salads Recipe #1" text.

11 Click the font name in the Properties panel and type the letters **os** (for Oswald). Select the Oswald SemiBold font to apply it.

Fixing missing fonts ▶️

To learn how to fix missing fonts, check out the video *Fixing missing fonts,* which is part of the Web Edition. For more information, see the "Web Edition" section of "Getting Started" at the beginning of the book.

Changing font size

By default, typeface size is measured in points (a point equals 1/72 of an inch). In this section, you will change the font size of text and also see what happens to point type that is scaled.

1 With the Selection tool, click to select the "with chef Hodgman" text on the flyer artboard on the left.

Looking in the Task bar below the text, you'll see that the font size may not be a whole number. That's because you scaled the point type earlier by dragging. The number you see will be different, and that's okay.

2 Choose 72 pt from the Font Size menu in the Task bar.

Time for some practice!

3 Click the "Learn to cook!" text above the "with chef Hodgman" text.

4 Select the Text Size value in the Task bar, type in **165**, and press Return or Enter.

5 Click in the "Avocado beet salad..." text on the recipe card artboard, and practice by changing the font size to **48 pt**.

6 If the text disappears, it's too big to fit in the text box. Drag a corner until you can see the text.

7 Click the "Starters • Salads Recipe #1" to the left of the selected text, and change the font size to **24 pt**.

8 Again, if the text disappears, drag a corner until you can see the text.

Changing the color of text

You can change the appearance of text by applying fills, strokes, and more. In this section, you'll change the fill of selected text by selecting type objects—which means all of the text in the object will be the same color. If you select text with the Type tool, you can apply different color fills and strokes to text within the text object.

1 With the Selection tool (▶) selected, click the "Learn to cook!" text and Shift-click the "Avocado beet salad..." text to select both.

2 Click the Fill color box in the Properties panel. With the Swatches option (⊞) selected in the panel that appears, select the Purple swatch.

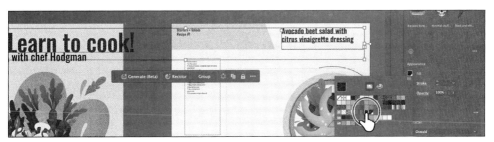

3 Click the text "with chef Hodgman" and Shift-click the "Starters • Salads Recipe #1" text to select both.

4 Click the Fill color box in the Properties panel. Select the swatch named Deep Pink.

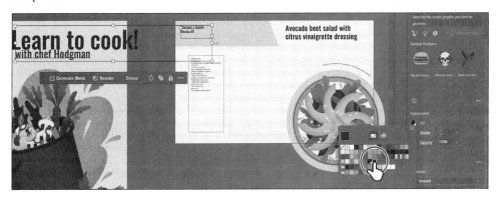

5 Choose Select > Deselect, and then choose File > Save.

Changing additional character formatting

In Illustrator, you can change a lot of text formatting besides font, font size, and color. As in InDesign or Microsoft Word, text attributes are split between character and paragraph formatting and can be found in the Properties panel, the Control panel, and two main panels: the Character panel and the Paragraph panel.

The Character panel, which you can access by clicking More Options () in the Character section of the Properties panel or by choosing Window > Type > Character, contains the formatting for selected text such as font, font size, kerning, and more. In this section, you will apply a few of the many possible attributes to experiment with the different ways you can format text.

▶ **Tip:** By default, text is set to a value called Auto for leading. When looking at the Leading value in the Properties panel, you can tell it's set to Auto if the value has parentheses around it, (). To return the leading to the default auto value, choose Auto from the Leading menu.

1   With the Selection tool (▶) selected, click the "Avocado beet salad..." heading on the recipe card artboard on the right.

2   Choose Type > Change Case > Title Case.

3   In the Properties panel, change Leading (▦) to 52 pt by selecting the value and typing **52** (or you can change to a similar value that looks good). Press Return or Enter to accept the value. Leave the text selected.

Leading is the vertical space between lines of text. Adjusting the leading can be useful for fitting text into a type object. Now, you'll make all of the headings capital letters.

4   Select the Type tool and select the word "With" and change it to lowercase "with."

5   With the Selection tool (▶) selected, select the "Learn to cook!" text and Shift-click the "with chef Hodgman" text to select both.

6   With the text selected, click More Options () (circled in the following figure) in the Character section of the Properties panel to show the Character panel. Click the All Caps button (TT) to capitalize the headings.

One of the benefits of point type versus area type is that no matter what formatting you throw at point type text, the box around it will always resize to show the text.

Changing paragraph formatting

As with character formatting, you can set paragraph formatting, such as alignment or indenting, before adding new text or changing the existing text appearance. Paragraph formatting applies to entire paragraphs rather than just selected content and can be found in the Properties panel, Control panel, or Paragraph panel.

1 With the Type tool (**T**) selected, click in the threaded text in the artboard on the left.

2 Press Command+A (macOS) or Ctrl+A (Windows) to select all of the text between the two type objects.

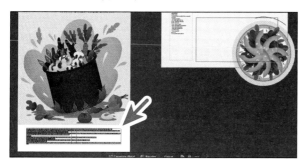

3 With the text selected, click More Options (•••) in the Paragraph section of the Properties panel to show the Paragraph panel options.

4 Change Space After Paragraph (⊞) to **10 pt** in the Paragraph panel.

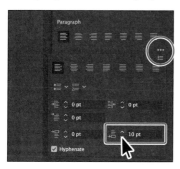
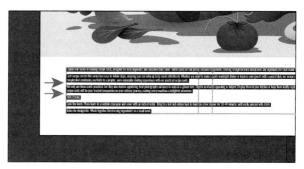

Setting a spacing value after paragraphs, rather than pressing the Return or Enter key, helps you maintain consistency and makes editing easier.

5 Select the Selection tool, click the "Learn to cook!" text, and then Shift-click the "with chef Hodgman" text to select both.

6 To center align the text, click Align Center in the Paragraph section of the Properties panel.

7 Choose Select > Deselect, and then choose File > Save.

Working with glyphs

To learn about working with the Glyphs panel, check out the video *Working with the Glyphs panel*, which you'll find in the Web Edition. For more information, see the "Web Edition" section of "Getting Started" at the beginning of the book.

Vertically aligning area type

You can align or distribute lines of text in a frame vertically or horizontally when using vertical type. You can align text to the frame's top, center, or bottom using each paragraph's leading and paragraph spacing values. You can also justify text vertically, evenly spacing lines regardless of their leading and paragraph spacing values. Here are the different types of vertical alignment you can apply to text:

Align top   Align center   Align bottom   Vertically Justify

Next, you'll vertically align one of the headings to more easily align between the bottom of the text and the bottom of a shape.

Note: You can also access the vertical text align options in the Area Type Options dialog box (Type > Area Type Options).

1 With the Selection tool (▶) selected, click the "Avocado beet salad..." heading on the recipe card artboard on the right.

2 Zoom in to the text by pressing Command and + (macOS) or Ctrl and + (Windows) a few times.

3 In the Area Type section of the Properties panel, click Align Bottom to align the text to the bottom of the text area.

4 Drag the text area so the bottom of the text box looks aligned with the bottom of the pink shape to the left of it.

Using glyph snapping ▰◀

To learn about glyph snapping, check out the video *Working with glyph snapping*, which you'll find in the Web Edition. For more information, see the "Web Edition" section of "Getting Started" at the beginning of the book.

Resizing and reshaping type objects

You can create unique type object shapes by reshaping them using a variety of methods, including adding columns to area type objects or reshaping type objects using the Direct Selection tool. To start this section, you'll place some more text on artboard 1 so you have more text to work with.

Creating columns of text

You can easily create columns and rows of text by using the Type > Area Type Options command. This can be useful for creating a single type object with multiple columns or for organizing text, such as a table or simple chart, for instance. Next, you'll add a few columns to a type object.

> Our home repair expertise makes your fix-it project simpler and faster. From old home restorations to new builds, we have the know-how to fill in the blanks on what
>
> you need and how to get it done. With our network of qualified specialists, we can also refer you to home repair technicians who can complete the parts of the process you'd

Area type with columns

1 Choose 1 Flyer from the Artboard Navigation menu below the document, if not already selected.

2 Choose View > Fit Artboard In Window.

3 With the Selection tool (▶) selected, click the text at the bottom of the artboard.

4 Zoom in to the text by pressing Command and + (macOS) or Ctrl and + (Windows) a few times.

> ▶ **Tip:** You will also see the Vertical option for vertically aligning text that you explored earlier in the lesson.

5   Choose Type > Area Type Options. In the Area Type Options dialog box, change Number to **2** in the Columns section, and change Gutter to **54 px**. Select Preview to see the change, and then click OK.

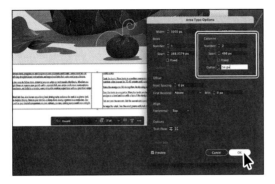

The text box is now split into two columns. There may not be enough text to flow into the recipe card artboard to the right. You'll fix that later.

Reshaping type objects

In this section, you'll reshape and resize a type object to better fit text.

1   With the Selection tool (▶) selected, click the "Avocado beet salad..." heading on the recipe card artboard on the right.

2   Press Command and + (macOS) or Ctrl and + (Windows) several times to zoom in to the text.

3   Select the Direct Selection tool (▷). Click and release on the upper-left corner of the type object to select the anchor point.

4   Drag that point to the left to adjust the shape of the path so the text follows the contour of the pink shape to its left.

5   Select the Selection tool and drag the text closer to the pink shape, if necessary.

Creating and applying text styles

Text styles allow you to save text formatting to apply it consistently and to be updated globally. Once a style is created, you only need to edit the saved style, and then all text formatted with that style is updated. Illustrator has two types of text styles.

- **Paragraph**—Retains character and paragraph attributes and applies them to an entire paragraph.

- **Character**—Retains character attributes and applies them to selected text.

Creating and applying a paragraph style

You'll start by creating a paragraph style for the body copy.

1 Navigate to the flyer artboard on the left.

2 Double-click in the paragraphs of text at the bottom to switch to the Type tool and insert the cursor.

3 Choose Window > Type > Paragraph Styles, and click the Create New Style button (▣) at the bottom of the Paragraph Styles panel.

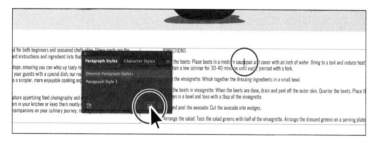

A new paragraph style appears in the panel and is called Paragraph Style 1. To create a paragraph style from text, you don't have to select the text. You can insert the cursor in the text when making a paragraph style. The text formatting attributes are saved from the paragraph that the cursor is in.

4 Double-click the style name Paragraph Style 1 in the list of styles. Change the name of the style to **Body**, and press Return or Enter to confirm the name inline.

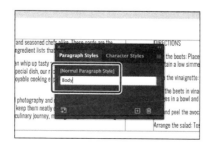

By double-clicking the style to edit the name, you apply the new style to the paragraph (where the cursor is). This means that if you edit the formatting for the Body paragraph style, only this paragraph will update.

Now you'll apply the style to all of the text in the threaded frames.

5 With the cursor in the paragraph text, choose Select > All to select it all.

6 Click the Body style in the Paragraph Styles panel to apply the formatting.

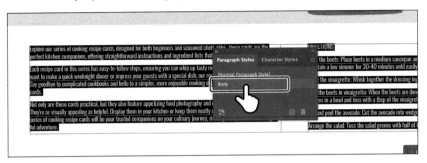

Sampling text formatting

Using the Eyedropper tool (✐), you can quickly sample type attributes from text and apply those attributes to other text.

1 Choose 2 Recipe Card from the Artboard Navigation menu below the document.

● **Note:** Your text may be a different size than the figure. That's okay because you're about to change it!

2 With the Type tool (T) selected, select the text "INGREDIENTS" at the top of the text column on the left. See the following figure.

3 To sample and apply formatting from other text, select the Eyedropper tool (✐) in the toolbar.

4 Click in the "Starters • Salads Recipe #1" text above it to apply the same formatting to the selected text.

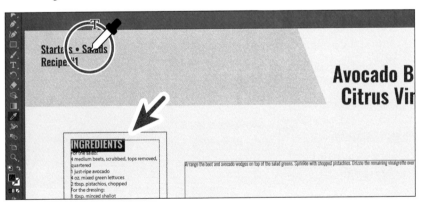

5 Leave the "INGREDIENTS" text selected.

6 Choose File > Save.

Practicing paragraph styles

With one paragraph style made, you'll practice by creating another for a few of the headlines in the document.

1   With the "INGREDIENTS" text still selected, to make a new paragraph style, click the Create New Style button (■) at the bottom of the Paragraph Styles panel.

Note: If you see the overset text icon (⊞) in the out port of the type object, with the Selection tool selected, drag the corner to make it larger so you can see all of the text.

2   Double-click the new style name Paragraph Style 2 (or whatever the name you see is) in the list of styles. Change the name of the style to **Subheading**, and press Return or Enter to change the name.

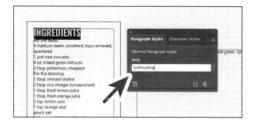

3   With the Type tool (T) selected, in the flyer artboard on the left, select the text "DIRECTIONS" in the threaded text at the bottom.

4   Click the Subheading style in the Paragraph Styles panel to apply the style to the text.

The Subheading formatting will override the Body style formatting.

Editing a paragraph style

After creating a paragraph style, you can easily edit the style formatting. Then anywhere the style has been applied, the formatting will be updated automatically. Next, you'll edit the Body style to see firsthand why paragraph styles can save you time and maintain consistency.

Tip: There are many more options for working with paragraph styles, most of which are found in the Paragraph Styles panel menu, including duplicating, deleting, and editing paragraph styles. To learn more about these options, search for "paragraph styles" in Illustrator Help (Help > Illustrator Help).

1   Click in any of the paragraphs of text with the Body style applied on either artboard to insert the cursor.

2   To edit the Body style, double-click to the *right* of the style named Body in the Paragraph Styles panel list (otherwise you will just edit the name inline).

3   In the Paragraph Style Options dialog box, select the Basic Character Formats category on the left side of the dialog box.

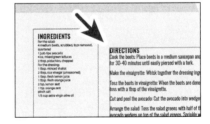

4   Change the Size to **19 pt**.

5   In the dialog box, select the Indents And Spacing category on the left side of the dialog box, and change the Space After Paragraph ( ) to **14 pt**.

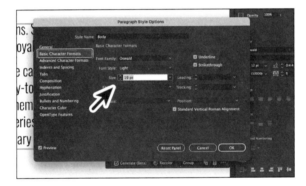

Since Preview is selected by default, you can move the dialog box out of the way to see the text change everywhere the Body style is applied.

6   Click OK.

7   Zoom out to see the flyer and recipe card artboards.

Tip: If the "DIRECTIONS" text is in the text area on the flyer artboard (the artboard on the left) and you want to push it to the next column, you can also insert the cursor before "DIRECTIONS" and press Return or Enter until it is there.

We want the "DIRECTIONS" heading to be at the top of the text on the recipe card artboard on the right. If it is not, you can make the text area at the bottom of the flyer artboard shorter to push the "DIRECTIONS" heading over to the other artboard.

Working with character styles ▇◢

To learn about working with the character styles, check out the video *Working with character styles*, which you'll find in the Web Edition. For more information, see the "Web Edition" section of "Getting Started" at the beginning of the book.

Creating text lists

In Illustrator you can add bullet and number lists to your text easily. They work just as they do in other apps in which you can add bullets—click a button and they're applied! There are some options, like appearances and sublists, so let's get to it and add a list to our recipe card.

Applying text lists

1 Zoom in to the recipe card artboard to the right of the flyer.

2 With the Type tool (**T**) selected, select *all* of the text below the "INGREDIENTS" heading in the left column.

3 Select the Body style from the Paragraph Styles panel to apply the formatting.

4 With the text selected, click More Options (**⋯**) in the Paragraph section of the Properties panel to show the Paragraph panel options.

5 Change Space After Paragraph (▦) to **4 pt** in the Paragraph panel.

6 In the Properties panel, click the Bullets button (▤▾) to convert the text in the box to a bullet list.

▷ **Tip:** To remove the bullet list, you could click the same Bullets button in the Properties panel!

Editing text lists

Now let's set up a few options for the list.

1 Click the arrow to the right of the Bullets button (▤▾). Try selecting a different bullet appearance.

▷ **Tip:** The None option (looks like a red slash, /) removes the bullets, but the text is still a bullet list.

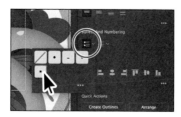

2 Drag across "4 medium beets…" and "2 tbsp. pistachios, chopped" to select all of the paragraphs between.

3 Click the arrow to the right of the Bullets button (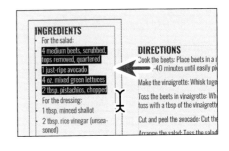). Click more options (•••) in the menu to open the Bullets And Numbering dialog box.

4 In the Bullets And Numbering dialog box, change Level to **2** and try a different bullet appearance. Click OK.

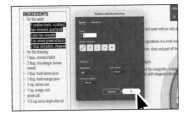

▷ **Tip:** To work smarter, you could save the level 2 bullet list as a paragraph style or sample the formatting using the Eyedropper tool!

5 Do the same for all of the text after "For the dressing:" Select all of that text, and change the bullet list level to 2, following the previous few steps.

6 Choose Select > Deselect and then File > Save.

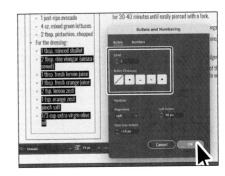

Wrapping text

In Illustrator, you can wrap text around objects, such as imported images and vector artwork, to avoid text running over those objects or to create interesting design effects.

Next, you'll wrap text around artwork. In Illustrator, as in InDesign, you apply text wrap to the content that the text will wrap around.

Text wrapping around a logo.

1 Choose View > Fit Artboard In Window to fit the recipe card in the window.

2 Select the Selection tool (▶), and click the avocado salad graphic in the lower-right corner of the artboard.

Text wrap needs to be applied to the object(s) that the text will wrap around.

3 Choose Object > Text Wrap > Make. Click OK if a dialog box appears.

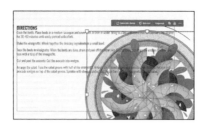

To wrap text around an object, that object must be in the same layer as the text that will wrap around it, and the object must also be located above the text in the layer hierarchy.

4 With the artwork selected, click the Arrange button in the Properties panel, and choose Bring To Front.

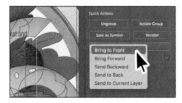 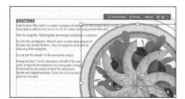

The salad artwork should now be on top of the text in the stacking order, and the text should be wrapping around it.

5 Choose Object > Text Wrap > Text Wrap Options. In the Text Wrap Options dialog box, change Offset to **30 pt**, and select Preview to see the change. Click OK.

▶ **Tip:** Try dragging the selected artwork to see how the text flows.

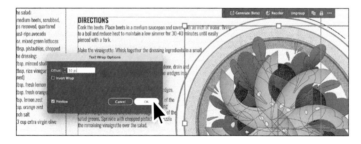

Curving text on a path

In addition to having text in point and type objects, you can have type along a path. Text can flow along the edge of an open or closed path and can lead to some uniquely creative ways to display text. In this section, you'll add text to an open path.

Text on a path.

1 With the Selection tool (▶), select the black curved path above the avocado salad graphic you just applied text wrap to.

2 Press Command and + (macOS) or Ctrl and + (Windows) a few times to zoom in.

3 Select the Type tool (T), and move the cursor over the left end of the black path to see an insertion point with an intersecting wavy path (⌶) (see the figure). Click when this cursor appears.

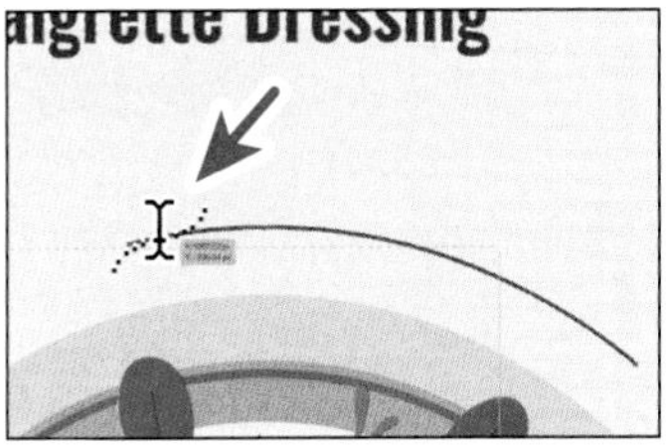

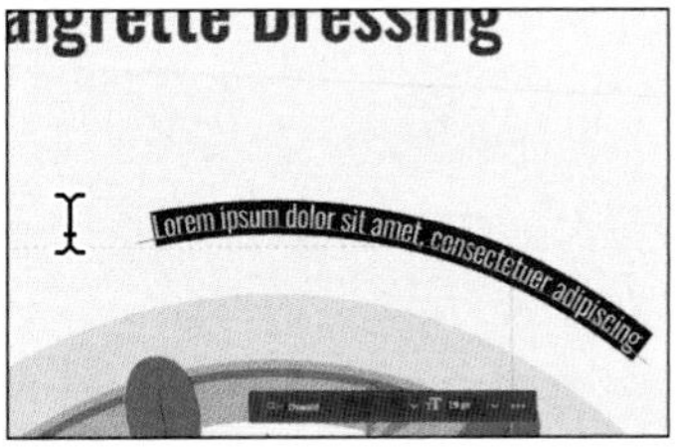

Placeholder text is added to the path, and it starts where you clicked. Your text may have different formatting than you see in the previous figure, and that's okay.

4 Click the Body style in the Paragraph Style panel to re-apply the formatting.

5 Type **EAT HEALTHY**!

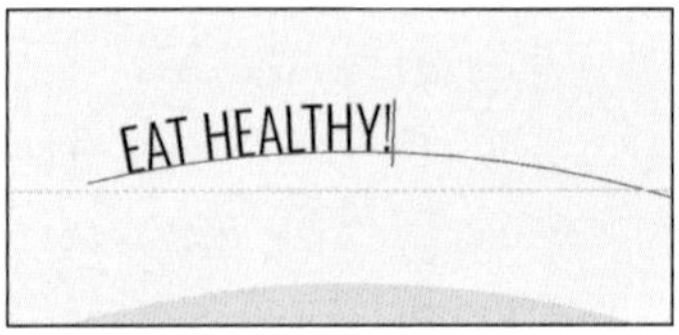

6 Select the Selection tool, and move the pointer over the line on the left edge of the text (just to the left of the "E" in EAT). When you see this cursor (⊢), drag to try to center the text as best you can on the path. Use the figure as a guide.

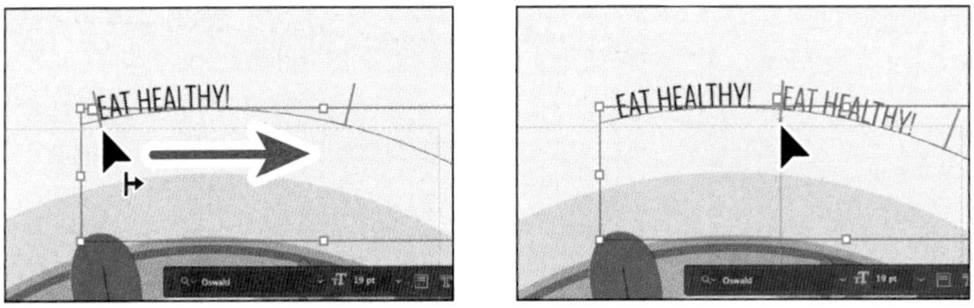

7 Change the font size in the Task bar beneath (or above) the text to something bigger.

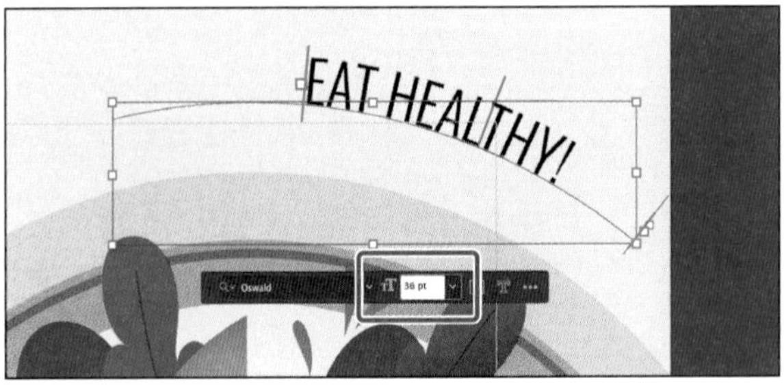

Warping text

You can create some original design effects by warping text into different shapes using envelopes (shapes). You can make an envelope out of an object on your artboard, or you can use a preset warp shape or a mesh grid as an envelope.

Warped text.

Reshaping text with a preset envelope warp

Illustrator comes with a series of preset warp shapes that you can warp text with. Next, you'll make a creative heading by applying a preset warp shape.

1 Choose View > Fit All In Window.

2 With the Selection tool selected, click the "LEARN TO COOK!" text.

3 Zoom in to the text by pressing Command and + (macOS) or Ctrl and + (Windows) a few times.

4 Choose Object > Envelope Distort > Make With Warp.

5 The Warp Options dialog box appears, with Preview selected. Make sure Arc Upper is chosen from the Style menu.

6 Drag the Bend, Horizontal, and Vertical Distortion sliders to see the effect on the text. You may need to deselect and then select Preview.

7 Ensure the Distortion sliders are 0%, and make sure that Bend is 40%. Click OK.

Editing the content of the envelope warp

If you want to make any changes, you can edit the text and shape that make up the envelope warp object separately. Next, you will edit the text and then the warp shape.

1 With the envelope object still selected, click the Edit Contents button (⊞) at the top of the Properties panel.

The Edit Contents button is so you can select what is inside of the warp—in this case, the text.

2 Select the Type tool (T), and move the pointer over the warped text. Notice that the unwarped text appears in blue. Change the "LEARN TO COOK!" text to **LEARN TO COOK** (*no* exclamation point).

You can also edit the preset shape, which is what you'll do next.

3   Select the Selection tool (▶), and make sure the envelope object is still selected. Click the Edit Envelope button (▦) at the top of the Properties panel.

▶ **Tip:** If you double-click with the Selection tool instead of with the Type tool, you enter Isolation mode. This is another way to edit the text within the envelope warp object. Press the Escape key to exit Isolation mode.

4   Click the Warp Options button in the Properties panel to show the same Warp Options dialog box you saw when you first applied the warp. Change the Style to Arch and the Bend to **25%**, and click OK.

5   With the Selection tool, drag the warped text and then the text "WITH CHEF HODGMAN" to center them above the pot artwork.

6   Choose Select > Deselect, and then choose File > Save.

Creating text outlines

● **Note:** Bitmap fonts and outline-protected fonts cannot be converted to outlines, and outlining text that is less than 10 points in size is not recommended.

Converting text to outlines means converting text into vector shapes that you can edit and manipulate like any other vector graphic. When you create outlines from text, that text is no longer editable as text. Text outlines allow you to change the look of large display type or send a file to someone when you can't or don't want to send the font. They are rarely helpful for body text or other text formatted at small sizes. If you convert all text to outlines, the file recipient doesn't need your fonts installed to open and view the file correctly.

You must also convert all text in a selection to outlines; you cannot convert a single letter within a type object. Next, you will convert the main heading to outlines.

1   Choose View > Fit All In Window.

2   With the Selection tool (▶) selected, click the "Avocado Beet Salad with Citrus Vinaigrette Dressing" text on the recipe card.

3   Choose Edit > Copy and then choose Object > Hide > Selection.

The original text is still there; it's just hidden. This way, you can always choose Object > Show All to see the original text if you need to make changes.

4 Choose Edit > Paste In Front.

5 Choose Type > Create Outlines.

The text is no longer linked to a particular font. Instead, it is now editable artwork.

6 For a last bit of cleanup, zoom in to the bottom of the flyer artboard on the left.

7 If you see a single word on a line that is the end of a paragraph (an arrow is pointing to one in the first part of the figure), select the Type tool and insert the cursor before the word on the line above. Then, add a soft return by pressing Shift+Return (macOS) or Shift+Enter (Windows).

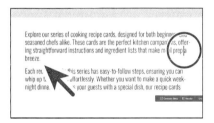

8 Select the Selection tool (▶) and select the pink background shape. Drag to make it taller to fit the artboard.

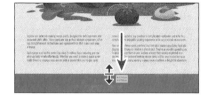

9 Choose File > Save.

Exploring Retype (Beta)

With Retype, Illustrator can identify the fonts of text found in raster images and outlined texts. Once they're identified, you can apply the font to text and convert the text to live text that is editable. Retype is a Beta feature, which means the functionality and user interface options may change. As you go through this section, keep that in mind!

1 Choose 3 Retype from the Artboard Navigation menu below the document to fit that artboard in the Document window.

2 With the Selection tool (▶), select the artwork.

Note: Currently Retype (beta) supports Latin scripts only. Also, on macOS 11, font identification from the image works fine. But to be able to edit the text, consider updating to macOS 12 or higher.

Everything you see on the artboard is an image. With Retype, you can find out what font is used for some of the text, apply new fonts, and edit the text!

● **Note:** Currently you will see "Beta" next to Retype in the menu.

3 Choose Type > Retype (Beta).

The Retype (Beta) panel will open and start working right away.

4 *If* you see an option to download a part of the feature set at the bottom of the panel, click Download.

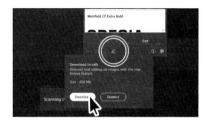

You do this only once, ever. If this option doesn't appear, click the Download button () at the bottom of the panel and click Download.

When the download is complete, you are ready to work with the feature.

5 Click any of the text on the artboard.

In the panel, you will see a listing of font matches. The top font in the list is the best match. I know for a fact that the text uses Rajdhani—so the first match (I see) is correct.

▶ **Tip:** If you select a font in the list and click Apply, the text is converted to editable text, and the font is applied!

6 Click the text "SPECIALISTS."

7 To edit the text, converting it to live text, double-click the "SPECIALISTS" text.

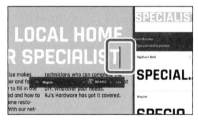

8 Select the Type tool (**T**) and change the word from "SPECIALISTS" to **SPECIALIST** (with no "S").

9 Close the Retype (Beta) panel.

10 Choose View > Fit All In Window.

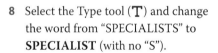

11 Choose File > Save, and then choose File > Close for all open files.

Review questions

1 Name a few methods for creating text in Adobe Illustrator.

2 What is overflow text?

3 What is text threading?

4 What is the difference between a character style and a paragraph style?

5 What is the advantage of converting text to outlines?

6 Name two things that the Retype feature can do.

Review answers

1 The following methods can be used for creating text:

- With the Type tool (T), click the artboard, and start typing when the cursor appears. A point type object is created to accommodate the text.

- With the Type tool, drag to create a type area object. Type when a cursor appears.

- With the Type tool, click an open path or closed shape to convert it to text on a path, or click in a type object. Here's a tip: Option-clicking (macOS) or Alt-clicking (Windows) when crossing over the stroke of a *closed* path creates text around the shape.

2 Overflow text is text that does not fit within an area type object or path. A red plus sign (⊞) in an out port indicates that the object contains additional text.

3 Text threading allows you to flow text from one object to another by linking type objects. Linked type objects can be of any shape; however, the text must be entered in an area or along a path (not at a point).

4 A character style can be applied to selected text only. A paragraph style is applied to an entire paragraph. Paragraph styles are best for indents, margins, and line spacing.

5 Converting text to outlines eliminates the need to send the fonts along with the Illustrator file when sharing with others and makes it possible to add effects to type that aren't possible when the type is still editable (live).

6 With Retype, Illustrator can identify the fonts of text found in raster images and outlined texts. Once it's identified, you can apply the font to text and convert the text to live text that is editable.

10 ORGANIZING YOUR ARTWORK WITH LAYERS

Lesson overview

In this lesson, you'll learn how to do the following:

- Work with the Layers panel.

- Create, rearrange, and lock layers and sublayers.

- Name content.

- Locate objects in the Layers panel.

- Move objects between layers.

- Copy and paste objects and their layers from one file to another.

- Search and filter layers.

- Make a layer clipping mask.

 This lesson will take about 45 minutes to complete. To get the lesson files used in this lesson, download them from the web page for this book at *peachpit.com/IllustratorCIB2024*. For more information, see "Accessing the lesson files and Web Edition" in the Getting Started section at the beginning of this book.

Creating layers in your Illustrator artwork lets you organize your artwork and easily control how it is printed, displayed, selected, and edited.

Starting the lesson

In this lesson, you'll organize the artwork for cookie packaging for a fictitious company, Nom Nom Cookies, and explore various ways to work with layers in the Layers panel.

Note: If you have not already downloaded the project files for this lesson to your computer from your Account page, make sure to do so now. See the "Getting Started" section at the beginning of the book.

1 To ensure that the tools function and the defaults are set exactly as described in this lesson, reset the Adobe Illustrator preferences. See "Restoring default preferences" in the "Getting Started" section at the beginning of the book.

2 Start Adobe Illustrator.

3 Choose File > Open, and open the L10_end.ai file in the Lessons > Lesson10 folder, located on your hard disk.

The Missing Fonts dialog box may appear, indicating that fonts were used in the file that aren't on your machine. The file uses Adobe fonts that you most likely don't have activated, so you will fix these before moving on.

Note: For more information on activating fonts, visit helpx.adobe.com/ creative-cloud/help/add- fonts.html.

4 In the Missing Fonts dialog box, make sure any missing fonts are selected, and click Activate Fonts. After some time, the font(s) should be activated, and you should see a success message in the Missing Fonts dialog box. Click Close.

5 Choose View > Fit All In Window.

6 Choose Window > Workspace > Reset Essentials.

7 Choose File > Open. In the Open dialog box, navigate to the Lessons > Lesson10 folder, and select the L10_start.ai file on your hard disk. Click Open.

8 Choose File > Save As. If the Cloud Document dialog box opens, click Save On Your Computer.

9 In the Save As dialog box, name the file **CookiePackage.ai**, and select the Lesson10 folder. Leave Adobe Illustrator (ai) chosen from the Format menu (macOS) or Adobe Illustrator (*.AI) chosen from the Save As Type menu (Windows), and then click Save.

10 In the Illustrator Options dialog box, leave the Illustrator options at their default settings, and then click OK.

What are layers?

Layers are like invisible folders that help you hold and manage all the items that make up your project. You can't see the layers in the project, but they are there, ready to help you when needed.

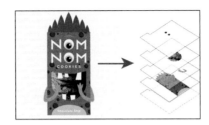

If you shuffle those folders (layers), you change the *stacking order* of your artwork. You learned all about stacking order in Lesson 2. The structure of layers in your document can be as straightforward or as complex as you want. You don't even need to use them. Maybe you have a straightforward design with only a few pieces, like an icon. Layers might not be beneficial in that case.

Once your design gets more complicated or involved, you will have more pieces. Then, it becomes challenging to select specific artwork, quickly move related items, or temporarily hide things you need to get out of the way for a minute. Using layers to organize your artwork can help you to deal with these issues and more.

For example, you could place text on a separate layer and lock that layer to focus on other artwork without affecting the text or have multiple languages that you can turn on and off.

With an idea of what layers are, let's get into the project and see how we can use them to our advantage when working with a design.

When should you use layers?

The short answer is, it's up to you and your project needs.

Here are a few of many scenarios where adding layers to your project makes sense:

- You have multiple design concepts or text with multiple languages and want to be able to show and hide the versions easily.
- Putting type, artwork, and design elements like background colors on separate layers makes it easier to lock and hide content.
- For web or app design, having all UI elements on their own layer can make exporting or hiding to work on other things much easier.

Creating layers

In this lesson, you'll add layers to organize *existing* content, making it easier to make selections and edit content in a packaging design. Before we begin, know that there is no "wrong" layer structure, but as you gain more experience with layers, you'll see what makes sense for you and your specific projects.

1 Choose View > Fit Artboard In Window.

2 To show the Layers panel, click the Layers panel tab on the right side of the workspace, or choose Window > Layers.

3 Click the triangle (▶) to the left of the Layer 1 thumbnail (▦) to show the content on the layer.

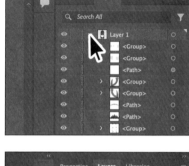

Everything in the document is listed in the Layers panel. By default, Illustrator names content to make it easier to see at a glance what is there. For instance, a group is named "<Group>," a raster image is named "<Image>," and so on.

4 Click the same triangle (▼) to the left of the Layer 1 thumbnail (▦) to hide the content on that layer so the panel doesn't look as busy.

The first thing you'll do is name Layer 1 something that makes sense.

5 In the Layers panel, double-click *directly* on the layer name Layer 1 to edit it inline. Type **Package** and then press Return or Enter.

● **Note:** In the figure, I split the very tall Layers panel, indicated by the dashed line. That way, you can see the top and bottom of the panel.

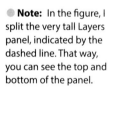

6 Click the Create New Layer button (▣) at the bottom of the Layers panel to make a new layer.

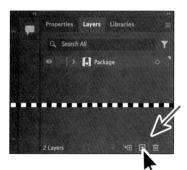

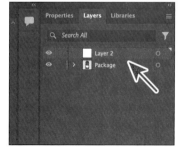

By default, the new layer is added above the currently selected layer in the Layers panel (Package, in this case) and becomes active. When you make a new layer, it's named in sequence, like Layer 1, Layer 2, and so on.

Notice that the new layer doesn't have a triangle (▶) to the left of the layer name. That's because it's empty to start with.

7   Double-click the empty layer thumbnail (the white box) to the left of the layer name "Layer 2" or in the blank area to the right of the name in the Layers panel.

8   In the Layer Options dialog box that opens, change the name to **Arms**, and notice all the other options available.

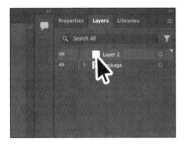
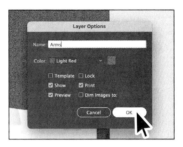

◖ **Note:** The Layer Options dialog box has a lot of the options you've already worked with, including naming layers, setting Preview or Outline mode, locking layers, and showing and hiding layers. You can also deselect the Print option in the Layer Options dialog box, and any content on that layer will not print.

9   Click OK.

Notice that the new layer has a different layer color (a light red). This will become more important later, as you select content. Next you'll practice by creating a new layer named Mouth.

10 Click the Create New Layer button (▣) at the bottom of the Layers panel again. Double-click the new layer name (Layer 3) and change the name to **Mouth**. Press Return or Enter to accept the change.

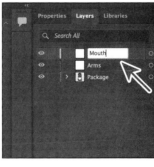

Creating a sublayer

Think of a sublayer as a subfolder within a layer—essentially, a layer nested within a layer. Sublayers can be useful for organizing content within a layer without having to group content.

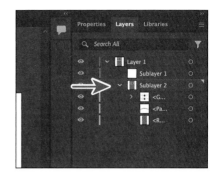

Next you'll create a sublayer to put teeth onto so that you can keep them together.

1   In the Layers panel, select the Mouth layer, if it isn't already.

Selecting a layer does not select the artwork that is on that layer, out on the artboard. It is only meant to do something to the layer, like move it, delete it, and so on.

2   Then, click the Create New Sublayer button (⊞) at the bottom of the Layers panel.

A new sublayer is created on that layer and is selected. You can think of this new sublayer as a "child" of the "parent" layer named "Mouth."

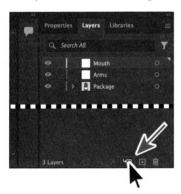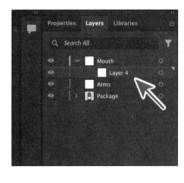

3   Double-click the new sublayer name (Layer 4, in my case), change the name to **Teeth**, and then press Return or Enter.

Creating a new sublayer opens the selected layer to show the content.

4   Leave the Teeth sublayer showing in the Mouth layer.

In the next sections, you'll add content to the Teeth sublayer.

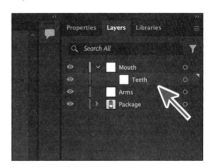

Editing layers and objects

As you create and add layers and sublayers, you'll move content between those layers to better organize it, and you'll rearrange the layers in the Layers panel to change the stacking order of objects in your artwork.

Locating content in the Layers panel

To start moving and editing content in the Layers panel, there may be times when you select something on the artboard and want to see where that content is in the Layers panel. This can help you determine how content is organized—whether it's on the right layer, for instance.

1 Drag the left edge of the Layers panel to the left to make it wider.

   When the names of layers and objects are long enough or objects become further nested one in another, the names can become truncated—in other words, you can't see all of them.

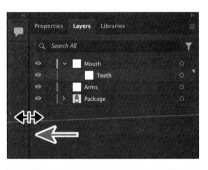

2 With the Selection tool (▶), click one of the teeth in the top part of the mouth to select a group of teeth.

3 Click the Locate Object button (🔍) at the bottom of the Layers panel to reveal the selected content within the Layers panel.

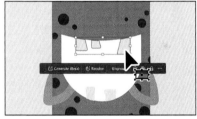

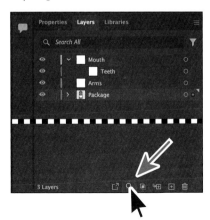

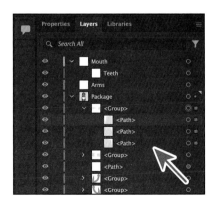

The layer that the teeth are on opens (if it wasn't already), and you should see each tooth listed (named <Path>) in a group (named <Group>) within the Package layer.

In the Layers panel, can you see the little selected-art indicators (■) to the far right of the teeth <Group>? They're circled in the figure.

Those little boxes mean that content is selected on the artboard.

4 So you don't see each individual tooth in the Layers panel, click the arrow to the left of the <Group> name to hide them.

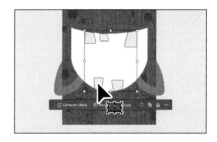

5 On the artboard, Shift-click a tooth in the bottom row of teeth to select that group as well.

In the Layers panel, you should see a selected-art indicator (■) to the far right of the other group of teeth. Each row of teeth is named <Group> in the Layers panel for an apparent reason—they are groups of individual shapes.

Also, look at the teeth artwork on the artboard. Notice that the color of the bounding box, paths, and anchor points of the selected artwork matches the layer's color (the small color strip [❙] you see to the left of the layer name in the Layers panel). When you select artwork on the artboard, you can tell what layer it's on by the color of the bounding box, paths, or anchors.

6 Choose Select > Deselect.

In the next section, I will ask you to select those same groups in the Layers panel.

Dragging content between layers

There are several ways to move content from one layer to another. Next you'll move artwork to different layers using a few different methods to take advantage of the layers and sublayers you've created.

1   In the Layers panel, click one of the teeth <Group> names; then Shift-click the other <Group> name.

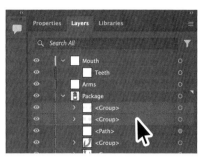

Notice that this does not select the teeth on the artboard! All you are doing is selecting the layer groups within the Layers panel so you can move them, rename the groups, and more.

2   Drag one of the layer names straight up onto the Teeth sublayer in the Mouth layer. When the sublayer shows a highlight, release to add the layer.

3   Click the arrow to the left of the Teeth sublayer, and you can now see both groups nested in there.

Now for some practice!

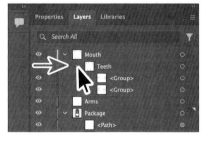

4   Click the white mouth shape on the artboard so you can see where that shape is listed in the Layers panel.

5   On the Package layer, click the name of that selected path to select it in the layer list.

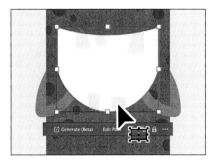

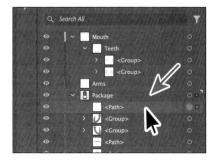

6 In the Layers panel, find the
<Image> object on the Package layer.
Command-click (macOS) or Ctrl-click
(Windows) its name in the Layers
panel to select it as well.

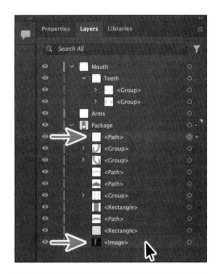

7 Drag either the selected <Path>
or <Image> layer directly onto the
Mouth layer. Release when the layer
is highlighted.

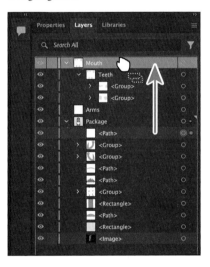

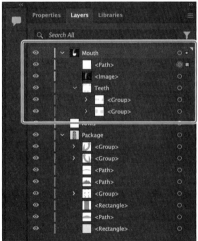

Be careful! Don't drag either of them onto the Teeth sublayer or they will go into
that sublayer, which we don't want, because they are not teeth!

Notice that the white mouth shape and image are covering the teeth and the
arms in the design. Any content that is dragged to another layer or sublayer is
automatically at the top of the layer or sublayer ordering. You'll fix that shortly.

8 Select the image out on the artboard.

9 To hide it, choose Object >
Hide > Selection.

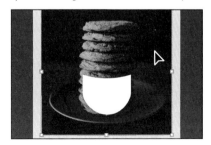

You'll learn how to hide layers in the
Layers panel in a later section.

Trying another method for dragging content to a layer

Now you'll try another way to move something from one layer to another. This other method can be faster at times, especially if you can't see where the content is in the Layers panel—maybe because none of the layer content is showing.

Let's move the arms onto the Arms layer!

1 Click the arrows to the left of the Package layer and Mouth layer names in the Layers panel to hide the content.

Hiding the layer content is a great way to make the Layers panel less visually cluttered.

2 Select one of the orange arms on the artboard.

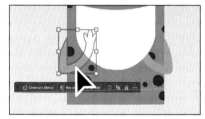

You should see a blue selected-art indicator (■) to the right of the Package layer in the Layers panel. That little indicator tells you that the arm is on the Package layer without having to reveal the content of that layer!

3 Drag that blue selected-art indicator straight up in the same column of the panel to the Arms layer—you won't have to drag very far.

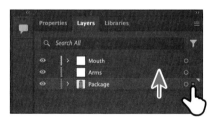 

The one arm is now on the Arms layer, and you should see that the bounding box is now the same color as the Arms layer—red!

4 Practice by selecting the other orange arm on the artboard and dragging the selected-art indicator from the Package layer to the Arms layer. Both arms are now on the Arms layer.

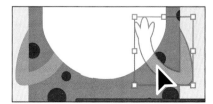 

5 Click the triangle (▶) to the left of the Arms layer to show the arms in the list.

6 With the one arm still selected on the artboard, Shift-click the other arm. Group them by clicking the Group button in the Task bar.

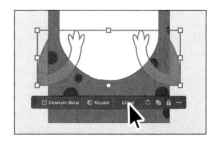

Looking in the Arms layer, you should now see a <Group> object and, if you were to click the arrow to the left of the <Group> name, the separate arms within the group.

7 Click the triangle (▶) to the left of the Arms layer to hide the content.

8 Choose Select > Deselect, and then choose File > Save.

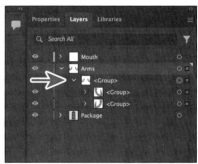

Locking and hiding layers

In Lesson 2, you learned about locking and hiding content. When you lock and hide content using menu commands or keyboard shortcuts, you can see the result in the Layers panel. The Layers panel also lets you hide or lock content. The best part about hiding or locking in the Layers panel? You can perform these actions on layers, sublayers, or individual objects. In this section, you'll lock some content and hide other content to make it easier to select things.

1 Click the background light-brown colored rectangle on the artboard.

2 Click the Locate Object button (🔍) at the bottom of the Layers panel to find it in the layer list.

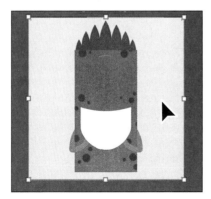

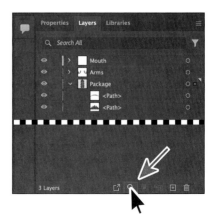

See the empty column to the right of the eye icon (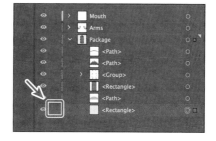) for that object in the list? This is where you can lock content and also see if something is locked.

3 Choose Object > Lock > Selection.

The rectangle is locked, so you can't accidentally move it. In the Layers panel, the empty column for the <Rectangle> object now shows a little lock icon (🔒).

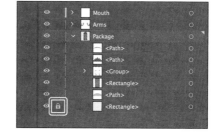

> **Tip:** To unlock content, you can click the lock icon (🔒) in the Layers panel.

We need to rearrange the mouth and arms and work on them a little. It would be easier if the rest of the content were locked—so let's do that.

Now you'll see the power of using the Layers panel after all of this setup!

4 In the Layers panel, click the empty column lock column to the right of the eye icon (👁) for the Package layer.

This action locks all of the objects on the Package layer, including the background shape, so you cannot select them on the artboard.

5 To temporarily hide the content on the Package layer, in the Layers panel, click the eye icon (👁) for the layer.

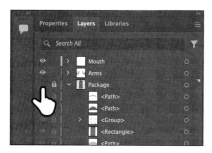

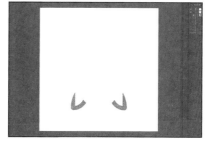

Without the colorful packaging showing, you can really only see the arms, because the mouth shape is white on the white artboard. In the next section you'll rearrange things so the mouth is behind the arms.

Reordering layers and content

In earlier lessons, you learned that objects have a stacking order, depending on when and how they were created. You used arrange commands like Bring To Front and Send To Back to reorder artwork.

Those arrange commands apply to each of the layers in the Layers panel independently. With multiple layers in your document, you can more quickly control how overlapping objects are displayed. Next, you'll fix the arms and teeth so they are no longer underneath the white mouth shape.

1 To view the artwork in Outline mode, press Command+Y (macOS) or Ctrl+Y (Windows).

   You should now see the teeth, mouth, and arms! Now you'll put the teeth on top of the mouth shape.

   Notice the eye icons (👁) in the Layers panel now. They indicate that the content on those layers is in Outline mode.

2 On the artboard, click the edge of the mouth shape to select it.

   In the Layers panel, notice the selected-art indicator for the Mouth layer, telling you what layer it's on (highlighted in the following figure).

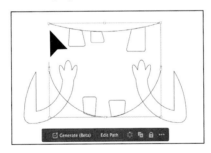

3 In the Layers panel, click the arrow (▶) for the Mouth layer so you can see what is on the layer.

   Looking in the Layers panel, you can now see that the mouth <Path> is at the top of the Mouth layer.

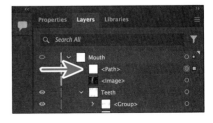

4 Choose Object > Arrange > Send To Back so the white shape is behind the teeth.

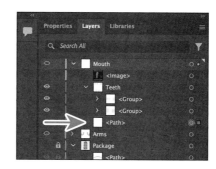

The arrange commands arrange content only within the layer that the object is on! If you want the mouth to go behind something on the Package layer, either the mouth shape would have to be on the Package layer or you could move the entire Mouth layer beneath the Package layer in the Layers panel.

5 Press Command+Y (macOS) or Ctrl+Y (Windows) to exit Outline mode.

You can now see the teeth! But we still have a problem. The arms are still behind the mouth. We cannot use arrange commands to fix this, because the arms and mouth are on different layers. To fix this, we need to reorder the layers themselves.

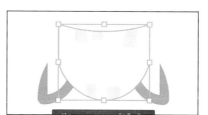

6 In the Layers panel, click the triangle (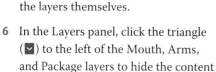) to the left of the Mouth, Arms, and Package layers to hide the content for each.

This will make it easier to drag layers.

7 Choose Select > Deselect.

I deselect out of habit so I don't accidentally move something I don't intend to.

8 In the Layers panel, drag the Mouth layer down beneath the Arms layer. When a line appears below the Arms layer, release to put the mouth below the arms on the artboard.

You could have also dragged the Arms layer up above the Mouth layer—either would have worked.

9 In the Layers panel, show the Package layer content by clicking where the eye icon () was.

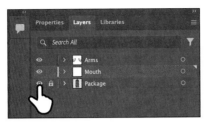

Viewing individual layers or objects as outlines

In Outline mode, you see all artwork without appearance attributes. But sometimes you may only need to see some of the artwork in Outline mode while retaining the strokes and fills for the rest of the artwork. In the Layers panel, you can display layers or individual objects in either Preview or Outline mode. In this section, you'll learn how to discover a hidden object on the Package layer using Outline mode so you can easily select it.

1 In the Layers panel, click the triangle (▶) for the Package layer so you can see what's on the layer.

▶ **Tip:** Displaying a layer in Outline mode is also useful for selecting the anchor points or center points of objects.

2 Command-click (macOS) or Ctrl-click (Windows) the eye icon (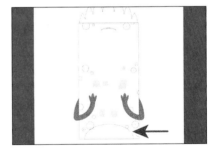) to the left of the Package layer name to show the content for *only that layer* in Outline mode.

You should be able to see the rounded shape near the bottom of the packaging. An arrow is pointing to it in the previous figure. To select it so you can bring it to the front of the other layer content, the layer needs to be unlocked.

3 Click the lock icon (🔒) in the Layers panel to unlock the Package layer content, except for the background shape.

4 With the Selection tool (▶) selected, on the artboard click the edge of the rounded shape or drag across part of it to select it.

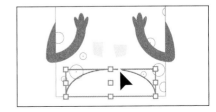

5 Command-click (macOS) or Ctrl-click (Windows) the eye icon (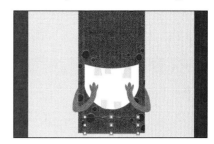) to the left of the Package layer name to show the content for that layer in Preview mode again.

You can still see the outline and bounding box of the shape on the artboard because it's still selected.

6 In the Layers panel, drag the selected <Path> by its name up above the top object in the layer. When you see a line appear, release.

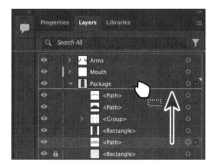

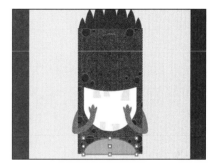

In this case, you could have also used the Object > Arrange > Bring To Front command. It would have come to the same result.

7 Click the triangle () to the left of the Package layer to hide the layer content.

8 Choose Select > Deselect and then File > Save.

Pasting layers from another document

Sometimes you need to bring artwork from outside of your project into your project. If you paste content into your project from another Illustrator document that has layers, you can preserve those original layers in the document you are pasting into.

In this section, you'll add the final content to the packaging artwork by pasting text from another document into your project.

1 Choose Window > Workspace > Reset Essentials.

2 Choose File > Open. Open the Packaging_text.ai file in the Lessons > Lesson10 folder on your hard disk.

3 Choose View > Fit Artboard In Window.

4 Click the Layers panel tab to show the panel and the layers.

5 Choose Select > All.

6 Choose Edit > Copy to copy the content to the clipboard.

7 Choose File > Close to close the Packaging_text.ai file *without* saving any changes.

8 Back in the CookiePackage.ai file, in the Layers panel, click the menu (≣) icon and choose Paste Remembers Layers.

A checkmark next to the option indicates that it's selected.

Paste Remembers Layers is not selected by default, which means new content you paste goes onto whatever layer is selected when pasting. With Paste Remembers Layers turned on, the layers from the original document are added to the document you are pasting into at the top of the Layers panel list.

9 Choose Edit > Paste to paste the content into the center of the Document window.

The Paste Remembers Layers option causes the layers from the Packaging_text.ai document to be added to the top of the Layers panel.

10 If you see a Swatch Conflict dialog box, ensure that Merge Swatches is selected, and click OK.

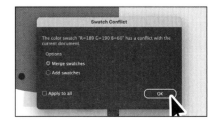

There is at least one color in the artwork you are pasting that is the same as a color in the CookiePackage.ai file. Merging will merge the incoming swatches using the color values of the existing swatches.

11 Drag the selected artwork on the artboard down into position, like you see in the figure.

12 Choose Select > Deselect.

Merging layers into a new layer

At times, you may want to simplify your layers and combine a few of them. You just pasted text from an outside document that has two layers into your project. It might make more sense to have a single layer named Text. So you'll merge the content from those two layers into a single layer.

1   In the Layers panel, select the Brand Text layer in the list. Shift-click the Cookie Type layer as well to select both.

2   Click the Layers panel menu icon (▤), and choose Merge Selected.

The content from the two selected layers is now merged into one of the layers.

3   Double-click the new sublayer name (mine is Brand Text, yours might be Cookie Type), and change the name to **Text**. Press Return or Enter.

We could have left the layers as is, but like I said, having a single layer for all of the text, in this case, will probably make it easier for us to select, hide, and lock it all at once.

Searching and filtering layers

When you spend enough time working with layers, you eventually find yourself trying to find specific content in the Layers panel. Using Locate Object, like you've used so far in this chapter, is a great way to see where *selected* content is in the Layers panel. But what if you need to find *all* the text—maybe to change the font? Or maybe to find *any* artwork with effects applied to remove them?

You can search for a layer or object name or use the layer and object filters in the Layers panel to locate specific layers and objects quickly. Let's change the color of the eyes in the text.

1   In the Layers panel, type **Iris** into the search field at the top (see the figure).

2   Click the arrows to the left of the Text layer and the <Group> to see the objects named Iris.

The Layers panel content is filtered to show only items named Iris.

3   To select both Iris objects, click the Selected Indicator column in the panel. See the figure to the right. Shift-click the same column for the other Iris object to select both.

Selecting in this way is sometimes easier—especially when the items you want to select are buried in groups.

4   Open the Properties panel and change the Fill color to something different.

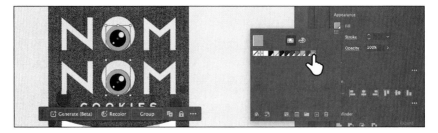

5   Back in the Layers panel, click the X to the right of the "Iris" text you typed in to clear the results.

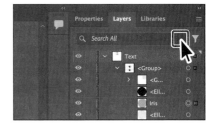

Creating a clipping mask

In the Layers panel, you can control whether artwork on a layer is hidden or revealed using a clipping mask. A clipping mask is an object or group of objects that masks (hides) artwork below it in the same layer or sublayer so that only artwork within the shape is visible.

Now, you'll take the image you hid and use the white mouth shape as a mask. We want it to look like the cookies are in the bag and you can see them through the little mouth opening.

1. In the Layers panel, click the Apply Filter button and choose Images from the menu. It's circled in the following figure. Click away from the menu to hide it.

    Only images will now be listed in the Layers panel.

2. To show the cookie image on the artboard, click the visibility column. See the second part of the following figure.

3. Click the Apply Filter button again and select Clear All to see all layer content again.

4. Choose Select > Deselect.

5. In the Layers panel, click the triangle (⌄) to the left of the Arms, Text, and Package layers to hide the content for each. If necessary, click the triangle for the Mouth layer to see the content for that layer.

    You will see <Image> listed at the top. We will use the *white mouth shape* as the mask. In the Layers panel, a masking object must be above the objects it masks. In the case of a layer mask, the masking object must be the topmost object on a layer.

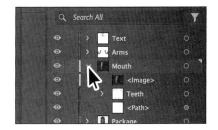

6 In the Layers panel, drag the white mouth shape up in the layer stack, above the image.

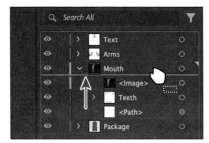 

This mouth shape will be used as the clipping mask for all of the content on the layer, so it needs to be at the top of the layer stack.

▶ **Tip:** To release the clipping mask, you can select the Mouth layer again and click the Make/Release Clipping Mask button (⬜).

7 In the Layers panel, click the name of the Mouth layer to highlight it.

8 Click the Make/Release Clipping Mask button (⬜) at the bottom of the Layers panel. The figure shows the button just before clicking.

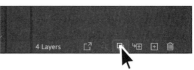

If you look in the Layers panel at the Mouth layer, you will see that the name of the mouth shape is now <Clipping Path> and is underlined. Both indicate that it is the masking shape.

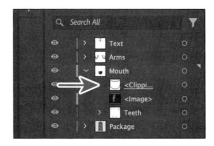

9 Click the cookie image on the artboard and choose Object > Arrange > Send To Back so the image is behind the teeth.

On the artboard, the mouth shape has hidden the parts of the image that extended outside of the shape.

10 Choose File > Save, and then choose File > Close.

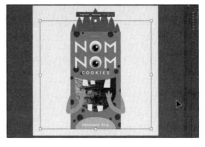

Review questions

1 Name at least two benefits of using layers when creating artwork.

2 Describe how to reorder layers in a file.

3 What is the purpose of changing the color for a layer?

4 What happens if you paste a layered file into another file? Why is the Paste Remembers Layers option useful?

5 How do you create a layer clipping mask?

Review answers

1 The benefits of using layers when creating artwork include organizing content, selecting content more easily, protecting artwork that you don't want to change, hiding artwork that you aren't working with so that it's not distracting, controlling what prints, and applying effects to all of the content on a layer.

2 You reorder layers by selecting a layer name or its selected-art indicator in the Layers panel and dragging the layer to its new location. The order of layers in the Layers panel controls the document's layer order—topmost in the panel is frontmost in the artwork.

3 The color for a layer controls how selected anchor points and direction lines are displayed on a layer and helps you identify which layer an object resides on in your document.

4 The Paste commands paste layered files or objects copied from different layers into the active layer by default. The Paste Remembers Layers option keeps the original layers intact when the objects are pasted.

5 Create a clipping mask on a layer by selecting the layer and clicking the Make/Release Clipping Mask button (▣) in the Layers panel. The topmost object in the layer becomes the clipping mask.

11 GRADIENTS, BLENDS, AND PATTERNS

Lesson overview

In this lesson, you'll learn how to do the following:

- Create and save a gradient fill.

- Apply and edit a gradient on a stroke.

- Apply and edit a radial gradient.

- Adjust the opacity of color in a gradient.

- Create and edit freeform gradients.

- Blend the shapes of objects in intermediate steps.

- Modify a blend.

- Create smooth color blends between objects.

- Modify a blend and its path, shape, and color.

- Blend with the Blend tool.

- Create and apply patterns.

This lesson will take about 60 minutes to complete. To get the lesson files used in this lesson, download them from the web page for this book at *peachpit.com/IllustratorCIB2024*. For more information, see "Accessing the lesson files and Web Edition" in the Getting Started section at the beginning of this book.

To add depth and interest to your artwork in Illustrator, you can apply gradient fills, patterns, or shapes. In this lesson, you'll explore how to work with each of these to complete a presentation slide.

Starting the lesson

In this lesson, you'll explore various ways to work with gradients, blend shapes and colors, and create and apply patterns. Before you begin, you'll restore the default preferences for Adobe Illustrator. Then you'll open a finished art file to see what you'll create.

Note: If you have not already downloaded the project files for this lesson to your computer from your Account page, make sure to do so now. See the "Getting Started" section at the beginning of the book.

1   To ensure that the tools function and the defaults are set exactly as described in this lesson, delete or deactivate (by renaming) the Adobe Illustrator preferences file. See "Restoring default preferences" in the "Getting Started" section at the beginning of the book.

2   Start Adobe Illustrator.

3   Choose File > Open, and open the L11_end.ai file in the Lessons > Lesson11 folder on your hard disk.

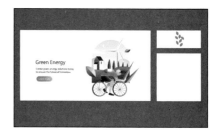

4   Choose View > Fit All In Window. If you don't want to leave the document open as you work, choose File > Close.

To begin working, you'll open an art file that you need to finish.

5   Choose File > Open. In the Open dialog box, navigate to the Lessons > Lesson11 folder, and select the L11_start.ai file on your hard disk. Click Open to open the file.

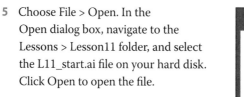

6   Choose View > Fit All In Window.

7   Choose File > Save As. If the Cloud Document dialog box opens, click Save On Your Computer.

8   In the Save As dialog box, name the file **Presentation.ai**, and select the Lessons > Lesson11 folder in the Save As menu. Leave Adobe Illustrator (ai) chosen from the Format menu (macOS) or Adobe Illustrator (*.AI) chosen from the Save As Type menu (Windows), and then click Save.

9   In the Illustrator Options dialog box, leave the Illustrator options at their default settings, and then click OK.

10 Choose Reset Essentials from the workspace switcher in the Application bar.

Note: If you don't see Reset Essentials in the workspace switcher menu, choose Window > Workspace > Essentials before choosing Window > Workspace > Reset Essentials.

Working with gradients

A *gradient* is a graduated blend of two or more colors, and it always includes a starting color and an ending color. You can create three different types of gradients in Illustrator. At their simplest, here they are described:

- **Linear**—One color blends into another color along a straight line.
- **Radial**—A beginning color radiates outward, from the center point to an ending color.
- **Freeform**—A graduated blend of color stops within a shape in an ordered or random sequence that gives the blending a smooth appearance, like natural color.

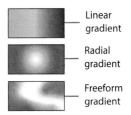

Linear gradient

Radial gradient

Freeform gradient

You can use gradients provided with Adobe Illustrator or create your gradients and save them as swatches for later use (except for freeform gradients). Using gradients, you can create blends between colors, add volume, or add a light and shadow effect to your artwork. As you go through this lesson, you'll see examples of each type of gradient and understand why you use each.

Applying a linear gradient to a fill

To begin the lesson, you'll apply a linear gradient fill that comes with Illustrator to a background shape, and then edit the colors to give the idea of a sunset.

1 Choose 1 Presentation Slide from the Artboard Navigation menu below the Document window to fit the first artboard in the window.

2 With the Selection tool (▶) selected, double-click the larger pink shape behind the crescent moon in the background.

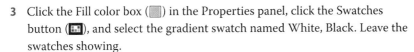

This is a great way to enter Isolation mode for a single shape so you can focus on the pink shape without the other content on top of it.

3 Click the Fill color box (▦) in the Properties panel, click the Swatches button (▦), and select the gradient swatch named White, Black. Leave the swatches showing.

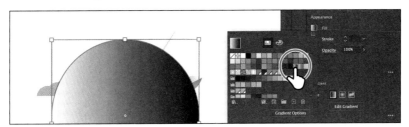

Editing a gradient color

Next, you'll edit the colors in the default black-and-white gradient you applied.

1 With the Swatches panel still showing (click the Fill color box if it's not still showing), click the Gradient Options button at the bottom of the panel to open the Gradient panel (Window > Gradient).

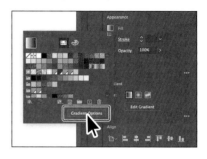

2 Do the following in the Gradient panel:

- Click the Fill box so it's selected.

If the icon is on top of the stroke icon, then it is already selected. With the fill selected, you will edit the fill color and not the stroke color.

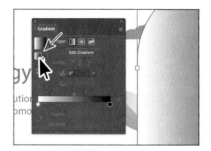

- In the panel, double-click the black color circle—called a *color stop*—on the right side of the gradient bar to edit the color in the Gradient panel. It's circled in the figure.

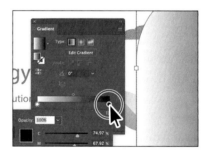

- In the panel that appears, click the Swatches button (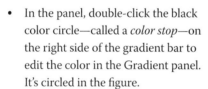) to show swatches. It's circled in the figure.
- Select the yellow swatch in the folder at the bottom of the panel.

You will be using the colors in that folder for the rest of the lesson.

- Press the Escape key after selecting the swatch to close the Swatches panel.

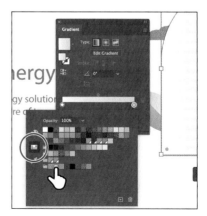

3 Leave the white color on the left side of the gradient slider white.

If you want to try practicing, change the white color by double-clicking the white, leftmost gradient stop to edit the starting color of the gradient. Know that your gradient won't match what you see in the rest of the chapter.

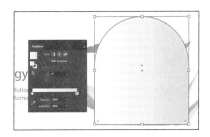

Saving a gradient as a swatch

Next, you'll save the gradient as a swatch in the Swatches panel. Saving a gradient is a great way to be able to apply it to other artwork easily and maintain consistency in the gradient appearance across artwork.

1 Click the Fill color box (▢) in the Properties panel. In the Swatches panel that opens, click the New Swatch button (⊞) at the bottom of the panel.

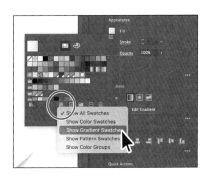

▷ **Tip:** You can also save a gradient from the Gradient panel. In the panel, click the Gradient menu arrow (▼) to the left of the word "Type," and click the Add To Swatches button (⬙) at the bottom of the panel that appears.

2 In the New Swatch dialog box, type **Background** in the Swatch Name field, and then click OK.

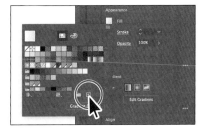

You should now see the new gradient swatch in the Swatches panel. It's usually at the end of the main color list and should be highlighted, since it's applied to the selected shape.

3 Click the Show Swatch Kinds Menu button (🞑▾) at the bottom of the Swatches panel, and choose Show Gradient Swatches from the menu to display only gradient swatches in the Swatches panel.

The Swatches panel lets you sort colors based on type, like gradient swatches.

4   With the shape still selected on the artboard, apply some of the different gradients to the shape fill by selecting them in the Swatches panel.

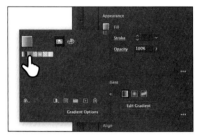

5   Click the gradient named Background (the one you just saved) in the Swatches panel to make sure it's applied.

6   Click the Show Swatch Kinds Menu button (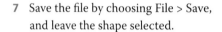) at the bottom of the Swatches panel, and choose Show All Swatches from the menu.

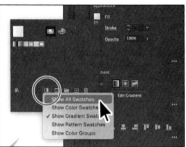

7   Save the file by choosing File > Save, and leave the shape selected.

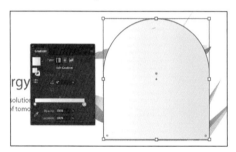

Adjusting a linear gradient fill

Not only can you adjust the color of a gradient, but you can adjust the gradient's direction, origin, and beginning and endpoints using the Gradient tool.

Now you'll adjust the gradient fill in the selected shape so the colors look more like a bright sky in the shape.

● **Note:** If you no longer see that the shape is in Isolation mode after saving, double-click the shape again.

1   With the shape still selected and the Gradient panel still open (Window > Gradient), make sure that the Fill box is selected in the panel (circled in the following figure) so you can edit the gradient applied to the fill.

2   Change the Angle value to 90 by choosing it from the menu.

Make sure the gradient shows yellow on top and white at the bottom.

3   In the Gradient panel, drag the white color stop (the circle) to the right to shorten the gradient.

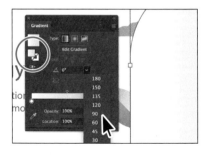

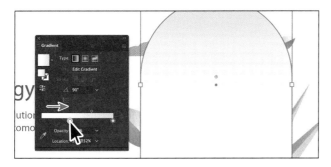

The transition from white to yellow will now happen over a shorter distance in the shape. Now you will see how to *visually* adjust the gradient in a shape so you can do it directly on the artwork using the Gradient tool.

4 Press the Escape key to exit Isolation mode.

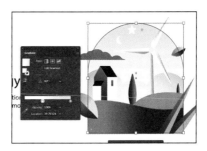

5 With the Selection tool (▶) selected, double-click the dark rolling hill shape to isolate it.

6 Select the Gradient tool (▣) in the toolbar.

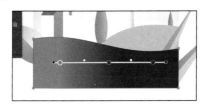

With the Gradient tool, you can apply a gradient to an object's fill or edit an existing gradient fill.

Notice the horizontal gradient bar in the middle of the artwork now? Similar to the one found in the Gradient panel? That bar is called the *gradient annotator*.

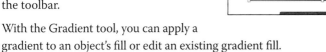

The gradient annotator indicates the color, direction, and length of the gradient. You can use the gradient annotator on the art to edit the gradient without opening the Gradient panel. The color circles represent the color stops. The tiny black circle on the left shows the starting point of the gradient, and the tiny square on the right is the ending point. The diamonds you see between the color stops are the midpoints between each color.

7 With the Gradient tool selected, starting just above the top of the shape, press the Shift key and drag down to just below the bottom of the shape.

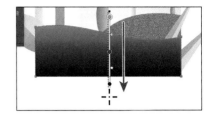

You just changed the angle and length of the gradient. It is now perfectly straight up and down in the shape.

Where you begin dragging is where the first color starts, and where you end is where the last color stops. As you drag, you see a live preview of the gradient as it's adjusted in the object.

Now you'll redraw the gradient so you can change the angle to follow the contour of the hill better.

8 With the Gradient tool, move the pointer above the left side of the shape. Drag down and to the right, at an angle. Release when it looks good.

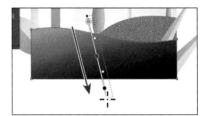

You can keep redrawing the gradient as many times as you want!

9 Select the Selection tool, and press the Escape key to exit Isolation mode.

Applying a linear gradient to a stroke

You can also apply a gradient to the stroke of an object. Unlike with a gradient applied to the fill of an object, you cannot use the Gradient tool to edit a gradient for a stroke. However, a gradient on a stroke has more options available in the Gradient panel than does a gradient fill. Next, you'll add colors to a stroke to give wheels on a bike a funky look.

1 Choose 3 Bike from the Artboard Navigation menu below the Document window to fit that artboard in the window.

2 With the Selection tool (▶) selected, click one of the black bike wheels. The wheel is actually a path with a stroke.

3 Click the Stroke box at the bottom of the toolbar on the left.

4 Click the Gradient box below the Stroke box in the toolbar to apply the last used gradient for the current session.

Note: After clicking the Stroke box in the toolbar, the Color panel group may open. If it does, you can close it.

Editing a gradient on a stroke

For a gradient applied to a stroke, you can choose different alignments on the stroke: within, along, or across. In this section, you'll explore how to align a gradient to the stroke and edit the gradient's colors.

1 In the Gradient panel (Window > Gradient), set the following:

- Ensure that the Stroke box is selected (an arrow is pointing to it in the figure) so you can edit the gradient applied to the stroke.

- Leave Type as Linear Gradient (![icon]).

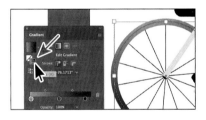

- Click the Apply Gradient Across Stroke button (![icon]) to change the Stroke type.

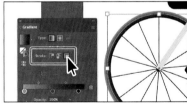

- Click the Reverse Gradient button (![icon]) so the darkest color (indigo) is on the left side of the gradient ramp in the panel.

With this type of path, aligning the gradient across the stroke can give the path a three-dimensional appearance.

Now to change the colors in the gradient!

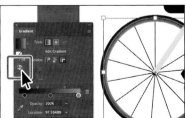

2 Double-click the middle blue color stop on the gradient annotator (also called a *slider*) in the panel, and with the Swatches option selected, select the swatch named Magenta to apply it.

3 Double-click the green color stop on the right end of the bar, and with the Swatches option selected, select the swatch named Light Blue to apply it.

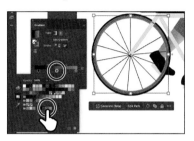 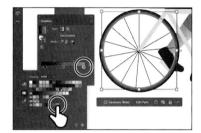

4 In the Gradient panel, click the middle Magenta color stop. Choose 50% from the Location menu.

The color stop is now 50% between the end and beginning of the annotator. You could also have dragged the color stop to change the Location value. Next you'll add a new color to the gradient to experiment a little.

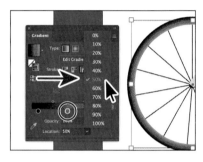

5 In the Gradient panel, move the pointer below the gradient slider, between two color stops. When the pointer with a plus sign (▷₊) appears, click to add another color stop, as you see in the first part of the following figure.

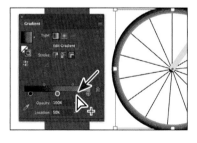 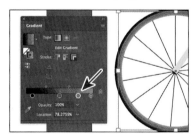

6 Double-click that new color stop, and select any other color.

7 Press the Escape key to hide the swatches and return to the Gradient panel.

When experimenting, sometimes you want fewer colors, rather than more. Next, you'll remove the color you just added.

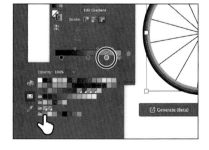

8 Drag the color stop that you just added down and away from the gradient slider. When you see that it's gone from the slider, release the mouse button to remove it.

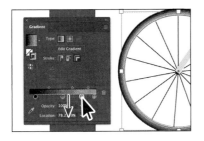 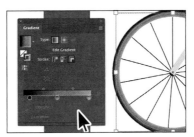

I wound up setting the Stroke option in the Gradient panel to Apply Gradient Within Stroke because it looked better to me.

Note: The gradient you see in your wheel may be rotated differently. You can change the Angle setting just below the Stroke option in the panel to rotate the gradient.

There are two wheels on the bike. Why don't you practice by applying the gradient to the other black wheel shape to the right? You could save the gradient as a swatch and apply it to the other wheel.

9 Choose File > Save.

Applying a radial gradient to artwork

With a radial gradient, the starting color is the center of the fill. That color radiates outward to another color. Radial gradients are useful for giving elliptical shapes a circular type of gradient. Next, you'll sample a gradient to fill another shape that is part of the rolling hills in the scene.

1 Choose 1 Presentation Slide from the Artboard Navigation menu below the Document window to fit that artboard in the window.

2 With the Selection tool (▶) selected, click the pink hill shape.

3 Select the Eyedropper tool (✐) in the toolbar or press I.

4 Click the rolling hill shape you adjusted the gradient in earlier.

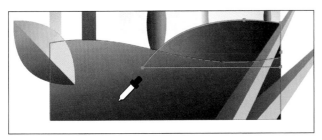

Tip: You could also have used the Eyedropper tool to sample the gradient from the bicycle wheel and apply it to the other wheel at the end of the previous section!

The same gradient is applied to the shape. We want the gradient to follow the contour of the hill, which would require the gradient to be an elliptical gradient. Next, you'll turn the gradient into an elliptical gradient.

5　In the Gradient panel, ensure that the Fill box is selected (an arrow is pointing to it in the figure). Click the Radial Gradient button to convert the linear gradient to a radial gradient.

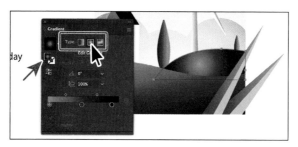

Editing the colors in the radial gradient

Previously in this lesson, you edited gradient colors in the Gradient panel. You can also edit the colors directly on artwork with the Gradient tool, which is what you'll do next.

1　Select the Gradient tool (🔲) in the toolbar.

2　In the Gradient panel, with the shape still selected, click the Reverse Gradient button (🔲) to swap the colors in the gradient.

3　To zoom in to the shape, press Command and + (macOS) or Ctrl and + (Windows) a few times.

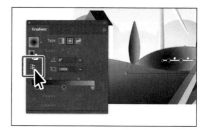

Notice how the gradient annotator starts from the center of the gradient and points to the right. Move the pointer over the annotator and a dashed circle appears around it. That circle indicates that it's a radial gradient. You can set additional options for radial gradients using it, as you'll soon see.

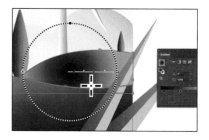

4　Move the pointer over the gradient annotator in the shape, and double-click the lighter green color stop on the right end of the annotator to edit the color (it's circled in the following figure). In the panel that appears, click the Swatches button (🔲), if it's not already selected. Select the swatch named Purple.

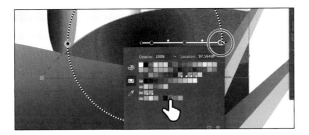

5 Press Escape to hide the Swatches panel.

6 Choose File > Save.

Adjusting the radial gradient

Next, you'll adjust the size, aspect ratio, and radius of the radial gradient so it follows the contour of the shape better.

1 With the Gradient tool (▨) selected in the toolbar and the shape still selected, move the pointer toward the bottom center of the shape (see the first part of the following figure).

2 Drag up to the top of the shape to change the gradient.

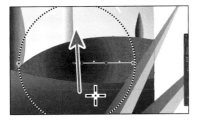
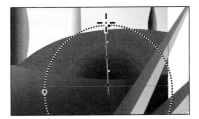

3 Move the pointer over the gradient annotator on the artwork so you can see the dashed ring around the gradient.

You can rotate this ring to change the angle of the radial gradient. The black point on the ring (⊙) is for changing the shape of the ring (called the *aspect ratio*), and the double-circle point (⊚) is for changing the size of the gradient (called the *spread*).

4 Move the pointer over the black circle (⊙) on the left side of the dashed ring. When the pointer changes (⬈), drag to make the gradient wider. Drag so the gradient follows the edge of the shape.

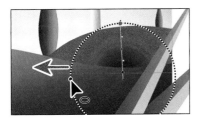
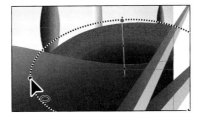

In the Gradient panel, you just changed the aspect ratio (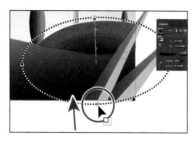) by dragging the black circle. The aspect ratio changes a radial gradient into an elliptical gradient and makes the gradient better match the shape of the artwork.

5   Move the pointer over the double-circle on the dashed circle (⊚) (see the first part of the following figure). When the pointer changes (⬝), drag to make the gradient larger or smaller—whichever looks best to you. I made it a little smaller.

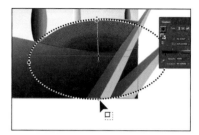

6   Leave the Gradient panel open.

7   Choose Select > Deselect, and then choose File > Save.

Applying gradients to multiple objects

You can apply a gradient to multiple objects by selecting all the objects, applying a gradient color, and then dragging across the objects with the Gradient tool to unify them. Now you'll apply a linear gradient fill to the yellow frame of a bike.

1   Choose 3 Bike from the Artboard Navigation menu below the Document window to fit that artboard in the window.

▶ **Tip:** I selected the frame shapes by Shift-clicking them. I then saved that selection by choosing Select > Save Selection.

2   With the Selection tool (▶) selected, choose Select > Bike Frame to select the five yellow parts of the bike frame.

3   Click the Fill box in the Properties panel. In the panel that appears, make sure the Swatches button (▦) is selected, and select the Background gradient swatch.

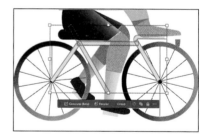

4 Select the Gradient tool () in the toolbar.

You can see that every object now has the gradient fill applied separately. With the Gradient tool selected, you can see that each object has its own annotator bar.

5 Looking at the following figure for guidance, start from off the left side of the left bike wheel and drag across to the right.

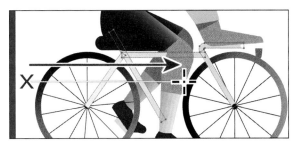

Note: In this case, where you start dragging is pure white. We don't want the frame to "disappear" (white on white), so we don't start dragging from the leftmost edge of the frame. If you start dragging farther from the left, by the time you drag into the frame, it's already transitioning to a light yellow.

Dragging across multiple shapes with the Gradient tool allows you to apply a gradient across those shapes.

Adding transparency to gradients

By specifying varying opacity values for the different color stops in your gradient, you can create gradients that fade in or out and that show or hide underlying artwork. Next, you'll apply a gradient that fades to transparent in a cloud shape.

1 Choose 1 Presentation Slide from the Artboard Navigation menu below the Document window to fit that artboard in the window.

2 Select the Selection tool (▶), and click the red cloud in the design.

3 Click the Fill color box in the Properties panel. Select the Background gradient.

4 Select the Gradient tool () in the toolbar. Drag from below the cloud up past the top edge at a slight angle.

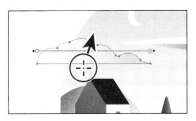 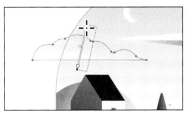

5 With the pointer over the shape, double-click the yellow color stop at the top of the annotator bar.

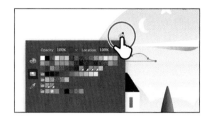

6 In the panel that opens, make sure the Swatches button ( ) is selected, and then select the white color from the swatches.

7 Choose 0% from the Opacity menu. Press the Escape key to hide the swatches.

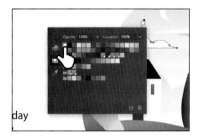

The color is completely transparent at the end of the gradient.

8 Drag the bottom color stop up to shorten the gradient a little.

9 Select the Selection tool and make a cloud copy by Option-dragging (macOS) or Alt-dragging (Windows) the cloud to the right.

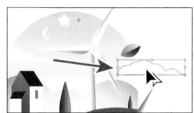

10 Choose File > Save.

Applying a freeform gradient

Aside from creating linear and radial gradients, you can also create freeform gradients. Freeform gradients are made of a series of color stops that you can place anywhere within a shape randomly or as a path. The colors blend between the color stops to create a freeform gradient.

Freeform gradients help add color blends that follow the contour of a shape, adding more realistic shading, and more, to artwork. Next, you'll apply a freeform gradient to the jersey of the bike rider.

1 Choose 3 Bike from the Artboard Navigation menu below the Document window to fit that artboard in the window.

2 Select the Selection tool ( ), and select the bright green jersey on the rider.

3 Choose View > Zoom In.

4 Select the Gradient tool (◧) in the toolbar.

5 Click the Freeform Gradient option (▥) in the Properties panel on the right.

6 Ensure that the Points option is selected in the Gradient section of the Properties panel (an arrow is pointing to it in the figure).

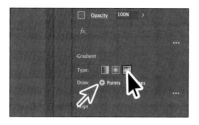

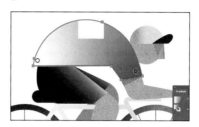

● **Note:** By default, Illustrator chooses color from surrounding artwork. This is because the preference Illustrator > Settings > General > Enable Content Aware Defaults (macOS) or Edit > Preferences > General > Enable Content Aware Defaults (Windows) is on by default. You can deselect this option to create your own color stops.

By default, a freeform gradient is applied in Points mode. Illustrator automatically adds individual solid colors that blend into each other. As with a linear or radial gradient, the colors are called *color stops*. The number of color stops Illustrator automatically adds depends on the shape and surrounding artwork. The color for each stop and the number of stops you see may not be the same as what is shown in the figures, and that's okay!

Editing a freeform gradient in Points mode

With Points mode selected, you add, move, edit, or delete individual color stops to change the overall gradient. In this section, you'll edit the color stops in your freeform gradient.

● **Note:** If you don't see the color stops shown in the next figure, know that you can drag color stops so they are in the same position to start, or you can click to add a new color stop.

1 Double-click the color stop on the arm of the jersey to show the color options.

2 With the swatches showing, select the Magenta swatch to apply it.

3 Press the Escape key to hide the panel.

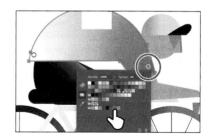

4 Drag the color stop up higher on the shoulder.

You can see that the gradient blending changes as you drag it. With each color stop, you can drag it, double-click to edit its color, and more.

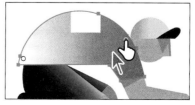

5 Double-click the color stop at the back of the jersey (mine is white), and change the color to the Dark Green swatch.

6 Drag the (now) dark green color stop to the right a little.

Dragging this color stop closer to the other adds more green and shortens the color transition from green to magenta. Next, you'll add a few color stops.

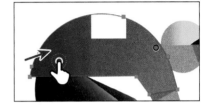

7 Add two more color stops by clicking in different areas of the jersey.

The new colors are the same color (mine are green).

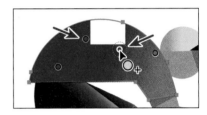

Tip: If you want to remove colors from the gradient, you could select one of the color stops on the back and press Delete or Backspace to remove it!

8 Double-click each color stop, one at a time, to edit the individual color. You can choose whatever colors you like. I chose purple and yellow.

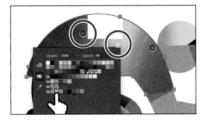

9 Drag a few of the color stops around to experiment with blending. You can see the result I came up with.

10 Move the pointer over the magenta color stop by the neck of the jersey. When you see the dotted circle appear, drag the widget at the bottom of the circle away from the color stop.

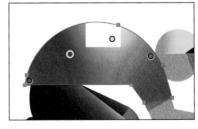

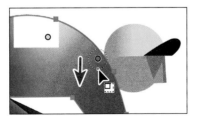
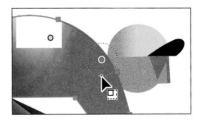

The color from that stop will "spread" farther away from the color stop.

Applying color stops in Lines mode

You can also add multiple solid colors that blend along a line in Lines mode. In this section, you'll add more color to the rider's jersey using Lines mode to add a darker shading.

1. Click near the end of the sleeve to add a new color stop.

2. Double-click the new color, and change the color to the swatch named Purple.

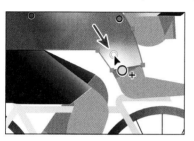 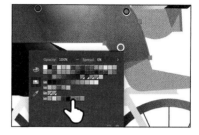

Note: The first part of the figure at left shows a white color stop added. Yours may be a different color, and that's okay.

3. In the Gradient panel or Properties panel, select the Lines option to be able to draw a gradient along a path.

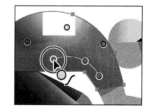

4. Select the last purple color stop you just added to the sleeve.

   You start a path with a single color stop, so you need to either select the stop you want to start with or make a new one.

5. Move the pointer up, and you'll see the path preview. Click to create a new color stop. You should see that it's the same purple color.

6. Click to make a final color stop down the jersey. The color stops are part of a curved path.

7. Try dragging any of the color stops on the path to reshape it.

   The color gradient follows the new path.

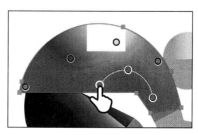

8. Close the Gradient panel.

9. Choose Select > Deselect, and then choose File > Save.

Creating blends

You can take two or more objects and "blend" them together. In a simple type of blend, Illustrator will create and distribute shapes evenly between those two objects. The shapes you blend can be the same or different. Here are a few examples of what is referred to as a "step" or "specified step" type of blend:

Blend between two of the same shape.

Blend between two of the same shape along a path.

Blend between two of the same shapes, each with a different color fill.

Blend between two different shapes with different fill colors.

You can also blend between two open paths to create a smooth transition of color between them, or you can combine blends of colors and objects to create color transitions in the shape of a particular object. Here are examples of this "smooth color" type of blend:

Smooth color blend between two stroked lines (original lines on left, blend on right).

Smooth color blend between two shapes with different color fills.

When you create a blend, the blended objects are grouped and called a *blend object*. If you move one of the original objects or edit the anchor points of the original object, the blend changes accordingly.

Creating a blend with specified steps

When objects are blended, you can choose from two options to blend them: Specified Steps and Smooth Color. In this section, you'll blend two trees to create a series of trees using specified steps.

1   Choose 1 Presentation Slide from the Artboard Navigation menu.

2   Zoom in to the trees on the right side of the artboard using any method.

3   With the Selection tool (▶) selected, select both trees.

4   Choose Object > Blend > Make.

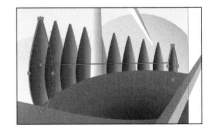

You should now see a series of copies of the trees, each copy changing in size from one tree to the next. Now you'll edit the blend settings to change the number of trees.

5   With the blended object still selected, choose Object > Blend > Blend Options.

6 In the Blend Options dialog box, choose Specified Steps from the Spacing menu. Change Specified Steps to **3** to see what it looks like—there are three copies between the two trees. You may need to deselect and select Preview to see the change. Click OK.

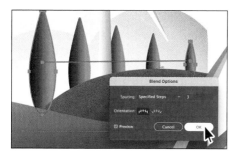

Modifying a blend

Now you'll edit one of the trees in the blend as well as the "spine" of the blend you just created so the shapes blend along a curve.

1 Select the Selection tool (▶) in the toolbar, and double-click anywhere on either tree in the blend object to enter Isolation mode.

The trees are temporarily ungrouped so you can edit each independently like any other group in Isolation mode.

2 Choose View > Outline.

Can you see the line between the trees? That is called the *spine.* The spine is a path along which the steps in a blended object are aligned. By default, the spine is a straight line. In Outline mode, you can see the outlines of the two original trees and the spine between them.

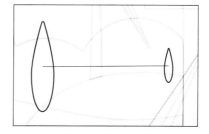

● **Note:** In the figure, I dimmed everything except the blend objects so you can see them better.

These three objects are what a blend object is composed of, by default.

3 Click the edge of the larger tree to select it. Shift-drag a corner to make it taller.

4 Choose Select > Deselect, and remain in Isolation mode.

Next, you'll curve the spine (path) that the blend follows.

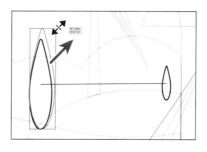

5 Select the Pen tool (✐) in the toolbar. Press the Option key (macOS) or Alt key (Windows), and move the pointer over the path between the trees. When the pointer shows this next to it: (✐), drag the path up so the path follows the contour of the hill beneath it, as in the figure.

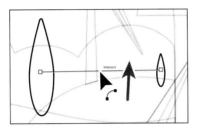 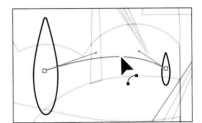

6 Choose View > Preview (or GPU Preview).

7 Press the Escape key to exit Isolation mode.

8 Choose Select > Deselect.

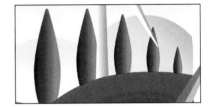

Creating a smooth color blend

When making a blend, if you choose the Smooth Color option for the blend when you edit the blend options, Illustrator combines the shapes *and* colors of the objects into many intermediate steps, creating a smooth, graduated blend between the original objects, as you see in the figure above.

Now you'll combine two stars to create a smooth color blend between them so they look like a shooting star.

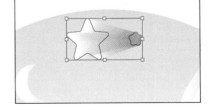

▶ **Tip:** You can also click the Blend Options button in the Properties panel to edit the options for a selected blend object.

● **Note:** Creating smooth color blends between paths can be difficult in certain situations. For instance, if the lines intersect or the lines are too curved, unexpected results may occur.

1 Select the Selection tool (▶), and in the yellow sky, above the trees, click the larger white star; then Shift-click the smaller orange star on the right to select both.

You may need to pan with the Hand tool.

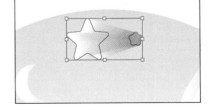

2 Choose View > Zoom In.

3 Choose Object > Blend > Make.

4 With the blend object still selected, double-click the Blend tool (◥₀) in the toolbar.

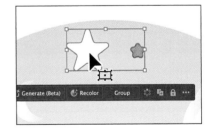

5 In the Blend Options dialog box, make sure that Smooth Color is chosen from the Spacing menu. Click OK.

6 Choose Select > Deselect.

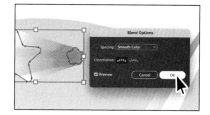

Editing a smooth color blend

Next, you'll edit the paths that make up the blend.

1 Select the Selection tool (▶), and double-click either star to enter Isolation mode.

2 Click the smaller star on the right to select it. Drag it into the center of the larger star. Notice that the colors are now blended.

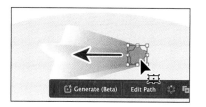

> **Note:** When you create the smooth blend and drag the smaller star, it may not look right, depending on your version of Illustrator. This known issue should be fixed in later versions of Illustrator. It may look right after you resize the star.

3 Change the fill color of the smaller star in the Properties panel to a yellow.

4 Press the Escape key to exit Isolation mode.

5 Choose Select > Deselect.

6 Select the star blend again, and Shift-drag to make it a little smaller.

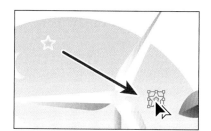

7 Option-drag (macOS) or Alt-drag (Windows) the star to another part of the sky to make a copy. Release the mouse button and then the key.

8 To see the artboard again, choose View > Fit Artboard In Window.

9 Choose File > Save.

Blending with the Blend tool 🎥

To learn another way to create a blend using the Blend tool, check out the video *Blending with the Blend tool*, which you'll find in the Web Edition. For more information, see the "Web Edition" section of "Getting Started" at the beginning of the book.

Getting creative with patterns

In addition to colors, spot colors, and gradients, you can also make and save patterns as swatches. A *pattern* is repeating artwork that can be applied to the stroke or fill of an object. Illustrator provides sample swatches of each type in the default Swatches panel as separate libraries and lets you create your own patterns as well. In this section, you will focus on creating, applying, and editing patterns.

Applying an existing pattern

You can design patterns from scratch or customize existing patterns with any of the Illustrator tools. Next, you'll apply a pattern that comes with Illustrator to the bicyclist's jersey.

1 Choose 3 Bike from the Artboard Navigation menu below the Document window to fit the artboard in the window.

2 With the Selection tool (▶) selected, click to select the rider's colorful jersey.

3 Choose Window > Appearance to open the Appearance panel.

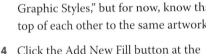

You'll learn a lot more about the Appearance panel in Lesson 13, "Exploring Creative Uses of Effects and Graphic Styles," but for now, know that you can add multiple strokes and fills on top of each other to the same artwork in the panel!

▶ **Tip:** You can drag the bottom of the panel down to see more of the panel content.

4 Click the Add New Fill button at the bottom of the Appearance panel.

This adds a new black fill to the shape that is layered on top of the colorful fill that you saw.

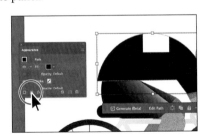

5 Choose Window > Swatch Libraries (near the bottom of the menu) > Patterns > Basic Graphics > Basic Graphics_Dots to open a library of patterns you can use.

6 Select the swatch named *6 dpi 40%*.

The pattern swatch fills the shape, replacing the black, as a second fill on top of the first.

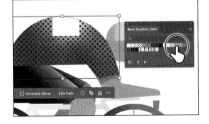

7 In the Appearance panel, click the arrow to the left of the *top* word "Fill" to show "Opacity," if you don't see it already.

8 Click Opacity to open the Transparency panel. Choose Screen from the Blend mode menu. Press the Escape key to hide the panel.

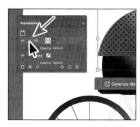 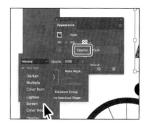 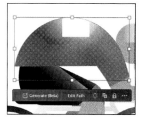

9 Choose Select > Deselect, and leave the Appearance panel open.

Creating your own pattern

In this section, you'll create your own custom pattern from leaves. Each pattern you create is saved as a swatch in the Swatches panel for the document you're working in.

1 Choose 2 Pattern from the Artboard Navigation menu below the Document window to fit the artboard in the window.

2 With the Selection tool (▶) selected, drag across the leaves to select them.

3 Choose Object > Pattern > Make.

You don't need to have anything selected when you create a pattern. You can add content to a pattern when editing in Pattern Editing mode, as you'll see.

4 Click OK in the dialog box that appears.

When you create a pattern, Illustrator enters Pattern Editing mode, which is similar to the Isolation mode you've worked with.

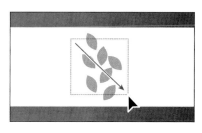

> **Note:** A pattern can be composed of shapes, symbols, or embedded raster images, among other objects that you can add in Pattern Editing mode. For instance, to create a flannel pattern for a shirt, you can create three overlapping rectangles or lines, each with varying appearance options.

Pattern Editing mode allows you to create and edit patterns while previewing the changes to the pattern. All other artwork is hidden and can't be edited in this mode. The Pattern Options panel (Window > Pattern Options) also opens, giving you all the necessary options to create and edit your pattern.

See the blue box around the darker leaves in the center? An arrow is pointing to it in the figure. I made it bolder so you could see it more easily. That box is the *pattern tile*—the area that repeats.

The series of lighter-colored leaves around the artwork in the center are generated copies that you can't edit. They are there for a preview and are a little dimmed so you can focus on the original.

5 Choose Select > All On Active Artboard to select the leaves.

6 In the Pattern Options panel, change Name to **Jersey Leaf**.

The name in the Pattern Options panel becomes the name of the swatch saved in the Swatches panel.

7 Try choosing different options from the Tile Type menu to see the effect on the pattern. Before continuing, make sure Grid is chosen.

Tile Type determines how the pattern is tiled. You have three main Tile Type choices: the default grid pattern, a brick-style pattern, and a hex pattern.

8 Choose 1 x 1 from the Copies menu at the bottom of the Pattern Options panel.

You will see only the original artwork now, not the repeat, so you can temporarily focus on it.

9 Deselect the leaves by choosing Select > Deselect.

10 Click to select the top, bottom, and far-right leaves. Delete them.

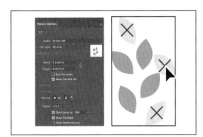

11 In the Pattern Options panel, choose 5 x 5 from the Copies menu to see the repeat again.

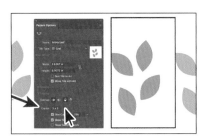

Notice how the blue tile box stayed the same size, even after deleting the leaves? By default, the tile won't change in size. But the pattern needs to have less space around the artwork—so you'll make the tile smaller.

12 Select the Size Tile To Art option in the Pattern Options panel.

The Size Tile To Art selection fits the tile area to the bounds of the artwork, changing the spacing between the repeated leaves, in this case.

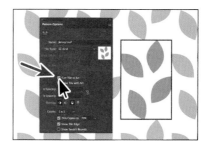

> **Tip:** With Size Tile To Art unselected, you could manually change the width and the height of the pattern definition area in the Width and Height fields to include more content or edit the spacing between.

13 To bring the leaves close together, change the V Spacing (vertical spacing between the tiles) to **–0.5** inches in the Pattern Options panel.

The H Spacing and V Spacing values can be either positive or negative, and they move the tiles apart or bring them closer together either horizontally (H) or vertically (V).

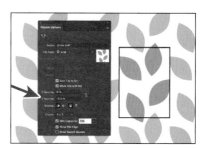

14 Click Done in the bar along the top of the Document window. If a dialog box appears, click OK.

15 Choose File > Save.

You'll still see the original art on the artboard that the pattern was made from!

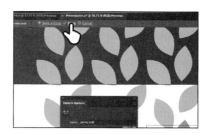

> **Tip:** If you want to create pattern variations, you can click Save A Copy in the bar along the top of the Document window when in Pattern Editing mode. This saves the current pattern in the Swatches panel as a copy and allows you to continue creating.

Applying your pattern

You can assign a pattern using a number of different methods. In this section, you'll use the Fill color box in the Properties panel to apply your pattern.

1 Choose 3 Bike from the Artboard Navigation menu below the Document window to fit the artboard in the window.

2 With the Selection tool (▶), click the rider's colorful jersey.

3 In the top "Fill" row of the Appearance panel, click the Fill color box to show a panel of swatches. You might need to click a few times. Select the Jersey Leaf pattern swatch you just made!

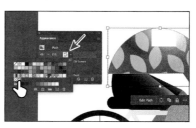

4 Close the Appearance panel.

Editing your pattern

Next, you'll edit the Jersey Leaf pattern swatch in Pattern Editing mode.

1 With the jersey shape still selected, click the Fill box in the Properties panel.

2 Double-click the Jersey Leaf pattern swatch to edit it in Pattern Editing mode.

3 Press Command and + (macOS) or Ctrl and + (Windows) to zoom in.

4 Choose Select > All to select the leaves.

5 In the Properties panel, change the fill color to the indigo swatch.

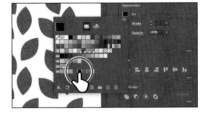

6 Click Done in the gray bar along the top of the Document window to exit Pattern Editing mode.

7 Select the jersey again and choose Object > Transform > Scale.

8 In the Scale dialog box, make sure that Transform Objects is deselected (we aren't trying to scale the jersey itself). Select Transform Patterns so the pattern will scale. Set the Uniform Scale to **60%**. Click OK.

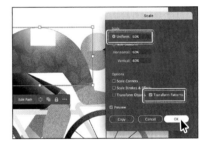

Putting it all together

In this last section, you will put the artwork for the presentation together.

1 Choose Select > All On Active Artboard to select all of the rider artwork.

2 Group it by clicking the Group button in the Properties panel.

3 Choose View > Fit All In Window.

● **Note:** If your artwork goes behind the artwork on the presentation artboard, click the Arrange button in the Properties panel and choose Bring To Front.

4 Drag the bicycle rider group onto the larger artboard on the left and arrange it like you see in the following figure.

5 You might want to make the bicycle rider group smaller by Shift-dragging a corner and then dragging it to fit in the presentation slide area better.

6 Choose File > Save, and then choose File > Close for all open files.

Review questions

1 What is a *gradient*?

2 How do you adjust the blend between colors in a linear or radial gradient?

3 Name two ways you can add colors to a linear or radial gradient.

4 How can you adjust the direction of a linear or radial gradient?

5 What is the difference between a gradient and a blend?

6 When you save a pattern in Illustrator, where is it saved?

Review answers

1 A gradient is a graduated blend of two or more colors or tints of the same color. Gradients can be applied to the stroke or fill of an object.

2 To adjust the blend between colors in a linear or radial gradient, with the Gradient tool (▣) selected and with the pointer over the gradient annotator or in the Gradient panel, drag the diamond icons or the color stops of the gradient slider.

3 To add colors to a linear or radial gradient, in the Gradient panel, click beneath the gradient slider to add a gradient stop to the gradient. Then double-click the color stop to edit the color, using the panel that appears, to mix a new color or to apply an existing color swatch. You can select the Gradient tool in the toolbar, move the pointer over the gradient-filled object, and then click beneath the gradient annotator that appears in the artwork to add or edit a color stop.

4 Drag across artwork with the Gradient tool to adjust the direction of a linear or radial gradient. You can also rotate the gradient using the Gradient tool and change the radius, aspect ratio, starting point, and more.

5 The difference between a gradient and a blend is the way that colors combine—colors blend together within a gradient and between objects in a blend.

6 When you save a pattern in Illustrator, it is saved as a swatch in the Swatches panel. By default, swatches are saved with the currently active document.

12 USING BRUSHES TO CREATE AN AD

Lesson overview

In this lesson, you'll learn how to do the following:

- Use four brush types: Calligraphic, Art, Pattern, and Bristle.

- Apply brushes to paths.

- Paint and edit paths with the Paintbrush tool.

- Change brush color and adjust brush settings.

- Create new brushes from Adobe Illustrator artwork.

- Work with the Blob Brush tool and the Eraser tool.

This lesson will take about 60 minutes to complete. To get the lesson files used in this lesson, download them from the web page for this book at *peachpit.com/IllustratorCIB2024*. For more information, see "Accessing the lesson files and Web Edition" in the Getting Started section at the beginning of this book.

The variety of brush types in Adobe Illustrator lets you create a myriad of effects by painting with the Paintbrush tool or drawing with the drawing tools. You can work with the Blob Brush tool; choose from the Art, Calligraphic, Pattern, Bristle, and Scatter brushes; and create new brushes based on your artwork.

Starting the lesson

In this lesson, you will learn how to work with the different brush types in the Brushes panel, change brush options, and create your own brushes. Before you begin, you'll restore the default preferences for Adobe Illustrator. Then you'll open the finished art file for the lesson to see the finished artwork.

● **Note:** If you have not already downloaded the project files for this lesson to your computer from your Account page, make sure to do so now. See the "Getting Started" section at the beginning of the book.

1 To ensure that the tools function and the defaults are set exactly as described in this lesson, delete or deactivate (by renaming) the Adobe Illustrator preferences file. See "Restoring default preferences" in the "Getting Started" section at the beginning of the book.

2 Start Adobe Illustrator.

3 Choose File > Open. In the Open dialog box, navigate to the Lessons > Lesson12 folder, and select the L12_end.ai file on your hard disk. Click Open to open the file.

4 If you want, choose View > Zoom Out to make the finished artwork smaller, and then adjust the window size and leave the artwork on your screen as you work. (Use the Hand tool [✋] to move the artwork to where you want it in the Document window.) If you don't want to leave the artwork open, choose File > Close.

To begin working, you'll open an existing art file.

5 Choose File > Open. In the Open dialog box, navigate to the Lessons > Lesson12 folder, and select the L12_start.ai file on your hard disk. Click Open to open the file.

6 Choose View > Fit All In Window.

7 Choose File > Save As. If the Cloud Document dialog box opens, click Save On Your Computer to save it locally.

8 In the Save As dialog box, name the file **UpLiftAd.ai**, and select the Lesson12 folder. Leave Adobe Illustrator (ai) chosen from the Format menu (macOS) or Adobe Illustrator (*.AI) chosen from the Save As Type menu (Windows) and then click Save.

9 In the Illustrator Options dialog box, leave the Illustrator options at their default settings, and then click OK.

● **Note:** If you don't see Reset Essentials in the workspace switcher menu, choose Window > Workspace > Essentials before choosing Window > Workspace > Reset Essentials.

10 Choose Reset Essentials from the workspace switcher in the Application bar to reset the workspace.

Working with brushes

You can decorate paths with patterns, figures, brush strokes, textures, or angled strokes using brushes. You can also modify the brushes provided with Illustrator and create brushes.

You can apply brush strokes to existing paths or use the Paintbrush tool to draw a path and apply a brush stroke simultaneously. You can change the color, size, and other brush features, and you can edit paths after brushes are applied (including adding a fill).

Types of brushes

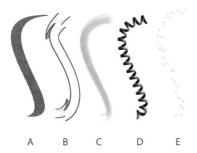

A. Calligraphic brush
B. Art brush
C. Bristle brush
D. Pattern brush
E. Scatter brush

There are five types of brushes that appear in the Brushes panel (Window > Brushes): Calligraphic, Art, Bristle, Pattern, and Scatter.

In this lesson, you will discover how to work with all except the Scatter brush.

▶ **Tip:** To learn more about Scatter brushes, search for "Scatter brushes" in Illustrator Help (Help > Illustrator Help).

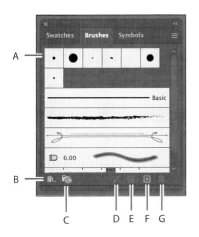

A. Brushes
B. Brush Libraries Menu
C. Libraries panel
D. Remove Brush Stroke
E. Options of selected object
F. New Brush
G. Delete Brush

Using Calligraphic brushes

The first type of brush you'll learn about is the Calligraphic brush. Calligraphic brushes resemble strokes drawn with the angled point of a calligraphic pen. Calligraphic brushes are defined by an elliptical shape whose center follows the path, and you can use these brushes to create the appearance of hand-drawn strokes made with a flat, angled pen tip.

Calligraphic brush examples.

Applying a Calligraphic brush to artwork

To get started, you'll filter the types of brushes shown in the Brushes panel so that it shows only Calligraphic brushes.

1 Choose Window > Brushes to open the Brushes panel. Click the Brushes panel menu icon (☰), and choose List View.

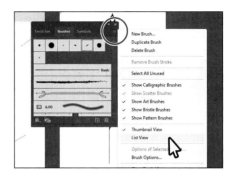

2 Click the Brushes panel menu icon (☰) again, and deselect the following, but leave the Calligraphic brushes visible:

- Show Art Brushes
- Show Bristle Brushes
- Show Pattern Brushes

A checkmark next to the brush type in the Brushes panel menu indicates that the brush type is visible in the panel. You can't deselect them all at once, so you'll have to keep clicking the menu icon (☰) to access the menu.

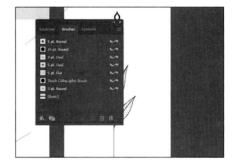

Your panel will wind up looking like the figure at right.

3 Select the Selection tool (▶) in the toolbar, and click the pink text object at the top of the artboard to select it. The text has been converted to paths because it was edited to create the appearance you see.

4 To zoom in, press Command and + (macOS) or Ctrl and + (Windows) a few times.

5 Select the 5 pt. Flat brush in the Brushes panel to apply it to the Puremental text shapes.

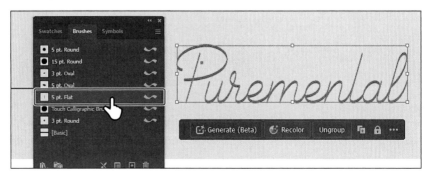

6 Change the Stroke weight to **5 pt** in the Properties panel to see the effect of
the brush.

As with an actual calligraphic pen, when you apply a Calligraphic brush, such as
the 5 pt. Flat brush, the more vertically you draw a path, the thinner the path's
stroke appears.

7 Change the Stroke weight to **1 pt**.

8 Click the Stroke color in the Properties panel, make sure the Swatches option
(▦) is selected, and select Black. Press the Escape key to hide the Swatches
panel, if necessary.

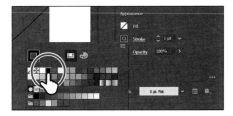 

9 Choose Select > Deselect, and then choose File > Save.

Editing a brush

To change the options for a brush, you can double-click the brush in the Brushes
panel. When you edit a brush, you can also choose whether to change artwork that
the brush has been applied to. Next you'll change the appearance of the 5 pt. Flat
brush you've been painting with.

1 In the Brushes panel, double-click
the brush thumbnail to the left
of the text "5 pt. Flat" or to the
right of the name in the Brushes
panel, to open the Calligraphic
Brush Options dialog box.

 Note: The edits you make will change the
brush for this document only.

2 In the dialog box make the following changes:

- Name: **8 pt. Angled**

- Angle: **35°**

- Choose Fixed from the menu to the right of Angle, if it isn't already. (When Random is chosen, a random variation of brush angles is created every time you draw.)

- Roundness: **15%** (This setting makes the brush stroke more or less round.)

- Size: **8 pt**

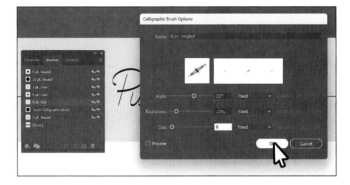

3 Click OK.

4 In the dialog box that appears, click Apply To Strokes so the brush changes will affect the text shapes that have the brush applied.

5 Choose Select > Deselect, if necessary, and then save the file by choosing File > Save.

Drawing with the Paintbrush tool

The Paintbrush tool allows you to apply a brush as you paint. Painting with the Paintbrush tool creates vector paths that you can edit with the Paintbrush tool or other drawing tools. Next you'll use the Paintbrush tool to paint part of the "t" in the text with a Calligraphic brush from a brush library.

1 Select the Paintbrush tool (✐) in the toolbar.

2 Click the Brush Libraries Menu button ([IMG]) at the bottom of the Brushes panel, and choose Artistic > Artistic_Calligraphic.

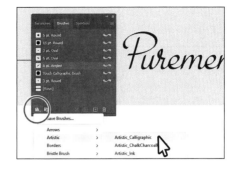

A brush library panel with various brushes appears.

Illustrator comes with a host of brush libraries that you can use in your artwork. Each brush type, including those discussed previously, has a series of libraries to choose from.

3 Click the Artistic_Calligraphic panel menu icon (☰), and choose List View. Click the brush named 15 pt. Flat to add it to the Brushes panel.

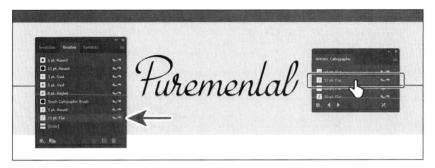

4 Close the Artistic_Calligraphic brush library panel.

Selecting a brush from a brush library, such as the Artistic_Calligraphic library, adds that brush to the Brushes panel for the active document only.

5 Make sure the fill color is None (▱), the stroke color is Black, and the stroke weight is 1 pt in the Properties panel.

With the pointer in the Document window, notice that the Paintbrush pointer has an asterisk next to it (✎₊), indicating that you are about to paint a new path.

6 Move the pointer to the left of the "t" in Puremental (see the first part of the following figure). Paint a curving path from left to right.

> **Note:** This Calligraphic brush creates random angles on the paths, so yours may not look like what you see in the figures, and that's okay.

7 Select the Selection tool, and click to select the new path you drew. Change the stroke weight to **0.5 pt** in the Properties panel on the right.

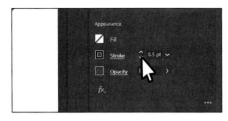 

8 Choose Select > Deselect (if necessary), and then choose File > Save.

Editing paths with the Paintbrush tool

Now you'll use the Paintbrush tool to edit paths.

1 With the Selection tool (▶) selected, click to select the Puremental text shapes.

2 Select the Paintbrush tool (✐) in the toolbar. Move the pointer over the capital "P"; see the figure for where. An asterisk will not appear next to the pointer when it's positioned anywhere over a selected path. Drag to redraw the path. The selected path is edited from the point at which you began drawing.

Notice that the letter shapes are no longer selected after you finish drawing with the Paintbrush tool. By default, paths are deselected.

3 Press and hold the Command (macOS) or Ctrl (Windows) key to toggle to the Selection tool, and click to select the curved path you drew on the letter "t." After clicking, release the key to return to the Paintbrush tool.

4 With the Paintbrush tool, move the pointer over some part of the selected path. When the asterisk disappears next to the pointer, drag to the right to redraw the path.

Next you'll edit the options of the Paintbrush tool to change how it paints.

5 Double-click the Paintbrush tool (✏) in the toolbar to display the Paintbrush Tool Options dialog box, and make the following changes:

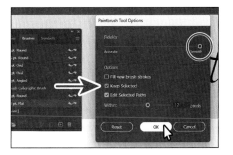

Note: This figure was created on Windows. The OK and Cancel buttons are flipped on macOS.

- Fidelity: Drag the slider all the way to Smooth (to the right).

- Keep Selected: Selected.

6 Click OK.

The Paintbrush Tool Options dialog box changes the way the Paintbrush tool functions. For the Fidelity option, the closer to Smooth you drag the slider, the smoother the path will be, and the fewer points it will have. Also, because you selected Keep Selected, the paths remain selected after you finish drawing them.

7 With the Paintbrush tool selected, once again press and hold the Command (macOS) or Ctrl (Windows) key to toggle to the Selection tool, and click to select the curved path you drew on the letter "t." Release the key. Try repainting the path once more.

Notice that now, after painting, the path is still selected, so you could edit it further if you needed to. Know that if you want to draw a series of overlapping paths with the Paintbrush tool, setting the tool option to *not* remain selected after you finish drawing paths is best. That way, you can draw overlapping paths without altering previously drawn paths.

8 Choose Select > Deselect, if necessary, and then choose File > Save.

Removing a brush stroke

You can easily remove a brush stroke applied to artwork where you don't want it. Now you'll remove the brush stroke from the stroke of a path.

1   Choose View > Fit Artboard In Window to see everything.

2   Select the Selection tool (▶), and click the black path with what looks like a chalk scribble down its length (see the following figure).

> When creating the artwork, I was trying out different brushes on the artwork. The brush applied to the stroke of the selected path needs to be removed.

▶ **Tip:** You can also select the [Basic] brush in the Brushes panel to remove a brush applied to a path.

3   In the Brushes panel, click the Remove Brush Stroke button (▨) at the bottom to remove it.

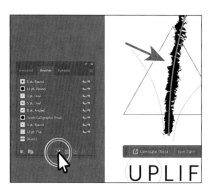 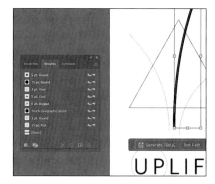

Removing a brush stroke doesn't remove the stroke color and weight; it just removes the brush applied.

4   Change the stroke weight to **1 pt** in the Properties panel.

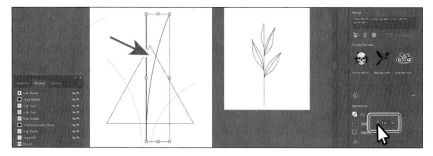

5   Choose Select > Deselect, and then choose File > Save.

Using Art brushes

Art brushes stretch artwork or an embedded raster image evenly along the length of a path. As with other brushes, you can edit the brush options to affect how the brush looks and is applied to paths.

Applying an existing Art brush

Next you'll apply an existing Art brush to the lines on either side of the text you edited at the top of the ad.

Art brush examples.

1 In the Brushes panel, click the Brushes panel menu icon (▤), and deselect Show Calligraphic Brushes. Then choose Show Art Brushes from the same panel menu to make the Art brushes visible in the Brushes panel.

2 Click the Brush Libraries Menu button (▣) at the bottom of the Brushes panel, and choose Decorative > Elegant Curl & Floral Brush Set.

3 Click the Elegant Curl & Floral Brush Set panel menu icon (▤), and choose List View. Click the brush named Floral Stem 3 in the list to add the brush to the Brushes panel for this document.

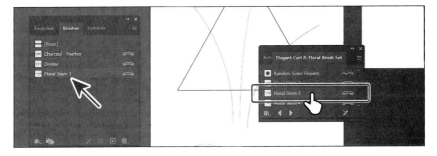

4 Close the Elegant Curl & Floral Brush Set panel group.

5   With the Selection tool selected, click the path to the left of the Puremental text.

6   To zoom in, press Command and + (macOS) or Ctrl and + (Windows) a few times.

7   Shift-click the path to the right of the text to select it as well.

8   Click the Floral Stem 3 brush in the Brushes panel.

9   Click the Group button in the Task bar beneath (or above) the artwork to keep them together.

10 Choose Select > Deselect, and then choose File > Save.

Creating an Art brush

In this section, you'll create a new Art brush from existing artwork. You can make Art brushes from embedded raster images or from vector artwork, but that artwork must not contain gradients, blends, other brush strokes, mesh objects, graphs, linked files, masks, or text that has not been converted to outlines.

1   Choose 2 from the Artboard Navigation menu in the Properties panel to navigate to the second artboard with the tea leaves artwork on it.

2   With the Selection tool (▶) selected, click the leaves artwork to select it (see the following figure).

3   In the Brushes panel, with the artwork still selected, click the New Brush button (⊞) at the bottom of the Brushes panel.

    This begins the process of creating a new brush from the selected artwork.

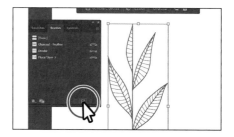

▶ **Tip:** You can also create an Art brush by dragging artwork into the Brushes panel and choosing Art Brush in the New Brush dialog box that appears.

4   In the New Brush dialog box, select Art Brush, and then click OK.

5 In the Art Brush Options dialog box that appears, change the name to **Tea Leaves**. Click OK.

6 Choose Select > Deselect.

7 Choose 1 from the Artboard Navigation menu in the Properties panel to navigate back to the first artboard.

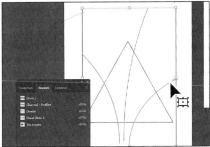

8 With the Selection tool selected, Shift-click to select the three vertical curved lines over the triangle in the center of the artboard.

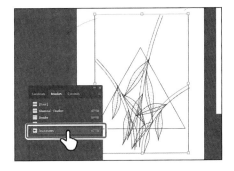

9 Click the brush named Tea Leaves in the Brushes panel to apply it.

Notice that the original tea leaf artwork is stretched along each path. This is the default behavior of an Art brush. Unfortunately, it's upside-down from how it should be. You'll fix that next.

Editing an Art brush

Next you'll edit the Tea Leaves brush you applied to the path and update the appearance of the paths on the artboard.

1 With the paths still selected on the artboard, in the Brushes panel, double-click the brush thumbnail to the left of the text "Tea Leaves" (or to the right of the name in the Brushes panel) to open the Art Brush Options dialog box.

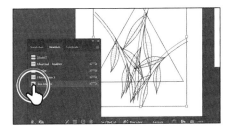

2 In the Art Brush Options dialog box, select Preview to see the changes on the artboard as you make them, and move the dialog box so you can see the line with the brush applied. Make the following changes:

- Stretch Between Guides: Selected. These guides are not physical guides on the artboard. They are used to indicate the portion of the art that stretches or contracts to make the Art brush fit the path length. Any part of the art that is not within the guides will be able to stretch or contract. The Start and End settings are how you indicate where the guides are positioned on the original art.

- Start: **7.375 in** (It's where the straight part of the leaves start)

- End: **10.8588 in** (default setting)

- Flip Along: **Selected**

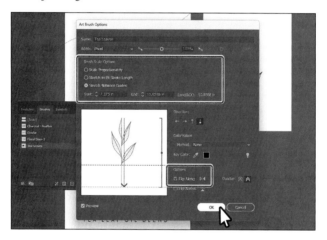

3 Click OK.

4 In the dialog box that appears, click Apply To Strokes to apply the change to the paths that have the Tea Leaves brush applied.

   Now you'll make a copy of the brush and make it so the artwork on the center path stretches along the path like it does without the guides set in the options.

5 Choose Select > Deselect and then click the larger, center path with the Tea Leaves brush applied (see the following figure).

6 In the Brushes panel, drag the Tea Leaves brush to the New Brush button at the bottom to make a copy.

7 Double-click the Tea Leaves brush *copy* thumbnail in the Brushes panel to edit it.

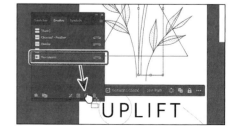

8 In the Art Brush Options dialog box, select Scale Proportionately from the Brush Scale Options section so artwork is scaled proportionally along the path.

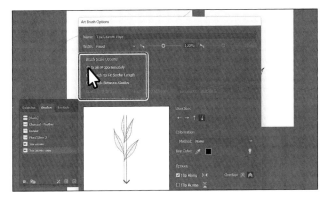

9 Click OK.

10 In the dialog box that appears, click Apply To Strokes to apply the change to the one path that has the Tea Leaves Copy brush applied.

11 Deselect the path.

12 Shift-click the remaining paths around the artboard and apply either the Tea Leaves or Tea Leaves Copy brush. Arrows are pointing to the paths in the figure.

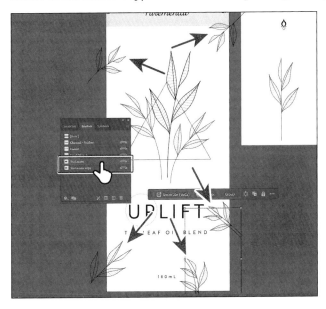

13 Choose Select > Deselect.

Using Pattern brushes

Pattern brushes paint a pattern made up of separate sections or tiles. When you apply a Pattern brush to artwork, different tiles of the pattern are applied to different path sections, depending on where the section falls on the path—the end, middle, or corner.

There are hundreds of interesting Pattern brushes that you can choose from when creating your projects, from grass to cityscapes. Next, you'll apply an existing Pattern brush to a triangle in the middle of the ad.

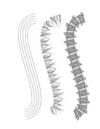

Pattern brush examples.

1 Choose View > Fit Artboard In Window.

2 In the Brushes panel, click the panel menu icon (▤), choose Show Pattern Brushes, and then deselect Show Art Brushes.

3 With the Selection tool (▶) selected, click the triangle in the middle of the ad.

4 Click the Brush Libraries Menu button (▯▮) at the bottom of the Brushes panel, and choose Borders > Borders_Geometric.

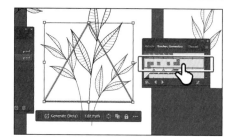

5 Click the brush named Geometric 17 to apply it to the paths and add the brush to the Brushes panel for this document.

6 Close the Borders_Geometric panel group.

7 Change the stroke weight in the Properties panel to **2 pt**.

Next, you'll edit the brush options only for the selected path.

▶ **Tip:** You'll also see the Options Of Selected Object button (▤) in the Properties panel.

8 Click the Options Of Selected Object button (▤) in the Brushes panel.

9 Select Preview in the Stroke Options (Pattern Brush) dialog box. Change the Scale to **120%** either by dragging the Scale slider or by typing in the value. Click OK.

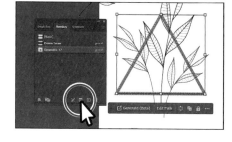

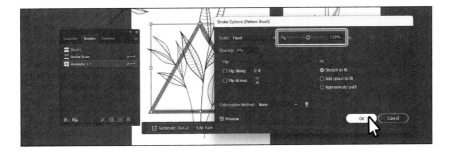

When you edit the brush options of the selected object, you see only some of the brush options. The Stroke Options (Pattern Brush) dialog box is used to edit the properties of the path with the brush applied without updating the corresponding brush.

10 Choose Select > Deselect, and then choose File > Save.

Creating a Pattern brush

You can create a Pattern brush in several ways. For a simple pattern applied to a straight line, for instance, you can select the content that you're using for the pattern and click the New Brush button () at the bottom of the Brushes panel.

To create a more complex pattern to apply to objects with curves and corners, you can select artwork in the Document window to be used in a pattern brush, create swatches in the Swatches panel from the artwork that you are using in the Pattern brush, and even have Illustrator autogenerate the Pattern brush corners.

The pattern you will create.

In Illustrator, only a side tile needs to be defined. Illustrator automatically generates four different types of corners based on the art used for the side tile. These four autogenerated options fit the corners perfectly. Next, you'll create a Pattern brush for decoration around the "UPLIFT" text.

1 With nothing selected, choose 2 from the Artboard Navigation menu in the Properties panel to navigate to the second artboard.

2 With the Selection tool (▶) selected, click to select the artwork at the top of the artboard.

3 To zoom in, press Command and + (macOS) or Ctrl and + (Windows) a few times.

4 Click the panel menu icon (▤) in the Brushes panel, and choose Thumbnail View.

Notice that Pattern brushes in the Brushes panel are segmented in Thumbnail view. Each segment corresponds to a pattern tile.

5 In the Brushes panel, click the New Brush button (⊞) to create a pattern out of the artwork.

6 In the New Brush dialog box, select Pattern Brush. Click OK.

 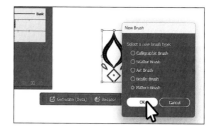

A new Pattern brush can be made regardless of whether artwork is selected. If you create a Pattern brush without artwork selected, it is assumed that you will add artwork by dragging it into the Brushes panel later or by selecting the artwork from a pattern swatch you create as you edit the brush. You will see the latter method later in this section.

7 In the Pattern Brush Options dialog box, name the brush **Decoration**.

Pattern brushes can have up to five tiles—the side, start, and end tiles, plus an outer-corner tile and an inner-corner tile to paint sharp corners on a path.

You can see all five tiles as buttons below the Spacing option in the

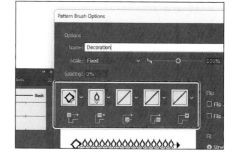

dialog box. The tile buttons let you apply different artwork to different parts of the path. You can click a tile button for the tile you want to define, and then you select an autogenerated selection (if available) or a pattern swatch from the menu that appears.

▶ **Tip:** Move the pointer over the tile squares in the Pattern Brush Options dialog box to see a tool tip indicating which tile it is.

▶ **Tip:** Selected artwork becomes the side tile, by default, when creating a Pattern brush.

8 Under the Spacing option, click the Side Tile box (the second tile from the left).

The decorative artwork that was originally selected is in the menu that appears, along with None and any pattern swatches found in the Swatches panel.

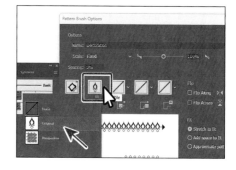

9 Click the Outer Corner Tile box to reveal the menu. You may need to click twice, once to close the previous menu and another click to open this new one.

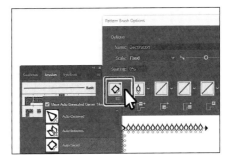

The outer-corner tile has been generated automatically by Illustrator, based on the original decorative artwork. In the menu, you can choose from four types of corners that are autogenerated:

- **Auto-Centered:** The side tile is stretched around the corner and centered on it.
- **Auto-Between:** Copies of the side tile extend all the way into the corner, with one copy on each side. They are then stretched into shape.
- **Auto-Sliced:** The side tile is sliced diagonally, and the pieces come together, similar to the miter joint at each corner of a wooden picture frame.
- **Auto-Overlap:** Copies of the tiles overlap at the corner.

10 Choose Auto-Between from the Outer Corner Tile box menu.

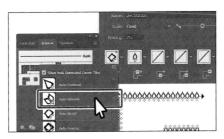

This generates the outer corner of any path that the Pattern brush will be applied to from the selected decorative artwork.

11 Click OK.

The Decoration brush appears in the Brushes panel.

12 Choose Select > Deselect.

Applying a Pattern brush

In this section, you'll apply the Decoration Pattern brush to a circle around the text in the center of the first artboard. As you've seen, when you use drawing tools to apply brushes to artwork, you first draw the path with the drawing tool and then select the brush in the Brushes panel to apply the brush to the path.

1 Choose 1 from the Artboard Navigation menu in the Properties panel to navigate to the first artboard with the ad artwork on it.

2 With the Selection tool () selected, click the circle around the "UP" text in "UPLIFT."

3 Choose View > Zoom In a few times to zoom in.

4 With the path selected, click the Decoration brush in the Brushes panel to apply it.

5 Choose Select > Deselect.

The path is painted with the Decoration brush. Because the path does not include sharp corners, outer-corner and inner-corner tiles are not applied to the path.

Editing a Pattern brush

▶ **Tip:** For more information on creating pattern swatches, see "About patterns" in Illustrator Help.

Now you'll edit the Decoration Pattern brush using a pattern swatch that you create.

1 Choose 2 from the Artboard Navigation menu in the Properties panel to navigate to the second artboard.

2 With the Selection tool (▶), click the same decoration artwork at the top of the artboard.

3 Change the stroke color to a light green color, as in the figure. Press the Escape key to hide the panel.

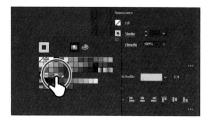 

4 Click the Swatches panel tab in the Brushes panel group to show the Swatches panel.

5 Drag the decoration artwork into the Swatches panel.

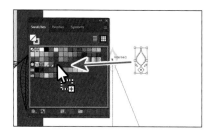 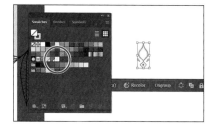

The artwork is saved as a new pattern swatch in the Swatches panel. After you create a Pattern brush, you can delete the pattern swatches from the Swatches panel if you don't plan to use them for additional artwork.

6 Choose Select > Deselect.

7 Choose 1 from the Artboard Navigation menu in the Properties panel to navigate to the first artboard with the main scene artwork on it.

8 Click the Brushes panel tab to show the panel, and double-click the Decoration Pattern brush to open the Pattern Brush Options dialog box.

9 Click the Side Tile box, and choose the pattern swatch named New Pattern Swatch 1, which you just created, from the menu that appears.

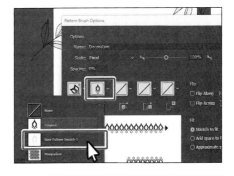

▶ **Tip:** You can also change the pattern tiles in a Pattern brush by pressing the Option (macOS) or Alt (Windows) key and dragging artwork from the artboard onto the tile of the Pattern brush you want to change in the Brushes panel.

10 Change Scale to **50%** so the pattern artwork is smaller.

11 Click OK.

12 In the dialog box that appears, click Apply To Strokes to update the Decoration brush and the brush applied to the circle.

13 With the Selection tool selected, click to select the triangle with the Geometric 17 brush applied. You may want to zoom in.

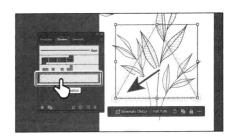

14 Click the Decoration brush in the Brushes panel to apply it.

Notice that the corners appear (an arrow is pointing to one in the figure). The path is painted with the side tile from the Decoration brush and the outer-corner tile.

15 Click to apply the Geometric 17 brush again.

16 Choose Select > Deselect, and then choose File > Save.

Using Bristle brushes

Bristle brushes allow you to create strokes with the appearance of a natural brush with bristles. Painting with a Bristle brush using the Paintbrush tool creates vector paths with the Bristle brush applied.

In this section, you'll start by adjusting options for a brush to change how it appears in the artwork and then paint with the Paintbrush tool and a Bristle brush.

Bristle brush examples.

Changing Bristle brush options

As you've seen, you can change the appearance of a brush by adjusting its settings in the Brush Options dialog box, either before or after brushes have been applied to artwork. In the case of Bristle brushes, it's usually best to adjust the brush settings before painting, since it can take some time to update the brush strokes.

1   In the Brushes panel, click the panel menu icon (▤), choose Show Bristle Brushes, deselect Show Pattern Brushes, and choose List View.

▶ **Tip:** Illustrator comes with a series of default Bristle brushes. Click the Brush Libraries Menu button (▣) at the bottom of the Brushes panel, and choose Bristle Brush > Bristle Brush Library.

2   Double-click the thumbnail for the default Mop brush, or double-click directly to the right of the brush name in the Brushes panel, to change the options for that brush. In the Bristle Brush Options dialog box, make the following changes:

- Shape: **Round Fan**

- Size: **10 mm** (The brush size is the diameter of the brush.)

- Bristle Length: **150%** (This is the default setting. The bristle length starts from the point where the bristles meet the handle of the bristle tip.)

- Bristle Density: **33%** (This is the default setting. The bristle density is the number of bristles in a specified area of the brush neck.)

- Bristle Thickness: **70%** (The bristle thickness can vary from fine to coarse [from 1% to 100%].)

- Paint Opacity: **75%** (This is the default setting. This option lets you set the opacity of the paint being used.)

- Stiffness: **50%** (This is the default setting. Stiffness refers to the rigidness of the bristles.)

3   Click OK.

Painting with a Bristle brush

Now you'll use the Mop brush to draw some strokes behind the artwork to add some texture to the background of the ad. Painting with a Bristle brush can create an organic, fluid path.

1 Choose View > Fit Artboard In Window.

2 With the Selection tool (▶) selected, click to select the "UPLIFT" text.

This selects the layer that the text shapes are on so that any artwork you paint will be on the same layer. The UPLIFT text shapes are on a layer that is beneath most of the other artwork on the artboard.

3 Choose Select > Deselect.

4 Select the Paintbrush tool (✐) in the toolbar. Choose the Mop brush from the Brushes panel or from the Brush menu in the Properties panel, if it's not already chosen.

5 Make sure that the fill color is None (☐) and the stroke color is the same light green from the Decoration brush, in the Properties panel.

6 Change the stroke weight to **5 pt** in the Properties panel.

7 Move the pointer to the right of the triangle in the middle of the page (see the figure). Drag slightly down and to the left, across the artboard, and then back again to the right to make a sideways V shape. Release the mouse button when you reach the end of the path you want to draw.

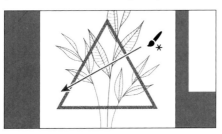 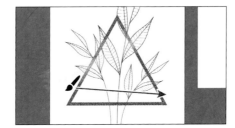

8 With the Paintbrush tool, use the Mop brush to paint more paths around the artboard.

These paths are meant to add texture to the ad. I added pink paths to the figure to show you where we added two more paths to the ad.

> **Note:** If your path winds up with a 1 pt stroke, with it still selected, change the stroke weight to 5 pt in the Properties panel.

Grouping Bristle brush paths

Next you'll group the paths you drew with the Mop brush to make it easier to select them later.

1 Choose View > Outline to see all of the paths you just created.

Next you'll select all of the Bristle brush paths you painted and group them together.

2 Choose Select > Object > Bristle Brush Strokes to select all of the paths created with the Paintbrush tool using the Mop brush. In the figure, I added pink paths to show you where my paths were.

3 Click the Group button toward the bottom of the Properties panel to group them together.

4 Choose View > Preview (or GPU Preview).

5 Choose Select > Deselect, and then choose File > Save.

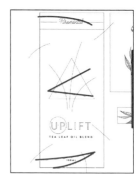

Working with the Blob Brush tool

You can use the Blob Brush tool () to paint filled shapes that intersect and merge with other shapes of the same color. With the Blob Brush tool, you can draw with Paintbrush tool artistry. Unlike the Paintbrush tool, which lets you create open paths, the Blob Brush tool lets you create a closed shape with only a fill (no stroke) that you can then easily edit with the Eraser or Blob Brush tool. Shapes that have a stroke cannot be edited with the Blob Brush tool.

Path created with the Paintbrush tool.

Shape created with the Blob Brush tool.

Drawing with the Blob Brush tool

Next you'll use the Blob Brush tool to add color to one of the leaf shapes.

1 With the Selection tool selected (▶), click the largest bunch of leaves in the center of the artboard (over the triangle).

2 Press Command and + (macOS) or Ctrl and + (Windows) a few times.

3 Deselect the leaves by clicking in an empty area of the artboard.

4 Press and hold down on the Paintbrush tool (✐) in the toolbar, and select the Blob Brush tool (🖌).

5 Click the Swatches panel tab in the Brushes panel group to show the Swatches panel. Select the Fill box to edit the fill color, and then select the same light green swatch you've been using up to this point.

6 Select the Stroke color box, and select None (□) to remove the stroke.

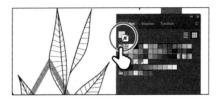

When drawing with the Blob Brush tool, if a fill and stroke are set before drawing, the stroke color becomes the fill color of the shape made by the Blob Brush tool. If only a fill is set before drawing, it ultimately becomes the fill of the shape created.

7 Move the pointer near the largest bunch of leaves in the center. To change the Blob Brush size, press the right bracket key ( ]) several times to increase the size of the brush.

Notice that the Blob Brush pointer has a circle around it. That circle indicates the size of the brush. Pressing the left bracket key ([ ) will make the brush size smaller.

8 Drag around the outside of the leaf shape to loosely draw another leaf shape.

When you draw with the Blob Brush tool, you create filled, closed shapes that can contain any type of fill.

9 Select the Selection tool and click the artwork you just made.

Notice that it's a filled shape, not a path with a stroke.

10 Click in an empty area of the artboard to deselect, and select the Blob Brush tool in the toolbar again.

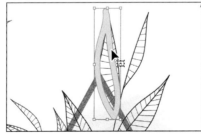

11 Drag to fill in the shape and maybe add a bit more to it.

As long as the new artwork is overlapping the existing artwork and it has the same stroke and fill, it will merge into one shape.

▶ **Tip:** If you want, try adding more shapes to the other leaves following the same steps.

Editing with the Eraser tool

▶ **Tip:** As you draw with the Blob Brush and Eraser tools, it is recommended that you use shorter strokes and release the mouse button often. You can undo the edits that you make, but if you draw in one long stroke without releasing the mouse button, undoing removes the entire stroke.

As you draw and merge shapes with the Blob Brush tool, you may draw too much and want to edit what you've done. You can use the Eraser tool (◆) in combination with the Blob Brush tool to mold the shape and to correct any changes you don't like.

1   With the Selection tool (▶), click to select the green shape you just made.

2   Click the Arrange button in the Properties panel, and choose Send To Back to put it behind the path with the Tea Leaves Copy brush applied.

Selecting the shape(s) before erasing also limits the Eraser tool to erasing only the selected shape(s). As with the Paintbrush or Blob Brush tools, you can also double-click to set options for the Eraser tool. In this case, you'll use it as is and simply adjust the brush size.

3   Select the Eraser tool (◆) in the toolbar. Move the pointer near the green shape you made. To change the eraser size, press the right bracket key ( ]) several times to increase the size of the brush.

The Blob Brush and Eraser tools both have pointers that include a circle that indicates the diameter of the brush.

4   Move the pointer just off the upper left of the green shape and, with the Eraser tool selected, press and drag along the edge to remove some of it. Try switching between the Blob Brush tool and the Eraser tool to edit the shape.

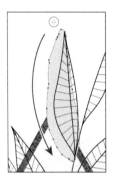 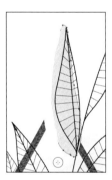 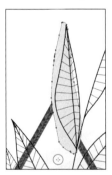

5   Choose Select > Deselect.

6   Choose View > Fit Artboard In Window.

In the figure, you can see that I added more green shapes I created with the Blob Brush and Eraser tools for some practice.

7   Choose File > Save, and close all open files.

Review questions

1 What is the difference between applying a brush to artwork using the Paintbrush tool (✐) and applying a brush to artwork that you made using one of the drawing tools?

2 Describe how artwork in an Art brush is applied to content.

3 Describe how to edit paths with the Paintbrush tool as you draw. How does the Keep Selected option affect the Paintbrush tool?

4 For which brush types must you have artwork selected on the artboard before you can create a brush?

5 What does the Blob Brush tool (✑) allow you to create?

6 How do you ensure that only certain artwork is erased when using the Eraser tool?

Review answers

1 When painting with the Paintbrush tool (✐), if a brush is chosen in the Brushes panel and you draw on the artboard, the brush is applied directly to the paths as you draw. To apply brushes using a drawing tool, you select the tool and draw in the artwork. Then you select the path in the artwork and choose a brush in the Brushes panel. The brush is applied to the selected path.

2 An Art brush is made from artwork (vector or embedded raster). When you apply an Art brush to the stroke of an object, the artwork in the Art brush, by default, is stretched along the selected object stroke.

3 To edit a path with the Paintbrush tool, drag over a selected path to redraw it. The Keep Selected option keeps the last path selected as you draw with the Paintbrush tool. Leave the Keep Selected option selected when you want to easily edit the previous path as you draw. Deselect the Keep Selected option when you want to draw layered paths with the paintbrush without altering previous paths. When Keep Selected is deselected, you can use the Selection tool (▶) to select a path and then edit it.

4 For Art (and Scatter) brushes, you need to have artwork selected to create a brush using the New Brush button (▣) in the Brushes panel.

5 Use the Blob Brush tool (✑) to create and edit filled shapes that you can intersect and merge with other shapes of the same color or to create artwork from scratch.

6 To ensure that only certain artwork is erased, select the artwork.

13 EXPLORING CREATIVE USES OF EFFECTS AND GRAPHIC STYLES

Lesson overview

In this lesson, you'll learn how to do the following:

- Work with the Appearance panel.

- Edit and apply appearance attributes.

- Duplicate, enable, disable, and remove appearance attributes.

- Reorder appearance attributes.

- Apply and edit a variety of effects.

- Add Photoshop effects.

- Work with 3D effects.

- Save and apply an appearance as a graphic style.

- Apply a graphic style to a layer.

- Scale strokes and effects.

This lesson will take about 60 minutes to complete. To get the lesson files used in this lesson, download them from the web page for this book at *peachpit.com/IllustratorCIB2024*. For more information, see "Accessing the lesson files and Web Edition" in the Getting Started section at the beginning of this book.

You can change the look of an object without changing its structure simply by applying attributes, such as fills, strokes, and effects, from the Appearance panel. Since the effects are live, they can be modified or removed at any time. This allows you to save the appearance attributes as graphic styles and apply them to another object.

Starting the lesson

In this lesson, you'll change the appearance of artwork for a birthday invite using the Appearance panel, various effects, and graphic styles. Before you begin, you'll need to restore the default preferences for Adobe Illustrator. Then you'll open a file containing the final artwork to see what you'll create.

Note: If you have not already downloaded the project files for this lesson to your computer from your Account page, make sure to do so now. See the "Getting Started" section at the beginning of the book.

1 To ensure that the tools function and the defaults are set exactly as described in this lesson, delete or deactivate (by renaming) the Adobe Illustrator preferences file. See "Restoring default preferences" in the "Getting Started" section at the beginning of the book.

2 Start Adobe Illustrator.

3 Choose File > Open, and open the L13_end.ai file in the Lessons > Lesson13 folder on your hard disk.

This file displays a completed illustration for a birthday card.

Note: You will need an internet connection to activate fonts.

4 In the Missing Fonts dialog box that most likely will appear, click Activate Fonts to activate all of the missing fonts. After they are activated and you see the message stating that there are no more missing fonts, click Close.

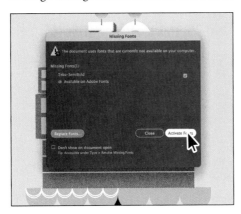

If you can't get the fonts to activate, go to the Creative Cloud desktop application and click the Fonts icon (f) in the upper right to see what the issue may be (refer to the section "Changing font family and font style" in Lesson 9 for more information on how to resolve it).

You can also just click Close in the Missing Fonts dialog box and ignore the missing fonts as you proceed. A third method is to click the Find Fonts button in the Missing Fonts dialog box and replace the fonts with a local font on your machine. You can also go to Help (Help > Illustrator Help) and search for "Find missing fonts."

5 If a dialog box appears referring to font auto-activation, then click Skip.

6 Choose View > Fit Artboard In Window. Leave the file open as a reference or choose File > Close to close it.

To begin working, you'll open an existing art file.

7 Choose File > Open. In the Open dialog box, navigate to the Lessons > Lesson13 folder, and select the L13_start.ai file on your hard disk. Click Open to open the file.

The L13_start.ai file uses the same fonts as the L13_end.ai file. If you've activated the fonts already, you don't need to do it again. If you didn't open the L13_end.ai file, then the Missing Fonts dialog box will most likely appear for this step. Click Activate Fonts to activate all of the missing fonts. After they are activated and you see the message stating that there are no more missing fonts, click Close.

8 Choose File > Save As. If the Cloud Document dialog box opens, click Save On Your Computer; otherwise, continue.

9 In the Save As dialog box, name the file **BirthdayInvite.ai**, and select the Lesson13 folder. Leave Adobe Illustrator (ai) chosen from the Format menu (macOS) or Adobe Illustrator (*.AI) chosen from the Save As Type menu (Windows), and then click Save.

10 In the Illustrator Options dialog box, leave the Illustrator options at their default settings, and then click OK.

11 Choose Reset Essentials from the workspace switcher in the Application bar to reset the workspace.

⬤ **Note:** If you don't see Reset Essentials in the workspace switcher menu, choose Window > Workspace > Essentials before choosing Window > Workspace > Reset Essentials.

12 Choose View > Fit Artboard In Window.

Using the Appearance panel

An *appearance attribute* is an aesthetic property—like a fill, stroke, transparency, or effect—that affects the look of an object but usually does not affect its basic structure. Up to this point, you've been changing appearance attributes in the Properties panel, Swatches panel, and more. Appearance attributes like these can also be found in the Appearance panel for selected artwork. In this lesson, you'll focus on using the Appearance panel to apply and edit appearance attributes.

To begin exploring appearance options, you'll see how to edit the color fill of the cake stand and then add another fill on top to give it more dimension.

1 Select the Selection tool (▶), and click to select the black base of the cake stand.

Tip: You can also choose Window > Appearance to open the Appearance panel.

2 Click More Options (•••) in the Appearance section of the Properties panel on the right (an arrow is pointing to it in the following figure) to open the Appearance panel.

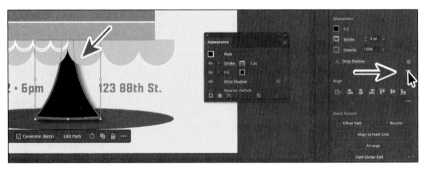

Tip: You may want to drag the bottom of the Appearance panel down to make it taller, as you see in the figure.

The Appearance panel (Window > Appearance) shows what the selected content is (a path, in this case) and the appearance attributes applied to it (stroke, fill, etc.). The different options available in the Appearance panel are shown here:

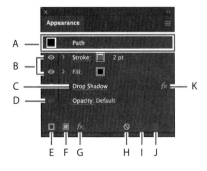

A. Appearance thumbnail and type of artwork selected

B. Example Attribute rows (Stroke and Fill)

C. Link to edit an effect

D. Visibility column

E. Add New Stroke

F. Add New Fill

G. Add New Effect

H. Clear Appearance

I. Duplicate Selected Item

J. Delete Selected Item

K. Indicates that an effect is applied

You can view and adjust the appearance attributes for a selected object, group, or layer in the Appearance panel. Fills and strokes are listed in stacking order; top to bottom in the panel correlates to the front to back in the artwork. Effects applied to artwork are listed from top to bottom in the order they are applied to the artwork. An advantage of using appearance attributes is that they can be changed or removed without affecting the underlying artwork or any other attributes applied to the object in the Appearance panel.

Editing appearance attributes

You'll start by changing the appearance of artwork using the Appearance panel.

1 With the cake stand selected, in the Appearance panel, click the black Fill box in the fill attribute row as many times as needed until the Swatches panel appears. Select the swatch named Aqua to apply it to the fill.

Note: You may need to click the Fill box more than once to open the Swatches panel. The first click of the Fill box selects the Fill row in the panel, and the next click shows the Swatches panel.

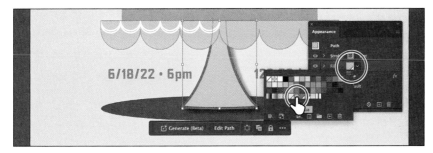

2 Press the Escape key to hide the Swatches panel.

3 Click the words "2 pt" in the pink Stroke row to show the Stroke Weight option. Change the stroke weight to **0** to remove it (the Stroke Weight field will be blank).

So far, everything you've changed could have been done in the Properties panel. Now you'll explore something unique to the Appearance panel—hiding an effect (not deleting it).

▶ **Tip:** You can view all hidden attributes (attributes you have turned off) by choosing Show All Hidden Attributes from the Appearance panel menu (▤).

4 Click the visibility column (👁) to the left of the Drop Shadow attribute name in the Appearance panel so the cake stand no longer shows a drop shadow.

I dragged the bottom of the Appearance panel down to make it taller in the figures. Appearance attributes can be temporarily hidden or deleted so that they are no longer applied to the selected artwork.

▶ **Tip:** In the Appearance panel, you can also drag an attribute row, such as Drop Shadow, to the Delete Selected Item button (🗑) to delete it.

5 With the Drop Shadow row selected (click to the right of the link "Drop Shadow" if it isn't selected), click the Delete Selected Item button (🗑) at the bottom of the panel to completely remove the shadow, rather than just turning off the visibility. Leave the shape selected.

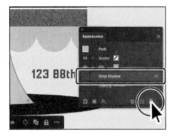

Adding another fill to content

Artwork and text in Illustrator can have more than one stroke and fill applied. This can be a great way to add interest to design elements like shapes and paths, and adding multiple strokes and fills to text can be a great way to make your text pop.

Next you'll add another fill to the cake stand to add texture over the color fill.

1 With the cake stand shape still selected, in the Appearance panel, click the Add New Fill button (▢) at the bottom of the Appearance panel.

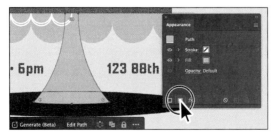

A second Fill row is added to the Appearance panel. By default, new fill or stroke attribute rows are added directly above a selected attribute row or, if no attribute rows are selected, at the top of the Appearance panel list.

2   Click the *bottom* (original) aqua Fill box in the fill attribute row a few times until the Swatches panel appears. Click the pattern swatch named 6 lpi 10% to change the fill.

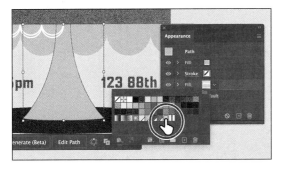

3   Press the Escape key to hide the Swatches panel.

The pattern doesn't show in the selected artwork because the second fill you added in the first step is covering the 6 lpi 10% fill. The two fills are stacked on top of each other.

4   Click the eye icon ( ) to the left of the top aqua Fill row to hide it.

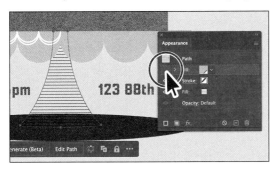

You should now see the pattern fill in the shape. In the next section, you'll reorder the attribute rows in the Appearance panel so the pattern is on top of the color fill.

5   Click where the eye icon was to the left of the top Fill attribute row to make it visible again.

6   Choose Select > Deselect, and then choose File > Save.

Adding multiple strokes and fills to text

Aside from adding multiple strokes and fills to artwork, you can also do the same for text. The text remains editable, and you can use a number of effects to achieve the look that you want. Now you'll take the "BIRTHDAY BASH!" text and make it pop with a few strokes and fills.

1   Select the Type tool (**T**), and select the text "BIRTHDAY BASH!"

Notice that "Type: No Appearance" appears at the top of the Appearance panel. That means there are no additional appearance properties added to the text beyond what you had applied initially in the Properties panel. You will also see the word "Characters." Formatting for the text (not the type object) is listed below the word "Characters." You should see the stroke (none) and the fill (pink).

Also notice that you cannot add another stroke or fill to the text, since the Add New Stroke and Add New Fill buttons are dimmed at the bottom of the panel. To add new strokes or fills to text, you need to select the type *object*, not the text within.

▷ **Tip:** You could also click Type: No Appearance at the top of the Appearance panel to select the type object (not the text within).

2   Select the Selection tool (▶). The type object will now be selected (not the text).

3   Click the Add New Fill button (▣) at the bottom of the Appearance panel to add a fill and a stroke above the word "Characters."

You might be wondering why adding a new fill *also* added a new stroke. That's because neither was there for the type object, and if you have a fill, you have to have a stroke, and vice versa.

The new black fill is covering the original pink fill of the text. If you were to double-click the word "Characters" in the Appearance panel, you would select the text and see the initial formatting options for it (fill, stroke, etc.).

4   Click the black Fill box a few times to see the Swatches panel, and select the pattern swatch named 0 to 50% Dot Gradation.

● **Note:** Why would I name a swatch 0 to 50% Dot Gradation? Actually, I didn't. That pattern swatch can be found in Illustrator by default (Window > Swatch Libraries > Patterns > Basic Graphics > Basic Graphics_Dots).

5   Press the Escape key to hide the swatches.

At this point, I will stop instructing you to close panels, hoping that this is becoming a habit.

When you apply a fill to a text object, an extra stroke with no color is also applied. You don't have to use it.

6   If necessary, click the triangle (▶) to the left of the Fill row to show other properties, like Opacity. Click the word "Opacity," which is indented below the fill row, to show the Transparency panel, and change Opacity to **40%**.

Each appearance row (stroke, fill) has its own opacity that you can adjust. The bottom Opacity appearance row in the panel affects the transparency for the entire selected object. Next you'll add two strokes to the text using the Appearance panel. This is another great way to achieve unique design effects with a single object.

7 Click the Stroke box () a few times in the Appearance panel to show the swatches. Select the white swatch.

8 Ensure that the Stroke Weight is **1 pt**.

9 Click the Add New Stroke button (■) at the bottom of the Appearance panel.

A second stroke, which is a copy of the original, is now added to the text. This is a great way to add interest to your designs without having to make copies of shapes and put them on top of each other to add multiple strokes and fills.

10 With the new (top) stroke attribute row selected, select the swatch named Orange to apply it.

11 Ensure that the Stroke Weight is **1 pt**.

12 Click the word "Stroke" in the same attribute row to open the Stroke panel. Click the Round Join option () in the Corner section of the panel to *slightly* round the corners of the stroke. Press the Escape key to hide the Stroke panel. Leave the type object selected.

Clicking underlined words in the Appearance panel, as in the Properties panel, shows more formatting options—usually a panel such as the Swatches or Stroke panel. Appearance attributes, such as Fill or Stroke, can have other options, such as Opacity or an effect applied to only that attribute. These additional options are listed as a subset under the attribute row and can be shown or hidden by clicking the disclosure triangle (▶) on the left end of the attribute row.

Reordering appearance attributes

The ordering of the appearance attribute rows can greatly change how your artwork looks. In the Appearance panel, fills and strokes are listed in stacking order—top to bottom in the panel correlates to front to back in the artwork. You can reorder attribute rows in a way similar to dragging layers in the Layers panel to rearrange the stacking order. Next you'll change the appearance of artwork by reordering attributes in the Appearance panel.

1 With the text still selected, press Command and + (macOS) or Ctrl and + (Windows) to zoom in.

2   In the Appearance panel, click the eye icon to the left of the white Stroke row to hide it temporarily.

3   Click the arrows to the left of all Stroke and Fill rows to hide the Opacity for each.

You may want to make the Appearance panel taller by dragging the bottom down.

4   Drag the orange stroke row in the Appearance panel down below the word "Characters." When a line appears below the word "Characters," release the mouse button to see the result.

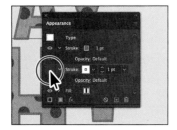 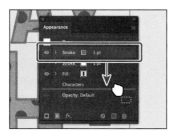 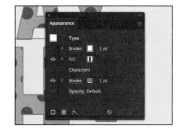

The orange stroke is now behind all fills and the white stroke. The word "Characters" represents where the stroke and fill (the pink color) of the text (not the text object) sit in the stacking order.

5   Click where the eye icon (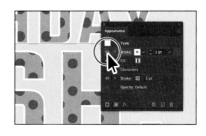) was for the white stroke row to show it again.

6   With the Selection tool (►) selected, click to select the cake stand you edited earlier.

You might need to select the Hand tool and drag in the window to see.

7   In the Appearance panel, drag the aqua Fill row down below the pattern Fill row, and release.

Moving the aqua fill attribute below the pattern fill attribute definitely changes the look of the artwork. The pattern fill is now on top of the solid color fill.

8   Choose Select > Deselect, and then choose File > Save.

Using live effects

Effects are how you apply the cool stuff to your artwork. Ever heard of a drop shadow (or just a shadow)? That's an effect. There are tons of effects, and they open up worlds of creative possibilities.

Artwork with a drop shadow effect applied.

In most instances effects alter the appearance of an object without changing the underlying artwork. They're added to the object's appearance attribute, which you can edit, move, hide, delete, or duplicate at any time, in the Appearance panel.

There are two types of effects in Illustrator: *vector effects* and *raster effects*. In Illustrator, click the Effect menu to see the different types of effects available.

● **Note:** When you apply a raster effect, the original vector data is rasterized using the document's raster effects settings, which determine the resolution of the resulting image. To learn about document raster effects settings, search for "Document raster effects settings" in Illustrator Help.

- **Illustrator effects (vector):** The top half of the Effect menu contains vector effects. You can apply most of these effects only to vector objects or to the fill or stroke of a vector object in the Appearance panel. The following vector effects can be applied to both vector and bitmap objects: 3D effects, SVG filters, Warp effects, Transform effects, Drop Shadow, Feather, Inner Glow, and Outer Glow.

- **Photoshop effects (raster):** The bottom half of the Effect menu contains raster effects. You can apply them to either vector or bitmap objects.

In this section, you will first explore how to apply and edit effects. You will then explore a few of the more widely used effects in Illustrator to get an idea of the range of effects available.

Applying an effect

Effects are applied using the Properties panel, the Effect menu, and the Appearance panel, and they can be applied to objects, groups, or layers. In this section, you'll apply a drop shadow to the cake stand to make it "stand" out.

1 Choose View > Fit Artboard In Window.

2 With the Selection tool (▶) selected, click the big aqua scalloped shape above the cake stand. Shift-click the aqua cake stand to select it as well.

3 Click the Group button in the Task bar below (or above) the selected artwork to group them.

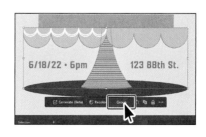

4 Click the Choose An Effect button (*fx.*) in the Appearance section of the Properties panel to apply effects.

5 Choose Stylize > Drop Shadow from the Illustrator Effects section of the menu that appears.

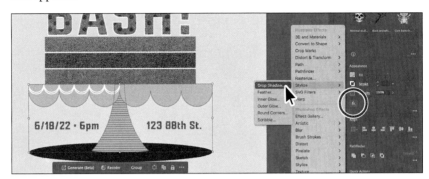

6 In the Drop Shadow dialog box that opens, select Preview and change the following options:

- Mode: Multiply (the default setting)
- Opacity: **20%**
- X Offset: **0 in**
- Y Offset: **0.03 in** (you'll need to type this value in)
- Blur: **0.03 in** (you'll need to type this value in)
- Color: Selected

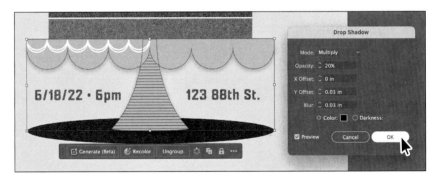

7 Click OK.

Since the drop shadow is applied to the group, it appears around the perimeter of the group, not on each object independently. If you look in the Appearance panel right now, you'll see the word "Group" at the top and the Drop Shadow effect applied.

The word "Contents" refers to the content within the group. Each object in a group can have its own appearance properties.

8 Choose File > Save.

Editing an effect

Effects are *live* and can be edited after being applied to an object. You can edit the effect in the Properties panel or Appearance panel by selecting the object with the effect applied and then clicking the effect's name, or in the Appearance panel, by double-clicking the attribute row. This displays the dialog box for that effect. Changes you make to the effect update in the artwork.

In this section, you will apply a shadow to the "BIRTHDAY BASH!" text, but with a twist. You'll apply it to one of the strokes, not to the whole object.

1 Click the "BIRTHDAY BASH!" text.

2 In the Appearance panel, select the white Stroke row.

This way, an effect you apply is applied only to the stroke.

3 Choose Effect > Apply Drop Shadow. If you need to, click the arrow to the left of word "Stroke" in the white Stroke row to see the drop shadow.

The Apply Drop Shadow command applies the last used effect with the same options set.

4 Zoom in to the selected text.

Note: If you attempt to apply an effect to artwork that already has the same effect applied, Illustrator will warn you that the same effect is already applied.

Tip: If you were to choose Effect > Drop Shadow, the Drop Shadow dialog box would appear, allowing you to make changes before applying the effect.

5 In the Appearance panel, click the text "Drop Shadow" beneath the white Stroke row to edit the effect options.

6 In the Drop Shadow dialog box, select Preview to see the changes. Change the following options:

- Opacity: **40%**
- X Offset and Y Offset: **0.01**
- Blur: **0.02 in**

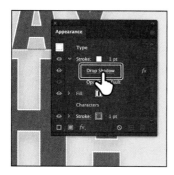
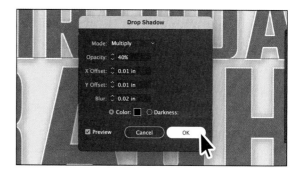

7 Click OK. Leave the text object selected.

Styling text with a Warp effect

Text can have all sorts of effects applied, including warp, as you saw in Lesson 9. The difference between the warp you applied in Lesson 9 and the Warp effect you are about to apply is that this one is an effect and can be turned on and off, edited, or removed easily. Next you will use the Warp effect to warp the "BIRTHDAY BASH!" text.

1 In the Appearance panel, click the word "Type" at the top of the panel. It's highlighted in the following figure.

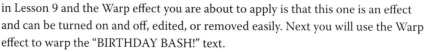

Clicking Type targets the text, not just the stroke or the fill. The more you apply effects, the more you realize how much flexibility you have when applying them.

2 With the text selected, click the Add New Effect button (*fx*) at the bottom of the Appearance panel.

3 Choose Warp > Rise from the menu.

This is another way to apply an effect to content and will be handy if you have the Appearance panel open.

4 In the Warp Options dialog box, select Preview to see the changes. Try choosing styles from the Style menu and then choose Arc Upper. Set Bend to **15%**.

5 Try adjusting the Horizontal and Vertical Distortion sliders to see the effect. Make sure that the Distortion values are returned to **0** and then click OK. Leave the text selected.

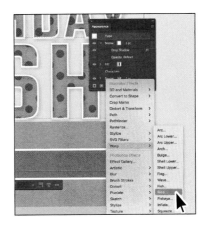

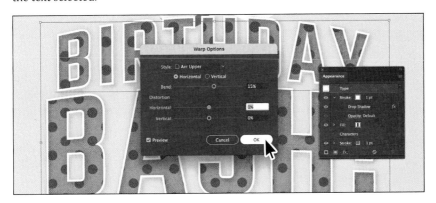

Temporarily disabling effects to make edits

You can edit text with a Warp effect applied, but sometimes it's easier to turn off the effect, make the change to the text, and then turn the effect back on.

1 With the text object still selected, click the visibility icon () to the left of the Warp: Arc Upper row in the Appearance panel to temporarily turn off the effect.

Notice that the text is no longer warped on the artboard.

► Tip: If your text is too wide, you can select it and change the font size, making it a bit smaller.

2 Select the Type tool (**T**) in the toolbar, and change the text to **BIRTHDAY PARTY** (without the exclamation point).

3 Select the Selection tool (▶) in the toolbar. This selects the text object, not the text.

4 Click the visibility column to the left of the Warp: Arc Upper row in the Appearance panel to turn on visibility for the effect.

The text is once again warped, but since the text changed, the amount of warp may need to be different because of the overall size of the text.

5 In the Appearance panel, click the underlined Warp: Arc Upper text to edit the effect.

6 In the Warp Options dialog box, change Bend to **30%**. Click OK.

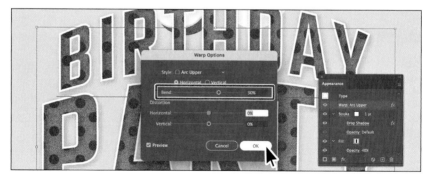

The text may have moved up after you clicked OK. If that is the case, you can drag the text down on top of the cake.

7 Close the Appearance panel for now.

8 Choose Select > Deselect, and then choose File > Save.

Applying a Photoshop effect

As described earlier in the lesson, raster effects generate pixels rather than vector data. Raster effects include SVG filters, all of the effects in the bottom portion of the Effect menu, and the Drop Shadow, Inner Glow, Outer Glow, and Feather commands in the Effect > Stylize submenu. You can apply them to either vector or bitmap objects. Next, you'll apply a Photoshop effect (raster) to the candle flames on top of the cake.

1   Choose View > Fit Artboard In Window.

2   Click the flame above the 3 candle and Shift-click the other flame, above the 0 (zero) candle, to select both.

3   Choose Effect > Texture > Grain.

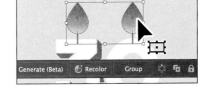

When you choose a raster (Photoshop) effect, the Filter Gallery dialog box opens for most, but not all, effects. Similarly to working with filters in Adobe Photoshop, where you can also access a Filter Gallery, in the Illustrator Filter Gallery you can try different raster effects to see how they affect your artwork.

4   With the Filter Gallery dialog box open, you can see the type of filter (Grain) displayed at the top. In the lower-left corner of the dialog box, click the plus sign (+) to zoom in to the art. I had to click it a bunch of times.

The Filter Gallery dialog box, which is resizable, contains a preview area (labeled A), thumbnails of effects that you can click to apply (labeled B), settings for the currently selected effect (labeled C), and the list of effects applied (labeled D). In the section labeled D, you can click an eye icon (👁) to turn off/on an effect. If you want to apply a different effect, expand a category in the middle panel of the dialog box (labeled B) and click an effect thumbnail.

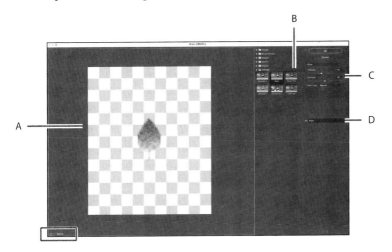

Note: The Photoshop effect will essentially rasterize your beautiful vector flame when you print or output the file. In the tip on the next page, I discuss setting it to display, print, and output at a higher resolution.

5 Change the Grain settings in the upper-right corner of the dialog box as follows (if necessary):

- Intensity: **51**
- Contrast: **100**
- Grain Type: **Contrasty**

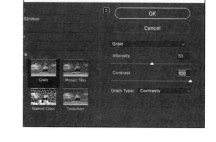

6 Click OK to apply the raster effect to the flames.

7 Choose Select > Deselect, and then choose File > Save.

▶ **Tip:** Does the flame art look pixelated after applying the effect? Choose Effect > Document Raster Effects Settings. In the dialog box that opens, choose High (300 ppi) from the Resolution menu, and click OK. *Better?* The resolution of all raster effects when you output (and preview) is controlled by the settings in that dialog box. While you're working, make sure to change the Resolution setting back to Screen (72 ppi) if Illustrator becomes slower and less responsive.

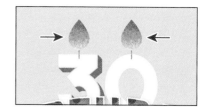

Applying 3D effects

You can apply powerful 3D effects to vector artwork to make objects look like realistic 3D graphics. After adjusting the lighting and applying materials like realistic textures, you can then render the artwork with ray tracing and export in a format that suits your needs. Next, you'll turn the purple shape below the aqua cake stand into a wood platter.

1 With the Selection tool (▶), click to select the purple ellipse below the cake stand (see the figure).

2 Choose Effect > 3D And Materials > Extrude & Bevel.

The Extrude effect is applied with default settings. Also, the 3D And Materials panel opens, where you will set the options for your 3D artwork. 3D effects are like other effects—they can be turned off, deleted, and edited later.

In the 3D And Materials panel, there are three main groups of settings:

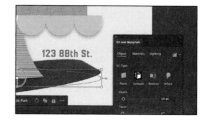

- **Object**—Here you can set the options for the basic shape and position of your object, like view angle (rotation), depth, whether you want a bevel, and more.

- **Materials**—You can apply default or custom materials and graphics to the surface of the 3D object.

- **Lighting**—Apply lighting options such as shadows, intensity, direction, and height.

3   In the 3D And Materials panel, with the Object category selected at the top, set the following:

- Depth: **15 pt**
- Bevel: **On** *(turn it on)*
- Bevel Shape: **Step**
- Width: **40%**
- Height: **30%**
- Repeat: **1** (the default setting)
- Rotation: X=**50°**, Y=**0**, and Z=**0**
- Perspective: **160°**

Note: You will have to do a lot of scrolling in the panel to see all the options you need to set.

With the main object settings finished,
experiment to see what you can come up with! Next, you'll explore materials and see what they're about.

4   In the 3D And Materials panel, click the Materials category at the top. It's circled in the following figure.

You can apply materials like fabrics or concrete or wood. You can also map your own vector artwork to the surface of the artwork.

5   Scroll in the All Materials & Graphics section of the panel to see all of the default materials you can apply. Select the material called Larch Wood Varnished.

The platter now looks like it's made of wood. Try other materials to see what they look like. Know that there are tons of options you can set to change the appearance. You'll do that next.

Tip: You can find a lot more materials on sites like *substance3d.adobe.com/community-assets*.

6 In the Properties section of the panel, below the materials list, change Repeat to **120**. You may need to scroll in the bottom half of the panel.

7 Click the Wood Color box (the brown square), and select a color in the Color Picker. Click OK. I chose a purple, similar to what was originally applied to the shape.

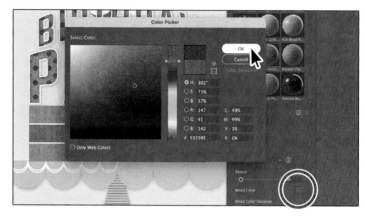

Next, you'll adjust the lighting.

8 In the 3D And Materials panel, click the Lighting category at the top. It's circled in the following figure.

9 Select the Diffuse preset.

This sets the lighting to be less harsh. You can now adjust the individual settings, like Height or Rotation.

10 Set Intensity to **100** to make it lighter overall.

11 To see the 3D artwork with realistic shading and lighting, click the Render With Ray Tracing button in the upper-right corner of the panel.

▶ **Tip:** You can export the 3D artwork for use in a 3D application like Substance if you choose File > Export Selection and choose the format you need, like OBJ, USDA, or GLTF.

It's best not to work with Ray Tracing on, since it may slow things down. But it's a great way to see what it will look like when exported or for showing off your artwork!

12 Close the 3D And Materials panel and drag the shape down a bit so the cake stand looks like it's in the middle.

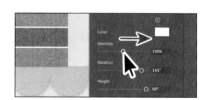

Using graphic styles

A *graphic style* is a saved set of appearance attributes that you can reuse. By applying graphic styles, you can quickly change the appearance of objects and text globally.

The Graphic Styles panel (Window > Graphic Styles) lets you create, name, save, apply, and remove effects and attributes for objects, layers, and groups. You can also break the link between an object and an applied graphic style to edit that object's attributes without affecting other objects that use the same graphic style.

For example, if you have a map that uses a shape to represent a city, you can create a graphic style that paints the shape green and adds a drop shadow. You can then use that graphic style to paint all the city shapes on the map. If you decide to use a different color, you can change the fill color of the graphic style to blue. All the objects that use that graphic style are then updated to blue.

You can also apply graphic styles to your artwork from graphic style libraries that come with Illustrator by choosing Window > Graphic Style Libraries.

Creating and applying a graphic style

Now you'll create a new graphic style from the number 3 candle and apply that graphic style to the number 0 candle.

1   With the Selection tool (▶) selected, click the number 3 candle on top of the cake.

2   Choose Window > Graphic Styles to open the Graphic Styles panel.

3   Click the New Graphic Style button (▣) at the bottom of the Graphic Styles panel.

   The appearance attributes from the selected candle are saved as a graphic style.

▶ **Tip:** When you make a graphic style by selecting an object, you can then either drag the object directly into the Graphic Styles panel or, in the Appearance panel, drag the appearance thumbnail at the top of the listing into the Graphic Styles panel.

4   In the Graphic Styles panel, double-click the new graphic style thumbnail. In the Graphic Style Options dialog box, name the new style **Candle**. Click OK.

5   Click the Appearance panel tab, and at the top of the Appearance panel you'll see "Path: Candle."

   This indicates that a graphic style named Candle is applied to the selected artwork.

6 With the Selection tool, select the number 0 candle.

7 In the Graphic Styles panel, click the graphic style named Candle to apply the styling.

Leave the candle selected.

Updating a graphic style

You can also update a graphic style, and all artwork with that style applied will update as well. If you edit the appearance of artwork that a graphic style is applied to, the graphic style is overridden, and the artwork will not update when the graphic style is updated.

1 With the candle still selected, look in the Graphic Styles panel; you will see that the Candle graphic style thumbnail is highlighted (it has a border around it), indicating that it's applied.

2 Click the Appearance panel tab.

3 With the candle selected, in the orange Fill row in the Appearance panel, click the Fill color box a few times to open the Swatches panel. Select the swatch named Aqua. Press the Escape key to hide the swatches.

Notice that the "Compound Path: Candle" text at the top of the Appearance panel just shows "Compound Path," telling you that the graphic style is not applied to the selected artwork.

4 Click the Graphic Styles panel tab.

Notice that the Candle graphic style no longer has a highlight (border) around it, which means that the graphic style is no longer applied.

5 Press the Option (macOS) or Alt (Windows) key, and drag the selected shape on top of the Candle graphic style thumbnail in the Graphic Styles panel. Release the mouse button when the thumbnail is highlighted, and then release the modifier key.

Both candles now look the same, since the Candle graphic style was applied to both objects.

6 Choose Select > Deselect, and then choose File > Save.

7 Click the Appearance panel tab. You should see "No Selection: Candle" at the top of the panel (you may need to scroll up).

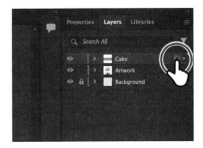

▶ **Tip:** You can also update a graphic style by selecting the graphic style you want to replace. Then you select artwork (or target an item in the Layers panel) that has the attributes you want to use and choose Redefine Graphic Style "Style name" from the Appearance panel menu.

Applying a graphic style to a layer

When a graphic style is applied to a layer, everything on that layer has that same style applied. Now you'll apply a drop shadow graphic style to the layer named Cake, which will apply the style to every object currently on that layer and anything you add later. Instead of applying the graphic style to each part of the cake, you are applying a graphic style this way to save time and effort.

1 Choose View > Fit Artboard In Window, if necessary.

2 Click the Layers panel tab on the right to show the Layers panel. Click the target icon (⊙) for the Cake layer.

This selects the layer content (the rectangles that are the cake layers) and targets the layer for any appearance attributes.

Note: If you apply a graphic style to artwork and then apply a graphic style to the layer (or sublayer) that it's on, the graphic style formatting is added to the appearance of the artwork—it's cumulative. This can change the artwork in ways you don't expect, since applying a graphic style to the layer adds to the formatting of the artwork.

▶ **Tip:** In the Layers panel, you can drag a target icon to the Delete Selection icon (🗑) at the bottom of the Layers panel to remove the appearance attributes.

3 Click the Graphic Styles panel tab, and then click the graphic style named Drop Shadow to apply the style to the layer and all its contents.

The target icon in the Layers panel for the Cake layer () is now shaded.

Also, in the Graphic Styles panel, graphic style thumbnails that show a small box with a red slash (⊘) indicate that the graphic style does not contain a stroke or fill. It may just be a drop shadow or outer glow, for instance.

4 Click the Appearance panel tab, and you should see, with all of the artwork on the Cake layer still selected, the words "Layer: Drop Shadow."

This is telling you that the layer target icon is selected in the Layers panel and that the Drop Shadow graphic style is applied to that layer.

5 Close the Appearance panel group.

6 With the Selection tool, drag across the flames and the candles to select them. Drag them up if necessary.

Applying multiple graphic styles

You can apply a graphic style to an object that already has a graphic style applied. This can be useful if you want to add properties to an object from another graphic style. After you apply a graphic style to selected artwork, you can then Option-click (macOS) or Alt-click (Windows) another graphic style thumbnail to add the graphic style formatting to the existing formatting, rather than replacing it.

Scaling strokes and effects

In Illustrator, by default, when scaling (resizing) content, any strokes and effects that are applied do not change. For instance, suppose you scale a circle with a 2-pt stroke from small to the size of the artboard. The shape may change size, but the stroke will remain 2 points by default. That can change the appearance of scaled artwork in a way that you didn't intend, so you'll need to watch out for that when transforming artwork. Next you'll make the white path on the cake larger.

1 Choose Select > Deselect, if necessary.

2 Click the white curvy lines on the aqua cake base (the scalloped shape).

3 In the Properties panel (Window > Properties), notice the stroke weight of 1 pt.

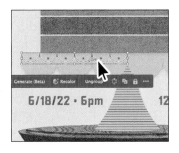

4 Click More Options (●●●) in the Transform section of the Properties panel, and select Scale Strokes & Effects at the bottom of the panel that appears. Press the Escape key to hide the options.

Without this option selected, scaling the artwork will not affect the stroke weights or effects when it is scaled. You are selecting this option, so the artwork will scale larger and not remain the same stroke weight.

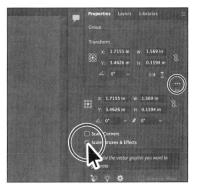

5 Pressing the Shift key, drag the lower-right corner of the path to make it larger. Drag until it's the width of the green scalloped shape it's on. Release the mouse button and then the key.

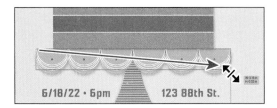

After scaling the artwork, if you look in the Properties panel, see that the stroke weight has gotten bigger.

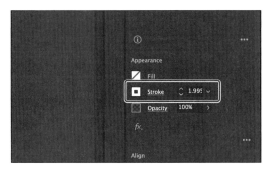

6 Choose Select > Deselect.

7 Choose File > Save, and then choose File > Close.

Review questions

1 How do you add a second fill or stroke to artwork?

2 Name two ways to apply an effect to an object.

3 When you apply a Photoshop (raster) effect to vector artwork, what happens to the artwork?

4 Where can you access the options for effects applied to an object?

5 What's the difference between applying a graphic style to a *layer* versus applying it to *selected artwork*?

Review answers

1 To add a second fill or stroke to artwork, click the Add New Stroke button (■) or Add New Fill button (▣) at the bottom of the Appearance panel. We didn't cover this in the lesson, but you can also choose Add New Stroke/Add New Fill from the Appearance panel menu.

2 You can apply an effect to an object by selecting the object and then choosing the effect from the Effect menu. You can also apply an effect by selecting the object, clicking the Choose An Effect button (*fx*) in the Properties panel or the Add New Effect button (*fx*) at the bottom of the Appearance panel, and then choosing the effect from the menu that appears.

3 Applying a Photoshop effect to artwork generates pixels rather than vector data. Photoshop effects include all of the effects in the bottom portion of the Effect menu and the Drop Shadow, Inner Glow, Outer Glow, and Feather commands in the Effect > Stylize submenu. You can apply them to either vector or bitmap objects.

4 You can edit effects applied to selected artwork by clicking the effect link in the Properties panel or Appearance panel to access the effect options.

5 When a graphic style is applied to a single object, other objects on that layer are not affected. For example, if a triangle object has a Roughen effect applied to its path and you move it to another layer, it retains the Roughen effect.

After a graphic style is applied to a layer, everything you add to the layer has that style applied to it. For example, if you create a circle on Layer 1 and then move that circle to Layer 2, which has a Drop Shadow effect applied, the circle adopts that effect.

14 CREATING ARTWORK FOR A T-SHIRT

Lesson overview

In this lesson, you'll learn how to do the following:

- Work with existing symbols.

- Create, modify, and redefine a symbol.

- Work with the Symbol Sprayer tool.

- Understand Creative Cloud libraries.

- Work with Creative Cloud libraries.

- Explore Mockup (Beta).

- Work with global editing.

 This lesson will take about 45 minutes to complete. To get the lesson files used in this lesson, download them from the web page for this book at *peachpit.com/IllustratorCIB2024*. For more information, see "Accessing the lesson files and Web Edition" in the Getting Started section at the beginning of this book.

In this lesson, you'll explore various valuable concepts for working smarter and faster in Illustrator: using symbols, working with Creative Cloud libraries to make your design assets available anywhere, and editing content using global editing.

Starting the lesson

In this lesson, you'll explore concepts such as symbols and the Libraries panel to create artwork for a T-shirt mockup. Before you begin, you'll restore the default preferences for Adobe Illustrator. Then, you'll open the finished art file for this lesson to see what you'll create.

● **Note:** If you have not already downloaded the project files for this lesson to your computer from your Account page, make sure to do so now. See the "Getting Started" section at the beginning of the book.

1 To ensure that the tools function and the defaults are set exactly as described in this lesson, delete or deactivate (by renaming) the Adobe Illustrator preferences file. See "Restoring default preferences" in the "Getting Started" section at the beginning of the book.

2 Start Adobe Illustrator.

3 Choose File > Open, and open the L14_end1.ai file in the Lessons > Lesson14 folder on your hard disk.

● **Note:** You may see a warning dialog box about a missing Mockup add-on. If that is the case, simply click OK.

You're going to create artwork for a T-shirt design using some features in Illustrator meant to help you work smarter.

4 Choose View > Fit All In Window and leave the file open for reference, or choose File > Close.

5 Choose File > Open. In the Open dialog box, navigate to the Lessons > Lesson14 folder, and select the L14_start1.ai file on your hard disk. Click Open to open the file.

6 Choose View > Fit All In Window.

7 Choose File > Save As. If the Cloud Document dialog box opens, click Save On Your Computer.

8 In the Save As dialog box, navigate to the Lesson14 folder, and name the file **TShirt.ai**. Leave Adobe Illustrator (ai) chosen from the Format menu (macOS) or Adobe Illustrator (*.AI) chosen from the Save As Type menu (Windows), and click Save.

9 In the Illustrator Options dialog box, leave the Illustrator options at their default settings, and then click OK.

10 Choose Reset Essentials from the workspace switcher in the Application bar.

Working with symbols

A *symbol* is a reusable art object stored in the Symbols panel (Window > Symbols). For example, if you create a symbol from a flower you drew, you can quickly add multiple instances of that flower symbol to your artwork, saving you from having to draw each flower.

All instances in the document are linked to the original symbol in the Symbols panel. When you edit the original symbol, all instances of that symbol (a flower, in this example) that are linked to the original are updated. You can turn all those flowers from one color to another instantly!

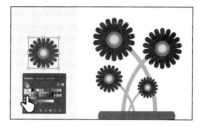

Using default Illustrator symbol libraries

You'll start by adding a symbol to your project from one of the many symbol libraries that come with Illustrator.

1   Select the Selection tool (▶) in the toolbar and click in the larger artboard to make it the active artboard.

2   Choose View > Fit Artboard In Window to fit the active artboard in the window.

3   Click the Hide Smart Guides button in the Properties panel to turn the Smart Guides off temporarily.

▶ **Tip:** You can also choose View > Smart Guides to turn them off.

4   Choose Window > Symbols to open the Symbols panel.

5   Click the Symbol Libraries Menu button (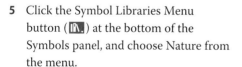) at the bottom of the Symbols panel, and choose Nature from the menu.

The Nature library opens as a free-floating panel. The symbols in this library are not part of the file you are working on, but you can import any symbols into the document and use them in your project.

Tip: If you want to see the symbol names along with the symbol pictures, click the Symbols panel menu (▤) and then choose Small List View or Large List View.

6 Move the pointer over the symbols in the Nature panel to see their names as tool tips. Scroll down in the panel, if necessary, and click the symbol named Trees 1 to add it to the Symbols panel.

Symbols added to the Symbols panel in this way are saved only with the document you are working on.

7 Close the Nature panel.

8 With the Selection tool (▶) selected, drag the Trees 1 symbol from the Symbols panel onto the artboard.

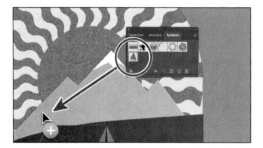

9 Drag the same symbol out once more so there are two sets of trees on the artboard.

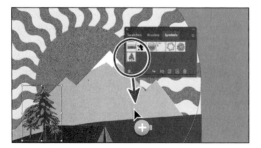

Each time you drag a symbol like the trees onto the artboard, an *instance* of the original symbol is created. With the symbol instance still selected on the artboard, notice that, in the Properties panel, you see "Symbol (Static)" and symbol-related options.

Transforming symbol instances

A symbol instance is treated like a group of objects and can change only certain transformation and appearance properties (scale, rotate, move, transparency, and more). You cannot edit the artwork that makes up an instance, because it's linked to the original symbol. Next, you'll resize the symbol instances and make a copy.

1 With one of the tree instances selected, Shift-drag a bounding point away from the center to make it bigger while also constraining its proportions. Release the mouse button and then the key.

2 Resize the other tree instance to make it much larger as well.

Note: Are you finding it challenging to select and move the trees without selecting the background art? If you are, maybe you could practice things you learned in earlier lessons, like temporarily hiding or locking art!

3 Drag the two tree instances into position, as in the following figure.

4 Choose Select > Deselect, and then choose View > Zoom Out so you can see more of the gray canvas area.

5 Make a copy of either tree instance by pressing Option (macOS) or Alt (Windows) and dragging it to the right of the artwork, off to the side. Release the mouse button and then the key.

Creating a copy of an instance is the same thing as dragging an instance of a symbol from the Symbols panel.

6   Turn on the Smart Guides by choosing View > Smart Guides.

7   To resize the new tree instance, Shift-drag a bounding point to make it much smaller. Release the mouse button and then the key.

You'll move it onto the main artwork shortly.

8   Choose Select > Deselect and then File > Save.

Editing a symbol

The Trees 1 symbol has three trees in it. It would look less crowded if there were only two trees. To change all instances at once, you can edit the original symbol. In this next section, you'll remove a tree from the original Trees 1 symbol, and all instances in the document will be updated.

1   With the Selection tool (▶) selected, double-click one of the larger tree instances on the artboard. A warning dialog box appears, stating that you are about to edit the original symbol and that all instances will update. Click OK.

▶ **Tip:** There are lots of ways to edit a symbol. You can select the symbol instance on the artboard and then click the Edit Symbol button in the Properties panel, or you can double-click a symbol thumbnail in the Symbols panel.

This takes you into symbol editing mode, so you can't edit any other objects on the page. The Trees 1 symbol instance you double-clicked will show as the size of the original symbol artwork. That's because in symbol editing mode, you are looking at the *original* symbol artwork rather than the transformed instance (if you double-clicked one that was resized). You can now edit the artwork that makes up the symbol.

2   Double-click the trees a few times to isolate the groups. Select the smallest tree in the group. See the first part of the following figure.

3   Press Delete or Backspace to remove it.

4   Double-click away from the symbol content, or click the Exit Symbol Editing Mode button () in the upper-left corner of the Document window, until you exit symbol editing mode so that you can edit the rest of the content.

Notice that all of the Trees 1 symbol instances on the artboard have been changed.

Working with dynamic symbols

As you just saw, editing a symbol updates all of the instances in your document. Symbols can also be *dynamic*, which means you can change specific appearance properties of individual instances using the Direct Selection tool without editing the original symbol. In this section, you'll make the Trees 1 symbol dynamic and edit one instance separately.

1   In the Symbols panel, select the Trees 1 symbol thumbnail, if it's not already selected. Click the Symbol Options button (▦) at the bottom of the Symbols panel.

2   In the Symbol Options dialog box, select Dynamic Symbol, and click OK.

The symbol and its instances are now dynamic.

You can tell if a symbol is dynamic by looking at the thumbnail in the Symbols panel. If there is a small plus sign (+) in the lower-right corner of the thumbnail, it is a dynamic symbol. You can also see the words "Symbol (Dynamic)" at the top of the Properties panel when a symbol instance is selected, telling you it's a dynamic symbol.

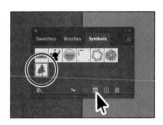

3   With the Direct Selection tool (▷) selected, drag across the smaller trees on the right.

Why the Direct Selection tool? To select individual parts of a dynamic symbol and not the whole symbol instance, you need to use the Direct Selection tool.

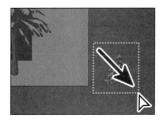

4 Click the Fill box (■?■) in the Properties panel. With the Swatches option (▦) selected, change the fill color to a darker green color in the Swatches panel.

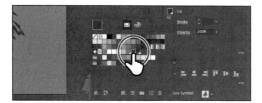

5 Choose Select > Deselect so you can see the color of those trees.

One set of trees now looks different from the others. Know that if you were to edit the original Trees 1 symbol, like you did previously, all symbol instances would update, but the smaller trees you just changed would keep the fill color change you just made.

6 Select the Selection tool and drag the selected trees onto the art in the middle of the artboard.

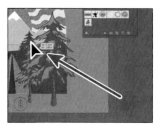

Creating a symbol

Illustrator also lets you create and save your own symbols. You can make symbols from objects, including paths, compound paths, text, embedded (not linked) raster images, mesh objects, and groups of objects. Symbols can even include active objects, such as brush strokes, blends, effects, or other symbol instances. Next, you'll create a symbol from existing artwork.

1 Choose 2 Symbol Artwork from the Artboard Navigation menu in the Status bar.

2 With the Selection tool (▶) selected, click the bird on the artboard to select it.

3 Click the New Symbol button (▣) at the bottom of the Symbols panel to make a symbol from the selected artwork.

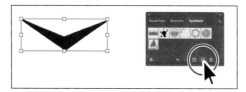

4 In the Symbol Options dialog box that opens, change the name to **Bird**. Ensure that Dynamic Symbol is selected, just in case you want to edit the appearance of one of the instances later. Click OK to create the symbol.

In the Symbol Options dialog box, you'll see a note explaining that there is no difference between a movie clip and a graphic export type in Illustrator. If you don't plan on exporting this content to Adobe Animate (formerly Flash), you don't need to worry about choosing an export type. After creating the symbol, the bird artwork on the artboard becomes an instance of the Bird symbol, and the symbol appears in the Symbols panel. You'll create another symbol by dragging artwork into the Symbols panel.

▶ **Tip:** You can drag the symbol thumbnails in the Symbols panel to change their ordering. Reordering symbols in the Symbols panel has no effect on the artwork. It is simply a way to organize your symbols.

5   Drag the cloud artwork into a blank area of the Symbols panel.

6   In the Symbol Options dialog box, change the name to **Cloud** and click OK.

7   Choose 1 T-Shirt from the Artboard menu in the Status bar.

8   Drag the Bird symbol from the Symbols panel onto the artboard twice, and position the instances in the sky above the mountains.

9   Resize and rotate each of the bird instances on the artboard using the Selection tool, making them different sizes. Make sure to press the Shift key to constrain the proportions as you scale.

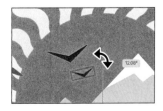

10 Choose Select > Deselect and then File > Save.

Practice editing a symbol

Time to practice by editing a symbol. You'll remove the stroke from the Cloud symbol.

▶ **Tip:** If you wanted to easily select all symbol instances from the same symbol, you could choose Select > Same > Symbol Instance. This could be useful if you put a whole bunch of trees in your project and wanted to group them together to be able to select them more easily or move them as a group.

1 With the Selection tool (▶) selected, drag a few copies of the Cloud symbol on top of the other artwork already on the artboard. Arrange them in the sky.

2 Select each Cloud symbol instance and resize it. Don't forget to Shift-drag a corner to resize proportionally!

3 Select one of the cloud instances and click the Flip Horizontally button () in the Properties panel to flip it.

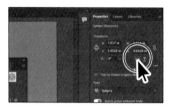 

4 Double-click one of the cloud instances.

5 Click OK to edit the Cloud symbol artwork.

6 When in Isolation mode, select the cloud shape.

7 In the Properties panel, change the Stroke Weight to **0** (zero).

 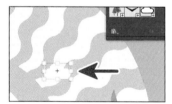

8 Press the Esc key to exit Isolation mode. Neither cloud should any longer have the stroke applied.

9 Choose File > Save.

Breaking a link to a symbol

Sometimes, you'll need to edit a specific instance on the artboard in ways that require you to break the link between the original symbol artwork and that instance.

As you've learned, you can make specific changes, such as scaling, opacity, and flipping, to a symbol instance, and saving the symbol as dynamic lets you edit only certain appearance attributes using the Direct Selection tool. When you break the link between a symbol and an instance, that instance will no longer update if the symbol is edited. Next, you'll see how to break the link to a symbol instance so you can change just that one.

1   Select the larger tree symbol instance on the right.

2   In the Properties panel, click the Break Link button.

Tip: You can also break the link to a symbol instance by selecting the symbol instance on the artboard and then clicking the Break Link To Symbol button (▨) at the bottom of the Symbols panel.

That symbol instance is now a group of paths, and you'll see "Group" at the top of the Properties panel. You should be able to edit the artwork directly now. This content will no longer update if the Trees 1 symbol is edited.

3   Choose Select > Deselect.

4   With the Selection tool selected, double-click the trees to enter Isolation mode.

5   To select the smaller tree, double-click several more times, and then click to select it.

6   Drag the smaller tree to the right so it doesn't interfere as much with the tent.

7   Press the Esc key to exit Isolation mode.

8   Choose Select > Deselect.

Working with the Symbol Sprayer tool 🎥

Suppose you need to add a lot of the Trees 1 symbol to your artwork. Instead of dragging them all from the Symbols panel, you could spray them onto the artboard using the Symbol Sprayer tool. To learn how to work with the Symbol Sprayer tool, check out the video *Working with the Symbol Sprayer tool,* which is part of the Web Edition. For more information, see the "Web Edition" section of "Getting Started" at the beginning of the book.

Replacing symbols

You can easily swap a symbol instance in the document with another symbol. Also, if you change a dynamic symbol instance, like a bird, you can replace that instance with the original symbol. That way, the symbol instance matches the original symbol artwork again. Next, you'll change one of the Cloud symbol instances to try it. Then you'll replace it so it looks like the others.

1   With the Direct Selection tool (▷), select one of the cloud instances.

Since the Cloud symbol is dynamic, you can select one of the cloud shapes to change its appearance.

Note: After making edits to a dynamic symbol instance with the Direct Selection tool, you can reselect the entire instance with the Selection tool and click the Reset button in the Properties panel to reset the appearance to the same as the original symbol.

2 Click the Fill box in the Properties panel. With the Swatches option (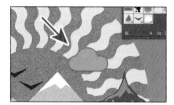) selected, change the fill color to something else, like a blue.

Now suppose you want to go back to the original Cloud symbol, or maybe instead of a cloud, you want a bird in its place? You could replace the symbol instance.

3 Select the Selection tool and click away from the cloud instance to deselect it. Then click to select it again. This way, the instance and not just the cloud shape within is selected.

Note: If the original symbol instance you are replacing had a transformation applied, such as a rotation, the symbol instance replacing it would have the same transformation applied.

4 In the Properties panel, click the arrow to the right of the Replace Symbol field to open a panel showing the symbols in the Symbols panel. Click the Bird symbol in the panel.

The cloud instance has been replaced by the Bird symbol.

5 With the bird instance still selected on the artboard, in the Properties panel click the arrow to the right of the Replace Symbol field and select the Cloud symbol in the panel.

6 Choose Select > Deselect, and close the Symbols panel group.

Working with Creative Cloud libraries

Creative Cloud libraries are an easy way to gather project elements that you can use—such as images, colors, text styles, Adobe Stock assets, and more—between applications like Adobe Photoshop, Illustrator, InDesign, and Adobe mobile apps.

Creative Cloud libraries connect to your Adobe profile, giving you instant access to your saved assets in Illustrator. When you create content in Illustrator and save it to a Creative Cloud library, it's available to use in all your Illustrator files. Library assets sync automatically and can be shared with Creative Cloud account users. Your shared library assets stay current and are accessible across Adobe desktop and mobile apps, ready for use in your projects.

Note: To use Creative Cloud libraries, you will need to be signed in with your Adobe ID and have an internet connection.

Adding assets to a Creative Cloud library

The first thing you'll learn about is how to work with the Libraries panel (Window > Libraries) in Illustrator, and then you'll add assets to a Creative Cloud library from another document you will open.

1   Choose File > Open. In the Open dialog box, navigate to the Lessons > Lesson14 folder, and select the Sample.ai file on your hard disk. Click Open.

Note: The Missing Fonts dialog box will most likely appear. Click Activate Fonts to activate all the missing fonts. After they are activated and you see the message stating that there are no more missing fonts, click Close.

2   Choose View > Fit Artboard In Window.

From this document, you'll capture artwork and colors to be used in the TShirt.ai document.

3   Choose Window > Libraries, or click the Libraries panel tab to open the Libraries panel.

4   In the Libraries panel, click Your Library (or "My Library" if you see it) to open the default library, if it isn't already open.

Note: In earlier versions of Illustrator, the default library was named My Library. If you don't see a library named Your Library, feel free to use another library or create a new library by clicking + Create New Library and naming it.

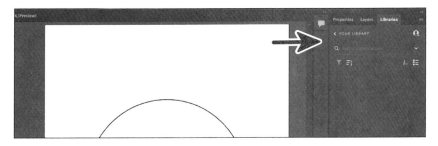

If it's open, you'll see "Your Library" at the top of the Libraries panel with an arrow pointing to the left. You can add your design assets to this default library and even create more libraries—maybe to save assets for specific clients or projects.

5 Choose Select > Deselect, if anything is selected.

6 Select the Selection tool (▶), and click the group that contains the text "MOUNTAIN EXPLORER."

The group is made of two text objects—one of which is warped.

7 Drag the group into the Libraries panel to save it in the library.

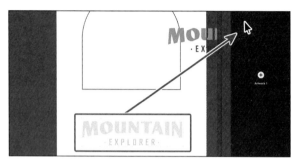

The text is still editable as text—retaining the text formatting as well. As you'll see, when you save assets and formatting in the Libraries panel, the content is organized by asset type (Graphics, Text, Color, etc.). The new library item you just saved is considered a "graphic" because it is a group of content.

8 To change the name of the saved group, double-click the name Artwork 1 in the Libraries panel and change it to **Text**. Press Return or Enter to accept the name change.

You can change the names of other assets, like graphics, colors, character styles, and paragraph styles, saved in the Libraries panel as well. In the case of character and paragraph styles you save, you can also move the pointer over the asset and see a tool tip that shows the saved formatting.

Next you'll save the color from the "MOUNTAIN" text.

9 With the text group still selected on the artboard, double-click the "MOUNTAIN " text to enter Isolation mode. Select the "MOUNTAIN" text within the group.

10 Click the plus sign (+) at the bottom of the Libraries panel, and choose Text Fill Color from the menu to save the green color.

11 Press the Esc key twice to switch to the Selection tool and to exit Isolation mode.

12 Click the shape on the artboard above the MOUNTAIN EXPLORER group.

You'll simply copy this artwork, since you will use it to mask or hide parts of the artwork.

13 Choose Edit > Copy.

14 Choose File > Close to close the Sample.ai file and return to the TShirt.ai file. Don't save the file if asked.

Notice that even with a different document open, the Libraries panel still shows those assets in the library. The libraries and their assets are available no matter which document is open in Illustrator.

15 Choose Edit > Paste to paste the shape. Drag it to the right of the artwork.

Using library assets

Now that you have some assets in the Libraries panel, once they sync with your Creative Cloud account, they will be available to other applications and apps that support libraries as long as you are signed in with the same Creative Cloud account. Next, you'll use some of those library assets in the TShirt.ai file.

1 While still on the 1 T-Shirt artboard, choose View > Fit Artboard In Window.

2 Drag the Text asset from the Libraries panel onto the artboard.

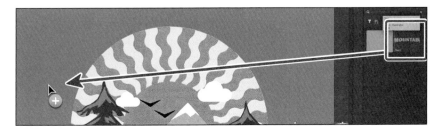

3 Click to place the group.

Note: To see the blue X, you will need to see the artwork edges (View > Show Edges).

Notice the blue X in the middle of the placed MOUNTAIN EXPLORER group? That means it is linked to the original library item. If you were to edit the item in the Libraries panel, as you'll see in the next exercise, the artwork you dragged out from the panel would update as well.

4 Choose Select > Deselect.

Updating a library asset

When you drag a graphic from your Creative Cloud library to an Illustrator project, it is by default placed as a linked asset. You can tell that an asset you dragged from a library is linked by the X that appears on the object bounding box when it's selected in the document. If you change a library asset, the linked instances will update in your projects. Next, you'll see how to update an asset.

Tip: You can also edit a linked library asset by clicking Edit Original () at the bottom of the Links panel (Window > Links).

1 In the Libraries panel, double-click the Text asset thumbnail.

The artwork will open in a new, temporary Illustrator document.

2 Select the Direct Selection tool (▷), and click to select the green text.

We selected the text with the Direct Selection tool because it is part of a group.

3 In the Properties panel, change the fill to an orange.

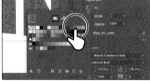

4 Choose File > Save, and then choose File > Close.

Note: If the graphic hasn't updated, with the Text graphic still selected on the artboard, click the text "Linked File" at the top of the Properties panel. In the Links panel that shows, with the Text graphic row selected, click the Update Link button (⟳) at the bottom of the panel.

In the Libraries panel, the graphic thumbnail should reflect the appearance change you made. Back in the TShirt.ai document, the Text graphic on the artboard should also have changed to orange.

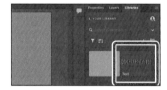

5 With the now orange Text graphic selected on the artboard, embed it by clicking the Properties panel tab to see the panel again. Click the Embed button in the Quick Actions section of the panel.

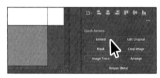

The asset is no longer linked to the library item and will not update if the library item is updated. That also means the artwork is now editable in the TShirt.ai document. Also notice that the X is gone from the artwork on the artboard.

6 Select the Selection tool (▶), and drag the white curved shape you pasted, on top of the artwork. Align its lower-left corner with the lower-left corner of the scene in the middle of the artboard.

7 In the Properties panel, click More Options () in the Transform section. Select Scale Corners so the radius of the corners of the shape will scale as you make it bigger.

8 Shift-drag the upper-right corner to make it bigger; release the mouse button and key when finished. The shape should be covering the artwork underneath it, except for parts of the trees.

The shape will be used to hide what's behind it.

9 Drag across the trees, clouds, bird, and white shape artwork to select them. Make sure not to select the three little icons lower on the artboard. If you do select any of them, Shift-click to deselect.

10 If your "MOUNTAIN" text is selected, Shift-click to deselect it.

11 Choose Object > Clipping Mask > Make.

The artwork that's outside the shape is now hidden.

12 Choose Select > Deselect.

● **Note:** If the clouds or birds disappear after choosing the Clipping Mask command, that means they were not selected. Choose Edit > Undo Make Clipping Mask and try selecting all of it again.

Creating a mockup

With Mockup, currently in beta, you can create high-quality mockups of vector artwork (only) on raster images of mugs, totes, T-shirts—whatever you can think of. When you apply vector art on a raster image using Mockup (Beta), Illustrator respects the object's curves and edges, and the vector art auto-adjusts onto the object non-destructively. You can edit the mockup further or release the art from the object if you want to rework it. Let's create a mockup by putting the logo on a T-shirt.

1 Drag the masked artwork, "MOUNTAIN EXPLORER" text, and icons like you see in the figure.

You will need to resize at least the text by dragging with the Shift key pressed.

With the artwork ready, you will now add it to a raster image to see what it looks like on a photo of someone wearing a T-shirt.

2 Choose Select > All On Active Artboard to select all of the artwork.

3 Choose Window > Mockup (Beta).

For the first iteration of this beta (prerelease software), you may see a dialog box asking you to install it. Later, as this feature matures, this may not happen.

4 If necessary, click Install to install the feature.

You can create a mockup with this feature in two main ways: use your artwork and a placeholder image from Adobe Stock that comes with the panel or use your artwork and an image you supply. We will use one of the supplied placeholder images from Adobe Stock to see how it works.

5 With the artwork still selected on the artboard, click the Mockup button in the panel.

You should now see the MOUNTAIN artwork on the images in the panel. You can select from a range of supplied product images for your mockup. Do you want it to show on a T-shirt? Or a mug?

6 Choose Apparel from the Category menu at the top.

7 To access the mockup, move the cursor over a thumbnail in the Mockup panel. Find the man in the black T-shirt (or something else, if you don't see that one). Click the Edit On Canvas button that appears.

8 Drag the MOUNTAIN artwork around, Shift-drag a handle to resize it proportionally, and more.

The artwork and the image are now grouped and are referred to as a Mockup object. Later, if you want to edit the artwork, you can double-click the image to access the artwork.

9 Close the Mockup (Beta) panel.

▶ **Tip:** Want the full-resolution image? Currently, you can move the cursor over the image thumbnail in the Mockup (Beta) panel, and click the Buy License icon.

● **Note:** In beta, the images, like the man in the black T-shirt, are coming from Adobe Stock and are low-resolution placeholder images with Adobe Stock watermarks.

Working with global editing

Sometimes, you create multiple copies of artwork and use it across multiple artboards within a single document. If you need to change an object everywhere it's used, you can use global editing to edit all similar objects. In this section, you'll edit icons in a document you open.

1 Choose File > Open, and open the L14_start2.ai file in the Lessons > Lesson14 folder on your hard disk.

2 Choose View >Fit All In Window.

3 With the Selection tool selected, click the black circle behind the larger microphone icon.

Suppose you need to edit all of the circles behind each icon. In that case, you can select them using several methods, including the Select > Similar commands, assuming they all share similar appearance attributes. You can also use global editing, which selects objects that share attributes, such as stroke, fill, or size, on the same or all artboards.

▶ **Tip:** You can also start global editing by choosing Select > Start Global Edit.

4 Click Start Global Edit in the Quick Actions section of the Properties panel.

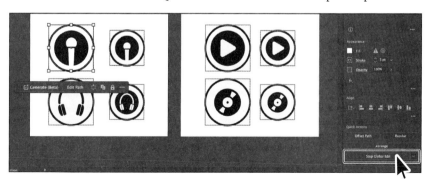

All circles (in this case) are now selected, and you can edit them. The object you originally selected has a red highlight, and the similar objects have a blue highlight. You can also use the Global Edit options to further narrow down the objects that will be selected, which is what you'll do next.

Note: The Appearance option is enabled by default when the selection includes plug-in art or mesh art.

5 Click the arrow to the right of the Stop Global Edit button to open a menu. Select Appearance in the Match section to select all of the circles with the same appearance attributes as the selected circle. Leave the menu showing.

6 Choose Match > Size from the Global Edit menu to further refine the search to include objects that have the same shape, appearance properties, and size. There should now be only two circles selected.

You can further refine your selection by choosing to search for similar objects on certain artboards.

Note: If you see a warning dialog box, click OK.

7 Click the Stroke color in the Properties panel, make sure the Swatches option is selected, and apply a color to the stroke.

8 Click away from the panel to hide it, and both of the selected objects should change appearance.

9 Choose Select > Deselect, and then choose File > Save.

10 Choose File > Close.

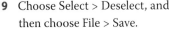

Review questions

1 What are three benefits of using symbols?

2 How do you edit an existing symbol?

3 What is a dynamic symbol?

4 In Illustrator, what type of content can you save in a library?

5 Explain how to embed a linked library graphic asset.

Review answers

1 Three benefits of using symbols are as follows:

   - You can edit one symbol to update all instances.

   - Using symbols reduces file size.

   - It is much faster to apply symbol instances.

2 To update an existing symbol, double-click the symbol icon in the Symbols panel, double-click an instance of the symbol on the artboard, or select the instance on the artboard, and then click the Edit Symbol button in the Properties panel. Then you can make edits in Isolation mode.

3 When a symbol is saved as dynamic, you can change certain appearance properties of instances using the Direct Selection tool (▷) without editing the original symbol.

4 Currently in Illustrator, you can save colors (fill and stroke), type objects, graphic assets, and type formatting.

5 By default, when a graphic asset is dragged from the Libraries panel into a document, a link is created to the original library asset. To embed a graphic asset, select the asset in the document and click Embed in the Properties panel. Once embedded, the graphic will no longer update if the original library asset is edited.

15 PLACING AND WORKING WITH IMAGES

Lesson overview

In this lesson, you'll learn how to do the following:

- Place linked and embedded graphics in an Illustrator file.
- Transform and crop images.
- Place Creative Cloud files. ▆◀
- Create and edit clipping masks.
- Mask with text. ▆◀
- Make and edit an opacity mask.
- Work with the Links panel.
- Embed and unembed images.
- Replace images. ▆◀

This lesson will take about 45 minutes to complete. To get the lesson files used in this lesson, download them from the web page for this book at *peachpit.com/IllustratorCIB2024*. For more information, see "Accessing the lesson files and Web Edition" in the Getting Started section at the beginning of this book.

Aside from creating vector art, you can also easily add images like JPEGs or PSDs (Photoshop documents) to an Adobe Illustrator file. Incorporating raster images into your vector artwork opens up a lot more creative potential!

Starting the lesson

Before you begin, you'll need to restore the default preferences for Adobe Illustrator. Then you'll open the finished art file for this lesson to see what you'll create.

● **Note:** If you have not already downloaded the project files for this lesson to your computer from your Account page, make sure to do so now. See the "Getting Started" section at the beginning of the book.

1 To ensure that the tools function and the defaults are set exactly as described in this lesson, delete or deactivate (by renaming) the Adobe Illustrator preferences file. See "Restoring default preferences" in the "Getting Started" section at the beginning of the book.

2 Start Adobe Illustrator.

3 Choose File > Open, and open the L15_end.ai file in the Lessons > Lesson15 folder that you copied onto your hard disk.

   This file contains social media images for a fictitious nursery company.

● **Note:** The fonts in the L15_end.ai file have been converted to outlines, and the images are embedded.

4 Choose View > Fit All In Window and leave it open for reference, or choose File > Close.

5 Choose File > Open. In the Open dialog box, navigate to the Lessons > Lesson15 folder, and select the L15_start.ai file on your hard disk. Click Open to open the file.

   This is an unfinished version of the social media ads for a nursery company. You will add graphics to each ad and edit those graphics in this lesson.

● **Note:** You need an internet connection to activate fonts. The process may take a few minutes.

6 The Missing Fonts dialog box *may* appear. Click Activate Fonts to activate all the missing fonts.

7 After they are activated and you see the message stating that there are no more missing fonts in the same dialog box, click Close.

   If you see another dialog box asking about font auto-activation, click Skip.

8 Choose File > Save As. If the Cloud Document dialog box opens, click Save On Your Computer.

9 In the Save As dialog box, navigate to the Lesson15 folder and open it. Name the file **Nursery_social_posts.ai**. Leave Adobe Illustrator (ai) chosen from the

Format menu (macOS) or Adobe Illustrator (*.AI) chosen from the Save As Type menu (Windows), and then click Save.

10 In the Illustrator Options dialog box, leave the Illustrator options at their default settings. Click OK.

11 Choose Window > Workspace > Reset Essentials to reset the Essentials workspace.

Placing image files

You can combine Illustrator artwork with images from other graphics applications in a variety of ways for a wide range of creative results. This lesson steps you through the process of finishing social media designs for a nursery by combining bitmap images with vector art.

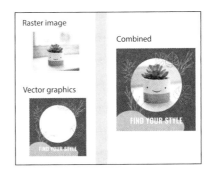

You can bring raster images, such as JPEG, PNG, PSD, and others, into Illustrator using the Open, Place, or Paste commands; drag-and-drop operations; and the Libraries panel. If you bring in Photoshop files, Illustrator supports most Adobe Photoshop data, including layer comps, layers, editable text, and paths. This means you can transfer files between Photoshop and Illustrator and still be able to edit the artwork.

Placing an image

First, you'll place a JPEG (.jpg) image in your document.

1 Choose View > Fit All In Window.

2 Choose File > Place.

3 Navigate to the Lessons > Lesson15 > images folder, and select the 01-Bring-some-life.jpg file. Make sure that the Link option is selected in the Place dialog box.

● **Note:** On macOS, you may need to click the Show Options button in the Place dialog box to reveal the Link option.

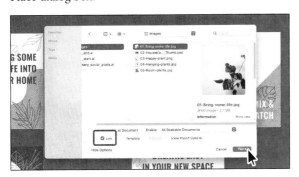

When placing a file using the File > Place command, it can be either embedded or linked, no matter what type of image file it is (JPEG, GIF, HEIC, PSD, AI, etc.). *Embedding* a file stores a copy of the image in the Illustrator file, whose size often increases to reflect the addition of the placed file. *Linking* files creates a link to external files, which are placed in Illustrator. A linked file does not add significantly to the size of the Illustrator file.

Linking to files can be a great way to ensure that image updates are reflected in the Illustrator file. The linked file must always accompany the Illustrator file or the link will break, and the placed file will not appear in the Illustrator artwork.

4   Click Place.

The pointer should now show the loaded graphics cursor. You can see "1/1" next to the pointer, indicating how many images are being placed (1 of 1), and a thumbnail so you can see what image you are placing.

5   Find the artboard with the text "BRING SOME LIFE INTO YOUR HOME."

6   Click to place the image to the left of that artboard. See the following figure. Leave the image selected.

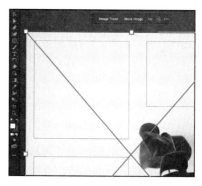

The image is 100% of its original size, with the upper-left corner placed where you clicked. Do you see the X on the image? That means that the image is linked (if you don't see the X, make sure the edges are on—View > Show Edges).

● **Note:** Your Properties panel may look different—with the Text to Vector Graphics (Beta) content showing.

Look in the Properties panel (Window > Properties). With the image selected, you see the words "Linked File" at the top, indicating that the image is linked to its source file.

By default, a placed image is linked to the source file, so if the source file is edited in a program like Photoshop, the placed image in Illustrator is also updated.

Transforming a placed image

You can transform placed raster images just like you do other objects in an Illustrator file. But unlike with vector artwork, with raster images you need to consider the *image resolution*, since raster images with lower resolution may look pixelated (bad) when printed. To learn more about resolution, check out the section "Welcome to Adobe Illustrator!" at the beginning of Lesson 1.

The image is pretty big, so in this section, you'll make it smaller and position it better.

1   With the image selected, choose View > Zoom Out three times or so.

    Since the image is selected, it is centered in the Document window when you zoom out, giving you better access to the bounding box handles.

2   With the Selection tool (▶) selected, drag the image so its lower-left corner is loosely in the lower-left corner of the artboard. Make sure the image covers the artboard. See the figure for how I placed it.

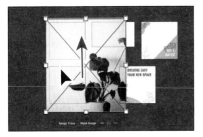 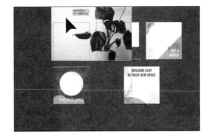

3   Shift-drag the upper-right bounding point of the image toward its center until it is just wider than the artboard. Release the mouse button and then the key.

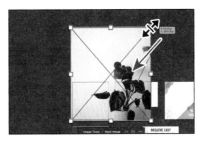 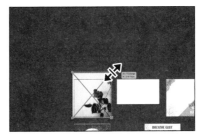

4   With the image still selected, at the top of the Properties panel click the text "Linked File" to show the Links panel. See the following figure.

5   With the 01-Bring-some-life.jpg file selected in the Links panel, click the Show Link Info arrow in the lower-left corner of the panel to see information about the image.

You can see the scale percentage as well as rotation information, size, and much more. Specifically, notice that the PPI (*pixels per inch*) value is approximately 150.

PPI refers to the current resolution of the image in Illustrator—how many color pixels fit horizontally (or vertically) in an inch. If you scale a placed raster image, like you just did, the resolution of the image in Illustrator will change. The resolution of the image outside of Illustrator is 72 ppi. Since you made the image smaller, the resolution in Illustrator is now higher (around 150 ppi). Illustrator makes the pixels smaller if you make the image smaller or bigger if you make the image bigger—so more or fewer pixels fit in an inch (PPI).

6 Press the Escape key to hide the panel.

7 Choose View > Zoom In a few times. (I zoomed three times.)

8 Click the Flip Horizontally button (⬕) in the Properties panel to flip the image horizontally, across the center.

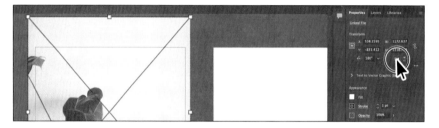

9 Leave the image selected, and choose File > Save.

Cropping an image

▶ **Tip:** You can turn off the Content Aware feature by choosing Illustrator > Settings > General (macOS) or Edit > Preferences > General (Windows) and deselecting Enable Content Aware Defaults.

In Illustrator, you can mask (*temporarily hide*) part of an image, as you'll learn about in this lesson, but you can also crop images to *permanently* remove part of them. When cropping an image, on Windows 64-bit and macOS, Illustrator automatically identifies the visually significant portions of the selected image, called Content-Aware cropping.

While cropping an image, you can also change the resolution by lowering it, which can be a useful way to reduce file size and improve performance. Next you'll crop part of the image so it fits better on the artboard.

1 With the image selected, click the Crop Image button in the Properties panel.

2 Click OK in the warning dialog box that appears.

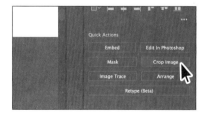

Linked images, like this plant image, become embedded after you crop them—that's basically what that dialog box told you. Illustrator shows a default cropping box with handles on the image that you can adjust if needed. The rest of the artwork is dimmed, and you cannot select it until you are finished cropping. The crop you see initially is what Illustrator thinks are the visually significant portions.

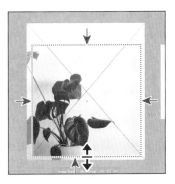

▶ **Tip:** To crop a selected image, you can also choose Object > Crop Image or right-click the image and choose Crop Image from the context menu.

3 Drag the crop handles so the crop boundary stops at the edges of the artboard.

When you drag a handle close to an artboard edge, you will feel it lightly snap or pull to it.

▶ **Tip:** You can also define a size in the Properties panel (width and height) to crop to.

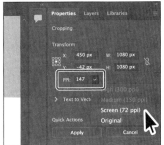

4 Click the PPI (resolution) menu in the Properties panel and choose Screen (72 ppi).

As mentioned, the PPI is the resolution of the image. Any options in the PPI menu that are higher than the original resolution of the image are disabled (dimmed). You cannot *raise* the resolution with the PPI menu. You lowered the resolution because this is a social media graphic and those types of graphics are typically web resolution (72 PPI).

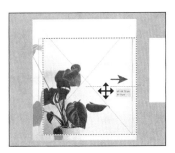

The maximum value that you can enter equals the resolution of the original image, or 300 PPI for linked artwork. Choosing a lower resolution than the original can be useful if you want to save file size but may result in an image that is not suitable for printing.

5 Move the pointer over the center of the image, and drag the crop area to the right to cut off more of the plants on the left.

► **Tip:** You can press Return or Enter to apply the cropping or press the Escape key to cancel the cropping process.

6 Click Apply in the Properties panel or press Return or Enter to *permanently* crop the image.

Since the image is embedded when cropping, the crop does not affect the original image file you placed.

7 Drag the image into the center of the artboard, as in the following figure.

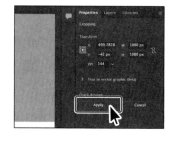

8 To send the image behind the other content on the artboard, click the Arrange button in the Properties panel and choose Send To Back.

9 Choose Select > Deselect, and then choose File > Save.

Placing a Photoshop document

When you place a Photoshop file as either a local document (.PSD) or cloud document (.PSDC) with multiple layers in Illustrator, you can change image options when it's placed. For instance, if you place a Photoshop file, you can choose to flatten the image or even to preserve the original Photoshop layers in the file. Next you'll place a Photoshop file, set import options, and embed it in the Illustrator file.

1 Choose View > Fit All In Window.

2 Choose File > Place.

3 In the Place dialog box, navigate to the Lessons > Lesson15 > images folder, and select the 02-Houseplant_Youtube_Thumb.psd file.

4 In the Place dialog box, set the following options (on macOS, if you don't see the options, click the Show Options button):

- Link: **Deselected** (Deselecting the Link option embeds an image file in the Illustrator file. Embedding a Photoshop file allows for more options when it is placed, as you'll see.)

- Show Import Options: **Selected** (Selecting this option will open an Import Options dialog box where you can set import parameters before placing.)

5 Click Place.

The Photoshop Import Options dialog box appears because you selected Show Import Options in the Place dialog box and because the file has multiple layers.

Note: The Import Options dialog box will not appear if the image contains only a locked Background layer, even though you select Show Import Options in the Place dialog box.

6 In the Photoshop Import Options dialog box, set the following options:

- Show Preview: **Selected**

Note: You may not see a preview in the dialog box, even after turning it on, and that's okay.

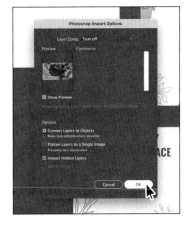

Tip: To learn more about layer comps, check out *Adobe Photoshop Classroom in a Book*!

- Layer Comp: **Text off** (In Photoshop, I hid the text and saved a layer comp that I named "Text off." A layer comp is a snapshot of a state of the Layers panel that you create in Photoshop. In Photoshop, you can create, manage, and view multiple versions of a layout in a single Photoshop file. Any comments associated with the layer comp in Photoshop will appear in the Comments area.)

- Convert Layers To Objects: **Selected** (This option and the next one are available only because you deselected the Link option and chose to embed the Photoshop image.)

- Import Hidden Layers: **Selected** (to import layers hidden in Photoshop).

7 Click OK.

8 Move the loaded graphics cursor into the upper-left corner of the blank artboard. Drag down to just past the lower-right corner of the artboard to place and size the image. Make sure it covers the artboard.

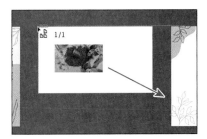

Dragging to place an image allows you to size it as you place it. Also, rather than flatten the file, you converted the 02-Houseplant_Youtube_Thumb.psd Photoshop layers into Illustrator layers and sublayers. When placing a Photoshop file in particular, if you had left the Link option selected (to link to the original PSD file), the only option in the Options section of the Photoshop Import Options dialog box would have been to flatten the content.

Notice that, with the image still selected on the page, the Properties panel shows the word "Group" at the top. The Photoshop layers, now Illustrator layers, are grouped when preserved and placed.

9   Open the Layers panel (Window > Layers). Drag the left edge of the Layers panel to the left to make it wider so you can read the names.

10 To reveal the image content in the Layers panel, click the Locate Object button (🔍) at the bottom of the panel.

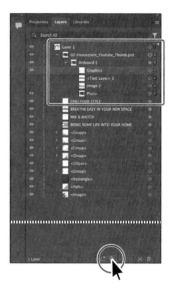

Notice the sublayers of 02-Houseplant_Youtube_Thumb.psd. These sublayers were layers in Photoshop and appear in the Layers panel in Illustrator because you chose not to flatten the image when you placed it.

When you place a Photoshop file with layers and you choose to convert the layers to objects in the Photoshop Import Options dialog box, Illustrator treats the layers as separate sublayers in a group. The Photoshop image had some text in it, but we chose to place the layer comp in which the text was hidden.

Now let's show the text that came with the Photoshop file along with one of the images.

11 In the Layers panel, click the visibility column for the left of the <Text Layer> 3 sublayer and the Image 2 sublayer to show them both.

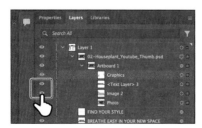

12 Choose Select > Deselect, and then choose File > Save.

Placing multiple images

In Illustrator you can also place multiple image files at one time. Next you'll place several images at once and position them for different social media graphics.

1   Choose View > Fit All In Window so you can see everything now that the Layers panel is so wide.

2   Choose File > Place.

3   In the Place dialog box, in the Lessons > Lesson15 > images folder, select the 03-Happy-plant.png file.

4   Shift-click the image named 05-Room-plants.jpg to select *three* image files.

5   Deselect Show Import Options, and make sure that the Link option is *not* selected to embed the images.

6   Click Place.

7   Move the loaded graphics cursor to the right of the artboard with the "FIND YOUR STYLE" text. Press the Right or Left Arrow key (or Up or Down Arrow key) a few times to see that you can cycle between the image thumbnails. Make sure that you see the smiling plant image thumbnail.

Whichever thumbnail is showing in the loaded graphics cursor when you click or drag in the Document window is the image that is placed.

> **Tip:** To discard an asset you see in the loaded graphics cursor (not place it), use the arrow keys until you see the asset in the cursor, and then press the Escape key.

8   Drag to place the image to fill the gap between the artboards, as you see in the following figure.

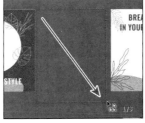

9 Move the loaded graphics cursor just off the upper-left corner of the artboard with the "MIX & MATCH" text. Make sure the hanging plants image is showing in the loaded graphics cursor (you can see which one, to the left). Drag just past the lower-right corner of the artboard to place and scale the image.

10 Move the loaded graphics cursor just off the artboard with the "BREATHE EASY…" text. Drag to the lower-right corner of the artboard to place and scale the image.

11 Choose File > Save.

Placing Creative Cloud files 🎥

To learn how to place Adobe Photoshop cloud files, check out the video *Placing Creative Cloud files*, which is part of the Web Edition. For more information, see the "Web Edition" section of "Getting Started" at the beginning of the book.

Masking content

Earlier in this lesson, you cropped an image and *permanently* removed parts of that image. You can also temporarily hide parts of any content, including an image, using what we call a *mask* (also called a *clipping mask*).

● **Note:** You will hear people use the phrases *clipping mask*, *clipping path*, and *mask*. Usually they mean the same thing.

A mask is a shape that masks, or hides, other artwork, so only content within the shape are visible. In the first part of the figure to the right is an image with a white circle on top. The white circle was applied as a mask in the second part of the figure to "mask" or hide part of the image.

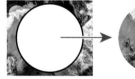

An image with a white circle on top.

The image, with part of it now masked (hidden) by the circle.

Only vector objects can be clipping paths; however, any artwork can be masked.

Masking content with a shape

Like you read in the previous explanation, you can mask any content (vector, raster image, both) with a shape that you create. In this section, you'll take a circle and mask the smiling plant image with it to give the image a more interesting appearance.

1   Select the white circle on the artboard with the "FIND YOUR STYLE" text. Drag it to the smiling plant image to its right.

    The circle will be behind the image because the image was added after the circle.

2   To zoom in to the circle, press Command and + (macOS) or Ctrl and + (Windows) a few times.

3   To arrange the circle on top of the image, click the Arrange button in the Properties panel, and choose Bring To Front.

    ● **Note:** If you accidentally selected the image, you can arrange the image behind the circle instead!

4   Make sure the circle is not bigger than the image. If need be, make the circle smaller.

5   Shift-click the smiling plant image beneath the circle to select it as well.

6   To mask the image with the circle, click the Make Clipping Mask button in the Quick Actions section of the Properties panel.

▶ **Tip:** It doesn't matter what color the shape is that you will use to make the mask. The stroke and fill are removed when it becomes a mask.

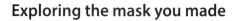

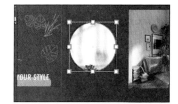

Exploring the mask you made

That mask (circle) and the image are now treated like a special group, called a *clip group*. At the top of the Properties panel, you'll see "Clip Group." As with a regular group, you can edit what's in the group by double-clicking it and editing in Isolation mode.

1 Open the Layers panel (Window > Layers).

2 Click the Locate Object button (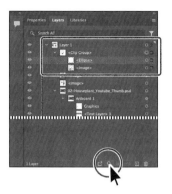) at the bottom of the panel.

Do you see the <Clip Group> sublayer? Within it, you'll find two things:

- <u>\<Ellipse\></u>
- \<Image\>

The <u>\<Ellipse\></u> is the circular mask shape, the \<Image\> is the smiling plant image.

Notice the underline applied to <u>\<Ellipse\></u>? That underline means it's a mask.

Editing the mask and image

The smiling plant image is probably not centered in the circular mask. Now you'll edit the image and the mask separately by double-clicking the mask group.

1 To move and resize the image, double-click the smiling plant image to enter Isolation mode.

You will now see the edge of the blue bounding box for the image, and if you move the cursor over the edge of the circle, you will see that thin blue circle as well.

2 Move the pointer over the image, and when you see its blue edges, click to select it, and then drag it until the smiling plant is more centered. Make sure the entire mask shape is filled with the image.

The plant image needs to be bigger. So that you'll have room to scale the image by dragging, you'll zoom out.

3 Zoom out by pressing Cmd and – (macOS) or Ctrl and – (Windows) twice.

4 Shift-drag the top, middle bounding point to make the image bigger so the smiling plant fills more of the circle. Release the mouse button and then the key.

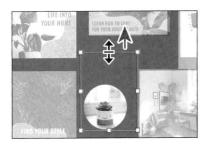 

If the plant isn't centered, at this point, you can drag it so it is.

5   Press the Escape key to exit Isolation mode.

6   Click away from the image to deselect it, and then drag the masked image into the center of the artboard with the "FIND YOUR STYLE" text to the left.

Note: You clicked away to deselect because only the image was selected previously, not the whole thing.

7   Choose Select > Deselect.

Automatic masking for an image

In this section, you'll see that Illustrator can create a simple mask for you, automatically, on an image so that you can hide parts of that image. Masking in this way means Illustrator will create a shape, like a rectangle, the exact size of the image. It will then apply that shape as a mask. Nothing will be hidden to start, but you can edit the shape (mask) to hide parts however you want!

1   Choose View > Fit All In Window.

2   Select the hanging plants image. See the following figure for which one.

3   In the Properties panel (Window > Properties), click the Mask button in the Quick Actions section.

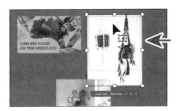  

What did this accomplish? Here's what Illustrator did:

*   Made a rectangle shape *exactly the same size* as the image.

*   Selected both the rectangle and the image and made the rectangle a mask (that is currently hiding *nothing*).

Note: Look at the top of the Properties panel and you'll see the "Clip Group" like you saw with the smiling plant image mask you made.

4   Deselect the image by choosing Select > Deselect, and then select the image again.

Editing the image mask

▶ **Tip:** Clicking the Isolate Mask button in the Properties panel does the same thing as double-clicking. It enters Isolation mode.

To edit the mask, the image, or both, you could double-click the image to enter Isolation mode, as you did previously. But in this case, it will be a little more challenging to select the mask shape because it's exactly the same size as the image. To select the shape, you would have to click directly on its edge or select it in the Layers panel. Let's try an easier way that you can use to edit any mask you make.

1   At the top of the Properties panel, click the Edit Contents button (⊙).

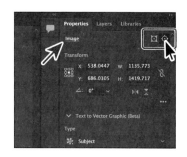

Clicking that button selects the image (the *content* of the mask) without having to go into Isolation mode. Looking to the left of the buttons in the Properties panel, you will now see the word "Image." An arrow is pointing to it in the figure.

2   Shift-drag the image up so its bottom is almost aligned with the bottom of the artboard.

Pressing the Shift key while dragging will constrain the movement. Notice that part of the top of the image is now gone because the mask is hiding it.

3   Click the Flip Horizontal button (⧗) in the Properties panel to flip the image.

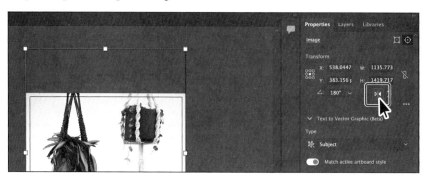

4   At the top of the Properties panel, click the Edit Clipping Path button (▣) to the left of the Edit Contents button.

The mask *shape* is now selected!

5 Drag the corners of the selected mask shape so it snaps to the edges of the artboard and masks a little of the image edges.

You may want to zoom in to the image. You may find that the edges you are dragging are snapping to content other than the artboard. Zooming in will help to snap to the artboard more easily.

6 Click away from the image, and then select it again to select the whole thing.

You should see "Clip Group" at the top of the Properties panel.

7 Choose Object > Arrange > Send To Back to send it behind everything else.

8 Choose Select > Deselect, and then choose File > Save.

Masking with text

To learn how to mask content with text, check out the video *Masking with text*, which is part of the Web Edition. For more information, see the "Web Edition" section of "Getting Started" at the beginning of the book.

Creating an opacity mask

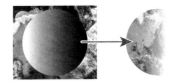

An image with a gradient-filled circle.   The circle applied as an opacity mask.

So far, the masks you've been making show or hide parts of content. What if you wanted to fade away part of an image or artwork—maybe to make a reflection? Or maybe to fade one image into another?

You would make an opacity mask. An *opacity mask* is technically just a mask—a shape masking parts of other content—but the shape for an opacity mask has a gradient applied to the fill. See the figure above. Opacity masks are made using the Transparency panel—rather than the way you've been using up to this point. In this section, you'll create an opacity mask for the last image so that it fades out and you can more easily read text.

1 With the Selection tool (▶) selected, select the last image you placed.

You may want to zoom out to see it.

2 Select the Rectangle tool (▭) in the toolbar, and starting about a quarter of the way down from the top, drag to create a rectangle that covers the image.

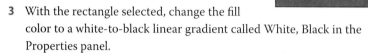

This will become the mask. Don't worry if there is no fill color. Next, you'll apply a gradient fill.

3 With the rectangle selected, change the fill color to a white-to-black linear gradient called White, Black in the Properties panel.

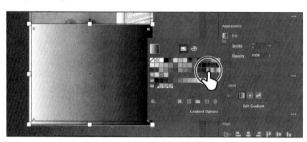

4 Select the Selection tool (▶) and, while pressing the Shift key, click the image beneath the rectangle to select it as well.

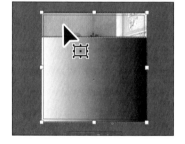

Note: If you had wanted to create a mask with the same dimensions as the image, instead of drawing a shape, you could have simply clicked the Make Mask button in the Transparency panel.

5 In the Properties panel, click the word "Opacity" to open the Transparency panel. In the panel, click the Make Mask button, and leave the artwork selected and the panel showing.

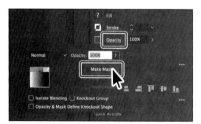

After clicking the Make Mask button, the same button now shows as "Release." If you were to click the button again, the image would no longer be masked. You'll also see that where there is white in the rectangle shape (mask), the image is showing, and where there is black, it is hidden. The gradient mask gradually reveals the image.

Editing an opacity mask

Next you'll adjust the opacity mask that you just created by turning it on and off, resizing the mask shape, and refining the gradient fill.

1 Choose Window > Transparency to open the Transparency panel.

You'll see the same panel you did when you clicked Opacity in the Properties panel. In the panel, you'll see the image thumbnail on the left and the mask shape on the right.

2 In the Transparency panel, Shift-click the mask thumbnail to disable the mask.

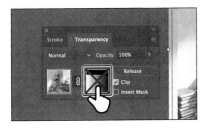

> **Tip:** To disable and enable an opacity mask, you can also choose Disable Opacity Mask or Enable Opacity Mask from the Transparency panel menu.

Notice that a red X appears on the mask in the Transparency panel and that the entire image reappears on the artboard. Hiding the mask can be useful to see all of the masked object again if you need to do anything to it.

3 In the Transparency panel, Shift-click the mask thumbnail to enable the mask again.

4 Now, just click the mask thumbnail on the right side of the Transparency panel to select it. If the mask isn't selected on the artboard, click to select it with the Selection tool (▶).

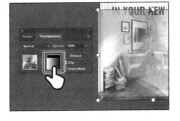

Clicking the opacity mask in the Transparency panel selects the mask (the rectangle) on the artboard. With the mask selected, you can't edit other artwork on the artboard. Also, notice that the document tab above the image shows (<Opacity Mask>/Opacity Mask), indicating that you are now editing the mask.

> **Tip:** To show the mask by itself (in grayscale if the original mask had color in it) on the artboard, you can also Option-click (macOS) or Alt-click (Windows) the mask thumbnail in the Transparency panel.

5 Make sure that the Fill box toward the bottom of the toolbar is selected.

6 Select the Gradient tool (▨) in the toolbar.

7 Move the pointer into the center of the image—above or below the horizontal gradient bar that now appears in the image. Drag up to the top of the mask shape.

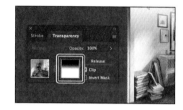

Notice that the mask thumbnail in the Transparency panel shows the new gradient appearance. At this point, if you wanted to make the mask fit the artboard better, you could resize it with the Selection tool selected.

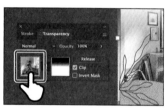

▶ **Tip:** To move the image or the mask separately, you can click the link icon (⬛) between the image thumbnail and the mask thumbnail in the Transparency panel.

8 In the Transparency panel, click the image thumbnail so you are no longer editing the mask.

9 Choose Object > Arrange > Send To Back.

10 Close the Transparency panel group.

11 Choose Select > Deselect, and then choose File > Save.

Working with image links

Whether you link to images or embed them, you can see a listing of all the images in your document in the Links panel. With the Links panel you can manage all linked or embedded artwork. The Links panel displays a small thumbnail of the artwork and uses icons to indicate the artwork's status. From the Links panel, you can view the images linked to and embedded, replace a placed image, update a linked image that has been edited outside of Illustrator, or edit a linked image in the original application, such as Photoshop.

Finding link information

When you place an image, it can be helpful to see where the original image is located, what transformations have been applied to it (such as rotation and scale), and more. Next, you'll explore the Links panel to discover image information.

1 Choose Window > Workspace > Reset Essentials.

2 Choose Window > Links to open the Links panel.

3 Select the 03-Happy-plant.png image in the Links panel list.

4 Click the Show Link Info arrow in the lower-left corner of the Links panel to reveal the link information at the bottom of the panel.

▶ **Tip:** If you see a cloud icon (☁) in the Links panel, that means a graphic was placed from a Creative Cloud library or cloud document and is linked to that asset.

Looking at the top part of the Links panel, you'll see a listing of all the images you've placed. In the link info area below the image list, you'll see information about the image, such as the fact that it's embedded (Embedded File), the resolution, the transformation information, and more.

5 Click the Go To Link button (⊞) below the list of images.

The 03-Happy-plant.png image will be selected and centered in the Document window.

6 Choose Select > Deselect, and then choose File > Save.

Embedding and unembedding images

An embedded (not linked) image means that the image data is stored within the Illustrator document. You can always embed a linked image later. You might want to use embedded images elsewhere, perhaps outside of Illustrator, or even edit them in an application like Photoshop. You can unembed images, which saves the embedded artwork to your file system as a PSD or TIFF file and automatically links it to the Illustrator file. Next, you will unembed an image in the document.

1 Choose View > Fit All In Window.

2 With the Selection tool (▶) selected, click to select the 05-Room-plants.jpg image (the image with the alpha mask) on the lower-right artboard.

3 Look in the Links panel, and you'll see (Embedded File) in the link info.

The 05-Room-plants.jpg image was embedded when you originally placed it.

You may decide that you need to edit an embedded image in a program like Photoshop. To do that, you need to unembed the image to make edits to it, which is what you'll do next to the image.

▶ **Tip:** You can also choose Unembed from the Links panel menu (☰).

▶ **Tip:** Want to *embed* a linked image? You can choose Embed Image(s) from the Links panel menu (☰).

4 Click the Unembed button in the Properties panel.

5 In the dialog box that appears, navigate to the Lessons > Lesson15 > images folder (if not already selected). Make sure Photoshop (*.PSD) is chosen from the File Format menu (macOS) or the Save As Type (Windows) menu, and click Save.

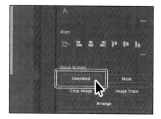

As you learned earlier, the X that now shows on the image on the artboard means the image is linked and not embedded. If you were to edit the image in Photoshop, it would be updated in Illustrator, since it is linked. Also notice the link icon (🔗) that now shows in the Links panel next to the image name!

6 Choose Select > Deselect.

7 Choose File > Save, and then choose File > Close as many times as necessary to close all open files.

Replacing images 🎬

To learn how to replace images in your designs, check out the video *Replacing images*, which is part of the Web Edition. For more information, see the "Web Edition" section of "Getting Started" at the beginning of the book.

Review questions

1 Describe the difference between linking and embedding in Illustrator.

2 How do you show options when importing images?

3 What kinds of objects can be used as masks?

4 How do you create an opacity mask for a placed image?

5 Describe how to replace a placed image with another image in a document.

Review answers

1 A *linked file* is a separate, external file connected to the Illustrator file by a link. A linked file does not add significantly to the size of the Illustrator file. The linked file must accompany the Illustrator file to preserve the link and to ensure that the placed file appears when you open the Illustrator file. An *embedded file* becomes part of the Illustrator file. The increased Illustrator file size reflects the addition of the embedded file. Because the embedded file is part of the Illustrator file, no link can be broken. You can update linked and embedded files using the Relink button (🔗) in the Links panel.

2 When placing an image using the File > Place command, in the Place dialog box, select the Show Import Options option. Selecting this will open the Import Options dialog box, where you can set options before placing. In macOS, if you don't see the options in the Import Options dialog box, click the Show Options button.

3 A mask can be a simple or compound path, and masks (such as an opacity mask) may be imported with placed Photoshop files. You can also create layer clipping masks with any shape that is the topmost object of a group or layer.

4 You create an opacity mask by placing the object to be used as a mask on top of the object to be masked. Then you select the mask and the object(s) to be masked and either click the Make Mask button in the Transparency panel or choose Make Opacity Mask from the Transparency panel menu.

5 *This question can be answered by watching a video!* See the section "Replacing images" on the previous page. *Answer*: To replace a placed image with a different image, select the image in the Links panel. Then click the Relink button (🔗) (or the Relink From CC Libraries button [⬚]), and locate and select the replacement image. Click Place or Relink (if you clicked the Relink From CC Libraries button).

16 SHARING PROJECTS

Lesson overview

In this lesson, you'll learn how to do the following:

- Package a file.
- Create a PDF.
- Use the Export For Screens command.
- Work with the Asset Export panel.
- Invite others to edit.
- Share for review.

 This lesson will take about 30 minutes to complete. To get the lesson files used in this lesson, download them from the web page for this book at *peachpit.com/IllustratorCIB2024*. For more information, see "Accessing the lesson files and Web Edition" in the Getting Started section at the beginning of this book.

In this lesson, you'll explore various methods for sharing and exporting your projects as PDFs and for optimizing your Illustrator content for use on the web, in apps, and in onscreen presentations.

Starting the lesson

Before you begin this lesson, you'll restore the default preferences for Adobe Illustrator and open the first lesson file.

Note: If you have not already downloaded the project files for this lesson to your computer from your Account page, make sure to do so now. See the "Getting Started" section at the beginning of the book.

1 To ensure that the tools function and the defaults are set exactly as described in this lesson, delete or deactivate (by renaming) the Adobe Illustrator preferences file. See "Restoring default preferences" in the "Getting Started" section at the beginning of the book.

2 Start Adobe Illustrator.

3 Choose File > Open. In the Open dialog box, navigate to the Lessons > Lesson16 folder. Select the L16_links.ai file, and click Open.

4 In the warning dialog that appears, select Apply To All, and then click Ignore.

There is at least one image, 04-Hanging-plants.jpg, linked to the Illustrator document that Illustrator can't find on your system. Instead of replacing the missing image(s) from this dialog box, later in the lesson you will open the Links panel so you can see which are missing and replace them there.

5 *If you skipped Lesson 15,* the Missing Fonts dialog box will most likely appear. Click Activate Fonts to activate all missing fonts (your list may not match the figure). After they are activated and you see the message stating that there are no more missing fonts, click Close.

6 If a dialog box appears referring to font auto-activation, then click Skip.

7 Choose File > Save As. If the Cloud Document dialog box opens, click Save On Your Computer.

8 In the Save As dialog box, navigate to the Lesson16 folder, and open it. Name the file **SocialPlant.ai**. Leave Adobe Illustrator (ai) chosen from the Format menu (macOS) or Adobe Illustrator (*.AI) chosen from the Save As Type menu (Windows), and then click Save.

9 In the Illustrator Options dialog box, leave the Illustrator options at their default settings. Click OK.

10 Choose Window > Workspace > Reset Essentials to ensure that the workspace is set to the default settings.

11 Choose View > Fit All In Window.

Note: If you don't see Reset Essentials in the Workspace menu, choose Window > Workspace > Essentials before choosing Window > Workspace > Reset Essentials.

Fixing the missing image link

After the document is open, since you ignored the missing link dialog box when it opened, you should fix the missing images if you hope to print or export this document. If you create a PDF or print this document without fixing the missing link(s), Illustrator will use a low-resolution version of each missing image.

1 To open the Links panel, choose Window > Links.

2 In the Links panel, select the 04-Hanging-plants.jpg image.

You'll see it has an icon ( ) to the far right of its name telling you the image is missing.

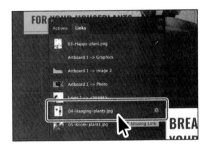

3 At the bottom of the panel, click the Go To Link button ( ) to show which image is missing.

To fix the missing link, you will relink the missing image to the original image.

4 At the bottom of the panel, click the Relink button ( ) to link the missing image to the original.

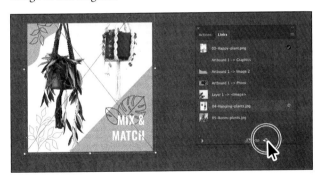

5 In the dialog box that opens, navigate to the Lessons > Lesson16 > images folder, select 04-Hanging-plants.jpg, and ensure that Link is selected. Click Place.

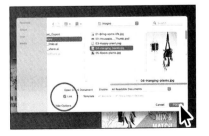

The 04-Hanging-plants.jpg image you just relinked will now show a link icon (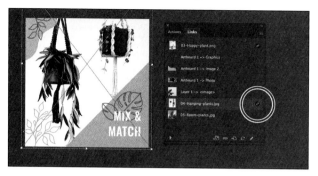) telling you it's linked to that image.

6 Choose Select > Deselect

7 Choose File > Save.

8 Close the Links panel group.

Packaging a file

Suppose you are working on an Illustrator project and you need to give someone else the file. If it's just vector content, you can just send them the file. But if you have linked content like images in your project, you need to send those with the Illustrator file so it will output correctly.

You can have Illustrator do this for you by collecting the file and everything linked to it. This is called *packaging*. When you package a file, Illustrator creates a folder that contains a copy of the Illustrator document, any necessary fonts, copies of the linked graphics, and a report that contains information about the packaged files.

Next you'll package the SocialPlant.ai file so you can send it to someone.

1 With the SocialPlant.ai file open, choose File > Package.

2 If you are asked to save the file, save it. In the Package dialog box, set the following options:

   • Click the folder icon (⬛), and navigate to the Lesson16 folder, if you are not already there. Click Choose (macOS) or Select Folder (Windows) to return to the Package dialog box.

   • Folder name: **Plants**

   • Options: Leave at default settings.

The Copy Links option *duplicates* all of the linked files to the new folder it creates. The Collect Links In Separate Folder option creates a folder called Links and copies the links into it. The Relink Linked Files To Document option updates the links within the Illustrator document to link to the new copies.

3 Click Package.

4 In the next dialog box, which discusses font licensing restrictions, click OK.

Clicking Back would allow you to deselect Copy Fonts (Except Adobe Fonts And Non-Adobe CJK Fonts).

5 In the final dialog box to appear, click Show Package to see the package folder.

In the package folder there should be a copy of the Illustrator document and a folder named Links that contains any linked images. The SocialPlant Report text file contains information about the document contents.

6 Return to Illustrator.

Creating a PDF

Portable Document Format (PDF) is a universal file format that preserves the fonts, images, and layout of source documents created on various applications and platforms. Adobe PDF is the standard for the secure, reliable distribution and exchange of electronic documents and forms worldwide. Adobe PDF files are compact and complete and can be shared, viewed, and printed by anyone with the free Adobe Acrobat Reader or other PDF-compatible software.

You can create different types of PDF files from within Illustrator. You can create multipage PDFs, layered PDFs, and PDF/X-compliant files. Layered PDFs allow you to save one PDF with layers that can be used in different contexts. PDF/X-compliant files ease the burden of color, font, and trapping issues in printing. Next, you'll save this project as a PDF so you can send it to someone else to view.

● **Note:** If you see the Cloud Document dialog box, click Save On Your Computer to save the file locally.

1 Choose File > Save As.

2 In the Save As dialog box, set the following:

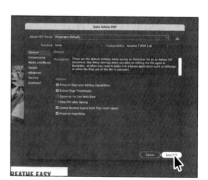

- Choose Adobe PDF (pdf) from the Format menu (macOS) or Adobe PDF (*.PDF) from the Save As Type menu (Windows).

- Navigate to the Lessons > Lesson16 folder, if necessary.

- Select All for the number of artboards.

● **Note:** If you see a dialog box that mentions sharing a link to your file for review, click Continue With PDF.

3 Click Save.

4 In the Save Adobe PDF dialog box, click the Adobe PDF Preset menu to see all of the different PDF presets available. Ensure that [Illustrator Default] is chosen.

There are many ways to customize the creation of a PDF. Creating a PDF using the [Illustrator Default] preset creates a PDF in which all Illustrator data is preserved. PDFs created with this preset can be reopened in Illustrator without any loss of data. If you are planning on saving a PDF for a particular purpose, such as viewing on the web or printing, you may want to choose another preset or adjust the options.

5 Click Save PDF.

6 Choose File > Close to close the PDF.

Exporting artboards and assets

In Illustrator, you can export entire artboards or selected assets using the File > Export > Export For Screens command and the Asset Export panel, perhaps to show a design in progress or to view selected assets.

You can export in several file formats: JPEG, SVG, PDF, PNG, OBJ, USDA, USDZ, GLTF, and WebP. These formats are optimized for use on the web, on devices, in onscreen presentations, and in 3D applications and are compatible with most browsers, yet each has different capabilities. Once selected, the artwork is automatically isolated from the rest of the design and saved as an individual file.

▶ **Tip:** To learn more about working with web graphics, search for "File formats for exporting artwork" in Illustrator Help (Help > Illustrator Help).

Exporting artboards

In this section, you'll see how to export artboards in your document, which can be helpful when you want to show someone a design you are working on or for capturing a design for use in a presentation, website, or app.

1   Choose File > Open. In the Open dialog box, navigate to the Lessons > Lesson16 folder. Select the SocialPlant.ai file, and click Open.

2   Choose View > Fit All In Window.

3   Choose File > Export > Export For Screens.

In the Export For Screens dialog box that appears, you can choose between exporting artboards and exporting assets. Once you decide what to export, you can set the export settings on the right side of the dialog box.

4   With the Artboards tab selected, look at the artboard thumbnails. Deselect the last two artboards and leave the first three selected. See the figure.

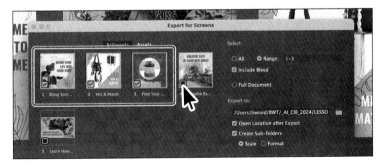

You can choose to export all or a specific range of artboards.

▶ **Tip:** Selecting Full Document will export all artwork in a single file.

5 Click the folder icon (📁) to the right of the Export To field. Navigate to the Lessons > Lesson16 folder, and click Choose (macOS) or Select Folder (Windows).

6 Click the Format menu, and choose JPG 80.

In the Formats section of the Export For Screens dialog box, you can set a Scale factor for the exported asset, create (or in this case edit) a suffix for the filename, and change the format. You can also export multiple versions with different scale factors and formats by clicking the + Add Scale button. You might need to scroll in the Formats area to see it.

▶ **Tip:** To avoid creating subfolders, like the folder "1x," you can deselect Create Sub-folders in the Export For Screens dialog box when exporting.

7 Click Export Artboard.

The Lesson16 folder should open, and you should see a folder named "1x" and, in that folder, the JPEG images.

8 Close the folder, and return to Illustrator.

Exporting assets

● **Note:** There are several methods for exporting artwork in a variety of formats. You can select artwork in your Illustrator document and choose File > Export Selection. This adds the selected artwork to the Asset Export panel and opens the Export For Screens dialog box.

Using the Asset Export panel, you can quickly and easily export individual assets in file formats such as JPEG, PNG, PDF, and SVG. The Asset Export panel lets you collect assets that you might export frequently and can be an excellent tool for web and mobile workflows because it allows for exporting multiple assets with a single click. In this section, you'll open the Asset Export panel and see how to collect the artwork in the panel and then export it.

1 Choose File > Open. In the Open dialog box, navigate to the Lessons > Lesson16 folder. Select the L16_share.ai file, and click Open.

2 Choose View > Fit Artboard In Window.

3 With the Selection tool (▶) selected, click to select the bird.

4 Press the Shift key, and click to select the TOUCAN text shapes.

5 With the artwork selected, choose Window > Asset Export to open the Asset Export panel.

The Asset Export panel is where you can save content for export now or later. It can work in conjunction with the Export For Screens dialog box to set export options for the selected assets, as you'll see.

6 Drag the selected artwork into the top part of the Asset Export panel. When you see a plus sign (+) appear, release the mouse button to add the artwork to the Asset Export panel. Each group or individual object is a different asset.

The assets are tied to the original artwork in the document. In other words, if you update the artwork in the document, the corresponding asset is updated in the Asset Export panel. Every asset you add to the Asset Export panel is saved with the panel and will stay there until you delete it from either the document or the Asset panel.

7 Click the TOUCAN text label below the thumbnail in the Asset Export panel and rename it **Text**. Click the bird thumbnail label and rename it **Bird**. Press Return or Enter to accept the last name.

> **Tip:** To add artwork to the Asset Export panel, you can also right-click the artwork in the Document window and choose Collect For Export > As Single Asset (or As Multiple Assets) or choose Object > Collect For Export > As Single Asset (or As Multiple Assets).

> **Tip:** If you Option-drag (macOS) or Alt-drag (Windows) multiple objects into the Asset Export panel, the selected content will become a single asset in the Asset Export panel.

If you drag artwork into the Asset Export panel, the asset name that appears is based on what the artwork is named in the Layers panel. Also, how you name assets in the Asset Export panel is up to you. For instance, they can be named according to what each asset is used for.

8 Select the Text thumbnail in the Asset Export panel.

Before exporting, you will need to first select the assets you'd like to export.

Note: If you are creating assets for use on iOS or Android, you could click iOS or Android to display a list of scaled export presets appropriate to each platform.

9 In the Export Settings area of the Asset Export panel, choose SVG from the Format menu, if necessary.

The Format setting you see to start, before choosing SVG, may be something different than what you see in the figure, and that's okay.

SVG is perfect for a website, but sometimes a co-worker may ask for a PNG version or some other format of the same logo as well.

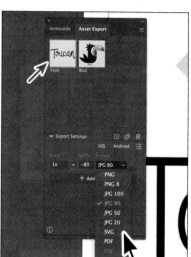

10 Click the + Add Scale button so you can export the artwork in another format.

Adding a scale makes the Scale value of the additional format something other than 1x, by default.

11 Choose 1x from the Scale menu so the second asset is exported at 100% of the size of the artwork on the artboard, and ensure that Format is set to PNG.

In this case, you have indicated that you want to export SVG and PNG files for the selected asset in the Asset Export panel. You can also set a scale (1x, 2x, etc.) if you need multiple scaled versions of the selected assets—perhaps for Retina and non-Retina displays for raster formats like JPEG or PNG. You can also add a suffix to the exported filename. A suffix could be something like "@1x" to indicate an exported asset's 100% scaled version.

12 With the Text thumbnail selected at the top of the Asset Export panel, click the Export button at the bottom of the panel to export the selected asset.

13 In the dialog box that appears, navigate to the Lessons > Lesson16 > Asset_Export folder, and click Choose (macOS) or Select Folder (Windows) to export the assets.

Tip: You can also click the Launch The Export For Screens Dialog button (▦) at the bottom of the Asset Export panel. This will open the Export For Screens dialog box, where you can adjust all the same settings, including a few more.

Both the SVG file and the PNG file are exported to the Asset_Export folder in a subfolder.

14 Close the Asset Export panel.

15 Choose Select > Deselect.

Inviting others to edit

If you want to work on an Illustrator project with someone else, you can invite them to edit your created document. To invite others to edit a document, you need to save that document as a cloud document. In Illustrator, only one collaborator can edit a cloud document at a time (called *asynchronous editing*).

For this next section, if you want to follow along, you will need the email address of someone you can share the file with.

1 With the L16_share.ai file still open, choose File > Invite To Edit.

If the document has yet to be saved as a cloud document (saved to your Creative Cloud account), it must be before moving on. The Share window will open in the upper-right corner of the app. If it is not open, don't click the Share button; instead, choose File > Invite To Edit again.

2 In the Invite To Edit dialog box, click Continue to save the file as a Creative Cloud document.

3 In the Save To Creative Cloud dialog box, click Save.

The Invite To Edit dialog box in the upper-right corner of the app will now contain two ways to invite people:

⬤ **Note:** If a user wants to edit the Illustrator document, they will need to have Illustrator installed and be signed in to Creative Cloud.

- You can invite users to edit the document by entering their email address, and they will receive an invite email and notification in the Creative Cloud desktop app. It's highlighted in **red** in the following figure.

- You can also invite users by sharing a link with them. Users will be taken to a browser where they can open the Illustrator document in Adobe Illustrator (if possible). It's highlighted in blue in the following figure.

To allow users that you share a link with to open the file in Illustrator, you need to choose Anyone With The Link Can Comment from the Who Has Access menu.

▶ **Tip:** You can set whether users can comment or download a copy by clicking the gear icon (⚙) in the upper-right corner of the Invite To Edit dialog box.

4 Enter an email address in the email field at the top. Press Enter or Return.

5 You can then enter a message (optional) and click Invite To Edit.

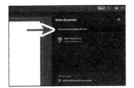 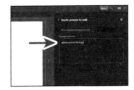 

The invited user will receive an email and a notification in the Creative Cloud desktop app.

6 Click away from the Invite To Edit dialog box to close it.

● **Note:** If you invite users via email, they will see the file on the Desktop Illustrator home screen (🏠) by clicking Shared With You. See the following figure.

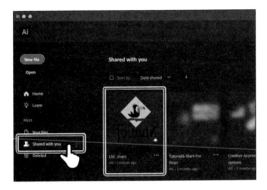

Sharing for review

If you invite someone to edit the Illustrator document, as you did in the previous section, they could also view the document in a browser or the Creative Cloud desktop app and comment on it (assuming the permissions are set for commenting).

You can also use Share for Review to share a document with someone with the express desire to have them review it rather than make edits. Share for Review is helpful if you want to share with someone who doesn't have Illustrator because the review can happen in the browser (or the Creative Cloud desktop app). Let's see how to share the previous file for review.

1 With the L16_share *cloud document* still open, click the Share button in the upper-right corner of the app.

Unlike with the Invite to Edit feature, if you intend to share a file for review, the document does not need to be saved as a cloud document first. That's because a link is generated from the document, and that link is what is shared.

Note: If you've used the Share for Review feature since you reset the application preferences, you may see a different dialog box. As long as there is a button to create a link, click it!

2 Click the Create Link button to make a shareable link.

As with the Invite to Edit feature, you can invite someone to review via email or by sending them the link.

If you invite people via email, they are sent an email and a notification in the Creative Cloud desktop app. If you want it so that only invited people (via email) can access the link destination, you will want to choose Only Invited People Can Comment from the Who Has Access menu. Otherwise, choose Anyone With The Link Can Access from the Who Has Access menu if you are okay with anyone reviewing—invited via email or sent a link.

3 Click the blue link you see in the Share dialog box to view the document in the browser.

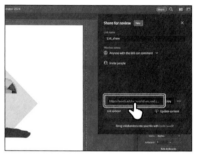

Note: You may see a small message pointing to the link; it contains help. You can click Skip.

At right is what someone who is reviewing the document in a browser will see.

4 Return to Illustrator.

One last thing to point out—and this is possibly the best part of Share for Review. Suppose you make changes to the document in Illustrator and want users to review the updated document. In that case, you can click Update Content, and the reviewers will see the latest version of the document!

5 Close the Share dialog box.

6 Choose File > Close for all open files without saving.

Review questions

1 Describe what packaging an Illustrator document does.

2 Describe how you export an artboard.

3 Name image file types that can be chosen in the Export For Screens dialog box and Asset Export panel.

4 Describe the generic process for exporting assets with the Asset Export panel.

5 How must an Illustrator document be saved to invite others to edit it?

Review answers

1 *Packaging* is used to gather all of the necessary pieces of an Illustrator document. Packaging creates a copy of the Illustrator file, the linked images, and the necessary fonts (if desired), and gathers those copies into a folder.

2 To export an artboard, choose File > Export > Export As (not covered in the lesson) or File > Export > Export For Screens. In the Export For Screens dialog box that appears, you can choose between exporting artboards and exporting assets. You can choose to export all or a specific range of artboards.

3 The image file types that can be chosen in the Export For Screens dialog box and the Asset Export panel are PNG, JPEG, SVG, PDF, OBJ, USDA, and GLTF.

4 To export assets using the Asset Export panel, the artwork to be exported needs to be collected in the Asset Export panel. Once it's in the panel, you can select the asset(s) to be exported, set the export settings, and then export.

5 For others to edit your Illustrator document, the file must be saved as a Creative Cloud document.

INDEX

S

sampling
    appearance attributes, 226
    colors, 106, 108, 231–232
    text formatting, 262
Save a Copy option, 325
Save To Creative Cloud dialog box, 444
saving
    colors as swatches, 216–217, 222–223
    documents, 11, 81–82, 83
    gradients, 303–304
    patterns, 325
    PDF files, 438
    selections, 66, 77
    workspaces, 42
Scale Strokes & Effects option, 136, 154, 165, 383
scaling
    effects, 154, 165, 383–384
    exported assets, 442
    objects, 153–154, 156
    patterns, 326
    strokes, 154, 156, 165, 383–384
    user interface, 41
    See also sizing/resizing
Scatter brushes, 331
Scissors tool, 115–116, 137
scrubbing across paths, 180–181
searching/filtering layers, 7, 294
segments, path, 61, 173, 188, 204
selected-art indicator, 282, 285
Selection Indicator, 34
Selection tool, 59–60, 62–63, 270, 398
selections
    bounding box of, 60
    exporting, 440
    marquee, 62–63
    Outline mode, 67
    rotating view to, 50

    saving, 66, 77
    similar object, 65–66
    tools for making, 59–63
Shape Builder tool, 15, 126–128, 137, 176
shape modes, 129–130, 137
shapes, 84–101
    color of, 87
    combining, 15, 126–130
    copying, 14
    creating, 12
    deleting, 127
    editing, 13, 115–126
    ellipses, 92–96
    lines and, 96–97
    Live, 85, 98, 111
    masking with, 421
    polygons, 98–100
    rectangles, 84–91
    rotating, 86
    stars, 100–101
    stroke alignment for, 94
    widgets for, 84, 88, 89, 99
Share button, 445
Share for Review feature, 445–446
shared library assets, 399
sharing
    files for review, 445–446
    links to documents, 444, 445–446
shearing objects, 156–157
shortcuts. *See* keyboard shortcuts
Show Activated Fonts button, 252
Show Rulers button, 150
Simplify command, 107–108, 125
sizing/resizing
    anchor points, 62
    artboards, 145, 165
    brushes, 353, 354
    fonts, 254
    gradients, 311, 312
    images, 413

Pearson's Commitment to Diversity, Equity, and Inclusion

Pearson is dedicated to creating bias-free content that reflects the diversity of all learners. We embrace the many dimensions of diversity, including but not limited to race, ethnicity, gender, socioeconomic status, ability, age, sexual orientation, and religious or political beliefs.

Education is a powerful force for equity and change in our world. It has the potential to deliver opportunities that improve lives and enable economic mobility. As we work with authors to create content for every product and service, we acknowledge our responsibility to demonstrate inclusivity and incorporate diverse scholarship so that everyone can achieve their potential through learning. As the world's leading learning company, we have a duty to help drive change and live up to our purpose to help more people create a better life for themselves and to create a better world.

Our ambition is to purposefully contribute to a world where:

- Everyone has an equitable and lifelong opportunity to succeed through learning.

- Our educational products and services are inclusive and represent the rich diversity of learners.

- Our educational content accurately reflects the histories and experiences of the learners we serve.

- Our educational content prompts deeper discussions with learners and motivates them to expand their own learning (and worldview).

While we work hard to present unbiased content, we want to hear from you about any concerns or needs with this Pearson product so that we can investigate and address them.

- Please contact us with concerns about any potential bias at https://www.pearson.com/report-bias.html.

Contributors

Brian Wood is an instructional designer, speaker/trainer, and author of the industry-leading Adobe Illustrator Classroom in a Book and numerous LinkedIn Learning courses and other content. He also works with the worldwide Marketing and Education teams and the Learn team at Adobe to create learning content, including speaking at various industry events. He enjoys designing and building unique, custom wood furniture in his spare time.

To learn more, check out www.youtube.com/askbrianwood or linkedin.com/in/brian-wood-training.

Production Notes

The *Adobe Illustrator Classroom in a Book 2024 release* was created electronically using Adobe InDesign 2023. Art was produced using Adobe InDesign, Adobe Illustrator, and Adobe Photoshop.

References to company names, websites, or addresses in the lessons are for demonstration purposes only and are not intended to refer to any actual organization or person.

Images

Photographic images and illustrations are intended for use with the tutorials.

Typefaces used

Adobe Myriad Pro and Adobe Warnock Pro are used throughout this book. For more information about OpenType and Adobe fonts, visit www.adobe.com/type/opentype/.

Team credits

The following individuals contributed to the development of this edition of the *Adobe Illustrator Classroom in a Book 2024 release*:

Writer: Brian Wood
Adobe Press Executive Editor: Laura Norman
Adobe Press Sponsoring Editor: Anshul Sharma
Adobe Press Senior Production Editor: Tracey Croom
Copy Editor: Scout Festa
Keystroke: Keith Gilbert
Technical Editor: Victor Gavenda
Project Design: Danielle Fritz, Birgit Palma, and Brian Wood
Compositor: Brian Wood
Proofreader: Kim Wimpsett
Indexer: James Minkin
Interior Design: Mimi Heft
Cover Illustration: Marte (Martina Galarza) behance.net/martevisual

Lesson project credits

The following individuals contributed artwork for the lesson files for this edition of the *Adobe Illustrator Classroom in a Book 2024 release*:

>**Danielle Fritz** (www.behance.net/danielle_fritz): Lessons: 00, 1–5, 8–10, 12, 13, 15, and 16.

>**Birgit Palma** (www.birgitpalma.com): Lessons 11 and 14.

Image credits

In Chapter 1, a photo of flowers by **Markus Winkler** on Unsplash.com is used: *unsplash.com/photos/34Dl4UKIItU/*

In Chapter 8, a photo of a basket with fruit by **Monika Grabkowska** on Unsplash.com is used: *unsplash.com/photos/VSYjkfzj3nw*

Throughout Chapter 10, the following is used:

>Photo by **Nathan Dumlao** on Unsplash.com: *unsplash.com/photos/M3dNCIPzdtg*

In Chapter 14, the **low-res placeholder image** (ONLY) of a photo of a man in a black T-shirt by **Creative Optiplex** on Adobe Stock is shown: *stock.adobe.com/images/young-model-shirt-mockup-boy-wearing-black-t-shirt-on-street-in-daylight-shirt-mockup-template-on-hipster-adult-for-design-print-male-guy-wearing-casual-t-shirt-mockup-placement-generative-ai/609688870*

Throughout Chapter 15 and 16, the following images are used:

>Photo by **Annie Spratt** on Unsplash.com: *unsplash.com/photos/green-leaves-on-white-background-aGev-rZ2rfw*

>Photo by **Faria Anzum** on Unsplash.com: *unsplash.com/photos/green-succulent-on-white-and-pink-pot-ONK9IlKizS4*

>Photo by **feey** on Unsplash.com: *unsplash.com/photos/green-plant-on-black-soil-ef8Xt_z_m1k*

>Photo by **feey** on Unsplash.com: *unsplash.com/photos/a-plant-hanging-from-a-rope-next-to-a-hanging-planter-oc5PhAv9Uw4*

>Photo by **Spacejoy** on Unsplash.com: *unsplash.com/photos/brown-wooden-table-with-books-on-top-3z_61bnbFhM*